0716

052191

Reporting
the Citizens'
News

Reporting the Citizens' News

Public Affairs Reporting in Modern Society

Ralph S. Izard
Ohio University

Holt, Rinehart and Winston

New York Chicago San Francisco Philadelphia
Montreal Toronto London Sydney
Tokyo Mexico City Rio de Janeiro Madrid

Library of Congress Cataloging in Publication Data

Izard, Ralph S.
  Reporting the citizens' news.

  Bibliography: p.
  Includes index.
  1. Reporters and reporting. I. Title.
PN4781.I96   070.4'3   81-6854
ISBN 0-03-057366-1   AACR2

CBS COLLEGE PUBLISHING
Holt, Rinehart and Winston
The Dryden Press
Saunders College Publishing

To Janet and Martha

CONTENTS

PREFACE

The immortal Rudyard Kipling, if one changes the context slightly, expresses well the idealistic intent of this book in his classic poem "If." It fits the journalistic dream to advise keeping one's head when everyone else has lost control, developing the ability to deal with kings and common people alike, depending on people but not trusting too much, and filling the hours of the day with productive and meaningful contributions.

Journalists need goals. We have some: objectivity, truth, fairness, ethical behavior. But the twentieth century has brought with it a broadened journalistic dream and new goals. News organizations are expected to provide citizens with accounts of important events and discussions of what those events mean. It may be impossible that any individual or news organization will achieve all that this may be construed to mean. But the existence of the effort is a significant fact, and even slight progress represents a step toward journalistic maturity.

These are equal ideals for reporters in whatever news medium—radio, television, newspapers, magazines or even newsletters. Of course, presentation techniques differ from one medium to another, and these techniques have impact upon methods of gathering information. But whatever the technique, it's inescapable that reporters through the remainder of the twentieth century and into the twenty-first century will have to know more about the subjects with which they are dealing. It's inescapable that news organizations will have to dedicate more funds and time for reporters to do the job expected of them.

This does not signal the death of general-assignment reporters. The necessary diversity of news media content requires aggressive individuals, strong in interviewing and writing skills, who tackle any assignment and rapidly produce understandable, meaningful, and interesting copy. Today's news events are important. Democratic society requires that citizens know what happens in their communities on a day-by-day basis. The talent to handle that diversity makes general-assignment reporters the very backbone of American journalism.

But, as the Commission on Freedom of the Press said in 1947, "It is no longer enough to report *the fact* truthfully. It is now necessary to report *the truth about the fact.*" The journalistic response to this challenge has been impressive. More and more reporters, usually those with general-assignment backgrounds, have been ticketed to step into expanded roles. These are journalistic specialists—or, as they are called in this book, expert reporters—who concentrate their attention on specific types of subject matter. Augmented by additional college training, continuing education and intensive on-the-job training, their special skills are designed to provide depth to coverage of single areas of journalistic and social concern.

It will be the combination of efforts by the expert reporters and the general-assignment reporters which will move the news media closer to the new ideals being set by themselves and by the public they serve.

This book is an effort to chronicle the development and role of the specialist, or expert reporter, in American journalism. It seeks to blend subject-matter description, performance analysis, and discussion of techniques. Even though a single author is listed, it is in many ways produced by a "committee," let us hope without the usual dreary results of committee reports. That committee is made up of those journalistic professionals who were willing to devote their time to being interviewed and to share their knowledge and experience with others. Many are cited in the text; others were used in general background ways. But all were valuable. I am grateful to be involved in a profession which thrives on the exchange of ideas and on a willingness to share. That's what it's all about. May I here express my debt and my thanks to the following persons who so capably represented that kind of dedication:*

Akron Beacon Journal: Richard Metchen, Doug Oplinger.
Arkansas Gazette: Ernie Dumas, Carol Griffee.
Arkansas Magazine: Bob Lancaster.
Associated Press: Dolores Barclay, Alton Blakeslee, Richard Carelli, Louise Cook, George Cornell, Linda Deutsch, Keith Fuller, Howard Graves, Jules Loh, Kevin McKean, Walter Mears, Brian Sullivan, Jonathan Wolman.
Athens Messenger: Herb Amey, Bob Ekey.

*Note: Journalists move around, sometimes rather rapidly. Frequent efforts were made to update information on the whereabouts of the individuals in this list. But many defy following. They are listed here with their last known news organization in the hope that at least most of the information will continue to be current.

Atlanta Journal: Mike Kautsch, Selby McCash, Charl Seabrook, Tom Walker.
Arizona Republic: Ira Fine.
Baltimore Sun: Lyle Denniston
Bridgeport Post: Frank Decerbo.
Charleston News and Courier: Jeff Watkins.
Chicago Tribune: Casey Bukro, Bruce Buursma, Ron Kotulak, Meg O'Connor.
Cincinnati Enquirer: Jim Delaney, George Hahn, John Kiesewetter, James B. Smith.
Cincinnati Post: John Leach.
Cleveland Plain Dealer: Steve Adams, Tom Diemer.
Cleveland Press: Brent Larkin, Bud Weidenthal.
Columbus Dispatch: David Lore, Robert McMunn.
Congressional Quarterly: John Felton
Cox Newspapers: Andrew Alexander, Doug Lowenstein.
Dallas Morning News: Tom Bayer, Tom Belden, Bill Choyke, Carl Freund, Dotty Griffith, Bill Kenyon, Linda Little, Anne Swardson.
Dayton Daily News: Dave Allbaugh, Michael Frisbee, Wes Hills.
Dayton Journal Herald: Cilla Bosnak, Fred Lawson, Cathy Martindale, Tom Price.
Denver Post: Gay Cook, Virginia Culver, Jim Duffy, Todd Engdahl, Carol Green, Chuck Green, Carl Miller, Dan Russel, Peggy Strain, Bob Threlkeld, John Toohey, Max Woodfin.
Detroit Free Press: Scott Bosley
Fairchild Publications: John Byrne.
Florida Times-Union: Margo Pope.
Fort Worth Star-Telegram: Anita Baker, Charlotte Guest, Glen Guzzo, Herb Owens, Phil Record, Z. Joe Thornton, Nancy Webman, Gerald Zenick.
Fredericksburg Free Lance-Star: Ed Jones.
Freelance writers: Jon Conroy, Jean McCann.
Freemont News Messenger: Roy Wilhelm.
Group W. Television: Val Hymes.
Hartford Courant: Robert Lamagdeleine.
Houston Post: Arthur Weise.
Jackson Clarion Ledger: Frederic Tulsky, David Phelps.
Knight-Ridder: Steven Dornfeld.
KOOL-TV, Phoenix: Burt Kennedy.
KOY, Phoenix: Paul McGonigle.
KPIX-TV, San Francisco: George Foulder.
La Crosse Tribune: David Offer.
Lexington Herald: John Carroll.
Los Angeles Times: Erwin Baker, Al Belugach, Dick Bergholz, John Dart, Frank del Olmo, Bruce Keppel, Claudia Luther, Jack McCurdy, Larry Pryor, Bob Rawitch, Carl Redburn, David Shaw, Gaylord Shaw, Don Speich.

Louisville Times: Dick Kaukas.
Louisville Courier-Journal: John Crocker, Phil Moeller, Bob Pierce.
Michigan State University: Mary Gardner.
Milwaukee Journal: Frank Aukofer, Paul Hayes, Larry Lohmann, Sam Martino, Joel McNally, Marie Rohde, Neil Rosenberg.
Mother Jones: Adam Hochschild.
New Haven Journal-Courier: John Mongillo.
Newsday: Rita Ciolli, B. D. Colen.
News Election Service: Janyce Katz
New York Times: Sheldon Binn, Kenneth Briggs, Jane Brody, Jerry Flint, Glenn Fowler, Henry Lieberman, Gene Maeroff, Louis Uchitelle.
Norfolk Virginian-Pilot: Margaret Edds, Michael Hardy.
Ohio University: Hugh Culbertson, Byron Scott, Richard Vedder.
Pittsburgh Post-Gazette: Stuart Brown, Dick Fontana, Susan Manella, Henry Pierce, Regis Stefanik.
Pittsburgh Press: Dolores Frederick, Caren Marcus, Sam Spatter, Wyndle Watson.
Peoria Journal Star: Shelley Epstein.
Religious News Service: Darrell Turner.
Reuters: Ingo Hertel.
Richmond Times-Dispatch: Bill Miller.
St. Louis Post-Dispatch: Gerald Boyd, Pamela Meyer, Jon Sawyer, Dana Spitzer, Susan Thomson, Victor Volland, Ron Willnow.
Seattle Times: Paul Andrews, Dean Katz, Hill Williams.
States News Service: Geoff O'Gara.
The Tennessean, Nashville: Frank Sutherland.
Topeka *Capital Journal:* Mary Ericson, Stephen Munro, Gene Smith.
Troy Daily News: Howard Wilkinson.
U.S. News & World Report: David Pike.
Wall Street Journal: Tim Metz, Priscilla Meyer, Jeffrey Tannenbaum.
Washington Post: John Berry, Warren Brown, William Greider, Rudy Maxa, Bill Richards, Charles Seib, Frank Swaboda.
WBBM-TV, Chicago: Eric Ober, Clarence Page.
Weatherford Democrat: Jim Golding.
WSGN, Birmingham: Les Coleman.
WSOL-TV, Charlotte: Doug Caldwell.
WTOP, Washington: Rich Adams.
Non-Journalists: Ralph Abernathy, civil rights leader; Dick Anderson, Battelle Memorial Institute; Ralph Derickson, Council of State Governments; Barbara Haas, Quaker Valley Schools, Pennsylvania; Thomas Hodson, Athens County, Ohio, Municipal Court; Richard Lamm, governor of Colorado; Elliot L. Lewis, Sanford R. Goodkin Research Corp.; U.S. Rep. Clarence Miller of Ohio; Ralph Nader, consumer advocate; Franklin Parisi, Getty Oil Co.; James Rogers, Consolidated Coal Co.; Rozanne Weissman, National Education Association.

    In writing a book of this nature, one accumulates a long list of individuals to whom special gratitude is owed. Cries for help were willingly answered, and it may be a cliche to say it, but this book would not be possible without the assistance of others. Among those to whom I offer special thanks are: Halina Czerniejewski, whose inquiring mind and editing skills helped make this book what it is; Jeff Brehm, Karen Cappone, Chris Celek, Mary Jo Crowley, Mary Beth Egland, Deena Ferguson, Cindy Fodor, Tom Hodson, Jim Jennings, Barbara Kaufmann, Peter King, John Kiesewetter, Sue Kiesewetter, Debbie Mansfield, Ed Miller, Stephen Munro, Randall Murray of California Polytechnic State University in San Luis Obispo, Mike Prager, Mary Quinn, Anne Saker, Patsy Smith, and the Ohio University chapter of the Society of Professional Journalists, Sigma Delta Chi.

    And, finally, I am grateful for financial support in the form of a Chairman's Discretionary Grant from the Ohio University Research Committee.

RIZ

Reporting
the Citizens'
News

Chapter 1

THE EXPERT
REPORTER

Journalists have always covered the experts. But times have changed. Now more reporters are being called upon to *be* experts themselves. They are responding. They get there by different routes, and they express different attitudes about what they are doing. Yet they share a common purpose—to provide deeper and broader coverage of citizen needs and of social efforts to meet those needs.

Explain the trend by whatever means seem appropriate: an effort to cope with increasing social complexity, acceptance of more journalistic responsibility, or a means of better informing citizens in a democratic society. News organizations depend heavily on general-assignment reporters. They always will, but they now are grafting to that system a cadre of individuals who have special skills and take opportunities to concentrate on providing more comprehensive explanations of subjects of citizen concern or need. For example:

Linda Deutsch, at age 26, was writing about movie stars for The Associated Press in Hollywood. She was doing what she had prepared for as an English major at Monmouth College. Then movie star Sharon Tate was brutally murdered, and Deutsch was called upon to write that story.

"As a result of that, I wound up writing about the [Charles] Manson trial, which was the most incredible form of theater I had ever covered," she says. "The Manson trial began as a brief assignment and wound up being almost a lifetime. When I finished the Manson trial, I figured if I could survive that, I could survive anything. And I was suddenly a trial specialist."[1]

Linda Deutsch of The Associated Press   Caren Marcus of the *Pittsburgh Press*

(Photo by Marlene Karas)

Caren Marcus didn't quite realize it at the time, but she used every available opportunity at Northwestern University to prepare herself for a career as an education writer.

"Every time I had to do a paper I always seemed to lean toward children or education. You really don't realize why you do that type of thing except you have an interest in it," she says. "When I came to the [Pittsburgh] *Press*, I did obits and everything, and whenever I had time to do a feature, I just happened to lean toward education. When the opening came up here, I think the *Press* realized it, and we just matched up. I wish I had more time to go to graduate school and get a master's in education."

Frank del Olmo of the *Los Angeles Times*   Ernie Dumas of the *Arkansas Gazette*

(*Los Angeles Times* photo)   (*Arkansas Gazette* photo by Larry Obstinik)

Frank del Olmo defines himself as a "specialist by default" or a "specialist by neglect" for the *Los Angeles Times*. He says candidly that he took on Chicano affairs out of a concern that his paper would not otherwise devote adequate attention to the Latin population of the area.

"I semivolunteered, semiagreed with the desk, to take on this area of coverage, but I've consciously made an effort not to get myself too deeply into the specialty because I don't really think it's a valid specialty. It's the kind of thing the paper should cover as a whole. I don't think I got it because I am a Chicano, but because I could speak Spanish. I enjoy it—obviously. I wouldn't do it if I didn't enjoy it. I can't totally complain because it's gotten me more opportunities than I might have had otherwise. But I'm a fairly young reporter, and I want to get a broad background in general assignment."

Ernie Dumas went to work for the *Arkansas Gazette* in 1960 as a general-assignment reporter and was called upon to assist in coverage of political campaigns. After five years, he had attracted enough attention to be assigned as a regular statehouse and political reporter, a job he held until becoming an editorial writer in 1979.

"It was not something I applied for or asked for, and I had made no real effort to prepare myself for it other than filling in when I was needed," he says. "But I was very pleased because it was what I wanted to do. I guess the statehouse is looked upon as a prestigious assignment."

THE SPREAD OF SPECIALIZATION

Specialization is not a new concept. Today's expert reporter represents an intensified application of an old idea—that the importance of the news media to democratic society lies in their ability to provide information upon which citizens make decisions. One might be tempted, in this age of skepticism about big government, big business, and big news media, to conclude that the process has become distorted. But the very faults of the media that feed such a conclusion also represent reasons that news media so hungrily adopted the idea that they needed journalistic experts to report on the social experts.

Citizens view with alarm the failures of American journalism: superficiality, emphasis on the events of the day without adequate regard to their broader meaning, blind acceptance of social leaders' pronouncements, inordinate dependence on special-interest groups. It's little wonder they question American journalism. Journalists see the flaws too. But it is not commonly accepted that they share the alarm.

In his classic essay, "The World Outside and the Pictures in Our Heads," famed syndicated columnist Walter Lippmann, as early as 1922, pointed out a need:

"I argue that representative government, either in what is ordinarily called politics, or in industry, cannot be worked successfully, no matter what the basis of election, unless there is an independent, expert organization for making the unseen facts intelligible to those who have to make decisions."[2]

Years later, in 1965, Lippmann expressed unbridled enthusiasm for the journalistic response—a trend toward greater use of specialized, more expert, reporters. He called it "the most radical innovation since the press became free of government control and censorship. For it introduces into the conscience of the working journalist a commitment to seek the truth which is independent of and superior to all his other commitments."[3]

This is not an isolated trend. Granted, specialists are more numerous and more conspicuous in more wealthy news organizations, but even small newspapers and broadcast stations may have individuals who, because of their special knowledge, cover specific assignments. Thus, the huge *Los Angeles Times* may label as much as 50 percent of its staff as specialists and devote thousands of dollars to their support, and this may represent the corporate extreme. But consider the Spokane, Washington, *Chronicle* with a circulation of about 62,000 and a total reporting staff of fifteen. In addition to such standard assignments as police and city hall, the paper has three reporters who devote most of their time to covering medicine, environment, and education from kindergarten through high school and higher education.

Although examples are not as numerous and the trend is not as pronounced, a parallel exists in broadcasting. At the network level, it's relatively common to hear specialized reports, for example, from NBC's Irving R. Levine on business, ABC's David Brinkley on politics, and Jules Bergman on science, and CBS's Fred Graham on law and Charles Kuralt on the human side of American life.

Larger local stations in metropolitan markets also designate several specialists on their new staffs as providing more comprehensive coverage of some social areas. Most frequent among these areas, says Eric Ober, news director of WBBM-TV in Chicago, are consumer affairs, health and medicine, business and economics, politics, and the arts. The smaller the station, of course, the less likely it will be able to afford the luxury of specialist reporters.

The fact that smaller newspapers and broadcast stations do not emphasize use of specialists should not be surprising. To provide an individual with the time and financial resources to work for days, weeks, or even months on a single story is out of the reach of smaller news organizations. It's not a matter of philosophy. The degree to which, say, one person on a staff of six or even fewer devotes time to a specialty is the degree to which coverage of important local activities must be reduced. Given the choice, it perhaps is better that smaller organizations concentrate on local news coverage and rely on news agencies and networks to discuss the major social issues of the day.

This is not to say that smaller organizations have no responsibility for comprehensive coverage of issues as well as events. The two simply cannot be done on the same level. The wise editor or news director, spotting issues which have particular local impact, occasionally will juggle the schedule to release a reporter to provide special coverage. And many do.

WHAT MAKES A SPECIALIST?

Who, then, are the specialists? How does the job they do differ from traditional expectations of reporters? Keith Fuller, president and general manager of The Associated Press, provides the most basic answer:

"When you define specialization, it's really more of a continuity of subject—just staying within the confines of a general subject. Your attention is not diverted to other things, and you get to know all the sources in that field, not only in a business sense but at their conventions and other activities. You win their confidence. They start opening up some really good material. You get to the point at which you can sense the slightest changes, the nuances that would be lost on the general reporter."

That provides an easy distinction between the specialist and the general-assignment reporter. The generalist covers many subjects and usually does not enjoy such a continuity of sources. But Fuller's statement does not explain how the specialist differs from the traditional beat reporter. The terms often are used interchangeably. But there is a difference, based on some fine lines, and often it is only a matter of individual performance.

For one thing, the specialist tends to have more time and flexibility. Beat reporters more often function under specific expectations of type and quantity of coverage. Specialists tend to have greater control over how they spend their time.

A beat typically is expressed in geographic or jurisdictional terms: city hall, county government, the school system, federal court, hospitals, police. Specialists deal with broad subject matter such as urban affairs, education, legal affairs, medicine, or law enforcement. The implications are more than semantic. They represent coverage philosophy. There's a big difference, for example, between covering activities at city hall—mayoral news conference, city council meetings, specific service programs, the budget—and relating those activities to the broad problems and directions of the community and to other communities.

And that emphasis on broader perspective constitutes a third general distinction. The specialist reporter is more likely to concentrate on process rather than activities. In journalistic terms, this leads reporters more into trend stories than spot news stories. This does not mean the specialist never covers spot news. Nothing could be further from the truth, and nothing, in the long run, could be more detrimental.

Says John Carroll of the *Lexington* [Kentucky] *Herald*, "Our feeling is that covering daily events provides good material for trend stories. If you just sit in the office and sort of abstractly try to think up trends without getting out and meeting people and covering events, pretty soon your stories are going to get pretty ethereal and aren't going to have much grounding in reality."

Most specialist reporters, therefore, will cover spot news and, when the need arises, they may be pressed into general service. However, this tends to occur less frequently for them. And the specialist usually controls spot news coverage, gaining more opportunities to concentrate on stories that relate the specifics to the general trends and help citizens better understand the implications of that spot news.

The distinction between the specialist and the beat reporter depends most on how reporters and their employers handle the assignments. It depends on the expectations and the approach. For example, city hall typically is considered a beat. But a thoughtful and knowledgeable reporter, given employer support, will be able to expand the focus. City hall may be a beat in which citizens are told what local government did today, or it may be a specialty in which the orientation is toward citizen understanding. Ot it may fall somewhere in between.

Whatever the organizational label, the expert reporter functions effectively if given the opportunity. In practical terms, specialists have more opportunities; beat reporters may create their opportunities; and even general-assignment reporters occasionally find themselves dealing with familiar material in a situation that makes such coverage possible. It's partly a matter of individual drive and desire, and it's partly a matter of knowledge and understanding gained through some combination of education and on-the-job training.

Education is a valuable component in the making of the expert reporter. But, surprisingly, it is uncommon to find journalists who emphasize the necessity of a specialized degree. Rather, they stress a broad liberal arts background, perhaps with a concentration of coursework in a specialized field (for example, several survey courses in different scientific or business disciplines). A master's degree may be an advantage, although it is seldom considered a requirement. Often, however, specialists will get the opportunity to participate in programs sponsored by specialist groups and colleges to improve their content background.

While a journalism education is accepted as a valuable means of gaining entry positions, it is assumed that the expert reporter will have supplemented that education or gained journalistic know-how through practical experience. Seldom will a new graduate move into a specialty slot. The route to finding one's place as a specialized expert is general-assignment experience. The *Denver Post*, for example, hires as specialists individuals with four to six years of reporting experience, most of which is in general assignment.

The idea is that, aside from simply having proven themselves and paid their dues before moving into a specialty, reporters benefit from the general experience by having the chance to develop basic skills and journalistic maturity. It helps young reporters develop tenacity, aggressiveness, and interview technique. This is common advice, typified by the experience of Georgie Anne Geyer, columnist for the Universal Press Syndicate:

"I had five years on society and local news, and I can't say how much I feel that slow, sort of everyday, repetition really trains in news judgment. But we talk about truth, and we are the ones who really can approximate more of the truth because we see it in front of us. It's not philosophical. It's the truth of what's going on around you. In order to do that, you have to sharpen your abilities to observe, and I think you do that in everyday work as a reporter."[4]

So, the expert reporter must have the basic skills of the general-assignment reporter: writing skills, reporting skills, and understanding of subject matter. The difference between the two lies in the specialist's emphasis on the latter and the opportunities the reporter gets to develop and use that content understanding.

The specialist, or expert reporter, tells the desk what stories he or she will cover, while the opposite applies to the generalist. And this has strong implications.

First, it means that story topics coming from a reporter are more likely to be oriented toward the practical problems of citizens or those who work within that subject area. Editors sitting in the office may lose touch with their readers and make assignments on the basis of long-standing personal prejudices. The field reporter daily confronts real life.

Second, it means greater diversity and depth of coverage. The expert reporter is in constant contact with sources and with the literature of the field, usually attends important meetings (both for coverage and informational purposes), and thus knows the issues and developments. Many stories that percolate from this process involve subjects that otherwise would have gone unnoticed. The expert reporter will find stories not obvious to the editor or the general reporter.

Third, relative autonomy allows the expert reporter to concentrate on stories in which he or she is interested. Any good reporter must be able to handle almost any assignment and often will work on uninteresting ones. That's the nature of journalism. But psychologists will agree that human beings do the best job on tasks that interest them. So, more frequent opportunities to do that must contribute to the quality of coverage and presentation.

Fourth, it means greater journalistic competition, the force that drives news organizations to the twin peaks of more and better. A specialist seeking the bigger picture should have a perspective that goes beyond the local community. While the point of coverage remains local, the processes of comparison and contrast force an outward orientation on area, state, or national subject matter. Specialists tend to know each other and to know that others across the country may be working on their own versions of the same story.

THE POTENTIAL PROBLEMS

Specialization is not new. Political, sports, business, education, and government reporters have been around for a long time. What is new is the application of the concept to important fields of social inquiry, to medicine, the environment, consumer affairs. And what is new is the overall emphasis and shifting of resources to support such specialized coverage. Yet in terms of its development, specialization is in no more than its adolescent stage. News organizations have seen how the expert reporter contributes diversity and depth in response to modern requirements. But they don't yet know the full potential. And they are at best only vaguely aware of the potential problems.

However, even in this early stage, at least two important questions have arisen and haunt those responsible for running newsrooms. Could specialists become too expert, too close to their subjects and sources, and lose the journalistic edge of being outside observers? Could a reporter tire and become "burned out" on a subject?

Whether an indiviual reporter's expertise leads to conflicting interests, of course, depends upon the individual. Some with formal legal training, for example, find that education to be a valuable tool in their efforts to report comprehensively on the nation's criminal justice system. Others find they lose the ability to communicate with lay citizens and to think independently.

The reporter conceivably can become so much a part of the system that he or she identifies with sources and begins to communicate their specialized jargon or espouse their concepts. What is perfectly clear to source and reporter may be gobbledygook to readers, viewers, or listeners. To the petroleum engineer, 64 billion barrels of oil is a meaningful concept. To the public it means nothing. In education, implications of "educating the whole child," perhaps apparent on the surface, have ramifications that escape all but the professional educator.

And specialists, like generalists, may commit errors of omission. *Los Angeles Times* media writer David Shaw cites the media's missing, or being late to cover, whole movements such as civil rights, feminism, or environmentalism.

"It was not so much a matter of the newspaper consciously trying to protect its friends by suppressing bad news," Shaw says. "It was more a matter of the men running the newspaper and the men running the city often sharing the same perceptions—and the same misperceptions. They just didn't see the story early enough. Sometimes, proximity, mutuality and personal relationships can combine with journalistic skepticism to distort one's judgment."[5]

There is a more specific version of this—reporters becoming what social scientists call "co-opted" by their sources. At its least, this is overdependence on certain talkative, informative, and trustworthy sources. A reporter may become overly impressed with one campus or university and overuse these sources so that diversity is lacking. At its worse, co-opting results in the loss of stories because a reporter commiserates with sources and is too easily convinced that timing is wrong for publication or that publication would be detrimental. Those are valid decisions when made on journalistic grounds; they're not necessarily so when made according to the criteria of sources.

Such distortions are not going to happen in all cases, but news organizations have seen examples of individuals who stay in one subject area so long that they grow tired of it. They become opinionated or prejudiced, or overly enjoy a sense of power and prestige within the field. The editors' solution has been to transfer individuals from one specialty to another. On the surface, this is contradictory and distorts the concept of specialization. But the attitude is that, given sound writing and reporting skills and an opportunity for study, a good reporter can in a limited time pick up enough background knowledge for a new specialty.

One caution, however, is that the transfer must be accomplished between related disciplines. For example, it's quite easy to slide from writing about the environment to writing about energy because these topics are so intertwined and sources are frequently tuned to the same wavelengths. Likewise, to shift from science to medicine or among various levels of government is not overly difficult. But it's difficult to take someone from, say, religion, and put that person into a completely different specialty, such as science.

Within certain reasonable boundaries, transferring specialists is accomplished smoothly and with a minimum of lag time. And it is generally expected that such actions will result in a fresher journalistic perspective and possibly rejuvenate individual reporters by providing them with new challenges. But, of course, exceptions abound. Some reporters are so thoroughly professional and so journalistically fascinated with their subjects that they never tire of them.

WHAT THE BOSS OWES THE SPECIALIST

Assignment transfer is one institutional action designed to make the system work more effectively, but it is not the only requirement of the news organization that is serious about specialists. The organization must create an environment for its experts' effectiveness. This includes time, financial support, guidance, coordination, and opportunities for professional improvement and stimulation.

Predictably, one of the keys to effectively managing the expert reporter is good leadership. If specialists are selected with care, if they have the right training, if they have the right attitude, and if their relationships with editors or news directors are sound, most of the potential problems will never materialize. But editors must agree that time and money will be available, and they must place special emphasis on their functions of coordination and communication.

If a reporter does in fact use specialized jargon or concepts, it is the editor who remembers that the lay audience is being forgotten. And when specialties such as energy and environment are related, it is the editor who keeps tabs on what is being done and encourages communication to avoid duplication or even contradiction. And it is the editor who assures that what specialists produce is journalistically sound and within news organization policy.

The editor integrates specialists into the operation and achieves what sociologist Emile Durkheim called "organic solidarity" within the organization.[6] The components of news production depend upon each other, and the total impact depends upon the interrelationships of the individual parts. When an organization functions with division of labor, fine tuning is necessary to achieve the balance that provides greatest efficiency and maximum effect. And that balance comes through careful coordination.

For one thing, editors must ensure a proper balance between specialists and general-assignment reporters. The day-to-day spot news content provides much of the information citizens seek when they come to their newspaper or broadcast program. While emphasis on spot news and human interest coverage can become excessive, as can emphasis on specialty material, careful orchestration can achieve the blend suited to community needs and desires.

CONCLUSION: THE EXPERT REPORTER

Is it possible that by so wholeheartedly accepting the concept of the specialist or expert reporter, journalism is sowing the seeds of doubt among its audience? These are, after all, times of "a new distrust of the experts," says *Time* magazine essayist Frank Trippett. They are times in which most Americans are hostage to the superior knowledge of the expert, and the citizen has rediscovered that the best of experts will now and then launch an unsinkable Titanic.[7]

The answer to that question would be frightening were it not for the fact that the jounalistic expert exists not as part of the problem but as part of the rescue force. The expert reporter does not create new bodies of contradictory theory or new social programs or products which may go astray. The expert reporter exists as a means of helping the citizen understand what is being done and said by social and scientific experts.

The distinction is highlighted by the fact that even the popular terminology "journalistic specialist" is a misnomer. Few journalists actually are specialists. With the possible exception of those who work for highly technical publications, journalists by definition serve a general function, to facilitate the widespread dissemination of information. That function doesn't change even if the reporter deals exclusively with specialized sources of information. The job may be contrasted with that of a medical specialist. And the difference is like that between a megaphone and a funnel. They're similar in shape, but their function depends on which end is emphasized. The medical specialist starts with a broad education that is then funneled into a narrow channel at the point of contact with the public. The journalistic specialist starts with a narrow information base which is then broadly and generally distributed to the public. The information is specialized, but the communication is general.

The ability to understand and communicate remains the goal of journalists of all types. Coping with specialized, often highly technical or complex, information is the challenge of the expert reporter. The effort represents a desire by journalism to dig deeper, to be more comprehensive, to broaden the scope of public knowledge and understanding. To accomplish those goals, reporters themselves must know and understand. That's why American journalism and American citizens need the expert reporter.

NOTES

1. Linda Deutsch, panel discussion, Region 11 Conference, Society of Professional Journalists, Sigma Delta Chi, Costa Mesa, Cal., April 22, 1978.
2. Walter Lippmann, *Public Opinion* (New York: Free Press, 1922), p. 19.
3. As quoted in Jeremy Tunstall, *Journalists at Work* (Beverly Hills, Cal.: Sage Publications, 1971), p. 1.
4. Georgie Anne Geyer, panel discussion, Region 11 Conference, Society of Professional Journalists, Sigma Delta Chi, Costa Mesa, Cal., April 22, 1978.
5. David Shaw, "Why Papers Miss News Stories," *presstime,* October 1979, p. 26.
6. Emile Durkeim, *The Division of Labor in Society* (New York: Free Press, 1933), p. 131.
7. Frank Trippett, "A New Distrust of the Experts," *Time*, May 14, 1979, p. 54.

Chapter 2

FUNDAMENTALS OF COVERING LOCAL GOVERNMENT

For years, reporters have walked into city, township, county, metro, and other local governmental offices in their search for news. They have attended thousands, perhaps millions, of meetings of councils, boards, commissions, committees, departments, and agencies. They have interviewed countless local government officials and produced reams of copy.

Local government news may be the major contribution by newspapers and broadcast news departments to the life of the average person. In spite of greater impact by state and federal governments, the most immediate governmental effect comes through local programs. And the news media, as the principal source of public information, play an important role in local decision making. It's not exactly a mutual admiration society—this relationship between local officials and reporters—but both groups know they rely on each other and, more than that, they know the public benefits from both their working together and their moments of discord.

But the media are criticized because they too often simply funnel through what government officials say or what happened at last night's council meeting. They give little evaluation, little bigger meaning, and little explanation of the impact of a statement or action upon citizens.

The *Oakland Press* in Pontiac, Michigan, for example, recently made this criticism of itself. But it determined to change its course. The paper's content study showed that 45 percent of its news hole consisted of "dry, factual accounts

11

of local government and school board actions and non-actions," while general features made up less than 5 percent and school features under 2 percent.

"That isn't an ideal balance," the *Press* concluded. "There is nothing wrong with local government news, and it is not the intent . . . to phase it out of the newspaper. But there is something wrong when who-what-where stories from little meetings devour nearly half of our local news hole.

"What it all means is that all too often—for instance, all the time—we write news in the form of a resume of a boring meeting. It is accurate. It is factual. And it is pitifully dull." In a policy booklet, the *Press* told its staff, "If we look at the newspaper with the reader's critical eye, we ought to see two things: A lot of what we're writing doesn't belong in print at all, or should be there in barebones, short-as-possible form; a lot of what survives that test has to be written from a different slant. Where the subject is complex and inherently dull, it's not enough to tell the reader what happened. Tell him—and show him—why it happened and what difference it can make to him."[1]

Providing this additional twist is a burden to reporters.

First, it means they must provide more news from the reader's perspective. Presenting the viewpoint of government officials is not all bad, but in many instances it fails to satisfy readers who have a different perspective. It is not enough to report that a local tax increase will add so many thousands of dollars to the treasury. How much will it cost the individual reader? What will the reader, as a citizen, gain from government as a result?

Second, it means reporters must reduce their dependence upon news releases, handouts, news conference statements, and prepared remarks. Few will complain about use of such material, but it should not be the reporter's sole source.

The more efficient local government is, the more influence it tends to exert on the media. It regularly presents, in writing, a wide variety of materials: memos, staff studies, inter-office staff communications, background materials, and de-tailed explanations. Officials volunteer selected comments. And, as a result, some lazy reporters wait for the information to come rather than do the digging themselves. Some reporters will take all the paperwork or official comment with-out carefully evaluating it and perhaps never discovering an important, unmen-tioned angle of the story.

Third, it means reporters need to take a more evaluative attitude, based on their knowledge of the structure, functions, and organization of local government. If one simply reports what happened at the meeting or what the mayor said, there is little need for full understanding of the complexities of governing even a small town. But if the goal is to place governmental activities into a fuller perspective, reporters need a more aggressive and knowledgeable approach. That many re-porters do not know this is a cause for concern, according to David Burnham of the *New York Times.*

"It is my belief that many reporters in America, perhaps even a majority of them, approach their jobs too passively," he says, "because the polite and passive stance is what many of their editors and publishers actually want. It is partly because reporters rarely are given an opportunity to develop enough expertise in a single area to question intelligently the expert and his conventional wisdom. It is partly because some reporters are insecure in their personal lives and desire to be liked by the people and the institutions they are covering."[2]

Providing comprehensive coverage of the complicated maneuverings of even a small local government is difficult because reporters require quick access to so many resources. It doesn't make any difference whether it is city, county, state, or national government. Reporters need an expert's grasp on the power structure, the process, and the wide range of governmental subject matter. Even though government reporters may be defined as journalistic specialists, they actually must serve a generalist function. One day they may be writing about airports, the next day about a poverty or welfare program. Or dog licenses. Or housing, highways, or hospital rates.

The frequency of meetings, governmental style, amount of material to be covered, available time, and editors' attitudes all are factors in what reporters can do on a given assignment. The challenge is to know the system so well that daily happenings may be placed into a larger meaning.

OFFICIAL AUTHORITY COMES FROM THE STRUCTURE

The name of the game in the American system of local government is power. Who controls? Who influences? Who decides? A citizen or a reporter who can answer these questions is in a position to understand the forces that provide the flavor of any community. Textbooks say, correctly, that the American system is based on negotiation and compromise, resulting in complete satisfaction for no one, but also complete dissatisfaction for few. At the same time, however, one does not have to be a political scientist to know that some people get more from the system because either they help make the decisions or their opinions reach those who make decisions.

Getting a share of that power depends upon several things, including politics, personality, wealth, and social status. But official authority grows out of one's place in the governmental structure of the city, village, town, borough, or county. And it's here that reporters have to start in their quest to understand local issues, policies, and directions. Government is not a static entity. It's a process that depends upon interplay among those in authority.

Although forms of governmental organization vary according to state laws and local traditions, governmental textbooks list three traditional types.

The *mayor-council* type is characterized by an elected executive and an elected legislative body. In practice, this type takes two forms, with administrative authority providing the basis for the difference. One is the *strong mayor* structure, in which the mayor dominates administratively and the mayor and council share in policy making. The mayor carries out established policy, usually prepares the budget, proposes new programs, and supervises department heads whom he or she may have appointed. The council's major duties are budget approval and working with the mayor in setting policy.

The *weak mayor* form, older of the two and generally popular in smaller cities, gives the executive limited, frequently only ceremonial, authority. This person usually presides over council, but the council itself retains most of the power. Members sometimes serve in city departments, often prepare the budget, and may have the largest word in municipal appointments.

A most interesting feature of the *commission* form of government is that it violates the tradition of separation of powers. A small number of elected commissioners, usually five or seven, retains all legislative and executive authority. One of the commissioners usually serves as mayor, but he or she has limited additional powers, frequently only ceremonial. At times, especially in larger county governments, this form may feature an appointed administrative officer.

Council-manager governments consist of an elected council which appoints a professional administrator to guide the operations of city departments. Council members are responsible to the public for establishing policy and, ultimately, for the overall operation of the government. The administrator, usually called city manager, is responsible for seeing that programs are carried out. Managers usually have authority to hire and fire, prepare the budget for council approval, and serve at the will of the council. This form has tended to put municipal operation in the hands of trained, career professionals. If there is a mayor, his or her authority often is limited.

The reporter's relationship with officials in any of these systems depends on the official's structural authority and actual power. From a practical standpoint, the reporter's concern is getting good information from that person over a period of time. The system of professional managers tends to give an edge because these often are more comfortable in dealing with reporters and usually are sensitive to journalistic requirements.

"The professional manager, despite his high awareness, may himself not be more open, but the system usually is more open if you know how to work it," says Bill Miller of the *Richmond* [Virginia] *Times-Dispatch.* "You have to try to work one-on-one with the professional or whoever is willing to deal with you. You also have to learn the system of government and how the various pieces fit together and then plug, into that, the individual people at the departmental or bureaucratic level."

Dealing with professional managers may provide reporters with other challenges because a professional who understands how to cooperate with the press would know equally well how to control the flow of news. Most professional managers are ambitious and therefore careful. They're concerned about what image is conveyed.

Miller's experience is that strong mayors, even though they usually do not have managerial training, are likely to be like the professional, with a "very carefully outlined and functioning bureaucracy" and some general understanding of how the media operate.

A contrast is most apparent in the weak mayor and commission forms, termed "amateur governments" by some political scientists. Their approach often is secretive and distrustful. Officials react in either of two ways: They may try to become close to the reporter in the hope that, by establishing some sort of friendship, they can understand and deal trustingly with each other. Failing that, or as an alternative, the officials try to keep reporters at a distance.

"This," Miller says in understatement, "frequently leads to antagonism and mistrust and is dysfunctional."

Bruce Keppel of the *Los Angeles Times*

(*Los Angeles Times* photo)

Miller terms the commission, the most common form of county government, a "reporter's headache" because it lacks a central figure with whom reporters can work regularly. They must deal with the commissioners as a group and develop diplomatic working relations with all. If a county administrator or a commissioner emerges as spokesperson, the reporter may have some sort of centralized source. But, fundamentally, it is up to the reporter to do the necessary legwork, fit the pieces together, and provide analysis.

A commission gives reporters a real challenge because of the lack of dividing lines between administrative and legislative authority. Commissioners can do almost anything with three or four votes on a given day. That can be efficient, but the absence of checks and balances offers the opportunity to conduct business out of the public's eye. It also can mean less open conflict.

"This is a challenge to a reporter because it's difficult to write interestingly and clearly about noncontroversial stuff," says Bruce Keppel of the *Los Angeles Times.* "Well, they're controversial, but they're not the epithet-tossing sort of controversy. The controversy is in the method of resolving the problem, and it really is hard to write about that."

Whatever the form of government, the job of the reporter is to provide readers, viewers, and listeners with an understanding of what Keppel calls the "delivery end of government services"—what the local problems are, how they're resolved or why they're not resolved.

Much of the reporter's preparation for this assignment will involve lower-echelon individuals who perform the specific tasks of local government. The journalistic value of these officials will vary. Some are elected and thus are in a position to be independent in their comments unless controlled by political leaders. Appointees, however, may be cautious in dealing with reporters because of their dependence on top officials for their jobs. These are not hard and fast rules, though. In both cases, local political structure and personality factors may override the traditional expectations.

In any event, reporters have to deal with the following local officials.

Chief legal officer (city or county attorney, counselor, solicitor, counsel, or law director), who gives legal advice to city officials and represents the government in court. As adviser, this person has an impact upon policy decisions through helping establish legal boundaries on what a local government is permitted to do.

Clerk (clerk of council), who functions as the official caretaker of local records and often keeps formal minutes of council meetings. But, especially in smaller cities, clerks may be of greater journalistic assistance. Often, because they remain in their positions for long periods, they know more about the specifics of local government operation than anyone else, at times even being called upon for advice by officials.

Treasurer, although essentially a bookkeeper with no authority, may be an excellent source, as custodian of local funds. Treasurers account for every dollar, make deposits, pay bills on order, and, without doubt, are the most knowledgeable persons on the specifics of local finances.

Controller (comptroller) works in relative obscurity, but serves as the chief fiscal assistant to city officials. Controllers often actually prepare the administrative budget and, once it is approved, assume internal responsibility for administering it.

Assessor (board of assessors) has responsibility for determining valuation of property, which dictates the amount of property tax to be collected. Although assessors seldom have a direct role in establishing local policy, their responsibilities for making funds available may position them to influence that policy directly.

Auditor, the watchdog of the budget, generally serves as agent for the council in determining if administrative expenditures were made according to appropriation.

Planner (planning commission) may be an individual or a group, may consist of public officials or lay citizens. But, in any event, city and county planners are responsible for converting long-range goals into local policy. Planning is an effort to make most efficient and progressive use of available land and, as such, may have significant impact upon citizens' lifestyles.

But even in smaller communities the responsibilities incorporated into these offices do not cover the range of services local government attempts to provide. Reporters will spend varying amounts of time with the heads of specific departments. These contacts not only reduce dependency upon government's higher officials, but they have additional value since department heads usually have more specific knowledge about the "delivery end" of local government. It is at the departmental level that citizens have their direct contact with their local government.

And that contact is made when citizens have needs or problems with local government services which may include any of the following:

Police and fire protection
Construction and maintenance of streets, bridges, sidewalks
Medical care and/or promotion of good health practices
Public parks and recreation
Supply and distribution of water, electricity, and natural gas
Public transportation
Libraries, museums, and art galleries
Sanitation services, including sewage and solid-waste disposal
Noise pollution
Public education

How many of these functions will be included in the reporter's responsibilities depends upon news organization preference. Education, for example, usually is a separate entity and a separate beat. Law enforcement frequently is a separate journalistic assignment. The attention to each service depends on time available to the reporter, the philosophy of his or her news organization, and the reporter's specific assignment. But the degree to which the services are covered may well be the greatest determinant of quality in local government reporting, at least in terms of journalism's responsibility to report what is most significant to the citizens.

This is not an easy thing to do. Even small towns and counties often are active enough that individual reporters have problems effectively covering them.

"One of the biggest problems in covering county government," says Jim Golding of the *Weatherford* [Texas] *Democrat,* "is keeping up with the various offices, officials, and activities in addition to being aware of what all the commissioners are doing, along with the county auditor, the tax assessor, the county treasurer, county judge and agricultural extension people."

The magnitude of local government coverage—from Golding's job in Weatherford, Texas, to Keppel's assignment in sprawling Los Angeles County—explains why many reporters are tempted to limit the number of sources with whom they deal. But it is that magnitude which highlights the need for a broad base of sources and an issue orientation, not to the exclusion of spot news, but as a means of helping citizens understand their governments.

THEY'LL ALWAYS HAVE MEETINGS

The effort to find time and sources to provide information on local public trends is being applied by more reporters to the legislative side of government as well as the administrative side. Most news media tend to use some combination of three approaches to covering meetings of council, commission, or committee.

One, which may be labeled the *paper-of-record* approach, is characteristic of smaller communities where the relationship of local governments to their citizens is closer. Here the reporter makes a point to include practically all business conducted, not just the highlights. The idea is that even a relatively insignificant item is worthy of mention because some reader will have both an interest in and a need for that information.

Of course, detailed discussion is not provided for all agenda items. Often, a rather standardized "in-other-action" list at the end of the story summarizes lesser points.

However, not only small-town reporters need to take into consideration the desires and needs of portions of their audiences, and Bob Threlkeld of the *Denver Post* admits he has problems deciding how much to include in his stories. In the end, however, he too leans toward the paper-of-record approach.

"When you're a major city paper, then you obviously have space limitations, and you highlight that business which you think is citywide in nature," he says. "But you also realize that it's the local zoning case which has the most intense readership in a particular neighborhood. So I think that some of these 'little' topics—zoning is one—keep coming back. They should be reported more."

The second major philosophy of meeting coverage grows out of consideration of space and time and geographic area. The *major-business* approach rules broadcasting reporters, for example, who do not have the air time to discuss items of limited interest. It often is followed by newspapers whose reporters cover wide geographic areas involving numerous local governments, as well as specialized publications whose readers are interested only in certain parts of government business.

Partly, the major-business approach grows out of the notion that much of what governments do is routine, repetitive, and therefore boring. Reporters see little public value in writing about a routine transfer of funds from one budget category to another or about an item significant to a limited number of citizens. And the approach partly is a function of what can be accomplished given journalism's natural limitations. Simply put, ignoring many of the smaller news items gives reporters more time and space to devote to the major business.

From the reader's perspective, this approach can result in valuable—if not comprehensive—coverage of a meeting or other local government activity. Handled improperly, however, it can result in coverage which suggests that governmental decisions are too big to be directly related to individual readers. Such coverage may reinforce a general attitude that government is impersonal and distant.

Issue orientation—in which the function is more explanatory than a blow-by-blow account of a given meeting—is the third approach. The idea is to present the *meaning* of meetings and actions. This is the analytical approach Keppel talks about, and it's the advice given to local government reporters of the *Oakland Press*:

"Our story should not be a summary of what went on there. If participants babble about trivia while the real news is hiding nearby, we must find that news and ignore that babble. If the city council debates three hours about some fire truck bids, and five minutes about a contract with the mayor's brother-in-law, we are not obligated to give news space to each in proportion as the council gave each its time.

"Forget the smoke, forget the babble. Write the news. And write it for the guy who's worked hard all day, given most of what's left of it to his family, and hasn't the time, the background or the inclination to wade through a long dull governmental-handout type of story and try to guess what it means to him."[3]

The issue approach may mean holding the story until more research broadens the discussion. Or it may mean talking after the meeting with participants, or presenting some of the floor debate rather than simply recording the decision.

Many reporters regularly broaden a story by talking with council members, public representatives who participate in meetings, and individuals who may be affected by a decision. Of course, the extent of such may well be a function of deadline pressure, but reporters who make this questioning a practice, even if it is necessarily limited, find their stories improved.

"One of the major problems in covering the city council in some cases," says Erwin Baker of the *Los Angeles Times,* "is the bewildering course that the council might take on specific legislation. There may be various interpretations as to what action the council did, in fact, take. Often, even the council members, after they vote, are unaware of what they did. Many times you have to get an interpretation afterward from the city attorney as to what actually happened."

Although he admits it's time consuming, Baker uses a tape recorder to supplement his notes of the Los Angeles City Council meetings not only to assure accuracy of direct quotations but to help him present the testimony and discussion.

The reporter has to make the judgment, of course, as to whether the debate helps the reader understand the meaning of or alternatives to a council action. One does not include debate simply to liven a potentially dull story, although that is a valuable side effect.

The debate also may indicate openness of city officials and whether they are willing to consider alternative points of view and perhaps even citizen participation.

Reporters often have to deal with local officials who, although perhaps efficient and honest in their operation of government, are tight-lipped and reluctant to be quoted. Perhaps discussion is limited at council meetings. A resolution or ordinance is introduced and approved. Debate may have been private. Some officials believe open discussion hampers their effectiveness and, in spite of sunshine laws, they conduct a rather quiet, behind-the-scenes operation.

At the other extreme, perhaps, are governmental bodies that deal with a bewildering array of alternative points of view, changes of mind, backtracking, and amendments from officials committed to public debate. Deciding how much of this discussion to present is a headache for the reporter. It's one thing to show openness; it's another to indicate confusion. And it takes a reporter who fully understands what is happening to find the proper blend that shows citizens how their government functions as well as informs them of specific actions.

A similar type of difficulty for reporters, especially in smaller and rural towns and counties, is informality in meetings of councils and commissions. Reporters expect an agenda, formal business sessions, and periodic background materials. But it's not always that way, says Jim Golding of the *Weatherford* [Texas] *Democrat.*

Sam Martino of the *Milwaukee Journal*

(*Milwaukee Journal* photo)

"You sit in on a city commission meeting, and members will go through their agenda items, have discussion and make decisions in a very orderly and organized manner," he says. "When the county commission meets, you'll have the county judge's secretary bring coffee in. You'll have people who come in and out of the courthouse hallways and say hello to one of the commissioners, and they'll shake hands and talk a while. Then they'll go on with their agenda and then something else will happen."

Golding says that, despite the time involved, he likes this informality "because you pick up things that you wouldn't in a more businesslike setting. Not necessarily from the agenda, just other things that might be happening around the area."

Reporters usually have many opportunities to report on particular pieces of legislation. The legislative process is deliberately repetitious, with each step designed to give the public and officials chance to comment.

As Sam Martino of the *Milwaukee Journal* describes it, "You've got a lot of kicks at the cat, sometimes as many as nine kicks. What I mean by that is that you work with a spokesman, or a congressman, or a legislator or supervisor, and he does something or proposes something, and then it goes through the long road of the legislative process. You can write about that one particular proposal as it goes through committee meetings, through public meetings and debate, and when you get comments on it from important people in the community."

Reporters have to decide at what stage of this process they should intensify their journalistic attention and when they are overcovering an event or issue. The initial determination is based on newsworthiness when as issue first comes to the reporter's attention. The amount of follow-up depends on the controversy or reaction the first story may have stimulated. A particularly important or controversial issue may require constant and detailed coverage of the formal proceedings, supplemented by additional interview material.

An important part of this legislative process is committee meetings. Reporters will differ on how many committee meetings should be attended regularly, but they will agree that some require being on the scene. Often it is in committee session that disagreements are settled and final forms of proposals worked out. Whether such meetings require a reporter's presence depends on the importance of the issue and what is expected to occur during the meeting.

The practical problem with committee meetings is their numbers. There simply are too many. Also, much of the testimony at committee sessions will be repeated when the full council or commission gets together. Reporter attention to committee meetings is increased, of course, when the issue is important to the community. And, if it's not possible to attend a meeting, reporters often will pick up much of it by talking with the committee clerk or committee members.

If the reporter determines that the issue does not merit continued coverage, he or she will make a note to be sure to provide later coverage on the matter's resolution. Too many stories are never followed through, and the steady reader often is disappointed in efforts to follow an item of business to its conclusion. It's much too easy to let that follow-up slide, especially if the item is not controversial, in the pace of day-to-day activities.

SOMETIMES THEY WON'T COOPERATE

Information doesn't always come easily. Governmental officials have a long list of reasons—some good, some terrible—for not wanting to comment or cooperate with reporters. They may feel the information is too sensitive to be made public. They may not trust a reporter's ability to understand or report accurately. They may want to withhold information until it is to their political advantage to release it. They may not like the reporter. They may be seeking to protect negotiations that they think are best conducted quietly. They may be attempting to hide a wrongdoing.

Although not usually the case, some reporters will agree at times that it's best not to make certain information public. Seventy-two percent of reporters who responded to a survey by Paul L. Massa of the Ohio Department of Health, himself a former reporter and columnist, "expressed the belief that under certain conditions and in certain situations public information should not be published by the news media." However, the reporters strongly supported the notion that *they,* not governmental officials, should make the decision.[4]

This is an argument that will never be settled. In many ways, control of information is the ultimate political tool, and both reporters and officials will continue to guard jealously what they consider to be their right. They will always be in conflict, and therefore it behooves reporters to know how to do more than scream when public information becomes private.

Going to court is an obvious choice. Almost all states have open-meeting and open-records laws. Although content varies, they do give the news media the right in certain situations to sue for public access to governmental information.[5] And the federal Freedom of Information Act gives the public, including reporters, the right of access to public records of the executive branch of the federal government.

But more reporters and editors these days are urging that news organizations not be too quick to jump into court. A law suit plays into the hands of a legal system that would like to think it should make the decisions in journalistic-governmental conflicts. Reporters are not attorneys. They must understand the law, and they must know how to make it work for them. But going to court should be the last resort. They must first attempt to pry the lid off through more informal methods in time for the next deadline.

Part of the answer lies in good journalistic technique, specifically in development of additional sources who will provide information which the reporter will then confirm or, in special instances, use on an unattributed basis. Use of unidentified sources, however, should be restricted to unusual cases. Many reporters feel strongly that it is not often necessary.

There also is the argument that the audience should receive enough information, including the name and background of the source, that *it* can determine the validity of information. But, of course, that doesn't relieve the journalist of evaluating the source's credibility also.

David Burnham of the *New York Times* classifies all governmental employees according to usefulness as sources:

"The head of an agency, because of his position, must offer self-serving, overly optimistic portraits of his operations. The second and by far the largest group of government employees are so filled with bureaucratic fears that they never tell you anything—honestly or dishonestly. The third group, comprised of individuals I actively seek out, can be called the malcontents. These are the people who for varying motives, sometimes good, sometimes bad, sometimes a mixture of both good and bad, provide the reporter with leads, information, and documents that the head of the agency usually does not want a reporter to see."

Burnham warns, however, that information provided by a malcontent, like information from an agency head, never can be taken at face value. It must be supported by documents or statements from other people. In addition, he says, especially when performance is being challenged, a department or agency should be given an opportunity to answer the charges.[6]

But it is not sufficient for a reporter to merely get the information from another source when public records are withheld or a meeting is closed. Journalists must meet the situation head-on to discourage such occurrences in the future. Ernest Morgan of the University of Missouri surveyed 145 city editors for their suggestions on how to proceed:

Advise the presiding officer formally that you seek admission. Protest; cite provisions of the state statute.

Get names of the attending members of the public body. Ask if the decision to close was made in open meeting. Where? When?

Ask if the decision to close was made by a vote or by the presiding officer. If it was closed by vote, who voted how?

As for justification for closing any meeting to the public. Try to pin officials down for the record.

Make it clear that a story will be written about the closing of the meeting.

Keep calm. The news organization wants an open meeting, not a vendetta. If reporters lose their tempers, the fight is lost. If board members lose their tempers, so much the better for the story on the closing.

If, after the challenge, the meeting is still closed, call a news executive who will call the attorney.

Morgan says the media must recognize that reporters have to share in the blame for governmental secrecy because of superficial, inaccurate reporting.

"Officials complain, with reason, of emphasis on minor conflict, of a hunt for good guys and bad guys, of sheer ignorance of government, of carelessness, of a fascination for dramatic trivia, of significant material slighted or ignored because of its complexity, and inevitably of sensationalism," he says.

Editors, reporters, and journalism schools must confront this problem, he stresses, because ultimately the public's support will go to the group—journalists or governmental officials—it trusts most. And public trust for journalists will grow only out of professional reporting. As one midwestern editor told Morgan, "Good solid reporting is the best way to fight secrecy in government. But it is also necessary to use a strong open-meeting or open-record law occasionally. These do not replace good reporting; they supplement it."[7]

NOTES

1. "Covering Government: A New Testament to Newswriting," *Oakland Press,* Pontiac, Mich., 1976, p. 5.
2. David Burnham, *The Role of Media in Controlling Corruption* (New York: Criminal Justice Center, John Jay College of Criminal Justice), pp. 2–3. Reprinted with permission from the John Jay Press.
3. Covering Government," p. 13.
4. Paul L. Massa, "Ohio Municipal Officials and the Media," *Ohio Cities and Villages,* November 1975, p. 6.
5. Ernest Morgan, *Informal Methods of Combatting Secrecy in Local Government* (Columbia, Mo.: Freedom of Information Center, 1976), p. 2.
6. Burnham, p. 12.
7. Morgan, pp. 8–27.

Chapter 3

THE HEART OF LOCAL GOVERNMENT COVERAGE

"Follow the money." That's the most basic, yet comprehensive, advice veteran reporters give about covering government at any level. Strictly speaking, not all stories are financial stories. But the monetary path leads reporters into all sorts of interesting and important places. The presence or lack of funds, demands by citizens for satisfaction of certain needs, and governmental response to those demands are indicators of the degree to which citizen and governmental priorities mesh.

The very heart of local government coverage is made up of reports of official efforts to improve the quality of the lives of its citizens. It's people stories—where they live, the problems they face, their attitudes about each other, attitudes about their community and its leadership. And an integral part of all this is the question of whether money is available.

MONEY: THE NITTY AND THE GRITTY

The news media and textbooks devote countless columns, minutes, and pages to the fact that the American city is in trouble. The demand for services is not matched by funds to provide those services. Movement to suburbs, both by individuals and by industries, has reduced the likelihood of local goverments' meeting their financial needs. There are chronicles of financial defaults. There are

24

stories about officials cutting back on programs because, they say, funds are inadequate.

These are important stories. They are mandatory. The public must know of deteriorating cities, of the poor distribution of wealth between core cities and suburbs, of diminishing opportunities to fund special or even regular services. The U.S. system is based on accountability of governmental officials. They may or may not have caused the disease of cities because circumstances cannot always be controlled. But, regardless, the nature of government is that its officials answer to the public. And in most instances they answer only if reporters ask the right questions at the right times.

Sources of Local Government Revenue

That, of course, means more than crisis reporting. It also means paying close attention to local government finances on a day-in-day-out basis. It's a difficult ideal to achieve, but citizens should not be surprised when crises occur.

The story of funds for some time to come will be based on the problems with traditional sources: tax limitations which restrict local revenues, decreasing ability of property taxes to meet local needs, fluctuating trends of state and federal funds coming into the community. The story starts with the revenue sources: local taxes, intergovernmental revenue, nontax fees and service charges, and borrowing.

With few exceptions, local governments are restricted by state law in both the type of taxes they may impose and the levels of that taxation. The practical effect is that property taxes have been the major source of local money for local needs.

Several states permit local government to impose, among others, income or sales taxes, "wheel taxes" on automobiles, taxes on use of hotel and motel rooms, or such special taxes as those on cigarettes. In most cases, however, state limitations are such that income received does not solve the local financial problems. Since state and federal governments make extensive use of sales and income taxes, local areas have been forced mainly to rely on and struggle with administration of property taxes. These may apply to *real* property (buildings and land), *personal* property (possessions such as furniture, jewelry, and clothing), and *intangible* property (bank accounts, stocks, and bonds). The problem with such dependence is that property taxes are assessed on the value of a person's real estate rather than that person's ability to pay. And much of the property tax revenue comes from relatively low-income persons, especially retirees who own property but have fixed incomes.

In addition, any adjustments in the property tax formula must be submitted to the voters in the form of levies. But the growing "taxpayers' revolt" has led voters to become more reluctant to accept local governmental requests for maintenance or increases in the property tax formulas.

Partial relief has come from programs which funnel state and federal funds into the local communities. These programs are of two general types: grants-in-aid to finance specific community efforts such as crime control, housing, or special education programs, and federal revenue-sharing funds which may be used as local officials see fit within certain broad guidelines.

Aggressive local governments, through grants-in-aid, can provide citizens with many opportunities they would otherwise not be able to afford. Basically competitive, the system requires that the community develop a specific program and submit a grant proposal to the appropriate state or federal agency. These funds are meant to redistribute wealth, assist communities with large low-income population, or help solve particular problems. Some may stimulate local efforts to raise funds by including a matching requirement, often on a percentage basis.

Governmental grants, of course, come with strings attached and herein lies the basis for some considerable criticism. At the worst, critics charge, the grants threaten local self-government because external authority determines local policy on how and for what purposes certain funds will be spent. It can be broader than that since federal officials at times will threaten to withhold funds to achieve some unrelated goal, for example, the national fifty-five mile-per-hour speed limit.

Critics also say that, at best, the availability of grant funds changes priorities of local communities. Instead of emphasizing what their citizens feel are the most important issues, local officials often are inclined to attend to those programs for which they have some chance of securing external funding.

In 1972, the government implemented the federal revenue-sharing program as a partial response to these criticisms. Available to all general-purpose local governments, these funds were to replace some of the specific-purpose grants and permit local officials latitude in meeting local needs with programs they could otherwise not afford.

This program, too, is not without faults. The general nature of distribution of the funds means they also go to relatively prosperous areas, in addition to the problem areas. Regardless, revenue sharing has been an important part of the federal budget, although recent trends have placed its future in doubt.

On the local scene, governments have numerous opportunities to raise funds by charging fees for services they provide. The idea is that in many instances, for example, water, hospitals, and public housing, certain individuals or groups benefit more from a service. Thus, they should pay for that service. And this concept has come to be applied to other areas such as sewerage, garbage collection, street lighting and cleaning, snow removal, and weed cutting.

In some instances when municipalities operate gas, water, and electrical facilities, they can make a profit. But utilities seldom are important sources of revenue because they are very expensive to operate. Few public transportation systems, for example, meet operating expenses because they must serve all the people in the entire area. Thus, they often run nonrevenue routes in poorer parts of the city or offer reduced fares to senior citizens or low-income individuals.

Some communities may levy service charges for services provided as a means of making the tax level appear lower than it really is. For example, a sewerage charge added to the water bill will produce funds which otherwise would have been raised through taxes. Such charges also may be used to equalize local taxation or to reach local industries which are, for example, discharging a disproportionate amount of waste into the sewerage system. Or they may be a means for the local government to gain some funds from tax-exempt property.

Special assessments represent yet another means of charging citizens according to the benefit they receive from a city or village service. The most common of these is assessing persons in a neighborhood for all or part of the cost of new street paving, installation of water lines, construction of off-street parking areas and street lighting.

Local governments, like individuals, often find they have needs or desires, but they don't have the cash. Then they face the same decision: Do they wait until enough cash is available or do they borrow? While some officials believe even governments should operate on a cash-only basis, the dominant attitude is that it is most desirable to have the facility or program now and pay for it over time.

Despite some exceptions arising from emergencies, it generally is accepted that local governments should not borrow to meet current operating expenses. And when they borrow to pay for long-term local improvements or emergencies, it is in anticipation of future incoming funds.

Borrowing for a local government generally takes the form of issuing bonds, which are little more than a loan arrangement in which it is agreed that the money will be paid back with interest. They are purchased by banks or other financial institutions. Since interest received on a municipal bond is not taxable, local governments usually pay less than the standard rate of interest. In general, municipalities issue three types of bonds:

General-obligation bonds are supported by the full credit of the local government. In effect, they carry a promise that the resources of the community are available to pay them off and that the tax rate will be sufficient to pay the interest and eventually pay off ("retire") the bonds.

Mortgage bonds, like mortages on an individual's home, normally are used when the community wants to purchase or construct a utility, and the security for the loan is a mortgage on that utility.

Revenue bonds are issued when a community wants to construct a revenue-producing facility such as a toll bridge, tunnel, or electricity or water system. Revenue bonds say, in effect, that the funds to be obtained from operation of these facilities will be used to pay off the bond. Sometimes, bondholders, in addition, will get mortgages on the utilities.

Financial Planning: The Budget

Other than times of crisis, the occasion most likely to attract reporters' attention to governmental finances is the often long, stormy process of preparing and approving the budget. The complexity of the process will vary, of course, but the path toward approval involves a number of rather standardized steps, each of which gives reporters opportunities to weigh local priorities.

   Often the budget is prepared by the budget officer or controller under supervision of the chief executive. In consultation with department heads, the executive estimates revenues and determines priorities that influence allocation of those funds. This report usually contains a summary and a detailed breakdown of the anticipated revenues and expenditures. The spending pattern is divided into various funds, starting with the general fund and then listing others designed to meet special needs such as streets and highways. Often a separate capital improvements budget and perhaps special arrangements to pay off debts will be presented at a different time.

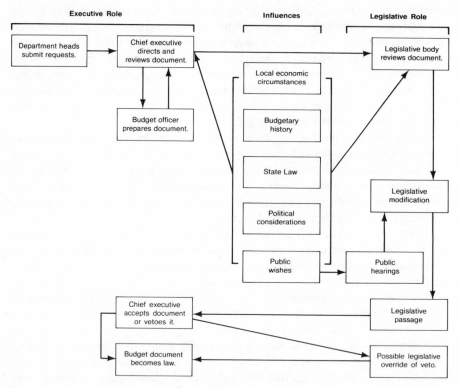

The Budgetary Process

   The document contains specific allocations of funds for specific purposes. Generally called a *line item budget*, it restricts the administration in rather precise ways depending upon the philosophy of the local government. Modern trends lean toward what may be called a *performance budget* or the *project approach,* in which the budget contains allocations of specific amounts for individual programs, but leaves room for administrative flexibility within those categories

   Once completed, this executive budget goes to the council or commission for discussion, modification, and approval. Included in the process at this stage are committee meetings and full-council discussion. Public hearings often will be held to allow citizens the opportunity to object to specific provisions or make special requests for funding of programs not included. Usually, persons who appear before the council represent interest groups rather than a cross-section of citizens. If the chief executive is weak administratively, department heads may appear before the council with requests for modifications.

The legislative body has the authority, then, to increase, reduce, delete, or add any specific item or amount. The document it ultimately approves returns to the chief executive, who often has the authority to veto any specific item. It then becomes a question of whether the council or commission has the desire and the votes to override a veto.

The process is designed to gain maximum input from all persons or groups who would be affected by funds spent on programs. The fact that such input usually comes only from a few who have strong interests and seldom involves the public at large is an accident of democracy which adds to the responsibilities of reporters covering the deliberations.

"How a governmental entity gets and spends its money is the nitty and the gritty of local news," says the *Oakland Press* of Pontiac, Michigan, in a booklet prepared for its staff. "But that doesn't mean the budget interests the reader, who long ago faced the fact that there's no way he can control what's in it. Who goes to public hearings on the budget anymore? No one, you say? An occasional eccentric, you say? You are right. Neither will the reader's interest be trapped by a newspaper story that is a rewrite of the budget book. These always come out as long lists of dollar signs and numbers that mean nothing to him and he won't, and shouldn't, remember."[1]

But the reporter who remembers that those dollar signs and numbers do mean something and who concentrates on that meaning instead of the numbers can produce story after story that will catch the reader's attention. A budget is, after all, a planning document, a statement of philosophy that sets the priorities for the coming year.

How much money will be spent on recreation and how does that compare with previous years and with facilities and programs now available? The answer tells the readers more about government's interest in providing community recreation than hundreds of official declarations. Specific appropriations may determine the treatment your dog will receive if picked up by the local dog catcher, whether you will be able to ride the city bus to work, whether the potholes on your street will be fixed, and what the likely political arguments will be in the next election.

Throughout the process, the story is not in the numbers. The story is in how those numbers relate to people. The story is in local priorities. Why does a department head so strongly support a new bond issue? Why does the mayor oppose it? Is the city manager more interested in constructing buildings or supporting social service programs? Why don't officials support a citizen request that a new street be built on the south side of town? Discussion of why certain groups or individuals make certain recommendations often is of greater significance than amounts of money. The behind-the-scenes negotiations or public debates probably are more political than financial, and that's the essence of good journalistic copy.

The good stories don't come only from the expenditure side of the budget. The estimates of revenue are pregnant with possibilities. Where does the city or county get its money? Is it simply milking the citizens through taxes? Or does it take advantage of numerous opportunities to get funding? Are federal revenue-sharing funds lost in the shuffle of day-to-day operations, or are they used to support special programs as originally intended? Do city services pay for themselves, or is there likely to be an increase in water rates next year?

The soul of any funding story will be people, and it should be couched in people terms. The reporter should be alert to the possibilities. A good first place to look is for dramatic increases or decreases in any of the major revenue categories: taxes; income from fines, permits, licenses, parking meters, etc.; federal and state grants; and payment for services. Potential tax increases are the most obvious, of course, but at times the suggestions may be more subtle. For example, an expected increase in revenue from contracting out fire department services could signal a major improvement in fire protection for residents of a nearby community.

SUBURBIA POSES SPECIAL PROBLEMS

Look at any metropolitan newspaper and you'll find traditional beat reporters who are the backbone of the city staff—city hall reporter who spends all day in city hall; police reporter stationed in the police department pressroom; court reporter who walks the halls of the courthouse, not the newsroom.

But if you look at any metropolitan area, you'll see that most of the population in the automobile-oriented decades since World War II has shifted from the aging, land-locked central city to the suburbs. These are rapidly developing cities and villages that are independent residential, recreational, and education centers, and regional economic centers. Mark the new air-conditioned shopping malls on a county map. Around these regional shopping complexes will be acres of new homes, fast-food restaurants, and new-car dealers—in short, the booming growth areas of news media audiences.

And reporters assigned to a metro desk find themselves dealing with not just one city hall or city school board, but with many cities, each with its own mayor, city administrator or clerk, elected city council, city services, fire/police chief, zoning and health codes, and sometimes a judicial system (mayor's court). For example, Cincinnati, Ohio, shares Hamilton County with thirty-seven other cities and villages, each with its own municipal administration and each with a mayor who is a very important figure in the community. Beyond the suburbs are sprawling subdivisions in the unincorporated area of the county. One of these, Colerain Township, has 80,000 residents and is three times larger than the largest suburban city. The township is run by three elected trustees with extremely limited powers, because townships were created 150 years ago as divisions of farmland in Ohio.

Who lives in the suburbs? These are the people who shop at those regional shopping malls, have children in one of the suburban school districts, probably work in a suburban industrial park near the interstate highway. They go to movies in the regional cinemas, eat at the McDonald's and Burger Kings, and go to the dentists and doctors near the regional hospitals. It's a fact of life that some city editors don't admit: Many people who live in the suburbs have all the goods and services they need within driving range, and they seldom have a reason to come into the central city. They aren't touched by the decisions made in city hall or by the city's board of education.

What, then, do suburban residents care about? How can reporters cover thirty-seven city councils when ten meet on the same night? And what do reporters find when they look hard at the suburbs? What you can find in any big city: police ineptitude, small-town political machines that run the small towns; nepotism; and very interesting and knowledgeable people who care about their cities and who know everyone by name.

A startling number of big-city problems (crime, labor disputes, hazardous wastes or working conditions), like the population, have drifted from the central city. The metro reporter also will have a share of major news stories. Airplanes crash in the suburbs because airports are built at the edge of the metropolitan area. Hazardous chemical wastes are hauled from city plants to rural, isolated landfills. The biggest Cincinnati story in recent years was a suburban story—162 persons were killed Memorial Day weekend, 1977, at the Beverly Hills Supper Club fire in Southgate, Kentucky. Beverly Hills was the regional big-name entertainment showplace, eight miles from downtown Cincinnati, just across the Ohio River. But Southgate is a city of fewer than 5,000 persons, with only a volunteer fire department.

The reporter assigned to cover suburbs first must find out what's there, cataloging the various traits of each community, its government structure, age, development potential, and wealth. Every suburb is not a flourishing row of new subdivision streets. Some are old mill towns that have been gobbled up by urban sprawl; some are affluent bedroom communities; some are working class bedroom communities; some are low-income havens for those who have fled the inner city slums; some are the new industrial parks and valleys.

A thorough understanding of the physical and economic traits of a community is vital to finding regional story ideas. The old mill towns are concerned with accommodating expanding, aging plants; redeveloping their decaying central business districts; and attracting young people. The new cities are suffering a variety of growing pains—battles usually fought over zoning and development— as developers plan apartments or shopping centers near $75,000 homes, or super-highways dump traffic into inadequate two-lane roads, or folks petition for a zone change to convert an old house into a shop for a butcher, baker, or candlestick maker.

People in the suburbs care about the same things city residents care about: zoning, sewers, water rates, crime, fire protection, traffic, and development of nearby land.

But getting that suburban news poses problems, says John Kiesewetter of the *Cincinnati Enquirer*. Of course, a reporter can't be stationed in every city hall every day. The reporter must develop good contacts in each suburb, and make those contacts feel important. Key sources of information will be police chief, fire chief, mayor, city manager, council clerk, and safety-service director. Often, the service director is the full-time administrator. It's important that reporters can reach these people at work and at home, because most elected suburban officials work daytime jobs and do their council politicking at night.

Just like the city hall reporter, the suburban reporter will find that covering meetings is a staple of the suburban beat. Periodic visits to council meetings show interest in the community and help maintain contacts. At the council meetings, reporters will get a spot news story or two. Also, citizens will talk about problems that could become topics of regional suburban stories, and reporters will hear about people and their business or other interests that could make good feature stories.

Attending meetings also gives reporters a firsthand look at the operation of the city. The potential for corruption or ineptitude is so much greater in the suburbs because the people running the city and its police/fire departments and other services often are making considerably less than major metropolitan officials. The suburban official, who has just as much power to run a city or its departments, *could* be much less qualified for that position than in the larger cities. Reporters also should watch for signs of overaggressive police who could be violating civil rights during arrests, of mayors who could conveniently change dispositions of cases during or after mayor's court sessions, of council members who pack city hall with friends and relatives, of ineptitude in city finances.

The suburban reporter must be alert to two distinct levels of story possibilities: regional, countywide trend stories and spot news stories pertaining to a single community. Most news organizations do both. They discuss the lack of low-income subsidized housing in the suburbs, but also cover the story on an individual basis. If a suburban city council votes Monday night to allow a low-income housing project to be built, the people expect to read about the council meeting on Tuesday morning. News organizations discuss dwindling school enrollments and closing schools, but also cover a specific school board meeting and report the next day on the board's decision to close two neighborhood schools and change attendance districts.

By talking to contacts and keeping an eye on suburban weeklies, reporters will know which meeting to hit and which to skip. They'll also see which topics are discussed by various cities, providing the news peg for a regional story.

Another staple of suburban coverage tends to be profiles. Reporters write about mayors, trying to use the story as an effort to describe the person as well as the characteristics of each community. They write about the people who run shops in the suburban business districts, people who are seen and heard often by fellow suburban residents. The suburbs are filled with people, and that has to be an important focus of the reporter. Those rows of houses are filled with people. The regional shopping malls and traffic congestion are people stories. They can't be covered by telephone. The suburban or metro reporter must be a foot soldier, getting out of the office, talking to the people. Listening.

POINTING THE JOURNALISTIC FINGER

For years, blacks were the subjects of a pattern of police harassment in Jackson, Mississippi. Fredric Tulsky and David Phelps of the Jackson *Clarion-Ledger* reported the story after tracking down witnesses from police records to support specific accusations.

Fighting a legacy of official obstruction, the *Philadelphia Inquirer* reporting team of Jonathan Neumann and William Marimow collected evidence of systematic police violence. The stories, accompanied by insights into the prevailing psychological makeup of the police themselves, were compelling and shocking.

Jay Lewis of the Alabama Information Network identified serious breaches of the public trust in state government in Alabama with a well-researched and well-delivered series on abuse of state-owned vehicles by state employees.

"Everyone knew" that many New York City police officers were sleeping on the job, but David Burnham of the *New York Times* documented the practice.

Things do go wrong in local government. Some individuals take advantage of their official positions. Some seek financial or other personal gain. Some simply seek ways to avoid doing the job for which they receive public funds. Shouldn't someone point an accusing finger?

"An examination of the problem of corruption—whether within a police department, the Central Intelligence Agency, or a major corporation such as ITT —shows that major sustained efforts to control the problem have almost always required an outside stimulus," says the *Times'* Burnham in a booklet titled *The Role of Media in Controlling Corruption.* That stimulus frequently has been the mass media. But despite numerous examples of media reporting about corruption, including the whole Watergate incident, Burnham feels reporters have not been doing the job adequately.

Covering—or uncovering—corruption in a local government cannot be accomplished, he says, by doing what too many reporters do best, that is, reporting what the politicians or administrators say. It requires energy and legwork. It requires hours of observation, of reading through documents, and of interviewing persons other than those in the highly placed official positions.

Burnham's story about "cooping," the New York City Police Department's time-honored expression for sleeping on duty, was documented between 2 and 6 A.M. on those occasions when he and a photographer prowled the docks, alleys, and parks of New York City. In another story, he determined that a large proportion of those arrested for robbery won almost immediate dismissal, that only a tiny fraction were brought to trial, and that those who pleaded guilty received sentences of well under a year. He gained this insight by pouring for many weeks over the "sloppily maintained filing system of the New York courts."

On another occasion, Burnham says, he decided to test the hypothesis that corruption and its easy tolerance profoundly influenced the performance of the police.

"I began interviewing literally hundred of New Yorkers from all over the city and from all walks of life," he says. "I interviewed—usually with a promise that they would not be quoted by name—bartenders, restaurant owners, liquor store owners, delicatessen operators, tow-truck drivers, building contractors, parking attendants, supermarket managers, numbers game operators, bookmakers, policemen, detectives, prosecutors, lawyers, judges, blacks, whites, and Spanish-speaking people."

These interviews consumed more than a year of evenings and free moments during the day. Combining them with an examination of the handful of corruption cases being prosecuted at that time, Burnham concluded that corruption did in fact dominate many of the activities of the New York City Police Department; and corruption, like cooping, had significantly decreased the effectiveness of the police.

The reactions to his stories about corruption, especially the cooping story, have led Burnham to what he terms "a fundamental truth about journalism": Most important stories concern widely known and generally accepted practices.

In this day of mass cynicism, too many reporters have learned to live with the existence of corruption. But the question, Burnham stresses, is not whether there always will be corruption, but why there seems to be more in one place than another, or at one time than another, and what steps can be taken to reduce it. Such considerations have led him to what he considers to be his job as a reporter: "to devote most of my energy to trying to describe those practices and procedures that stop a particular agency from achieving its stated goals."[2]

Most local government officials are honest and dedicated. But reporters owe it to themselves and to their public to be alert to the possibility that some are not. They must be willing to devote the time and effort required to documenting any story about practices and procedures that hamper the official effectiveness of an individual or an agency. Corruption stories are not written simply for their readership value; they are not written as an assertion of a journalist's power. They are written because it is the public that pays the financial, psychological, and sometimes physical price when government goes wrong. Whether it's corruption, incompetence, or simply faulty judgment makes little difference. Reporters are watchdogs, not lapdogs, of government.

COVERING THE CITY, NOT JUST THE HALL

Reporters have for years been covering city halls and county courthouses, and they have kept citizens at least relatively informed. But city hall and the county courthouse are more complicated now. Officials have greater responsibilities, they handle more money, and they often are tied together in cooperative programs, not only with each other, but with the state and federal governments. Coverage is difficult. And talented as they may be, individual reporters simply do not have the time and sometimes the resources to do the whole job. A new approach is needed.

Glenn Guzzo of the *Fort Worth Star Telegram*

(*Fort Worth Star Telegram* photo)

What has developed is two journalistic trends, both of which often are labeled *urban affairs reporting*.

Examples of one of these—called *cluster* or *team reporting*—have been on the journalistic scene for years, but their use is expanding as the media seek to broaden local government coverage. Team makeup will vary, of course, but it usually includes reporters responsible for city hall, county government, local politics, local courts, and sometimes police.

The move is partly one of efficiency; team members will cover for a fellow staffer on vacation or on special assignment. But, more important, it's a move designed "to provide time, to provide the opportunity and the encouragement for the reporters on the team to do enterprise work, and that is investigative stuff, in-depth stories, features to humanize the beat, trend stories, analyses, perspective pieces and diagnostic pieces," says Glenn Guzzo of the *Fort Worth Star Telegram*.

Guzzo heads a team of six. Every member is required to have a good knowledge of both the city and the county although each has a primary area of responsibility —two at city hall, two on county government, one on the county at large, and Guzzo himself, who covers city and county as necessary.

Assignment of team members to specific areas of responsibility seems to be necessary. Bill Miller of the *Richmond* [Virginia] *Times-Dispatch* says his paper once tried to assign a team to local government on a totally unstructured basis, but their sources complained.

"People in local government want someone clearly defined as their man or their woman," he says, "someone they could call and say, 'Here's a story I would like to get done.' "

Because team members can work together and cover for each other on the day-to-day breaking news requirements, they then can be freed to concentrate on broader stories which the normal city or county government reporter could seldom find the time to do.

"That translates to me into a more efficient operation," Guzzo says. "It's better stories, it's good reader pieces, it's digging, not just handling all the press releases, the public meetings and the governmental offices."

Another side of the urban affairs reporting coin, most frequently found at the nation's largest prestige newspapers and wire services, is the reporter with no day-to-day breaking news responsibilities who looks only at the big trends. Strictly speaking, this is a sociological rather than a governmental beat. Ask Jonathan Wolman, Washington-based urban affairs writer for The Associated Press, what he does, and he's rather hard-pressed to answer.

Dean Katz of the *Seattle Times*

(*Seattle Times* photo; copyright © Seattle Times Co.)

"Well, in Washington, an urban affairs writer keeps one eye on the cities and one eye on the federal government. With the federal government controlling about 33 to 36 percent of the city budgets, it has a pretty broad role to play. On the other hand, you don't want to get steeped in bureaucracy, so you want to spend some time in the cities, getting to know them."

Essentially, Wolman covers "issues of interest to every city and all the people who live in them."

This must include getting the broad picture of community problems which affect all residents, regardless of where they live or how much wealth they have accumulated. The effort to solve the significant urban problems of poverty, poor education, crime, and slums, for example, is costing billions of taxpayer dollars, and in a direct way affects the quality of all citizens' lives.

Another significant issue is the belated effort in this country, both locally and nationally, to carefully plan how available land will be used to achieve maximum life quality for a growing population. It, too, is a story that cannot be done in a narrow daily reporting sense. Dean Katz, working for the *Seattle Times* in one of the nation's fastest growing areas, stresses that it may be the most important story a reporter can tell.

"It is something that probably doesn't excite most people," he says, "but it is also something that affects their future more than anything else. It doesn't have sex appeal because it's sort of a long-term thing."

This land usage, or zoning, story involves community growth or, for those not likely to expand, development of present neighborhoods. In the case of Seattle and King County, Katz asks:

"What's the county going to look like twenty years from now? How much farm land is going to be left five years from now? What kind of restrictions are you going to place on new buildings? What about density? To what extent does the construction of 500 new homes out in a suburb east of Seattle affect the tax base of Seattle? Is it taking people out of the city and putting them in the suburbs? Does that mean the city is losing money?"

It's desirable, of course, that these stories be covered in detail from a local perspective, but officials and residents of one locale could benefit from knowledge of what others are doing about the same problem. As a news agency reporter, Wolman, for example, travels across the country to gain an understanding of one local problem and to compare that to the situations of other cities.

"I spent a week in Tulsa, Oklahoma, trying to figure out why that city is attracting industry at the rate it is," he explains. "And then I spent time in Detroit, Michigan, trying to figure out why its economy is falling apart at an equal rate."

Making comparisons, Wolman says, "always involves statistics. In our business, that's generally how you prove things. If it doesn't involve statistics, then it involves an awful lot of talking and listening."

Admitting that he worries about the necessity of statistics in his stories, Wolman says he sometimes will not put them into a story but will save them for "anybody who calls." Or he will use the standard journalistic technique of providing a realistic example that reflects the statistics and placing the two side by side.

"Sometimes we get lost in the numbers," he says. "But ultimately I think these are people stories. They tell us whether or not there's going to be a job and whether or not to live downtown."

NOTES

1. "Covering Government: A New Testament to Newswriting," *Oakland Press*, Pontiac, Mich., 1976, p. 14.
2. David Burnham, *The Role of Media in Controlling Corruption* (New York: Criminal Justice Center, John Jay College of Criminal Justice), pp. 1–14. Reprinted with permission from the John Jay Press.

Chapter 4

COVERING LAW
ENFORCEMENT

American people know about crime. They know about muggings, prostitution, bank robberies, murders, embezzlements, rapes, and shoplifting. They know about Saturday night specials. They know that more and more crimes are being committed these days. And they know it isn't safe to walk the streets at night anymore.

Most Americans, however, have never witnessed or been involved in a major crime. Their knowledge is second hand. That must mean American people are watching a lot of fictitious crime on television, which they are, or hearing about a lot of crime on broadcast news or reading about it in their local newspapers, which they are. Crime is a subject to which journalists, for a lot of good reasons and sometimes not so good reasons, have devoted a lot of attention.

Reporters have always been in the police stations and will continue to be there as long as law enforcement remains a necessary social activity. For as long as there is crime. The public is interested in crime and law enforcement, perhaps because of curiosity or because of a fear of what might happen to them someday, but in either case, because information about crime is essential to their understanding of their own community.

That's why journalistic interest in law enforcement is most likely to concentrate on local crime and local police. But jurisdictions of such agencies overlap, and from time to time reporters find themselves seeking information from various types of law enforcement officials.

For information on efforts to maintain the peace in rural areas and small communities, the focus may be on activities of a *township constable* or *village marshal.* Larger communities have professional *city police* whose efforts to enforce municipal ordinances and state statutes within city limits provide reams of journalistic copy.

At the county level, the principal official is the *sheriff,* and there may be *county police* who serve under the sheriff or are an independent agency with full powers. Sheriffs' authority has been declining nationally, but reporters follow their work in unincorporated areas and as caretaker of the county jail.

Called by varying names, *state police* may be restricted to highway patrol duties or serve general police functions, particularly in rural areas. Most states have an agency to investigate state crimes, keep records, and compile statistics. Generally know as the Bureau of Criminal Investigation, these agencies can provide a wealth of information for enterprising reporters.

The federal government has numerous law enforcement agencies, but reporters have most encounters with the Federal Bureau of Investigation, which has responsibility for looking into violations of federal laws.

SOURCES, TRUST, AND CONFIDENTIALITY

Veteran reporters know and young reporters learn very quickly that law enforcement officials at all levels and of all types can be very difficult to work with. Stories of conflict, usually ideological but sometimes physical, are legion. History may have never recorded the hour in which some police official somewhere was not refusing to give information to reporters. And, under many circumstances, that official was citing reporters' lack of dependability as the reason for the refusal.

Many journalists, such as Scott Bosley of the *Detroit Free Press,* say there is sufficient cause for reporters and officials to shoulder the blame for this perpetual conflict.

"A lot of these situations come up because we get carried away with our own importance, and that goes for both sides," he says. "I think that reporters from time to time in the pursuit of truth—and I'm not saying I'm innocent; on some days I haven't been—get a little huffy about getting something right now. At the same time, police officers, without any authority, will do things like tell a hospital emergency room, 'You can't give out any information. You can't even say who's here.' "[1]

George Faulder of KPIX-TV in San Francisco admits that reporters sometimes provide the major barrier to good cooperation with law envorcement agencies, especially in on-the-street incidents, in which officers already are under pressure. And he takes the pragmatic viewpoint under these circumstances that "when you're on the street, the rights that are guaranteed to you are the ones the cop is going to give you. It's just that simple." Faulder stresses, however, that his objection is to reporter belligerence, not to professional attempts to get information in situations that tempt officers to refuse to cooperate.

"What I've found is that if you are persistent, but polite, if you persevere, but at the same time stay within the realm of respectability, if you are courteous but firm, you don't have any problems with the people you work with," he says. "You may run into areas, and I have, where there is a long residue of bitterness, let's say, between the street cop and the reporter. But if you go around to the station, you'll find that there will be reporters who get along with them fine and who are getting stories. That means it's not the status quo. It's the personality involved."

It's the personality, yes, but it's also an atmosphere of trust, of knowing each other. It's building a good relationships with the sources used day in and day out. Without such sources, there will be no tips and few stories beyond the commonplace. Reporters who don't care about relationships with their sources will get maybe one good story. In some types of reporting, it may be possible to "burn" sources and not have to encounter them again. But in police reporting, the journalist who burns an officer will have to see the officer tomorrow and the day after that and after that.

The desire for trust based on continuity of relationship was emphasized in a survey conducted by The Associated Press Managing Editors. A whopping 81 percent of police chiefs indicated they felt frequent changes in news media personnel are not beneficial. They want to work with reporters they know. And editors apparently share the attitude because 82 percent of them indicated they do not shift police reporters frequently.[2]

If reporters stay on the job long enough, they develop contacts among people who move up the ranks. Today's officer is yesterday's beat cop. Experienced reporters have learned which officers are trusting and will permit a few liberties and which officers insist on a strict, according-to-policy relationship.

Developing sources is like making friends—a long process that involves a lot of trial and error. The reporter goes to the local police department and seeks out, for example, the desk officer. Introductions come first. Then a few exploratory questions and a little self-revelation. Over time, the reporter and source get to know each other's jobs and styles fairly well. And the relationship comes close to being a friendship. But a friendship it is not.

The reporter must walk the perennial tightrope between understanding the police officer and beginning to think too much like that officer. As in any professional situation, the reporter must keep a distance so that it will not be difficult for coverage to involve officers' mistakes as well as their successes.

Reporters must keep their function clear in their minds. Police gather information for successful prosecution of violators of the law. Reporters gather information to allow the public to judge the fairness and effectiveness of its government. To lose sight of the distinction is to erode the profession.

WHO NEEDS TO KNOW?

Even under the best of circumstances, one of the realities of journalistic and legal life is frequent disagreement over what information should be made public and under what circumstances. For example:

The chief judge of the Court of Common Pleas in Blair County, Pennsylvania, ordered the county's magistrates to provide no information to reporters. The judge gave no reason for his decree which, according to officials of the *Altoona* [Pennsylvania] *Mirror,* made it almost impossible for that newspaper to cover the news from those eight courts.[3]

Photographer Dan Rios of the Escondido, California, *Times-Advocate* was arrested by sheriff's deputies as he stood in the street taking pictures of an overturned oil truck. He was charged with resisting a public officer in the discharge of his duty. The prosecution said Rios had made it difficult for the accident area to be cleared. (Rios was acquitted by a municipal court jury.)[4]

Police officers in Myrtle Beach, South Carolina, would answer only general questions and would not give to reporters from the *Sun News* incident reports or summaries of routine police actions. Thus, reporters had no way to double-check when the police said nothing of importance was happening.[5]

The Oregon Legislative Assembly in 1976 passed a law prohibiting official public disclosure of criminal records, including records of "arrest, detention, indictments, information or other criminal charges . . . sentencing, correctional supervision, and release." The law created chaos, not only for reporters, but also for state government officials and police themselves. It was repealed four days later in a special session of the assembly.[6]

The roots of such instances grow from three attitudes of public law enforcement and legislative officials. One, of course, is the distrust and resentment many officials hold for reporters whom they consider to be meddling and obnoxious. The second is the arrogant sense of power held by some law enforcement officials. The third, especially in recent years, is rooted in growing feelings about the need to protect individual privacy and resulting federal and state actions which cause local police to put a lid on information.

An illustration of that last element is the administrative requirement of the federal Law Enforcement Assistance Administration (LEAA), which has provided millions of dollars to criminal justice agencies. Included in the requirements for receiving such funds is the stipulation that state and local governments and agencies which use LEAA money for record keeping must assure the privacy of those records. Individual states, permitted to submit their own plans, are very slow in doing that.[7] The result is confusion on the part of state legislatures and sometimes overreaction such as in the Oregon case mentioned earlier.

Concern over accessibility of police records was heightened by two congressional actions—the amended and expanded Freedom of Information Act, passed in November 1974, and the New Privacy Act, effected in 1975. Although their authors intended the acts to permit broader public access to documents from the day-to-day operation of federal agencies, they have thrown some law enforcement officials into such panic that they have destroyed records rather than make them public.

Locally, reporters and law enforcement agencies collide over the document known by various names but generally called the police blotter, a law enforcement agency's record of its actions. Police departments use different forms, sometimes a chronological listing, sometimes a card file, but included is a mixture of serious and not-so-serious complaints and subsequent police actions.

Depending on the policy of the individual agency, however, it may include less official information, such as speculation by an investigating officer. It may also have information which departmental policy dictates should be kept confidential, such as the name of an undercover agent. And among the thorniest pieces of information frequently on the blotter are the names of rape victims or juvenile offenders. It is general practice as well as police policy to avoid publicly naming rape victims on the grounds that they have innocently suffered enough, or juveniles on the grounds that publicity may reduce the chances for a return to a normal life. Often, the law solidifies the policy regarding juveniles.

However, journalists insist that, even in these cases, the information is public record, and journalists should decide whether to use it. Reporters have for years scanned these records daily, noted which items they wanted to pursue and then gathered more complete information for their stories by looking at other records or interviewing appropriate officers.

Reporters traditionally have analyzed and ignored much of what appeared in police records. In many instances, this continues to be the standard practice, but, as the use of computers by law enforcement agencies increases, some officials are becoming even more difficult. The fact is that modern technology has increased the dangers in using the information, according to Jay B. Wright of Syracuse University, executive director of the New York Fair Trial Free Press Conference.

"As governmental computerized information storage and retrieval systems are linked," he says, "it also becomes possible for the same system to hold records of arrests, convictions and dropped charges mixed with other records on the same individual which do not necessarily have any relationship to criminal activity."

Unfortunately, Wright explains, the records (1) can be factually inaccurate, (2) can be incomplete, and (3) taken out of context, can create an inaccurate picture.[8]

Bugs within the system itself do haunt reporters, who argue that such inefficiency is not reason to deny access. They say a person's criminal history, for example, is public record because it is part of a public arrest or public trial, because it is kept at taxpayer expense, and because it is kept at the mandate of the legislature or courts. If the government orders such record keeping, they say, it must be available for public access.

Reporters frequently use any of three methods to gain information from governmental records. One is the informal route of developing sources who will provide information, perhaps on an unattributed basis. This method, while at times effective and necessary, carries with it the usual potential danger of using secondary sources of information. Another is establishing trust, confidentiality, and professional respect—an atmosphere in which officials are much more likely to be cooperative. A third measure is taking legal action when state or federal freedom of information laws apply.

THE MATTER OF PUBLIC ACCOUNTABILITY

But there's another reason for maximum access to criminal records besides their being public record. Those involved in law enforcement themselves recognize that they are accountable to the public. And many argue in favor of the media's watchdog role in enforcing this accountability.

"If police practices had been more thoroughly aired by the press in past years —if even a fraction of the space given to repetitious stories of holdups and shootings had been devoted to charges of police brutality, corruption and high-handedness—then the people of our cities would have a better idea of the truth about their police," says J. Skelly Wright, judge of the U.S. Court of Appeals for the District of Columbia. "We would have a better idea of which charges were well-founded and which were baseless. Then we could have acted long ago to remedy what was revealed by accurate reports, and to ignore those who spread false reports.

"But in the absence of this reporting, word of mouth has been king. Baseless rumors have not been dispelled; well-grounded complaints have not been remedied."[9]

But it's not really that simple when reporters do try to fill that void. Ask reporters at KABC-TV in Los Angeles who staged a determined battle with the Los Angeles Police Department to get details of police shootings of civilians. It took more than a year of dedicated reporting and the support of a city council member and the *Los Angeles Times* before the police finally released the requested statistics. And the statistics showed that of 223 shootings of civilians over two years, thirty-five were judged to be below department standards.[10]

And ask members of a reporting team for the *Indianapolis Star* who weathered official foot dragging, threats of bodily harm, and an attempt by a prosecutor to have two members of the team prosecuted for alleged bribery. Formed by the paper on a suggestion from police reporter William Anderson, the team eventually produced more than 400 stories, which resulted in dismissal of the city's director of public safety and removal of the chief of police and virtually all ranking police officers.[11]

And ask Marie Rodhe of the *Milwaukee Journal,* who grew very upset over tactics used by Milwaukee police in their dealings with members of two motorcycle clubs suspected of being involved in the bombing death of a twelve-year-old.

"Police, being human, were out to solve this murder," she says. "But the methods they were using, I don't think you could really condone. One was that they would arrest somebody on Friday night on charges of first degree murder and hold him in jail until Monday morning, the first date of the court appearance for the case. Then they would say, 'We don't have enough information,' and would let him go."

Marie Rodhe of the *Milwaukee Jour-nal* (*Milwaukee Journal* photo by Dale Guldan)

Rodhe says that about the same time the police closed to reporters the records which showed the name, address, age, and official charge of everyone in jail.

The difficulty of getting official information on police activities is further demonstrated by a report from the Chicago Law Enforcement Study Group, a joint research project of Northwestern University's Center for Urban Affairs in cooperation with a number of community groups. The report underscores the lack of accountability under which many police departments function.

It recommends establishment of a Police Information Center which would collect and distribute information, especially statistical information, to provide an overview of police activities, accomplishments, and weaknesses. It specifically calls for statistics on incidence of crime in various parts of the city; a statistical breakdown of complaints, arrests, referrals to social welfare agencies, prosecutions, and convictions; complete statistics on juvenile crime; the disposition of cases in which calls to the police did not lead to arrests; number of complaints made against police officers by citizens; selection and hiring of police officers; awards presented; promotions granted; deaths resulting from police operations; weapon usage; and data on race involved in each circumstance.[12]

The justification for these requests was simply stated: "The Chicago Law Enforcement Study Group, from its inception, has been a consistent advocate of the public's right to know what its officials are doing."[13]

GETTING OUT ON THE STREET

Covering police activities is more than analysis of statistics and police records. It is—or it should be—getting out on the street to capture the drama of police activities and, more important, to keep in contact with citizens.

Covering criminal and law enforcement activities on the scene, especially in circumstances which pose potential danger for the reporter, creates its own set of problems, says Paul McGonigle of KOY radio in Phoenix, who has firsthand experience. He was cited by the Society of Professional Journalists, Sigma Delta Chi in 1977 for his twelve hours of coverage while a man held a hostage in the Yarnell, Arizona, bank.

"In a situation like that, the problem you're facing is time," McGonigle says. "You've got to get the facts and get them straight, and that's an extremely hard thing to do when you're under a pressure situation and you're faced with a considerable time problem in that it's happening right then and there.

"In the beginning it was rough. I couldn't get anybody to say anything. What I had to do was build a rapport and get their confidence that I was not going to do anything that would blow their position, that I was not going to be reporting things on the air that would give the gunman an idea of what they had planned or that would hurt the hostage or anything. Near the end, they were keeping us very, very completely informed."

Reporters on the scene also must rely on their own abilities to observe and make judgments about what is happening. They use their own sight, their own senses. They have to discover quickly whose word to accept because often there's no way to double check . They do not use rumors as information, however, but rather as tips to be checked out.

Good reporters are aware and wary of the natural tendency to isolate some part of the action or some especially moving human component and to emphasize that as if it were the total story.

"You may pick a focal point to exhibit the tensions, but you must demonstrate the scene in relation to the overall picture," cautions George Faulder, whose station, KPIX-TV in San Francisco, also won a 1977 SPJ, SDX Distinguished Service Award.

That coverage—of a confrontation between police and supporters of forty-five elderly residents who were being removed from a San Francisco hotel—provides an excellent example of professionalism. Pictures showed individuals being forcibly removed. But, on two occasions, the point was stressed that the police were not being excessively brutal in any way.

The broader perspective is important for all journalism, Faulder says, but it's especially significant for television reporters because of that medium's visual impact.

The on-the-scene problems for reporters are compounded, of course, in those situations involving hostages, especially if the major point of the whole incident is to gain publicity. The situation places journalists in two very awkward positions which force hard decisions. First, how do they avoid becoming the "captives" of terrorists, that is, how do they distinguish between covering an event and being used? Second, how do they cover such an event without informing terrorists of police strategy or providing information that may place hostages in even more jeopardy?

Law enforcement authorities tend to argue that journalists hamper their efforts in several ways: by (1) providing basic intelligence and tactical information for terrorists, (2) creating traffic problems at the scene, (3) tying up telephone lines with terrorists, (4) diluting police authority by talking directly with the terrorists and reinforcing their sense of power, (5) displacing authorities from their rightful role as negotiators, (6) nagging the police for information when they are occupied with saving hostages, and (7) either casting doubt on the veracity of the police or raising anxiety levels of the terrorists by broadcasting or printing inaccurate or premature reports.[14]

It's unlikely that journalists and officials will agree on everything in terrorist situations. But police and the news media can work, if not together, at least side by side, especially if they can gain understanding of how each must function.

One of the answers is training, with reporters sharing sessions with police officers. Another is experience. And news organizations have sought a third in developing internal guidelines to blunt the impact of the media on such stories, at the same time stressing that the reporter must cover the event independently.

"There can be no clearly defined policy for terrorist and kidnapping stories since the circumstances vary in each story," says Paul G. Eberhart, United Press International managing editor. "However, we have established a set of guidelines that we think are workable in most circumstances":

> Each story will be judged on its own and if a story is newsworthy it will be reported despite the dangers of contagion.
> Coverage will be thoughtful, conscientious and show restraint.
> Stories will not be sensationalized beyond the fact of their being sensational.
> Demands of terrorists and kidnappers will be reported as an essential point of the story but not provide an excessive platform for their demands.
> Nothing will be done to jeopardize lives.
> Reporters, photographers and editors will not become a part of the story.
> If staffers do talk to kidnappers or terrorists they will not become part of the negotiations.
> If there has been no mention of a deadline, kidnappers or terrorists will not be asked if there is one.
> In all cases apply the rule of common sense.[15]

DRUG ABUSE DESERVES ATTENTION

Another kind of street crime story, one in which participants are not seeking publicity, involves drugs: their use and abuse, their sale, their impact, the extent of their usage, and efforts of law enforcement and other governmental and private agencies to control them. More individuals are using illicit drugs now than at any other time. The drug abuse treatment industry employs 54,000 persons, by most responsible estimates, and governments at all levels spend millions of dollars on drug law enforcement.

"There is, in fact, a great deal left for the reporter who wants to develop interest in writing about drugs. But the stories are no longer the fascination pieces of the late sixties; they are stories about the expenditure of tax money, the competency and activities of the medical and social work professions and the progress of legislation; in other words, the kinds of reporting journalists have always done," says Allan Parachini of the *Chicago Sun Times* in a booklet for reporters published by the Drug Abuse Council.[16]

Dolores Barclay of The Associated Press

Reporters like Parachini and Dolores Barclay of The Associated Press who have worked extensively on drug stories insist that sources be developed among all interest groups concerned with drugs. And they stress that the sources are available and most usually are cooperative. Barclay suggests, as a beginning, the Drug Enforcement Administration, the National Institute on Drug Abuse, and local law enforcement officials.

"What usually happens with drug stories, as in any story, is that one source begats another. One should milk a source for all he or she is worth and try to get as much information and as many names as possible," she says.

Local clinics and treatment centers may be willing to help reporters gain an understanding of the medical and psychological problems related to drug abuse as well as, if handled properly, provide assistance in developing source inroads to users and sellers.

In addition, drug historians and researchers are tucked away in laboratories, frequently on university campuses, and may be consulted by the enterprising reporter. Pharmaceutical companies are also a source, although they may be somewhat defensive if they manufacture a drug that is being abused.

But regardless of the source, Barclay and Parachini agree that reporters must be especially cautious with any statistics or figures provided, especially "street value" of drugs. They point out that police have not, as a rule, been willing or able to assess accurately the value of what they have received, and news media have tended to pass along unverified police figures. The answer, of course, is in use of multiple sources—even, as Parachini suggests, consulting drug users about current street values.

One drug story still requiring some solid coverage, Parachini suggests, is drug treatment: "Few areas of medical endeavor have been permitted to function with so little critical review as the so-called 'drug abuse industrial complex.' Astonishingly, comparatively little reporting on the real effect of treatment programs has been done."

In this regard, he provides two suggestions:

Be dubious of the claims of treatment program operators, looking past their statistical statements of success at ulterior motives, including financial ones. Be especially skeptical of treatment officials who seem to imply indirectly or directly that one type of treatment (e.g., methadone) is suitable for all or even most drug users.

Demand proof of simple solutions and logical cause-effect categorizations such as linking heroin use and property crime. Some of the best stories in the field have grown from a reporter's disbelief of supposed axioms.[17]

THE TIGHT-LIPPED FBI

In a public program in which he discussed his coverage of an Arizona hostage situation, Paul McGonigle of KOY Radio in Phoenix drew laughter from his audience of fellow journalists when he told them of the arrival of FBI agents.

"That meant nothing was happening because when the FBI gets there, they like to pretend: 'What bank? What hostage? What gun?' But the FBI actually was, I thought, quite efficient."

That's a good summary. The FBI perhaps is the most tight-lipped, official-sources-only law enforcement agency most reporters will ever deal with. Field agents know the policy and, at least on the surface, live by it.

"The only person authorized to release information concerning an investigation is the agent in charge of the major field division or his authorized representative," says one agent who, true to form, would not speak at all unless it was agreed that his name would not be used.

The some 8,500 FBI agents in this country are organized into fifty-nine field offices and sprinkled in resident agencies sometimes consisting of one agent. Many cities and towns have no local agent. The reporter, then, might have to deal with field agents or media liaison officers hundreds of miles away.

And, more than that, it's difficult to get anything other than bare facts.

"Even in the criminal cases, if you contact the liaison officer, you do not get much of the color that you might be interested in because they're pretty restricted in what they can hand out: 'Yes, this individual by name and descriptive data was arrested on this charge pursuant to some indictment return,' and it's pretty much the technical description of what he was arrested for," an agent says. "It will not include anything concerning the evidence backing up the charge."

In a small town with a field office hundreds of miles away, the standard practice is for the local investigating agent to write a press release, which would be approved by the field office and made available locally.

That's officially. Unofficially, reporters and agents know that, like most other situations, it's possible to gain information from the FBI if trust has been built up.

"Trust," an agent stresses, "is the entire basis of my relationship with a given reporter." And that trust, as always, is built up as reporters demonstrate their accuracy and their dependability to maintain a confidence.

However, that's not the only means available to reporters. "As a practical matter," the agent says, "in almost all of these instances, we work very closely with the local [law enforcement] agency because we have concurrent jurisdiction. A bank robbery still is an armed robbery from the state perspective, and I work much more closely with police department officers and detectives than I work with our own agency."

Local police sources, therefore, should have the same information, and the reporter who has developed those sources, in most instances, will experience little difficulty.

IT'S NOT ALL MURDER AND RAPE

Public speakers seem to like the old line about the martians who base all their knowledge about life on Earth on what they read and view in the mass media. Here's another variation: If those martians—or indeed the American public— depend on the media for an understanding of local crime, the attitudes thus formed are likely distorted. Many critics charge that crime reporting in general does not distinguish journalism because of its overemphasis on the sensational, the bizarre, or the latest journalistic fad.

Research by two University of Houston political scientists indicates that during the month of their study less than 1 percent of local crime was reported by the *Houston Post* and the *Houston Chronicle*.

"This might not present a problem," the researchers say, "if the set of crimes reported in the press was generally representative of local crime. However, this is not the case. The distribution of crimes reported in the press is markedly dissimilar to the distribution of crimes known to police. Murder and rape are reported far out of proportion to their frequency of occurrence, while burglary, larceny and (in one paper) auto theft are substantially underreported."[18]

This poses a dilemma for the journalist who knows it is not possible to cover the thousands of minor crimes which occur annually. It's a fact of life that accounts of more dramatic crimes always will be a staple of American journalism. The problem is one of emphasis. Other kinds of less exciting crimes also affect citizens and have impact upon the quality of community life. They merit attention. Journalists have done this through a combination of two general approaches. It may represent what Marie Rohde of the *Milwaukee Journal* calls "human stuff," or it may be summaries, perhaps statistical, of crime in the community.

"Cops are human, victims are human, murderers are human, and I think it is interesting to see all those people from that perspective," Rohde says. This applies whether the crime is dramatic or not, and reporters could easily broaden and humanize their coverage with, say, a weekly story on how the spot news events affect the people involved.

Compared to this kind of human story, statistics may seem rather forbidding, but, handled properly, they can be helpful to readers, viewers or listeners. When the Chicago Law Enforcement Study Group called on police to compile and release statistics on the incidence of various types of crime in different parts of the city, the potential value was obvious. It could provide a warning of certain concentration or types of crime so that residents could, if they wanted, take necessary precautions.

Such stories need not concentrate on the more dramatic crimes. They can cut across the spectrum of what is happening in the community. They can inform readers about the less dramatic crimes in a way which would be otherwise impossible. And, when combined with interview material, they need not be overly numerical or dull.

Judge J. Skelly Wright of the U.S. Court of Appeals for the District of Columbia agrees that it is not enough to report the crime, the capture, and the punishment.

"Crime and trial reporting should cover additional aspects of the criminal process and, through their cumulative effect, increase the public's knowledge as to the causes of crime and the nature of society's responses to it," he says. "The causative factors behind entire classes of crime can make good material for the press—better material in the long run than the accidental circumstances of a particular crime. Some of the better newspapers, TV stations and networks have shown that stories of conditions causing crime can make good copy—stories about slums, illiteracy, poverty, unemployment and poor mental health."

Since most trials involve the poor and members of minority groups, Wright also suggests that the media focus widely to provide the proper perspective, particularly since crime is the exclusive propensity of no one group and since white collar crimes can be more socially harmful than a hundred petty thefts that provide exciting adventure stories. The judge also asks for better reporting of events following the trial, with particular attention to how prisons are managed.[19]

LOOKING TO THE FUTURE: CRIME PREVENTION

Some journalistic organizations have focused a portion of their efforts on crime prevention. Such programs would include WNAC-TV's "H.O.T. CAR" ("Hands Off This Car"), credited with reducing the incidence of car thefts in Boston,[20] and the Indianapolis *News'* Concerned Neighbors Crime Watch which similarly is said to have been a major factor in that city's 1976 crime rate reduction.[21]

Crime prevention how-to stories can be relatively simple. Stephen Munro of the Topeka, Kansas, *Capital Journal* once did a story on the fact that even if police recover stolen property, citizens might not recover it unless it's positively identified. The story suggested use of an electric engraving pencil or some other means to label goods.

Such a consumer approach can help overcome many of the weaknesses that have been evident in crime reporting over the years. A major value of such coverage is that it can supplement what Munro calls a "tendency for knee-jerk reportage of crime after it occurs."

NOTES

1. "Reporting the Criminal Process," all-day program, sponsored by the Ohio University Chapter, Society of Professional Journalists, Sigma Delta Chi, March 4, 1978.
2. "Police and the Press," *News Research for Better Newspapers,* Vol. VI (Washington: American Newspaper Publishers Foundation), pp. 94–95.
3. "Judge Imposes Restrictions on Crime News," *Editor & Publisher,* July 23, 1977, p. 13.
4. Jim Julian, "Letter to a Sheriff," *The Quill,* January 1977, p. 24.
5. "Access to Police Records Still Blocked; Privacy Fuels Movement for Secrecy," *FoI Digest,* July/August 1978, p. 5.
6. Barry Mitzman, "Too Much Privacy," *Columbia Journalism Review,* January/February 1976, p. 36.
7. Peggy Roberson, "What Are These LEAA Regulations and How Did We Get into This Mess?" *The Quill,* July/August 1976, pp. 19–22.
8. Jay B. Wright, "Adult Individual Criminal Records and the News Media: Inherent Problems for Access and Privacy," unpublished paper presented to the Law Division,

Association for Education in Journalism annual convention, Seattle, Wash., August 1978, pp. 3–4.

9. J. Skelly Wright, "A Judge's View: The News Media and Criminal Justice," *American Bar Association Journal,* December 1964, p. 1129. Excerpted with permission from *American Bar Association Journal.*

10. Glenn Esterly, "It's the Reporters Against the Cops," *TV Guide,* Nov. 12, 1977, p. 44.

11. "400 Stories on Police Corruption," *The Quill,* June 1975, p. 15.

12. Ralph Knoohuizen, *Public Access to Police Information in Chicago* (Evanston, Ill.: Chicago Law Enforcement Study Group, 1974), pp. 52–55.

13. Knoohuizen, p. i.

14. Walter B. Jaehnig, "Journalists and Terrorism: Captives of the Libertarian Tradition" unpublished paper presented to the Mass Communications and Society Division, Association for Education in Journalism annual convention, Seattle, Wash., August 1978, pp. 12–13.

15. "UPI News Guide for Covering Extremists Issued," *Editor & Publisher,* May 28, 1977, p. 46.

16. Allan Parachini, *Reporter's Guide: Drugs, Drug Abuse Issues, Resources* (Washington, D.C.: Drug Abuse Council, Inc., 1975), p. 12. Reprinted with permission of the Drug Abuse Council, Inc.

17. Parachini, pp. 3–25.

18. George E. Antunes and Patricia A. Hurley, "The Representation of Criminal Events in Houston's Two Daily Newspapers," *Journalism Quarterly,* Winter 1977, p. 758.

19. J. S. Wright, pp. 1128–1129.

20. Gerry Nadel, "Putting Car Thieves into Reverse," *TV Guide,* Dec. 24, 1977, pp. 26–28.

21. "Crime Watch Program Credited for a Decline in Crime Rate," *Editor & Publisher,* Jan. 29, 1977, p. 16.

Chapter 5

COVERING COURTS: THE ISSUES

It was the biggest show in Cleveland during the latter part of 1954 when Dr. Sam Sheppard was being tried on a charge of killing his pregnant wife. The trial had all the elements: murder and mystery, society, sex, and suspense.

It's an old example, but it's classic. The trial judge, a candidate for reelection, simply lost control of his courtroom. Reporters and photographers took advantage of the opportunity. They roamed the corridors, hounding participants. When the judge and attorney went into the judge's chambers, they had to fight their way back out again through the crowd of reporters jammed into the judge's anteroom.

At the trial, some twenty reporters got an up-close look from a table inside the bar within three feet of the jury box. Others occupied the first three rows. They used every room on the floor. One radio station set up broadcasting facilities in a room next to the jury room. The judge permitted himself to be interviewed on the courthouse steps. As they dashed in and out of the courtroom, reporters created so much confusion that it was difficult to hear even though a special loudspeaker system had been installed. Sheppard and his attorney had to leave the room if they wanted to talk privately.

All three Cleveland newspapers published the names and addresses of prospective jury members, and many received anonymous letters and telephone calls. The court permitted photographers to take group pictures in the jury box and individual pictures of the members in the jury room. During the trial, pictures of the jury appeared more than forty times in Cleveland newspapers.[1]

Twelve years later, the U.S. Supreme Court, in *Sheppard* v. *Maxwell*, over-turned the conviction, citing conduct at and outside the trial, including that of the news media. That decision, says Jack Landau of the Reporters Committee for Freedom of the Press, enshrined a legal and political crisis in the relationship between the news media and the courts.[2]

The continuing debate has its basis in two constitutional amendments, the first, guaranteeing freedom of the press, and the sixth, assuring a defendant the right to a public trial by an impartial jury. No one disagrees with either of these high principles. The problem arises over the question of how these amendments can coexist.

Doesn't publicity prejudice jurors and thus destroy the chances for a fair trial? Shouldn't judges have the power to control such publicity? But isn't the presence of the media the most effective means of protecting the accused from an arbitrary decision?

Attorneys express concern over "trial by newspaper" or "trial by television." They fear jurors will base their decisions on information gained from the news media, not in the controlled courtroom.

"A jury cannot be impartial if its members' minds have been poisoned against the defendant because of news accounts of his prior arrest record, or his con-fession, or evidence against him, or opinions expressed as to his guilt," says Whitney North Seymour Jr., former president of the New York State Bar As-sociation.[3]

And that's the context of the debate. While they generally accept—and some even defend—the right of the news media to report the facts of a criminal case, judges, lawyers, and even some reporters list at least six types of information which could be prejudicial.

Two of these stand out: confessions and a defendant's previous criminal record. Justice officials argue that publicity that an individual has admitted guilt or has been convicted before, especially on a similar charge, is very damaging. The court might not admit a confession as evidence. Officials first must determine whether it was voluntary, whether the accused had access to an attorney, and, in general, whether the confession was given according to proper legal procedures. Individu-als have been known to confess to crimes they did not commit. Likewise, informa-tion about the past misconduct of an individual usually is not admissible as evidence because it implies a predisposition toward criminal acts which should not be considered in the present case.

Also potentially prejudical to the defendant is publicizing opinions about an accused's character, guilt, or innocence; results of any examinations or tests, such as fingerprints, lie detector, ballistics, or laboratory tests; statements on the credibility of anticipated testimony in the case; and speculation on what evidence or argument will be used in the trial.[4]

Attorneys say jurors must apply the standard that the accused is innocent until proven guilty beyond a reasonable doubt. So they contend that the courtroom scene is structured to carefully screen facts and comments, giving the prosecution full responsibility for proving its case, and without the help of media-inspired prejudice.

Nevertheless, the potential for prejudicial publicity does not argue for the restriction of press coverage of trials. Claude Sitton of the Raleigh, North Carolina, *News & Observer* says it well:

"News coverage provides a strong shield for a defendant's Sixth Amendment right to a speedy trial by an impartial jury. It exposes abuses of police power. It encourages judges and prosecutors to perform properly and witnesses to tell the truth."

The lack of such openness, he adds, can have only one end: "Its poisonous fruits are secret investigation, secret arrest, secret trial and secret imprisonment. A free press could not exist for long under those circumstances. Neither could a free judiciary."[5]

The late C. William O'Neill stressed such public accountability as chief justice of the Ohio Supreme Court. In his efforts to reduce a backlog of cases in his state, he required judges to give progress reports every thirty days.

"But the real secret," he said, "is that we made those reports matters of public record. So we made judges accountable, but the important thing was we made their accountability public, and we brought the media into it so that they could look at the judge's report and know where he stood. When a candidate for judicial office has been on the bench, we know reporters can look at his record and find out what he's been doing very easily and publish it. And that has had a very salutary effect on the whole system."[6]

In a democracy, journalists serve as the public's representative. It's not the right of journalists that's at stake; rather, it's the public's right to know the activities of its government.

On the question of prejudicial publicity, journalists argue that those in the justice system are underestimating the abilities of jurors to make a fair decision. After all, they say, the system was established on the idea that a jury of peers, knowledgeable about the community and personal circumstances, would be in the best position to judge fellow human beings.

Landau, for example, notes many instances in which the impact of massive publicity seemed to have been negligible, at least three of those instances coming out of the Watergate affair. Former Attorney General John N. Mitchell was acquitted in his home city of New York in spite of publicity. And, in the face of claims of prejudicial publicity, U.S. courts of appeals affirmed the convictions of Watergate break-in defendant G. Gordon Liddy and Watergate coverup defendant Dwight Chapin.[7]

Landau and others point to the responsibility of trial judges to control their courts. They urge that before judges step on First Amendment rights by closing trials or restricting coverage, they should apply several other well-known remedies to the impact of prejudicial publicity:

Change of venue: moving the trial to another area where pretrial publicity has not been so great

Continuances: delaying the trial until possible impact has been reduced

Venire from another area: bringing in jurors from another area where publicity has been less

Voir dire: careful questioning of prospective jurors and excusing those who have developed attitudes

Admonition: a judge's instructions to jurors that they should not read or listen to media reports about the trial

Sequestering: keeping members of the jury out of public circulation while the trial is in progress

Severance: conducting separate trials for codefendants in a trial if one has received considerable publicity

Attorneys note that these remedies may be effective at times, but that many are time consuming and expensive and not as easily accomplished or as effective as journalists seem to think.

The result of this disagreement has been the refusal of more judges to allow reporters access to certain information and the closing of portions of the trial process. News organizations often win appeals in these situations, but only long after the timeliness of the story has diminished.

The debate has reached the U.S. Supreme Court on a number of occasions, and two recent decisions, although opposite in their impact, have stirred up the journalistic community. The first came in 1979 when the court, in *Gannett* v. *DePasquale*, held that neither the public nor reporters has an automatic right to attend pretrial hearings. The court followed that decision in 1980, however, with a ruling that the First Amendment guarantees the right of the public and reporters to attend criminal trial proceedings, except in the most unusual of circumstances. In addition, that decision (in *Richmond Newspapers Inc.* v. *Commonwealth of Virginia*) has been interpreted by some experts as going beyond trials and setting the tone for the opening up of all governmental proceedings.[8]

Many say the matter is hardly settled. The U.S Supreme Court will hear other cases, and it remains to be seen whether the justices will continue to move in the direction established by their Richmond decision. In the meantime, however, efforts will continue on the local and state levels to seek workable arrangements in which the rights of all parties can be preserved. In nearly half the states, representatives of the news media and the judicial system have drawn up voluntary guidelines [with the American Bar Association (ABA) providing the impetus] in cooperative efforts to at least blunt the possible impact of prejudicial publicity.

Journalists have mixed emotions about such guidelines. Many are concerned that news stories may prejudice a defendant's chances, and they appreciate guidance. But they fear judges will forget the voluntary nature of such guidelines and seek to enforce them. Likewise, they are concerned that once they begin to compromise their basic rights, even through voluntary agreements, the door will be open to those who would restrict press freedom.

By 1979, twenty-three states had voluntary bench-bar-press agreements. Landau characterizes these as "mostly ineffective."[9] Research at the University of Texas in 1978 found that nearly 68 percent of the crime stories examined contained at least one violation of such guidelines.[10] But the ABA itself has concluded the agreements are being "generally followed," that they have helped protect guarantees of fair trial and free press, and they have helped improve bar-media relations and understanding.[11]

The problem thus remains, and authorities such as Robert Kasanof, former attorney in charge of the Legal Aid Society, see no easy solution: "The press has a right almost amounting to a duty to report to the citizens what happens in their courthouses. Equally so, judges and lawyers have a duty to see that what happens in the courthouse proceeds according to law and no other way. The constitutional tasks of the press and the legal profession cannot be resolved with logical rigor."[12]

THE HUMAN SIDE OF CRIME COVERAGE

Reporters covering the criminal justice system face these issues daily. Their goal is to provide journalistically sound coverage of a specific case but, at the same time, they are not unaware of the need for sensitivity. Thus, they often temper their journalistic decisions with considerations of the human impact of what they are doing. They know they are dealing with serious problems. They know their coverage can have impact on individual lives. And they know that specific decisions cannot be made automatically. They must be based on careful consideration of a given case and the balancing of journalistic values with human considerations.

Drama Without the Sensational Overplay

Court reporters face a built-in dilemma. They, like any other reporter, do not have the time or the space to cover everything. In consultation with their editors, they decide, first of all, the significance of public interest in a case. Perhaps it is true that journalists overestimate at times the audience's attraction to the bizarre or the sensational. But even the most responsible news judgment will lead reporters to those cases which are inherently interesting.

"The kinds of cases that the press has time to cover in detail are going to be those that involve either a notorious defendant, a particularly ghastly crime or some other element of a bizarre set of facts," says Lyle Denniston of the *Baltimore Sun*.[13] "The press is not going to cover the routine case of a traffic court."

But this situation has two edges. The very circumstances which attract attention offer the greatest temptation for the reporter to overwrite.

Lyle Denniston of the *Baltimore Sun*

(*Washington Star* photo by Paul Schmick)

"One of the principal problems in covering cases that merely by themselves are going to be sensational is that the press does tend to exaggerate the use of words and descriptions that do arouse emotions in covering of criminal law," Denniston explains. "These cases are inherently interesting. They are inherently emotional, and the press gets caught up in them the same way that spectators do in the courtroom. I suppose the answer to that is simply that the press has to be more disciplined. If a case is sensational, if it is inherently fascinating to the public, it is not at all necessary to overwrite it, to use buzz words, to use highly selective material in order to create that fascination. It is there already."

One of the main causes of such overwriting and, curiously, also the cause of dull writing is the trap of limiting court coverage to the immediate. Such stories emphasize only what happened in the courtroom today, stressing the process rather than the human participants, the specific case rather than the issue. This is not to say day-to-day coverage should not be provided; it is necessary. But today's testimony is not an end in itself. The strongest reporting seeks a context, then zeros in on the problem involved rather than plodding through the actual details of the court system. What happens today has its maximum meaning when related to what happens outside the courtroom, the backgrounds of the participants, and the importance of the case to the community.

This is part of another valuable saving grace available in dealing with a dramatic case—the traditional journalistic goal of serving as an observer regardless of one's attitudes about the trial.

"Reporters need to stand away more and be a good deal more neutral in dealing with these cases than perhaps reporters or individuals as human beings are able to do," Denniston says. And he suggests that failure to stand back was a basic reason for the news media's problems in the celebrated Sheppard case.

"It wasn't that the press was fascinated, as was the public, with the bizarre crime itself," he says. "It was that the press suddenly acted as if it were an arm of the prosecution. I have no basic ethical objection to crusading journalism as such, but I do have a very fundamental, basic, and pervasive objection to the press in any way becoming a part of the state, certainly the prosecutorial arm."

When Not to Tell All

Simply because a fact is available does not mean it will be included automatically in a story or, indeed, that a story will be written. Journalistic tradition has it, for example, that there are times when the identity of a source may be withheld to protect that source. Many journalists will agree to withhold information about a police investigation if publication is likely to endanger the lives of undercover officers. And in times of war, it is conventionally accepted that publication of information about troop movements could result in disaster.

But even those decisions are not always automatic. Responsible and sensitive journalists will agonize over them, remembering their responsibility to inform the public. Some journalists argue, with some justification, that news organizations should not practice censorship, should not make value judgments. The reporter, they say, presents information without consideration as to whether it be good, bad, harmful, or beneficial. To do otherwise is to violate the principle of journalistic neutrality. And, they say, the policy of making information public in the long run will be more beneficial than harmful.

But that is rather naive. Journalists do make value judgments by the mere fact that a news story has space and time limitations. And journalists do withhold information, sometimes even information of potentially high readership. In covering the criminal system, it's possible to identify at least six broad reasons some reporters would consider not publishing specific information about a case:

The information is irrelevant to the specific case.
It is premature and therefore subject to change.
It is an unnecessary invasion of individual privacy.
Publication would place individuals' lives in jeopardy.
Publication is possibly libelous.
Individual human beings deserve compassion.

"In a lot of cases," says David Pike of *U.S. News and World Report*, "to get some guidance on this and also to protect yourself, you should consult with your editors. I know when I worked at the *Washington Star* for a dozen years—covered the courts for about four or five—I often discussed these matters with my editors. They generally were inclined to withhold publication if there was a question of damaging someone's reputation unnecessarily."

The knots begin to form over Pike's "unnecessarily," especially when applied to a common point of disagreement between journalists and law enforcement officials: previous criminal record. Pike relies on the relevance of the information.

"I think it depends. If the person, for example, is about to be tried for a bank robbery and has been convicted of 20 bank robberies, it's relevant, even if it does raise a problem of prejudicial publicity," he says. "Oftentimes, however, papers go overboard and reveal the number of arrests, for example, which I think is irrelevant. People get arrested all the time, but the charges are dropped because they're bad arrests or for whatever reason. Or the fact that this person who's on trial for bank robbery had some completely unrelated convictions—drunken driving, assault on his wife, or something else. I just think I would use it only if it were relevant to the case at hand."

Another circumstance in which reporters might withhold information—even at the risk of losing a good story—is when such information is premature. For example, suppose a reporter gets a clue or outright information from a judge or law clerk on the outcome of a civil case. The judge or clerk, working on an opinion to be released later, will say, "Yeah, I'm leaning toward A rather than B for this reason." Few reporters would jump in with a story at that point. It's too risky. The judge could change his or her mind, or the law clerk could discover a new case that bears on the decision.

Reporters also are exercising more professional judgment as to how far they will invade someone's privacy. This is particularly true with regard to domestic relations court or probate court—courts that involve emotion and deeply personal feelings. This also is true in juvenile court, where decisions can make or break a youngster's future. Or cases involving innocent victims, such as in sexual assaults.

Much of the consideration is not over whether a story is presented, but whether the individuals involved will be named. It is generally, although not universally, accepted that the names of juveniles charged with crimes will not be used, although there is greater likelihood the name will appear if the juvenile is close to the legal age of adulthood, if the offense is not the first and if the crime is particularly serious. It was this latter reason, for example, which prompted the *Charleston* [West Virginia] *Gazette* and *Charleston Daily Mail* to violate a state law by identifying a 14-year-old boy who was accused of murdering one of his classmates. The appeal ultimately found its way to the U.S. Supreme Court, where the West Virginia law was overturned.

Rita Ciolli of *Newsday*

(*Newsday* photo)

Identification of the victim of a sexual assault, likewise, often is not used in news accounts. Many journalists have concluded that sensitivity is necessary because of the potential harm publicity would bring to the innocent victim.

There is, of course, another side to this issue, one noted by *Newsday*'s Rita Ciolli:

"I think you have to take these one case at a time, depending on the victim," she says. "I had an attempted murder-rape case in which the victim was a 58-year-old woman. I talked with her before the trial and she said she would not be troubled at all by use of her name or anything else because she was able to reveal her life, and she felt she wanted just to talk about it. She had no problems because she felt it was so important for people to know that victims, especially of sex crimes, have to come to court and have to testify."

Protection of other individuals involved in the justice process prompted *Newsday* to take a different tack, however; the paper holds back some identifying facts about jurors in cases involving violent crime.

"It's a big problem when you know that the two people who are on trial are part of a group of dangerous people who are free," Ciolli says. "So now we're leaving out jurors' addresses, even their towns, just to make the jurors more comfortable."

Such compassion, under certain circumstances, may even be extended to the person accused of a crime, although that decision must be balanced by other community considerations. For example, a reporter may hear a number of police reports of an exhibitionist. At that point, without knowing who it is, the reporter probably would write a story, as a community warning. The reporter then must pursue the story to its conclusion, using the accused person's name. Likewise, if such a case were well known in the community and had become a subject of popular conversation, there would be a duty to provide coverage to ensure that the information traded among citizens be as factual as possible.

But in the absence of rumors and especially if it is the individual's first offense and he cooperates by taking psychological treatment, many reporters will agree there is no story.

"Where the press learns about an incident of that kind, where there are no victims other than individuals whose sensory sensitivities have been invaded, I think that the press might just as well forget those stories," Denniston says.

The distinction is thin, however, between omitting stories out of human compassion and becoming a part of the system or of going too far in protecting individuals from their own mistakes. Human considerations must be cautiously weighed in journalism. Reporters should be compassionate, but only while recognizing their ultimate responsibility to keep the public informed about important public matters.

SOFT ON THE JUDICIARY?

When city councils schedule executive sessions, reporters pound on the doors and demand admittance. When mayors avoid questions about sensitive public issues, reporters insist on explanations. When county commissioners spend federal funds on a special program, reporters want evidence the money was properly spent.

But when judges hold private hearings, too many reporters wait for information to come out of those hearings. Sometimes they wait impatiently. But they usually wait.

Further, when a decision by an appellate judge is unclear or contradictory, some reporters will write unclear or contradictory stories rather than seek explanations. It's puzzling, but undeniable. There is a tendency in journalism to permit the judicial branch privileges not usually afforded, thankfully, other branches of government.

According to Jerrold K. Footlick of *Newsweek* magazine, this is because judges —even those who are elected—are solidly entrenched. And the public, which may want to know more, doesn't really understand the judicial system well enough to open some of its age-encrusted windows.

"State courts are much easier to complain about than to change," Footlick writes. "Out-of-date laws, political maneuvering and tradition-bound judges handicap efforts to modify them from within. And the degree of community pressure that would force change seldom develops. Although almost half of all adult Americans have had contact with their local courts, in cases ranging from traffic violations to first-degree murder, state court systems receive precious little public attention,"[14]

As for the news media, tradition has bound reporters. Judges have created a forbidding atmosphere, and they've reinforced the assumption that it would be undignified or unethical for them to work closely with reporters. Compounding this is a lack of reporter training and a lack of time to give courts the same scrutiny other governmental agencies have received. The average reporter assigned to "the courthouse" often covers a large part of local government as well.

The belief that these are not really adequate excuses, however, is reflected in growing efforts in some of the larger news organizations to bring about a new journalistic specialty—legal affairs reporting. This new generation of reporters, many of whom have legal training or degrees themselves, is giving the same kind of attention to the judiciary that the news media traditionally have given executives and legislators. They're absorbed in getting the bigger picture. They want to chronicle the trends, the policies, the injustices, and the overall impact of courts on the average citizen.

"Generally, we try to take the trends that are developing in the courts and to reduce them to information on a consumer level," says Carol Green of the *Denver Post*. "We try to look at the courts as a consumer would—use of legal services, if you will. And so we look at things like the operation of the courts themselves, problems within the legal profession—fees, costs, parliamentary procedures. We cover a really wide gamut of affairs, such things as the emergence of minority groups as legal forces—for example, a feature on Mexican-American legal education and defense for them. So there is an extreme variety of hard news, features and interpretive pieces on the legal system."

An increasing professionalism about covering legal affairs is imperative today. There is, of course, the potential long-range impact such coverage could have in opening up the judicial system itself. But there is also the fact that so many persons these days end up in the courts one way or another, particularly in civil cases. Disputes that used to be settled in the family or in the neighborhood or in the church are ending up in court.

And the reach of the court's arm often extends beyond the participants themselves. Legal scholars have noted a greater tendency by courts, in effect, to write laws through powers to interpret constitutional issues. Perhaps the most far-reaching social issue of the twentieth century—desegregation of schools—gained its impetus not from legislative or administrative action, but from a decision of the U.S. Supreme Court.

The broader, improved coverage is an answer to criticism that news media concentrate on sensational trials. As attorney Whitney Seymour says, "When it comes to sensational trials, they are in the front row of the courtroom writing away, but when it comes to the steady trampling of the rights of poor defendants, there is rarely a line printed. It is a disservice to the public for the news media, on the one hand, to fail to report the very real flaws in the justice system, and then, on the other hand, to assert that legitimate effort to protect the rights of defendants is in fact a coverup for incompetence and corruption in the courts. This is a double wrong, which does a grave disservice to the public and due process."[15]

To know when judges are moving in new legal directions or how the system fails certain defendants requires a level of expertise that few reporters have achieved. An increasing number of reporters are responding to that challenge through legal training. And that, says Green, who has done it herself, has advantages and disadvantages.

"I think law training is helpful because it teaches you a second language," she says. "And so when you encounter the mystical jargon of the legal profession, you know right away whether they're trying to bullshit you or whether it's real. This gives you an edge. If you have penetrated into the inner circle, you have now defrocked the mystique. Beyond that, it gives you some understanding of the procedural operation, although you can get that from street experience."

On the other hand, Green admits the difficulty sometimes of combining the two professions, noting that when returning to reporting after her first full-time year of law school, she had to "deprogram." This is not simply a matter of avoiding the jargon. Legal training alters a reporter's thought process.

"The reporter is taught to synthesize and to centralize what's going on and try to boil it down to single thoughts or single small groups of thoughts. Something you can write a headline from," she says. "Law teaches you to scatter your thinking, to follow many paths in many directions, and look for alternatives and create your alternatives."

Reporters who can maintain the balance between these two perspectives can function with a foot in each world, probably to the benefit of both. But if they are unable to separate the functions, they fall into the very trap which leads many journalists to be suspicious of both the necessity and the value of formal legal training.

They are skeptical of the necessity because they feel strongly that a person with an inquiring mind and a reporter's curiosity can learn enough on the job, through personal study, and in occasional special seminars to cope with the mystique and the complexity of the legal process. They are skeptical of the value because they fear it may lead reporters into thinking like attorneys, into becoming too much a part of the system.

This is another journalistic debate that will never be settled. Perhaps it's enough to say that providing consumer-oriented coverage of the judicial process requires more of reporters. It requires a level of understanding which only a few in the past have been able to attain on their own. As in other coverage categories, a growing number of reporters will seek formal training as the basis of their efforts to go beyond being just reporters of events.

NOTES

1. All descriptive facts of the Sheppard case are drawn from the U.S. Supreme Court decision: 384 U.S. 333 (1966).
2. Jack C. Landau, "The Challenge of the Communications Media," *American Bar Association Journal*, January 1976, p. 56.
3. Whitney North Seymour Jr., "Framing the Issues," *Law and the Press*, p. 23. Copyright 1975 by the New York Bar Foundation. Reprinted with permission. All rights reserved by the New York Bar Foundation.
4. *Fair Trial/Free Press Voluntary Agreements* (Chicago: American Bar Association, 1974), p. 8.
5. Walter Putnam, "A Brief for the First and Sixth Amendments," *The Quill*, March 1976, p. 29.
6. C. William O'Neill, "Reporting the Criminal Process," all-day program sponsored by the Ohio University Chapter, Society of Professional Journalists, Sigma Delta Chi, March 4, 1978.
7. Landau, p. 60.
8. For discussions of these two cases, see: Lyle Denniston, "A Restrained Right," *The Quill*, September 1980, pp. 12–14; "Affirms Open Trial Guarantee," *The News and the Law*, August/September 1980, pp. 2–4; and "Press Hails Court's Richmond Ruling," *presstime*, August 1980, pp. 10–11.
9. Landau, p. 59.
10. Kent Middleton, James W. Tankard Jr., and Tony Rimmer, "Compliance With the American Bar Association's Voluntary Free Press-Fair Trial Guidelines: An Empirical Study," unpublished paper presented to the Law Division, Association for Education in Journalism annual convention, Seattle, Washington, August 1978, p. 7.
11. *Fair Trial/Free Press Voluntary Agreements*, p. 52.
12. Robert Kasanof, "How Not to Cover the Courts," *Law and the Press*, p. 58.
13. Denniston has written a detailed and excellent book on court coverage: Lyle Denniston, *The Reporter and the Law* (New York: Hastings House, 1980).
14. Jerrold K. Footlick, "Vox Populi," *Newsweek*, March 27, 1978, p. 87.
15. Seymour, *Law and the Press*, p. 19.

Chapter 6

THE WHERE AND THE WHO OF COURT REPORTING

"You act foolish once, but you learn," says Shelley Epstein of the Peoria, Illinois, *Journal Star*. "There's a common mistake made by young reporters, and I must say I did it once also: A fellow goes on trial, and the verdict comes back, 'not guilty,' and so you ask the prosecutor if he's going to appeal. Well, the prosecutor has no right to appeal in that instance."

Epstein stresses the importance of fully understanding not only the appeal process—circumstances under which it applies, procedures, time limitations—but the whole spectrum of legal proceedings.

"The more knowledge you have about the court system the better off you are," he says. "You need as much background as possible in the law. It can only help deal with those kinds of things that keep coming up again and again, specifically possible sentencing terms for different crimes, procedural matters so you don't have to keep running up and asking an attorney or the judge about things you really should know about."

STATE SYSTEMS: COURTS AND COURT ACTIONS

Courts serve two broad purposes: to facilitate criminal justice by providing decisions when individuals are accused of violating laws and to provide a forum for the settlement of civil disputes between individuals and/or groups within the society. To accomplish these goals, courts are organized first into trial courts, which have what is called original jurisdiction in that they provide the first (and usually the last) hearing of evidence and decision in a case. Individuals who feel an improper decision has been made or improper procedures have been followed can take the case to one of several appellate courts that evaluate the basic fairness of the trial court decision.

Shelley Epstein of the (Peoria) *Journal Star*

(*Journal Star* photo by Linda Henson)

In addition to the normal criminal and civil functions, courts handle other special duties that concern reporters. Depending on the size of the system, these may involve special departments or a temporary renaming of the court to perform the special duty. In either event, these special functions would include juvenile, probate, domestic relations, small claims, and equity.

Reporters, therefore, first need to know the purview of a given court, in terms of both its authority to handle certain types of cases and the geographic area it covers. This must include the distinction between serious crimes (felonies) and crimes of a lesser nature (misdemeanors). The distinction, although based on the severity of the offense, also determines the penalty allowed—the maximum fine or maximum imprisonment, and whether that separation from society is in a penitentiary or a local jail. In Montana, for example, a misdemeanor is punishable by a maximum fine of $500 and no more than one year behind bars.

Both state and federal courts are organized into hierarchies with the extent of the authority of each level carefully defined by geography and type of case with which they deal (jurisdiction). Although states have differing systems, a number of common strains run through the functions designated to particular courts.

Justice and Municipal Court

The lowest rung on the judicial ladder is occupied by elected justices of the peace, municipal court judges, or police court judges. Not a feature of all state systems, justices of the peace generally preside over rural areas and have limited jurisdiction. In metropolitan areas, municipal courts or police courts are similar although they may have slightly broader jurisdiction. These courts usually deal with both civil and criminal cases.

In civil cases, a court will handle those cases whose claims fall below a specific maximum amount. In California, for example, justice courts may hear civil claims of up to $1,000, municipal courts have civil jurisdiction up to $5,000, and both courts may hear small claims matters of $500 or less.[1]

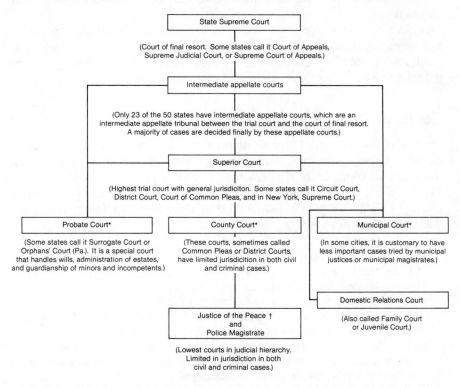

State Supreme Court

(Court of final resort. Some states call it Court of Appeals, Supreme Judicial Court, or Supreme Court of Appeals.)

Intermediate appellate courts

(Only 23 of the 50 states have intermediate appellate courts, which are an intermediate appellate tribunal between the trial court and the court of final resort. A majority of cases are decided finally by these appellate courts.)

Superior Court

(Highest trial court with general jurisdiciton. Some states call it Circuit Court, District Court, Court of Common Pleas, and in New York, Supreme Court.)

Probate Court*

(Some states call it Surrogate Court or Orphans' Court (Pa.). It is a special court that handles wills, administration of estates, and guardianship of minors and incompetents.)

County Court*

(These courts, sometimes called Common Pleas or District Courts, have limited jurisdicition in both civil and criminal cases.)

Municipal Court*

(In some cities, it is customary to have less important cases tried by municipal justices or municipal magistrates.)

Domestic Relations Court

(Also called Family Court or Juvenile Court.)

Justice of the Peace †
and
Police Magistrate

(Lowest courts in judicial hierarchy. Limited in jurisdiction in both civil and criminal cases.)

* Courts of special jurisdiction, such as Probate, Family or Juvenile, and the so-called inferior courts, such as Common Pleas or Municipal courts, may be seperate courts or may be part of the trial court of general jurisdiction.

† Justices of the Peace do not exist in all states. Their jurisdictions vary greatly from state to state where they do exist.

The State Judicial System

(Chart courtesy of West Publishing Co., St. Paul, Minn.)

In criminal cases, all three courts deal with misdemeanors and such matters as traffic offenses. They also conduct the initial hearing in which individuals arrested on felony charges are informed of the specific charge against them, of their right to counsel, of whether they may post bond, and of their right to either request or waive a preliminary hearing. The same official also may conduct the preliminary hearing, in which the magistrate determines whether a crime was committed and if there is "probable cause" to believe the accused committed that crime. If so, the magistrate will bind the defendant over to the proper court for trial or to the grand jury for further proceedings.

Small Claims Court

Another function of many municipal and justice courts is to provide an informal civil hearing that involves small sums of money. Designed to reduce the expense and delay of a normal trial, small claims courts are limited to suits under a state maximum.

It is a system which does not usually involve attorneys. Instead, both parties may represent themselves in suits for personal injury, property damage, labor, goods sold, money lent, a bad check, or a dented fender. No jury is involved; the judge or referee makes the decision and transcripts usually are not kept.

Courts of Original Jurisdiction

Journalists will have most of their dealings with the trial courts in the judicial districts. These courts have varying names, including superior court, circuit court, district court, court of common pleas, and, in New York, supreme court. The jurisdiction of these courts varies little from state to state and is well represented by California, which has established these functions for its trial court (called the "superior court"):

Civil: Superior courts have jurisdiction in civil matters in which money judgments of over $5,000 are sought. They also have exclusive jurisdiction, regardless of the amount involved, over such proceedings as probate matters and actions affecting the title to real property.

Criminal: Superior courts have jurisdiction over all crimes designated as felonies, or criminal offenses punishable by death or by imprisonment in a state prison.

Appeals: Superior courts may hear appeals from municipal and justice courts.

Equity: Superior courts hear special matters, such as injunction proceedings, administration of trusts, and foreclosure of mortgages.

Writs: Superior courts may grant what are called prerogative writs, for example, habeas corpus, to determine if a person is being legally held, as well as writs of mandamus, certiorari, and prohibition, all of which order someone to do or not do something.

Special: Superior courts have special jurisdiction in probate matters or the administration of wills, guardianships, and conservatorships; in domestic relations matters, including dissolution of marriage, legal separation, marriage annulments, enforcements of support, and paternity actions; in juvenile matters involving the correction and protection of minors and delinquent children; in adoption proceedings; and in psychiatric actions for the protection and custody of the mentally ill.[2]

Juvenile Court

Usually not a separate court, but a division of the court of original jurisdiction, the juvenile court is perhaps the most functional example of the philosophy behind the whole court system, namely, that it should be rehabilitative rather than punitive. Not that it works in all cases, of course, but when dealing with individuals under legal age, usually 18, the courts have demonstrated much more acute awareness of the impact of court action and of the need to give an offender the opportunity to start a new life.

In general, juvenile courts deal with persons under legal age and some adults who are charged with contributing to the legal problems of juveniles. Three types of juveniles fall under their domain: those who do not have a proper home or parental guidance or who are dangerous to the community because of a mental or physical problem; those who commit any felony or misdemeanor that would be a crime were the perpetrator an adult (generally charged with delinquency); and those who behave in a way that could be harmful to themselves or to the community, involving such actions as truancy, disobedience toward parent or guardian or custodian, and associating with disreputable people.

Probate Court

Also usually a department of the court of original jurisdiction, probate courts supervise administration of wills. They seek to ensure payment of debts and distribution of property to beneficiaries. In many states, probate courts also have responsibility for guardianships and for commitment of individuals to mental health institutions.

Domestic Relations Court

Efforts to settle domestic disputes usually involve, first, attempts at conciliation. If that fails, the court processes such matters as annulment, dissolution or divorce, child custody, visitation rights, division of property, and child and spouse support.

Appellate Court

Courts of appeal exist to ensure the basic fairness of the decisions made in trial courts, either in the application of specific laws or in procedures used in considering evidence and reaching decisions. To cut back on heavy case loads, thirteen states have established intermediate appellate courts and, in all states, a state supreme court stands at the top as the court of last resort.

Jurisdiction of intermediate appeals courts varies from state to state, but it usually includes the reviewing of decisions of courts of original jurisdiction and at times the consideration of appeals from municipal or justice courts. Intermediate courts usually have authority to issue writs of habeas corpus and writs of mandamus, certiorari, and prohibition.

The state supreme court has appellate jurisdiction over appeals from intermediate courts and judges disputes involving state constitutional interpretation. Its decisions bind courts within its state and in only one instance is there any avenue for further appeal—when federal law is involved. In such an instance, the proceedings leave the state level.

The Federal System

There's meaning to the common advice, "Don't make a federal case out of it." Federal courts function more stringently and formally than state courts, perhaps because these judges are selected with greater care because they are appointed for life or because of tradition.

David B. Offer of the *La Crosse Tribune*

(*La Crosse Tribune* photo)

"A federal judge is a king," says David B. Offer of the *La Crosse* [Wisconsin] *Tribune*. "A federal judge is so powerful and so important. He's got two or three full-time lawyers as clerks and assistants, and the little people insulate the judge more often than not."

The U.S. Constitution provided for establishment of the federal court system. It called for a supreme court and gave Congress authority to set up other courts. The result is a three-part federal system with functions similar to those of the state systems: trial courts, appeals courts, and special courts.

In the federal system, reporters deal most frequently with district courts in the country's ninety-one judicial districts. These are the federal trial courts. As courts of original jurisdiction, district courts handle most federal cases. They conduct the first hearing of almost all federal cases and the last hearing of a large majority of such cases.

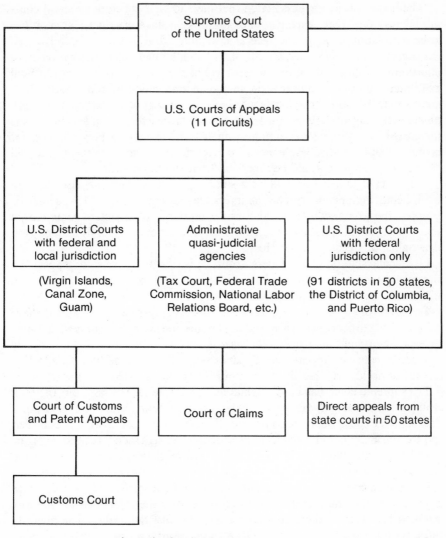

The Federal Judicial System

(Chart courtesy of West Publishing Co., St. Paul, Minn.)

Federal court jurisdiction is outlined in the Constitution (Article III, Section 2) and covers two types of cases that the state courts are not equipped to handle. The first involves interpretation of the U.S. Constitution as well as federal laws and treaties. The second includes cases affecting ambassadors, cases in which the United States is a party, and the so-called diversity-of-citizenship cases in which the dispute involves the U.S. government, different states, or individuals living in different states or other countries.

"There are criteria for jurisdiction that have to be met before a federal court will take a case," Offer explains. "For example, if it's a criminal matter, it has to be a violation of a specific federal law. Shoplifting is not a federal crime. Neither, generally, is murder. On the other hand, kidnapping is, bank robbery is, extortion can be depending on the elements of the crime, various kinds of mail fraud are, any crime committed on an Indian reservation is, and so on."

However, federal judicial officials can expand the list of criminal actions with which they may deal. If a murder is a state crime, for example, and it was committed by an individual acting in an official capacity (a police officer, for example), but the state doesn't choose to prosecute, federal officials can go in and investigate because it would be a possible civil rights violation.

Federal civil jurisdiction follows a similar pattern in that the cases tend to involve constitutional interpretation, interstate matters, or federal law. Thus, for example, the federal courts would consider questions of interstate commerce, a labor-management question covered under the National Labor Relations Act, civil rights, or freedom of the press.

Like some state systems, federal courts provide two levels for appeal, an intermediate level consisting of eleven circuits of the U.S. Court of Appeals and, at the top, the U.S. Supreme Court.

The courts of appeals have appellate jurisdiction only in cases that already have been tried in a lower court. An appeal might question either facts or law, but most appeals are brought on grounds that law is unconstitutional or was incorrectly applied. A court of appeals usually does not retry the case; it reviews court records to decide whether the lower court judge has applied the law properly.

The supreme court has both original and appellate jurisdiction, but the bulk of its work involves appeals from a federal district court, court of appeals, or a state supreme court. Supreme court justices select the cases they want to consider, and these usually fall into two classes: violations of federal constitutional rights or of federal law, and cases in which a state law or clause in a state constitution violates some federal law or the U.S. Constitution.

In supreme court cases, both parties submit written briefs, and each side then has one hour for oral argument and questions from the justices. After the case has been heard, the justices confer privately and cast their votes. The majority rules. Written explanations accompany each decision. If the decision is not unanimous, dissenting opinions may be written. Concurring opinions may be written by justices who agree with the majority or the minority, but for differing reasons.

Special Courts

Political scientists call the federal courts "constitutional courts" because they were created under authority granted by the constitution. Congress also has established a number of special courts that exercise jurisdiction only in certain cases. Labled "legislative courts," they have only the jurisdiction granted them by Congress.

Territorial courts function in the Virgin Islands, the Canal Zone, and Guam. They are defined as U.S. District Courts and have the same jurisdiction.

Court of claims hears suits for damages filed against the U.S. government. These suits are typical of those found in civil law, involving chiefly breaches of contract and torts (civil wrongs such as trespassing).

Customs court hears complaints from foreign importers who maintain the tariff they pay is excessive.

Court of customs and patent appeals hears two types of cases: (1) disputes that are appealed from the customs court and (2) controversies arising over decisions of the patent office.

Court of military appeals reviews all cases of court martial in which a general or admiral has been found guilty, or in which any member of the armed forces has been sentenced to death.

Reporters have few dealings with these special courts. They more often cover those quasi-judicial administrative agencies such as the tax court, Federal Trade Commission, and the National Labor Relations Board. These agencies conduct hearings and make decisions within their special area of concentration.

U.S. Commissioner

In effect, the U.S. Commissioner is a justice of the peace for the federal court system. U.S. commissioners provide a source of frequent contact for reporters. They are appointed by each district court, and their duties are to issue arrest warrants, take bail, and determine whether probability of guilt is sufficient to hold an accused person.

SOURCES OF INFORMATION

The barrage of discussion in journalistic trade publications about court secrecy prompts the belief that the reporter's life is filled with constant battles to gain information. The battles are there, but the average local reporter who understands how the court system works can find pertinent information easily and, with a little effort, can find even controversial information.

Information is gained in three general ways. The first is the documents of the court, these being public record. The second is what reporters see by sitting in a courtroom and watching the hearing or trial. The third is what reporters hear outside of the court.

That out-of-court information, of course, comes through interviews. In spite of professional codes, attorneys especially tend to be very willing, even anxious at times, to talk about a case with reporters. The same applies to judges, who, after all, in most instances, are facing reelection.

But a court system involves more than attorneys and judges, and Cathy Martindale of the Dayton *Journal Herald* suggests the value in going beyond the obvious.

Cathy Martindale of the Dayton *Journal Herald*

(*Journal Herald* photo)

"One general rule that not only applies to court reporting, but to almost any beat, is that the little people—bailiffs, court stenographers and the clerks in the clerk of court's office—are liable to know a heck of a lot more about what's going on and are going to be more accessible to you," she says. "You can get these people to trust you so that they know they are not going to be reported in the paper the next day as the source of information.

"They can tip you off to a lot of things that happen and are going to happen. 'Be here at 9 in the morning, Jack. Something interesting is going to happen.' Well, this guy never steered me wrong, so I'm there at 9 and, sure enough, somebody comes in and gives a plea to a case. I'm the only reporter there. I got it."[3]

Another instance in which the tip is valuable is a case in which the reporter originally was not interested, but something unexpected happens: an attorney wins a motion on a novel legal theory or there's an interesting twist to the case.

A 1978 survey with responses from nineteen nonmetropolitan Minnesota newspapers indicates the breadth of sources used by court reporters. All reporters in the survey said they use the county attorney and law enforcement officials. All but one listed court clerks; seventeen said they use judges; sixteen listed the city attorney and private attorneys; and eleven said they use civil action plaintiffs and defendants. In addition, nine said they use criminal defendants, seven mentioned public defenders, and six listed the official court reporter.[4]

As Marie Rohde of the *Milwaukee Journal* says: "I get tips all the time. This place is like one big grapevine, and everybody is a little grape on that vine."

Judges Can Be Cooperative

"For some reason, and I don't really understand it, a lot of reporters seem to be afraid of judges," says David Offer of the *La Crosse* [Wisconsin] *Tribune.* "I don't mean to demean judges when I suggest this, but all a judge is is a successful politician who wears a black robe. The same reporter who wouldn't stand for any kind of garbage from the mayor and would just demand accurate answers is absolutely terrified to go up and ask a judge if he's going to have court tomorrow."

Offer suggests that it's not proper to ask judges what their decision is going to be in a particular case, but the reporter may get information on scheduling, explanations about completed court proceedings, or, importantly, information about some of the legal issues involved in a complex case.

"At the very worst," he adds, "they'll tell you that they won't talk to you, but that doesn't hurt very much. The rudest that anyone has ever been to me is to tell me to get lost. But they can be exceptionally helpful. In lower courts, the judges are politicians. They usually are elected. They know the reporters who frequent the courts and they like to see their names in print. There's a camaraderie there that's not true of a federal court. Those judges are appointed by the president, they serve for life and they tend to be, for the most part, pretty unapproachable."

Of course, accessibility of a judge depends on the judge's personality, the nature of the case, and the reporter's questions. But that they often are accessible was confirmed by a University of Oregon master's thesis by F. Dennis Hale of the Idaho Falls *Post-Register.* Hale said nine justices of the Washington State Supreme Court indicated they were seldom approached by reporters, but they were willing to assist.

"Two thirds said that they would 'cooperate in explaining their own decisions to the press' or 'answering reporters' questions concerning general points of law, off the record or for background purposes only.' The justices emphasized that they would only comment on a case after the written decision had been filed. They made it clear that there were definite limits on what they would discuss.

" 'It's acceptable to attempt to clarify, but not to buttress what was said,' said Justice F. He added, 'If it is clearly written there will be no purpose for the inquiry.' Justice G observed, 'I won't tell what the decision said; they can read that. But I will tell what the decision doesn't say and how far it doesn't go.' Justice E commented, 'I don't mind explaining the impact of a decision, but not the why!' " [5]

The Minnesota study also found judges cooperative when reporters have trouble understanding documents or proceedings and when they need help using legal reference materials. [6]

In dealing with judges, however, reporters shouldn't be surprised when even the most cooperative expect to speak off the record. Judges hesitate to speak publicly about a particular case. But, off the record, some often will explain. Judges have even been known to evaluate efforts of a particular attorney in a particular case or to provide tips.

Attorneys Like to Talk

Lawyers, by definition, are advocates. It's the basis of their training, the basis of the system in which they work, and fundamentally, the basis of their relationship with reporters. They can be friendly, helpful, and valuable, but only to the reporter who exercises caution and who understands that a lawyer's adversarial background means he or she will be trying to use the media as another weapon in achieving a goal.

"My most trusted lawyer source I would only believe about 40 percent of the time," says Marie Rohde of the *Milwaukee Journal.* "Lawyers have so much to gain, and it is obvious that you have to be very, very careful with them. Also, attorneys, I think, because of their training, can take virtually any concept and justify it, which I find very irritating. They don't have to believe what they are saying, but they're trying to convince you that you should believe it."

But reporters can't do without attorneys. Given natural journalistic caution, they know lawyers can help in a wealth of ways. They are, first of all, principal sources for stories on the facts, issues, and approaches to the case.

Attorneys might be very helpful to the reporter who is covering more than just one trial, especially a reporter they know. If called in advance, they usually will respond to a reporter's "What are you likely to be doing today or tomorrow in court?" That's particularly helpful if the case is long and the reporter doesn't want to be in court every day. The lawyer may say, "Hey, you can skip today. It's going to be another dull witness, but tomorrow I'm going to do this, and maybe you should try to stop down at about 3 o'clock." Not all lawyers are so cooperative, but it makes sense to be in constant contact.

Because few journalists have legal training, it likewise can be helpful to have developed lawyer sources with whom they can discuss legal issues or specific cases informally. Perhaps the best way to learn about the intricacies of the judicial process is to spend a great deal of time covering the courts or simply observing them. In the absence of such experience, however, reporters can get a crash course by finding attorneys who will take the time to sit down and discuss the issues in general off-the-record terms: "OK, I think the strategy in this case is this, and I think Attorney X did this because he was trying to do that, and I think the judge's ruling was because. . . ."

But only the reporter who builds a reputation of trust will continue to get this type of help from attorneys.

"You have to treat these people very, very well," an attorney says, "and I don't mean buying them lunch. I gave a reporter background information once and then found myself quoted in a very controversial way in the paper the next day. That reporter would never get another thing out of me, and I'd do anything— I did everything I could—to make sure he never got anything out of anybody else. Attorneys do talk to each other about reporters."[7]

For specific on-the-record information, however, reporters find prosecuting attorneys more cooperative than defense attorneys. "A prosecuting attorney tends to be a person who's more used to the news media, better understands the needs of the news media," says Ed Jones of the Fredricksburg, Virginia, *Free Lance-Star*. "In our case, commonwealth attorneys in Virginia are subject to voters, so they have an interest in cooperating with the news media. And, I think defense attorneys, with the fate of their client at stake, just tend to be a little more conservative in what they have to say."

Actually, defense attorneys seldom do speak out at all, unless they think it would be to their own advantage. Quite clearly, they have enough problems taking care of a client who is fighting for his or her freedom. They don't need to take chances with potentially negative or derogatory publicity that suggests their client may have committed a crime.

Defense attorneys normally do not approach reporters with tips unless they think their client is being railroaded or they just won a preliminary victory and they want to make sure that the public knows about it.

The relationship with defense attorneys is double-edged. On the one hand, they need journalists to be watchdogs, to carefully scrutinize the prosecutor, the police, the judge to ensure they're doing their job and doing it fairly. On the other hand, they don't want to cooperate too much. They don't want to breach the confidence of their clients or disclose something that should not be disclosed until the trial.

Prosecutors, however, because they are elected officials and because many are politically ambitious, are more likely to answer specific questions with some candor and to be more open to publicity. And, because they are public officials, it's less easy for them to avoid answering reporters' questions.

Exceptions abound, of course. Individual personalities defy pigeonholing. Some prosecutors won't say anything beyond a recitation of the facts of a case. Some defense attorneys, such as F. Lee Bailey and Melvin Belli, enjoy national reputations because of their flamboyant personalities, their well-known clients, and the fact that they very skillfully orchestrate their dealings with the media.

In any event, it was a municipal judge, Thomas Hodson of Athens, Ohio, who suggested: "Being an attorney with a journalism background, I can see both sides to these issues. A lot of these attorneys talk about all the rules of professional responsibility and judicial conduct. That's fine for attorneys, and I'm bound to live up to them as an attorney. But as a journalist, you shouldn't really give a damn. Your job is to ask the questions. If the attorney wants to violate the rules, fine. That's his or her problem. Your problem is to get the story, and it's my view that you ought to ask the questions. Rules be damned."[8]

It's All in the Clerk of Courts' Office

Like most journalists, court reporters never have enough time. Shelley Epstein of the Peoria, Illinois, *Journal Star* doesn't just cover courts. He covers all county government, a common situation for reporters on smaller newspapers. But even at the *Los Angeles Times,* Bob Rawitch is responsible for proceedings being supervised by sixteen full-time judges, other federal agencies, and organized crime.

Bob Rawitch of the *Los Angeles Times*

(*Los Angeles Times* photo)

It isn't easy for either reporter. Epstein and Rawitch must know what's on the docket and daily decide their priorities. They must choose the several meetings or trials they will attend, and they must find some way to cover the rest of the day's activities. This process starts and sometimes ends at the office of the clerk of courts, who maintains public records of all judicial proceedings.

Without question, the clerk of courts can be the journalist's most valuable source. If for no other reason, the clerk is significant because he or she prepares the daily court calendar, which must be religiously checked by the journalist to determine the schedule of court activities. And, for the reporter who is unable to cover everything in person, the clerk's office contains all the written documents on which coverage may be based: applications, motions, petitions, pleadings, answers, and historic materials. Any routine news may be picked up here, and the enterprising journalist with time to review the records can uncover a treasure chest of information.

The clerk of court's office, in fact, contains more than any reporter can read carefully on a regular basis, even in metropolitan areas where several checks are made daily. That's why reporters work hard to ensure the cooperation of the clerk, deputy clerks, and other office staff. This is one place where the hurried reporter makes it a point to slow down and chat and perhaps have a cup of coffee. A friendly, cooperative staff with some understanding of news has saved more than one reporter.

This help may come in any of several forms. It may be as simple as a "nothing today, Sam" when the reporter enters the office. It may be a straightforward suggestion that the reporter check a particular file. It may be a telephone call to the office: "Sam, I know you're on a deadline, but you'd better check with Attorney Jones. He just filed something you're going to want today." Or it may be the kind of quiet tip which prompts the reporter to begin an investigation when something in the judicial system has gone awry.

Bailiff Keeps Tabs on Everything

Technically, a bailiff is a court attendant whose duties are to keep order in the courtrooms and to have custody of the jury. But to a reporter, the bailiff is much more. He or she may be a better source for the whole system than anyone, including the judge.

"The judge is tied up in a pretrial conference, and you want to know what's going on," says Cathy Martindale of the Dayton *Journal Herald*. "The bailiff is sitting out there, and he can tell you who is in the chambers with the judge, what they're talking about and when the meeting is likely to end."[9]

Reporters make a point to check regularly with bailiffs because they generally know not only what is going on in their courts but in everyone else's court too. It's a kind of intelligence system that develops in the courthouse, and bailiffs seem to be most willing to discuss courthouse politics. Because of their constant contact with lawyers, bailiffs often know what is going to happen before judges do.

Court Reporter Has the Quotes

The most quiet, and perhaps the busiest, person in the courtroom is the court reporter. This is the person, in the movies, who sits at the front of the room, looking uninspired, never glancing around, just tapping away with both hands on a machine. The function is to record and transcribe all testimony, objections, and rulings made during the court proceeding. For the journalist, that spells potential value in confirming direct quotes or covering missed material.

"It happens with all too much frequency, maybe once a week," Offer says, "there are two things going on simultaneously. I have to choose one. I'll go to the court reporter later for the other one, and he or she will almost invariably agree to read the pertinent parts, even though there really is no obligation to do it."

The detail of the court reporter's tape recording or transcript at times can prove a real blessing for reporters looking for something more than the legal facts of a case. Offer provides an example: "I had one case in which I couldn't attend the sentencing. So I stopped by to see the bailiff just to find out what the sentence was, and he said, 'You should have been here. That woman stood up and screamed and cried for her children and begged the judge not to send her to prison. The judge sentences her to 120 days, and she fainted.'

"I went to the court reporter who had all those screams down, as best as you can transcribe a scream in a stenographer's notebook, and she read back everything the judge had said, everything the woman had said. And I got a helluva story because the court reporter was willing to read it to me."

Interview the Defendant?

It was a story with the kind of twist that was certain to create controversy. A Bergen County, New Jersey, murder defendant had admitted killing his father, mother, and two brothers, and the confession had been reported locally. On the eve of the trial, the local newspaper, the *Record,* published a story in which the defendant retracted the confession, saying his brother had killed the members of his family, and he had killed that brother in a fit of temporary insanity.

The inevitable storm followed. The judge, citing pretrial publicity, postponed the trial indefinitely and criticized the *Record* and the defense attorney for permitting the interview. Later, staff writer Lucinda Fleeson wrote a story for her paper in which she put the whole matter into this perspective:

"Publication of the interview raises these questions: Should a newspaper judge a story by its newsworthiness or by its potential harmful effect on the criminal justice system? Also, does a defendant have a right to tell his side of the story outside the courtroom? The article also raises the question of whether it is impossible in a well-publicized criminal case to find a truly neutral jury."[10]

As usual, there are several sides to the issue. And journalists are not unanimous in their attitudes about whether statements outside the courtroom from the defendant should be made public. Some believe they should remain as detached as possible, confining their stories to reports of official statements and actions. To publicize confessions issued by police is playing into the hands of law enforcement officials, and to publicize private statements from the defense is becoming part of the defendant's strategy.

But, particularly if they believe their job is to tell the human story instead of simply providing the official facts, most journalists would use the statements, though cautiously.

"There are some problems with running a defendant interview," says Ed Jones of the Fredricksburg, Virginia, *Free Lance-Star.* "First of all, although normally an interview like this would be accompanied with the safeguard of the defendant's attorney being there, you always have the potential problem of a naive defendant or a naive attorney saying something that could very well prejudice a fair trial for the defendant.

"Also, you have the problem of a defendant very often wanting to use the news media as his way around the court system. So you have it on both sides, and it's difficult to get a good, usable interview with the defendant, at least while the proceeding is still going on."

However, Jones stresses that, despite his reservations, he thinks such stories can have a distinct value: "I believe an interview of this kind—and I put aside for a moment the question of timing—really brings out the story of a crime far better than you could if you were dealing with what third persons are saying about the facts."

Information Officer May Be Helpful

Like other government offices, courts in some states and at the national level often have public information officers available to assist reporters. Journalists evaluate the assistance provided by these individuals much as they would any source.

Reporters stress strongly that information officers are not an adequate substitute for contacts with other court officials. But they can be helpful by providing —as is the case with the U.S. Supreme Court—synopses of each decision tailored to fit the needs of the news media, background information on complicated legal issues, or suggestions of stories, especially feature stories, that reporters may choose to pursue.

NOTES

1. Albert G. Pickerell and Michel Lipman, "The Courts and the News Media," *Los Angeles Daily Journal Report,* Office of Criminal Justice Planning, 1975, p. 3.
2. Pickerell and Lipman, pp. 5–6.
3. "Reporting the Criminal Process," Ohio University seminar sponsored by the Society of Professional Journalists, Sigma Delta Chi, March 4, 1978.
4. Robert Drechsel, "How Nonmetropolitan Daily Newspapers Cover Courts in Minnesota," unpublished paper presented to the Mass Communication and Society Division, Association for Education in Journalism annual convention, Seattle, Wash., August 1978, p. 9.
5. F. Dennis Hale, "The Court's Perception of the Press," *Judicature,* December 1973, p. 187.
6. Drechsel, p. 16.
7. "Reporting the Criminal Process."
8. "Reporting the Criminal Process."
9. "Reporting the Criminal Process."
10. Information presented here is from excerpts of a report in the *Record* written by staffer Lucinda Fleeson, presented in "Defendant Interview Stirs Debate," *AP Log,* November 14, 1977, pp. 1, 4.

Chapter 7

MOST OF THE ACTION PRECEDES THE TRIAL

It is said by those who know about such things that the result of the 1932 baseball World Series was a foregone conclusion before the first game was played. The story goes that all activity on the Chicago Cubs' side of the field stopped, and players watched in awe as the New York Yankees took batting practice. The likes of Babe Ruth, Lou Gehrig, and Bill Dickey were hitting ball after ball out of the park.

That the Yankees won the series four games to none apparently was a surprise to very few.

It's not so much a matter of awe and intimidation, but the American justice system works the same way. Matters are settled long before the players—judges, lawyers, plaintiffs, and defendants—take to their field, the courtroom. That's how the system is structured.

JUSTICE AT A BARGAIN PRICE

One of the ways the system disposes of cases before they get to the trial stage is plea bargaining. It happens very frequently. A defendant is charged with selling cocaine and suddenly that charge is dropped, and he or she pleads guilty to possession of marijuana. It's a legitimate legal procedure, but it's an understatement to say it appears strange to the public.

There's a natural suspicion: Somebody is getting off easy. Somebody has been bought. Somebody didn't do the job. Such suspicions often are incorrect, but attorneys are nervous enough about plea bargaining that few really want to talk about it, especially if their comments are likely to reach the public.

From the prosecution standpoint, discussing plea bargaining for a defendant may suggest attorneys did not have a strong case against the defendant. And while it's true that building of a case may depend more on activities at the time of the arrest than any subsequent prosecutor investigation, attorneys know the public doesn't look at the situation that way. The prosecutor is held responsible, and it's a source of embarrassment to be forced by a reporter into detailed discussions. On the other side, when the defense discusses plea bargaining, it almost forces admission of guilt. The common feeling is, if innocent, why is the defendant willing to plead guilty to anything, even a minor charge that may bring little more than a suspended sentence?

Such attitudes ignore the fact that there are at least two good reasons for the existence of plea bargaining. One is related to the fact that the whole concept of American justice places the burden on the state to prove "beyond a reasonable doubt" that the defendant is guilty. Prosecutors know that's difficult at times, and they would rather be assured that an individual be found guilty of something— even a relatively minor offense—than to get off.

Attorneys also stress that most instances of plea bargaining occur, in the first place, in cases of relatively minor offenses. It would be impossible, they say, for a municipal court to go through the whole trial process for, say, every drunken driving charge. So prosecutors carefully select the cases they want to try and then seek to reduce the volume of the remaining cases through plea bargaining.

But attorneys still don't want to discuss it very much, and the reporter must understand the means they will use to avoid publicity, such as arranging for a judicial hearing before a judge at an unusual time. The whole process takes five minutes, the reporter doesn't know it's happening and the page one story still says this trial will open tomorrow.

"It's really embarrassing to walk in on the date of the trial and find the courtroom dark and nothing going on," says Cathy Martindale of the Dayton, Ohio, *Journal Herald.* "The reporter needs to understand the law, the system and the individual participants well enough to be on the alert for evidence of plea bargaining. That's why sources are so important.

"You can get a bailiff to say, 'Hey, the defense attorney for so-and-so and the prosecutor are in chambers with the judge, and this is the second time they've met.' So you begin probing around and you find out they're talking plea bargaining. And then one day pretty soon, it's bang, bam, thank you, 9 o'clock in the morning, the defendant, the defense attorney and the prosecutor will appear before the judge, and you have a five-minute plea-bargaining thing. 'We're going to plead guilty to manslaughter, and you're recommended for probation,' and it's over. And because you had your ear to the door, and you knew in advance that this was a likely thing to happen, you got it, and maybe the competition missed it."[1]

And unless the reporter is in the courtroom at the time of this process, the chances are slim he or she will get the parties to say much about it. The result and perhaps the legal reasons can be discovered through open court documents, but those don't always get to the heart of the situation. It's possible, for example, that plea bargaining may be used to keep facts of a situation from becoming public because only the decision may be announced, not the process or reasoning leading to it. A reporter needs sources, court documents, legwork, and needs to know the law and court personnel well enough to predict when plea bargaining is likely. In the meantime, it is indeed embarrassing to walk into an empty courtroom on the day of a trial.

COVERING THE CRIMINAL PRETRIAL PROCESS

Similar drive is needed to overcome problems created by the complexity of the judicial system. Certainly, many of the decisions are made during the pretrial process, but reporters do not have the time (or, sometimes, the interest) to give each step full attention. It is physically impossible and generally undesirable for any reporter to cover every hearing of every case. Take, for example, the situation of Jeff Watkins of the Charleston, South Carolina, *News and Courier*.

"There are seventeen magistrates who would hold preliminary hearings, and I'm the only court reporter," he says. "Therefore, unless it's a major case, I don't involve myself too much with initial appearances, bond hearings, or preliminary hearings. But cases that have received a lot of publicity—for instance, a policeman is shot on the beat—are closely scrutinized from the bond hearing all the way up to appearance in criminal court."

Court reporters, especially those who work for smaller news organizations and have responsibilities for more than the courtrooms, are daily faced with decisions about which of the numerous activities they are going to cover. And they base these decisions on standard news judgment values, trying to determine whether the people or the legal issues are of interest to the public, whether there are novel interpretations of the law or seldom used legal strategy or a great deal of money involved—just generally whether people are going to be either interested or affected by the judgment.

Reporters know, however, that because they must limit their coverage to certain cases they are missing a significant part of the judicial process for which they are responsible. This results in a great deal of legal activity conducted without public scrutiny. And they know they would better understand a specific trial or indeed the whole system if they could be more intimately involved with the pretrial processes of more cases, even if they don't get a daily story out of it.

The pretrial process provides a rehearsal of the witnesses and strategy of the case. It gives the reporter a better background and results in richer trial coverage. One reason for this is that participants in pretrial hearings generally are more open in what they say.

"You can see that if there is a confession and if it is suppressed by the judge why the district attorney's office might give someone a nice plea to a reduced charge if they don't have a strong case to go to trial," says Rita Ciolli of *Newsday,* herself an attorney. "In pretrial, you may have a judge saying, 'All you have in this case is a confession. Why didn't someone go and take fingerprints? Why didn't someone do this?' If there's no jury there, you find all the participants— I don't want to say talkative—but critical of each other, and it's a very good way to get a good look at the system and what's going on."

If there are procedural problems in the case against a defendant, they tend to be discovered early and, with some exceptions, are not likely to come up during a trial. Thus, covering pretrial hearings helps reporters let the public know why many cases are dismissed. Perhaps there was questionable police behavior such as an improper search or a wiretap without a warrant.

COMPLAINT

The undersigned complainant, being duly sworn, states that on or about _____, 19___, within _____ Ohio, _____
(county/city)   (defendant's
_____ did _____[1] in violation of _____.
name)   (ordinance/statute)

The complaint is based on _____[2]

_____
(Complainant's signature)

Sworn to and signed in my presence this _____ day of _____,
19___, at _____, Ohio.

_____
(Magistrate, Clerk, etc.)

[1]Recite essential facts constituting the offense, e.g., "failed to yield ... " *[or]* "assault (victim's name) ... "

[2]Here put "facts and circumstances known to Complainant," if there are no affidavits of persons other than Complainant. If there are other affidavits, put "the attached affidavit(s)."

Comment: A complaint is a written statement of the essential facts constituting the offense charged. It must state the numerical designation of the applicable statute or ordinance and be made upon oath before any person authorized by law to administer oaths.

Source: All court documents are courtesy of Anderson Publishing Co., Cincinnati, Ohio.

Publicity on cases that are dismissed because of improper police behavior is a sensitive issue to prosecutors, as elected officials. They don't like publicity that, in their opinion, overstates their role.

They point out that the most vulnerable part of a criminal case is the time immediately surrounding the arrest, and the prosecuting attorney may not be involved at that time. Perhaps the prosecutor's only alternative is to dismiss. Yet, when the story is reported, they say, it reads, "prosecutor dismisses case."

They're partly right. In other instances, though, the prosecutor controls the means through which charges are brought against an individual. For example, if police learn of the whereabouts of a suspect, the prosecutor often specifically coordinates efforts to check out information and to make an arrest.

The normal stimulus for an arrest is provided by either of two procedures, both of which are controlled by the prosecutor: an indictment returned by a grand jury or what is called a bill of information filed in court by the prosecutor. In either

---

WARRANT

To any law enforcement officer of _____.
(this city/this county)

WHEREAS, there has been filed with me a complaint stating that

_____ did _____
(defendant's name or description allowing reasonably certain identification)
_____[1] in violation of _____
(ordinance/statute)
_____, a copy of which is incorporated or attached hereto.

　　YOU ARE COMMANDED to arrest the above described person in this or any adjoining county you shall find him and bring him without necessary delay before this issuing Court to answer unto the charge set forth herein, or, if he be found in any other than this or any adjoining county, to arrest and take him before a court of record therein having jurisdiction of this offense, to be dealt with according to law.

　　Given under my hand this _____ day of _____, 19____.

_____
Judge/Clerk of Courts/etc.

[1]Give a description of the offense charged in the complaint.

Comment: The warrant must contain: 1. the name of the defendant or, if that is unknown, any name or description by which he can be identified with reasonable certainty; 2. a description of the offense charged in the complaint; and, 3. the numerical designation of the applicable statute or ordinance. The warrant shall command that the defendant be arrested and brought before the court issuing it without unnecessary delay. A copy of the complaint shall be attached to the warrant.

instances, the legal requirements are rather simple: The charge must set forth the time, date, and place of the alleged criminal act as well as the nature of the charge.

Initial Appearance

Once arrested, an individual generally first appears in municipal or justice court (in federal cases, before a U.S. commissioner), regardless of whether the crime is a misdemeanor or a felony. This first appearance has three functions: to determine (1) whether the accused gets his or her own attorney or whether the court needs to appoint one, (2) whether the accused wants a preliminary hearing, and (3) whether the accused is a good risk for bond.

News from this initial appearance concerns whether the accused is released and the amount of bond. In most states, a person charged with murder is not eligible for release on a bail bond. In other cases, the judge sets a figure in accordance with the severity of the crime. The idea is that rather than forfeit the bail amount, the individual will return for further proceedings. Practices vary, but generally the person is permitted to post 10 percent of the face amount. Often individuals

---

SUMMONS

To any law enforcement officer of _____.

(this city/this county)

WHEREAS, there has been filed with me a complaint stating that

_____ did _____
(defendant's name or description allowing reasonably certain identification)
_____ in violation of _____, a copy of which is incorpo-
(ordinance/statute)
rated or attached hereto.

YOU ARE COMMANDED TO SERVE THIS SUMMONS upon the above described person in this or whatever county you shall find him, advising him by these presents that he is to appear before _____

_____ on the ____ day of _____, 19____, at _____

o'clock ____ M., at _____, to answer said charge;
(building, address, etc.)
AND FURTHER ADVISING HIM that he may be arrested if he fails to appear as above set out.

You are to make return of this Summons according to law.

Given under my hand this ____ day of _____, 19____.

_____
Judge/Clerk of Courts/etc.

may engage professionals who for a fee will assume the financial obligation. Persons who cannot afford to post bail themselves or to borrow it will remain in jail until their cases are decided.

Alternatively, the magistrate may decide that an accused person is likely to appear in court for the trial. The judge can release such persons on their own recognizance, that is, on their own promise to appear.

Preliminary Hearing

Some states have both an initial appearance and a preliminary hearing; others combine all the functions in a single appearance, usually called the preliminary hearing. But in either event, the functions tend to be the same.

At the preliminary hearing, which may be requested or waived by the accused, the state presents evidence to convince the magistrate that there is sufficient reason to believe the accused probably committed the crime, so that a grand jury or trial court should consider the case. The role of defendants will vary from case to case, but they must be present at the preliminary hearing and may give evidence. However, many defense attorneys present no evidence, preferring instead to place the burden on the prosecution to show probable cause and not, at that stage, to reveal their case.

"The initial appearance or preliminary hearings I've seen are just a means of establishing probable cause, that there was a crime and there probably is reason to think that this particular person or persons were involved in it," says Jeff Watkins of the Charleston, South Carolina, *News And Courier.* "As part of that, they involve basically testimony from witnesses or police officers. As opposed to a trial, such hearings often allow hearsay evidence (perhaps one officer speaking of the involvement of other officers), which is not admissible, at least in South Carolina, as evidence in court. And it all is pretty one-sided for the prosecution."

This one-sided nature of the preliminary hearing makes it the core of the pretrial publicity controversy. And the 1979 Gannett decision by the U.S. Supreme Court makes it likely that more judges may be excluding reporters from these hearings. The issue is far from settled as news organizations continue to challenge such exclusions. In the meantime, most reporters advise continued efforts at coverage, under the assumption the hearings are open.

Depending on a state's system, the result of the preliminary hearing may be any of three possibilities. If magistrates decide the prosecution's evidence is inadequate, they may dismiss the case. If they conclude that the evidence merits further consideration, they may order the defendant bound over to the grand jury. Or, in some instances, they may send the case to the proper trial court.

The Grand Jury

The function of a grand jury, stated simply, is to look into crimes committed in the district and determine whether available evidence is adequate to bring an

FINDINGS ON PRELIMINARY HEARING

Preliminary hearing was conducted this ____ day of _____,
19____, on the charge of _____ [1] wherein the State by the
Prosecutor of _____ [2] offered its evidence in support of the
charge in the presence of

(circle applicable statement)
1. defendant and his counsel
2. defendant, unrepresented by counsel who
(circle applicable statement)
1. likewise offered countervailing evidence
2. after being advised according to Crim. R. 5(B)(3), likewise
    offered countervailing evidence
3. elected not to offer evidence at this time
and the Court having considered all of the foregoing,
FINDS:
(circle proper finding)
(a) That there is probable cause to believe the felony alleged has
     been committed and that the defendant committed it.

(b) That there is probable cause to believe that the felony ____
     _____ and not that alleged has been committed and that
     (title and statute)
     defendant committed it.

(c) That there is probable cause to believe that the misdemeanor
     _____ and not the felony alleged, has been
     (title and statute or ordinance)
     committed and that defendant committed it.

(d) That there is no substantial credible evidence showing probable
     cause as to any offense.
WHEREFORE
(circle proper orders)
(a) Defendant is bound over to the Court of Common Pleas,
     _____, Ohio, whose venue appears, and bail or the condi-
     tions of release here and before prescribed are continued and
     transferred to the Court of Common Pleas.
(b) Defendant is bound over to the Court of Common Pleas of
     _____ County, whose venue appears; the Prosecutor is in-
     structed to prepare and file a Complaint reflecting this finding;
     and bail or the conditions of release here and before prescribed
     are continued and transferred to the Court of Common Pleas.
(c) The prosecutor is instructed to prepare a new Complaint reflect-
     ing this Finding and the matter is retained for trial (or) _____
     Court of _____, Ohio for trial.

_____
Judge

[1]State the title of offense.
[2]"the City of _____, Ohio" *[or]* "_____ County."

accused person to trial. If grand jurors decide it is probable the accused did commit the crime, they will indict that individual by returning a "true bill." If they decide on the basis of evidence presented that such probability was not established, they will return a "no bill."

Although on some occasions a grand jury may undertake inquiries on its own, it most generally represents a forum for the prosecution. Members consider cases presented by the prosecutor and hear witnesses provided by the prosecutor. The defense has no opportunity to make statements, present witnesses, or cross-examine prosecution witnesses. The accused appears only if called as a witness.

Grand jury deliberations, to protect the rights of the accused, are secret. Reporters tend to show respect for this secrecy although there are many examples to the contrary, usually under very special circumstances. *Washington Post* reporters Carl Bernstein and Bob Woodward honored it when they were preparing to track down a member of the federal grand jury looking into the Watergate incident. In their book, *All the President's Men,* they said:

"Bernstein and Woodward consulted the *Post*'s library copy of the Federal Rules of Criminal Procedure. Grand jurors took an oath to keep secret their deliberations and the testimony before them; but the burden of secrecy, it appeared, was on the juror. There seemed to be nothing in the law that forbade anyone to ask questions. The lawyers agreed, but urged extreme caution in making any approaches. They recommended that the reporters simply ask the woman if she wanted to talk.

"[*Post* managing editor Ben] Bradlee was nervous. 'No beating anyone over the head, no pressure, none of that cajoling,' he instructed Woodward and Bernstein. He got up from behind his desk and pointed his finger. 'I'm serious about that. Particularly you, Bernstein, be subtle for once in your life.' "[2]

This respect does not mean that reporters ignore grand juries when they are in session, but it does mean they place special rigor on the usual journalistic cautions when information becomes available.

One type of grand jury information requiring a conservative stance is the fact that an individual has been called before a grand jury. Too often reporters want to write, "So-and-so was hauled in before the grand jury and questioned," which implies that this person is guilty of something. The truth is that often, when a grand jury is in a preliminary stage of its investigation, it calls in anyone who might have any information. A person might come in and have none and be dismissed.

Decisions on when to use stories about grand jury activities must be made on a case-by-case basis. And reporters should be considerate of an individual's reputation before they write a general story. They should do more legwork to gain more specific information and verification.

Witnesses also can be sources of information for reporters. Bob Rawitch of the *Los Angeles Times* points out that, while not so in most state grand jury proceedings, a witness before a federal grand jury is not bound to secrecy.

"But you have to treat that information very carefully because you may be getting a distorted picture from one witness as to who a potential target of the grand jury may be and who is a witness," he says. "It's very easy for someone to leak something from a grand jury, but you have to evaluate it very carefully. A prosecutor or a defense attorney or grand juror may be willing to tell you something off the record so that you can determine whether you should write the story on what you got from this one witness, or to keep it in the proper perspective."

The potential cooperation of court officials is always in the minds of reporters. This can come in the form of corroboration, or it may come as a direct leak, perhaps even in the form of actual grand jury documents. Even then, depending on the specific situation, many reporters are cautious.

"Maybe I shouldn't say this, but I am privy to indictments before they are presented to the grand jury," one says, "although I have been sworn that I can't

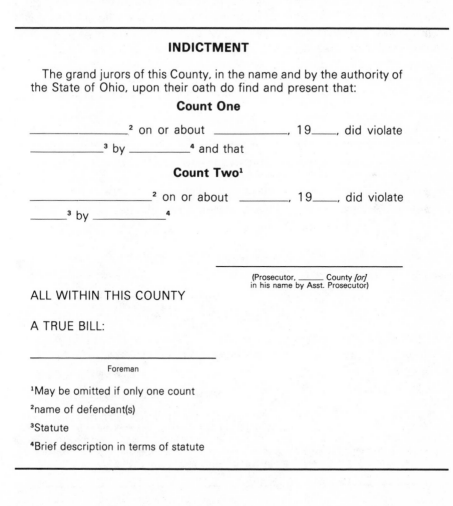

INDICTMENT

The grand jurors of this County, in the name and by the authority of the State of Ohio, upon their oath do find and present that:

Count One

_____² on or about _____, 19____, did violate

_____³ by _____⁴ and that

Count Two¹

_____² on or about _____, 19____, did violate

_____³ by _____⁴

_____
(Prosecutor, _____ County [or]
in his name by Asst. Prosecutor)

ALL WITHIN THIS COUNTY

A TRUE BILL:

_____
Foreman

¹May be omitted if only one count
²name of defendant(s)
³Statute
⁴Brief description in terms of statute

print them until they are passed by the grand jury. It took a while to build up trust. Only recently was I allowed to read a proposed indictment, and I was told in no uncertain terms that to print that ahead of time would be disastrous."

The reporter uses this advance knowledge to prepare background so that when the indictments are officially returned, he is ready with a detailed, well-researched report.

If the person indicted by a grand jury is not already in custody, the clerk of courts issues a warrant, and the arrest is made. Often, when the grand jury indicts, no preliminary hearing is held since their purposes are the same.

Arraignment

Of major interest to reporters during the arraignment is the plea of the defendant and the fact that, in many instances, this represents the end of the pretrial process. In some states, the arraignment and plea are separate proceedings, but in all cases the specific charges and rights are explained to defendants, who are then asked for their plea. Defendants have options that differ from state to state, but four are most standard.

If the defendant pleads *guilty* to a felony charge, the court will set a date for sentencing. For a misdemeanor, sentencing probably will occur at that time, although the judge has the option of delaying for additional study.

BILL OF INFORMATION

_____[1] the Prosecutor of this County, says by way of information that _____[2] the defendant, on or about _____ _____, 19____, did in this County violate _____[3] by _____ _____[4]

_____
(Prosecutor's signature by himself
or by an Asst. Prosecutor)

[1]Prosecutor's name.

[2]Defendant's name.

[3]Statute.

[4]Brief description in terms of statute, e.g., "assaulting _____ with intent to kill," etc.

Comment: The requirements of a bill of information are identical to those of an indictment. It must be signed by the prosecuting attorney or signed in his name by an assistant prosecuting attorney, and contain a statement that the accused has committed some public offense specified therein. Each count of the information shall also state the numerical designation of the statute which the defendant is alleged to have violated.

If the defendant pleads *no contest,* meaning no defense to the charge will be presented, he or she is at the mercy of the court, and a sentence usually will be handed down by the judge. This is a practical equivalent to a guilty plea except it cannot be used against the defendant in later court actions.

If the defendant pleads *not guilty,* the case is set later for trial.

If the defendant pleads *not guilty by reason of insanity,* the judge usually orders a series of psychiatric examinations before determining whether a trial should proceed. Most frequently used in homicide cases, this plea centers on a defendant's ability, either temporary or permanent, to distinguish between right and wrong.

Motion Hearings

Defense attorneys have a wide variety of special actions that they may request of the court. Their strategic success in using these could have significant impact upon the outcome of the case. At times, these motions are considered as part of a regular pretrial hearing, but such considerations frequently come at a special hearing scheduled by the trial judge, often at the request of the defense, or in an appellate court.

Perhaps the most significant of these is a *motion to suppress evidence* in the case. Usually presented on technical grounds, this motion questions acceptability of a law enforcement action. If the court accepts the motion, the evidence in question will not be used in court, thus possibly reducing—and sometimes destroying—chances for a guilty verdict.

Often, if their case is thus severely damaged, prosecutors will either drop their charges or be willing to plea bargain.

A major issue for journalists is whether they should report the evidence under consideration. An unanswered question is whether prospective jurors who know of the evidence will be able to dismiss it from their consideration. This is the issue of a 1979 U.S. Supreme Court decision, and the answer there is that judges may indeed exclude the public, including reporters, from the sensitive motion hearings.

Given the availability of information, however, most reporters do present it with the thought that any prospective juror likely to be influenced by such information will be excused from service for that particular trial.

Among other motions available to the defense are:

Motion to strike prior convictions: This would remove any consideration by the judge of prior convictions in the determination of the sentence.

Motion to set aside: This motion applies to an information presented by prosecutor or a grand jury indictment for procedural or factual deficiencies. The defense attorney may charge that the district attorney's complaint, based on evidence taken at the preliminary hearing, is not sufficient to prove what it charges.

Motion to dismiss due to lack of speedy trial: This usually is made by the defense when the prosecution or the court delays the start of the trial while preparing its case.

Motion to dismiss due to denial of due process: This may be made when the defendant did not receive the proper explanation of his or her rights at the time of the arrest.[3]

Motion for severance: This is presented when one of several jointly accused individuals believes the best defense would be separate from the trials of the other defendants. It is a request for a separate trial.

COVERING THE CIVIL PRETRIAL PROCESS

A clue to the nature of the criminal justice system is in the titles given to individual cases: *State* v. *John Jones.* The state, representing the citizens, is taking action against an individual or group accused of violating a law. Civil actions, on the other hand, usually are labeled with the names of individuals or groups, *Smith* v. *Jones.* Thus, a civil case is one in which an individual, business, or agency of government seeks payment for losses or injuries (damages) or asks that another party be forced by the court to do something or stop some action which is causing problems (relief).[4]

With notable exceptions, journalists do not pay as much attention to civil cases, and this means they are missing much that could be very important to their communities. Not only do civil cases constitute the great bulk of court activity, but it's in the civil court that, to put it broadly, the rules of society are being laid down.

"You miss the medical malpractice suits, the legal malpractice suits, the dispute between the legislative and executive branches of government," says Carol Green of the *Denver Post.* "You miss the racial discrimination issues, the methods in which the probate courts are handling the estates of hundreds of citizens, the job discrimination issues, the sex discrimination issues. Maybe probate courts touch more lives than most other courts, except traffic courts.

"You miss judges doing favors for law firms in the way they schedule cases and the way they treat motions. And it's in civil court where you find the school finance suits, where you find government condemnation suits that will cost taxpayers millions of dollars. You miss most of what's going on in the judicial system by confining coverage to criminal cases."

Claudia Luther of the *Los Angeles Times,* who covers nothing but civil activities, has the same opinion.

"Civil courts are becoming more and more of a forum for a wide variety of issues that are confronting society today," she says. "People are becoming more judicious. They are finding out that they can go to court and get some relief. The thing I like about civil cases is that the issues are a lot more complex, and they ultimately have much more effect on your life than the razzle-dazzle criminal case."

It's probably that very complexity which results in poor coverage, along with news judgment which fails to see the ramifications of what superficially is a simple dispute between two individuals or organizations.

Claudia Luther of the *Los Angeles Times*

(*Los Angeles* photo)

In civil cases, reporters may need to wade through vast piles of discovery motions. They may encounter appraisals in cases involving government purchasing, and the appraisals are very difficult to understand. The civil procedure is more complex in some ways because it's less familiar, and it's more apt to revert to Latin terminology.

It's also more difficult from a reporter's standpoint because a civil judge will see many different lawyers in a month. A criminal judge sees the same set of lawyers. And reporters who cover criminal court see those same lawyers regularly. They can build relationships that result in the ability to get information. In civil court, reporters may see on Tuesday one lawyer they have never seen before, and another new one on Wednesday. Unless they build a relationship with the judge and with the staff, they are less likely to have someone who is constantly around to act as a translator.

Another problem making civil case coverage difficult is the length of the proceedings. It often takes years before the full story of a civil proceeding develops.

"Judges have some duty to bring a criminal case to trial period," says David Lieberth, now an attorney but formerly of WHLO in Akron, Ohio. "But in a civil case involving product liability or personal injury, it may be as long as two years before the entire story can be told. A reporter in that case, I think, has to proceed under the burden that readers or viewers or listeners have no prior information about the case. And reporters have to keep retelling the story every time they do something with it. The updates in court may be as much as six or twelve or even twenty-four months since the last story."[5]

Despite problems of covering civil cases, reporters like Luther stress the need for giving more consideration to the potential long-term impact of civil decisions. She decides which of the multitude of cases she will cover based on possible effect on citizens and on topics that have broad interest. She still functions on advice written in 1975 by Myrna Oliver, her predecessor at the *Los Angeles Times:* "Look for rulings that change law, cost taxpayers, affect large numbers of people."[6]

Types of Civil Actions

Civil cases may be categorized into three broad groups, generally according to the request. In the first, one citizen seeks money damages from another; the second involves an effort to prevent or compel action (equity); and the third is a catch-all category for a whole group of special court responsiblities.

Termed cases "at law," civil actions in the first group result when one individual believes he or she has suffered damages when a second individual has committed a wrong. Examples are claims made by persons injured in accidents, disputes over property, breach of contract, and such individual offenses as trespass, assault, and defamation.

Individuals filing suit may ask the court to require payment of certain sums for three specific purposes: compensation for actual money or property lost, funds to help alleviate physical or psychological sufferings caused by the alleged action, and payment which serves as punishment for the action. If the suit gets to trial stage, the decision is made by a jury.

Equity proceedings, on the other hand, do not always involve demands for money. In addition to resulting from a wrong already committed, these cases also are efforts to prevent wrongs. For example, a company may ask the court for an injunction to limit picketing by a striking labor union, or an individual or firm may request the court to require another party to live up to the terms of a contract. Equity decisions usually are made by a judge, not a jury.

In addition, courts have been given the responsibility to supervise a number of other actions. These frequently differ in their procedures. Included, for example, are dissolution of marriage suits, to which the major journalistic attention often is only a periodic listing, and probate action. Separate stories may be written if prominent individuals or large sums of money are involved or the case contains some other unusual or significant circumstances.

Two other types of cases provide business news: bankruptcy proceedings and corporate reorganization, both of which fall under the jurisdiction of the U.S. District Court. Reporters seldom attend the hearings themselves, preferring to get information from documents filed in the clerk of court's office, unless large numbers of persons are involved or the actions contested.

Reporters are unanimous in their advice that the first requirement for anyone assigned to cover civil cases is to learn the system.

"One of the most important things is to get the procedure down," Green says. "And in a civil case, it's more important to talk to both sides and to talk to the judges because you're really more likely to make a mistake.

"And the same would apply to cases that fall into civil categories such as probate cases, domestic relations cases, and juvenile proceedings which are in that grey area between civil and criminal. They speak a different language, they're a different set of lawyers and a different set of judges. It's very difficult. And, for that reason, I think most reporters are intimidated by cases in those areas."

Focus of Civil Pretrial Coverage

Civil cases are like criminal cases in one important respect. Most never get to the trial stage, partly because judges make special efforts to accomplish as much as possible out of the courtroom and because going the full route can be very time consuming and expensive.

Given this, reporters try to be especially alert in the early stages to anticipate an early settlement, both so they won't be caught alseep if it occurs and to provide readers with the full perspective. Such coverage is accomplished through a combination of three methods: following the documents filed with the clerk of courts, interviewing parties in the case, and attending various hearings.

"Everything that goes on in court goes on in writing. Almost everything goes on in writing before it goes on out loud," says David Offer of the *La Crosse* [Wisconsin] *Tribune*. "That's not true at the final trial level, but a trial is the last thing that happens in court, and about 95 percent of all legal cases—criminal and civil—never get to a trial. So much of the coverage of courts is coverage of paperwork—covering law suits that are filed, answers, responses, interrogatories (written questions). I tend to spend much more time writing about paperwork than I do about trials."

It is important, therefore, that reporters know what documents are available and the fact that they almost always are public record. Any member of the public —including reporters—has only to walk into the clerk of court's office and ask for them.

It would be quite possible in most cases for a reporter to use the documents alone to produce readable and accurate stories about civil cases. But it's often desirable to supplement documentary material with conversations and attendance at hearings. The documents give the superficial, but not the undercurrent, the mood, in the courtroom. Attendance at selected hearings may facilitate putting legal points into simpler language. Lawyers will write in legalized style in their briefs, but they speak more plainly in the courtroom.

The Civil Pretrial Process

A civil case begins with a complaint in which a person charges he or she has suffered damage from a wrong action committed by another person. That petitioner is the plaintiff. After explaining what resulted from the alleged action, the plaintiff makes a specific request for damages, judgment, or other relief. Also requested is a summons to notify defendants of the allegations against them and to require that they appear in court.

This may cause problems for the reporter who checks the records frequently, perhaps several times a day.

As Dave Lieberth explains, "Very often the plaintiff and the lawyer file the suit even before they notify the defendant that he is being sued. Sometimes, the defendant learns that he has had a suit filed against him when the reporter calls

CIVIL COMPLAINT; Negligence, Automobile Accident

IN THE COURT OF COMMON PLEAS
OF FRANKLIN COUNTY, OHIO

Paul P. Patton
150 N. High Street
Columbus, Ohio 43214

Plaintiff

vs.   Case No. 13,875

David D. Doe
2861 Summit Avenue
Columbus, Ohio 43228

Defendant

Complaint
Jury Demand Endorsed Hereon

1. On February 16, 1970 at the intersection of East Main Street and College Avenue in Bexley, Ohio, the defendant negligently operated his motor vehicle into the motor vehicle owned and operated by plaintiff.

2. As a result plaintiff suffered injuries of the neck, back, shoulders and other parts of his body, causing pain and permanent damage.

3. Plaintiff has incurred medical and hospital expenses in the sum of $300.00 and expects to incur further such expenses.

4. Plaintiff has lost $600.00 earnings and expects to lose further earnings. His earning capacity has been permanently impaired.

5. Plaintiff's 1969 Chevrolet was damaged in the amount of $800.00.

WHEREFORE, plaintiff demands judgment against defendant in the sum of $16,500.00 and costs.

/s/ Alan Able
_____

Able and Ready
100 E. Broad Street
Columbus, Ohio 43215
Phone 221-4500
Attorney for Plaintiff

Jury Demand

Plaintiff demands trial by a jury in this action.

/s/ Alan Able
_____

Attorney for Plaintiff

Comment: This form can be used for all routine automobile accidents involving negligence. It is not important for the purpose of pleading whether the negligence is assured clear distance ahead, speed or for a reaction. If you're on deadline you have that special problem of how to treat the story fairly."[7]

Lieberth admits there is no standard answer. But most reporters would report the suit, point out that the defendant had no immediate reply, and hope balance would come over the long run.

It may well not be in time for a reporter's deadline, but the defendant's answer, called a pleading, is the next step in the process. It must be filed within a stipulated period, and if it is not, the plaintiff may then request a default judgment. If the answer is filed on time, the defendant has a number of alternative pleadings, which may include one or more of the following:

Motion to strike: Asks the court to rule that the plaintiff's petition contains irrelevant, prejudicial, or other improper matter. The court may order such matter deleted.

Motion to make more definite and certain: Requires the plaintiff to set out the facts of the complaint more specifically or to describe the injury or damages in greater detail so that the defendant can answer more precisely.

Demurrer or motion to dismiss: Questions whether the plaintiff's petition states a legally sound cause of action against the defendant, even admitting for the purpose of the pleading that all of the facts set out by the plaintiff in the petition are true.

Answer: This statement by the defendant denies the allegations in the plaintiff's petition, or admits some and denies other, or admits all and pleads an excuse.

Cross-petition or cross-complaint: May be filed by the defendant either separately or as part of the answer. It asks for relief or damages against the original plaintiff, and perhaps others. When a cross-petition is filed, the plaintiff may then file any of these same motions to the cross-petition, except a motion to quash service of summons.[8]

Most of these motions may be appealed, usually to a higher court, and that's part of the reason civil cases may take years. Each appeal sets off a whole new series of hearings and additional motions which must be taken care of before a trial date is set. And it often is at this stage that reporters lose contact with a case unless it happens to be a very big one or involves prominent community individuals.

any other cause as conclusionary allegations of negligence are the same in each case under the Civil Rules. Specific facts are to be ascertained through the discovery or pre-trial process.

Special damages are required to be set forth with particularity. The issue of what constitutes special damages is unchanged by the Civil Rules and includes specific injuries, medical expense, loss of earnings, permanency of injury, impairment of earning capacity and property damage. It is recommended that all applicable types of special damages be pleaded briefly as in this form. No technical form of allegation is required although the method of proof remains unchanged.

Reporters' attempts to deal with civil cases often include a personal filing system in which they keep notes and clips of cases they are attempting to follow. And, of course, the other part is helpful sources.

"There are hundreds and hundreds of documents filed here, and there's no way I can keep up with all of them," says Bob Rawitch of the *Los Angeles Times,* "so I have to rely a great deal on the attorneys and the other people who have contact with the case. I'll tell them in advance of a case I'm interested in and say, 'Hey,

---

ANSWER; General Form Combining a Denial Defense with Other Defenses and Objections

IN THE COURT OF COMMON PLEAS OF FRANKLIN COUNTY, OHIO

Paul P. Patton
Plaintiff

vs.   Case No. 14,264

David D. Doe
Defendant

Answer

First Defense
1. Defendant admits the allegations contained in paragraphs 1 and 2 of the complaint.
2. Defendant admits the allegations contained in paragraph 3 of the complaint except he denies that he was negligent.
3. Defendant alleges that he is without knowledge or information sufficient to form a belief as to the truth of the allegations contained in paragraphs 4 and 5 of the complaint.
4. Defendant denies all of the allegations contained in paragraph 6 of the complaint.

Second Defense
Plaintiff has failed to join the ABC Insurance Company as a plaintiff in this action. ABC Insurance Company has an interest or claim arising out of the same act for property damages subrogated to the aforesaid company.

Third Defense
If defendant is found to be negligent, which he expressly denies, plaintiff was contributorily negligent proximately resulting in his injuries.

/s/ John Jones _____

Jones and Smith
50 W. Broad Street
Columbus, Ohio 43215
Phone 228-2800
Attorney for Defendant

---

let me know when you file a trial memorandum or the defense plea in this case.' For the most part, they're willing to call me and tell me."

Good stories also are to be found in the rather freewheeling and potentially time-consuming process called discovery, which essentially is the paperwork of asking and answering questions. It's of obvious value to attorneys to know as much as they can about the other side's case, and it is through discovery that they obtain much of this information.

Attorneys are under few limitations in their use of discovery, being able to ask almost anything. It is up to the opposing attorneys to object to an improper request. Given such an objection, the judge decides whether a question or questions must be answered. In Ohio, for example:

"Parties may obtain discovery regarding any matter, not privileged, which is relevant to the subject matter involved in the pending action, whether it relates to the claim or defense of the party seeking discovery or to the claim or

---

PLEADINGS; Motion for Definite Statement

IN THE COURT OF COMMON PLEAS
OF FRANKLIN COUNTY, OHIO

Paul P. Patton
Plaintiff

vs.   Case No. 14,264

David D. Doe
Defendant

Motion for Definite Statement

Defendant moves the court for an order requiring plaintiff to provide a definite statement concerning the following particulars in his complaint as it is so vague and ambiguous that defendant is unable to frame an answer thereto:

1. By setting forth the date on which the accident alleged in the second paragraph of the first claim in the complaint occurred as time is material to the affirmative defense of the statute of limitations.

2. By setting forth items of special damage specially in the fifth paragraph of the first claim as required by Civil Rule 9 (G).

3. By setting forth the circumstances constituting mistake with particularity in the third paragraph of the second claim as required by Civil Rule 9 (B).

/s/ John Jones_____

Jones and Smith
50 W. Broad Street
Columbus, Ohio 43215
Phone 228-2800
Attorney for Defendant

defense of any other party, including the existence, description, nature, custody, condition and location of any books, documents, or other tangible things and the identity and location of persons having knowledge of any discoverable matter."[9]

An important part of discovery is what is known as an interrogatory, a list of written questions presented by an attorney to the other side which must be answered under oath. The questions may be of a background nature. For example, in a personal injury case resulting from an automobile accident, an attorney may ask for the driving record of the defendant, whether glasses are required, whether the defendant had been drinking, or what the defendant had done for the twenty-four hours prior to the accident.

Answering the questions may involve the expression of opinion, even if that opinion would not be allowed as evidence during the trial. Or the questions may be strategic in nature, such as a request for the amount of insurance the defendant carries so that the plaintiff's attorney can be guided in the amount of damages to request.

Attorneys even are permitted to ask for a list of witnesses who will appear with the stipulation that such a list be updated until the time of the trial.

In preparation for the trial or as part of pretrial activities, either side in a case has the right to take sworn out-of-court statements from the other party or from any witness. Called depositions, these statements often are needed because a court cannot require appearance at a civil trial of a person who lives outside the county. If a person who has given a deposition also testifies at the trial, attorneys may use that deposition to attack his or her credibility.

Depositions may consist of answers to written questions or of oral examination conducted before an authorized person. In either event, a transcript is made, although some courts permit recordings or even videotapes. And attorneys may cross-examine. Some reporters have found it possible in some jurisdictions to attend the session at which depositions are being taken, but generally they are not considered public record until made public by court order or introduced as evidence in a trial.

However, it is usually possible for reporters to get an advance look at the depositions because they often must be filed at least one day before being used in a hearing or the trial.

Offer, who formerly worked for the *Milwaukee Journal,* believes in paying careful attention to depositions. "We get great stories here [Milwaukee] from depositions, especially in civil rights cases," he says. "Our fire department is under orders to hire women, and officials keep taking depositions from people asking how these women are being found, and the answer is, they're not. Every time they do a deposition, I get a story."

In addition to interrogatories and depositions, attorneys have other methods of discovery that are used in special instances. Three used most frequently are requiring that documents, records, and books be presented or permission be given to enter someone's property for an inspection; requiring that a person involved

INTERROGATORIES: General Form to Corporation

IN THE COURT OF COMMON PLEAS
OF FRANKLIN COUNTY, OHIO

Paul P. Patton
Plaintiff

vs.   Case No. 28,253

ABC Corporation
Defendant

Interrogatories

To the ABC Corporation:

The following interrogatories are submitted herewith to you to be answered in writing under oath within 28 days after the date of service thereof upon you.

Instructions for answering:

1. You are required to choose one or more of your proper employees, officers or agents to answer the interrogatories, and the employer, officer or agent shall furnish such information as is known or available to the organization.

2. Where the word "accident" is used it refers to the incident which is the basis of this law suit unless otherwise specified.

3. Where an interrogatory calls for an answer in more than one part, the parts should be separated in the answer so that they are clearly understandable.

4. "Medical practitioner" as used herein includes any medical doctor, osteopathic physician, chiropractor or any other person who performs any type of healing art.

5. You are reminded that all answers must be made separately and fully and that an incomplete or evasive answer is a failure to answer.

6. You are under a continuing duty seasonably to supplement your response with respect to any question directly addressed to the identity and location of persons having knowledge of discoverable matters, the identity of any person expected to be called as an expert witness at trial, and the subject matter on which he is expected to testify and to correct any response which you know or later learn is incorrect.

QUESTIONS:

(Insert herein questions directed to the particular case)

1. ......
2. ......
3. ......
4. ......

/s/ John Jones

Jones and Smith
50 W. Broad Street
Columbus, Ohio 43215
Phone 228-2800

in the case take a physical or mental examination; and requiring that the other side admit or deny the genuineness of documents.

Once all of the various motions and discovery techniques have been used and the case is ready for trial, many states require one final step, a pretrial hearing. Basically an effort to reduce trial time, this hearing is designed to determine points of agreement (stipulations) among the parties. Participants usually are the attorneys and the judge. Generally, these agreements center on many of the facts of the case, although points of law may be included.

"The courts these days are trying to do as much out-of-court work as possible to get the issues defined," Offer says. "If there is a trial, in many federal cases what I'll do right beforehand is read the list of uncontested facts and the list of contested questions. This helps focus my attention."

NOTES

1. "Reporting the Criminal Process," Ohio University seminar sponsored by the Society of Professional Journalists, Sigma Delta Chi, March 4, 1978.
2. Carl Bernstein and Bob Woodward, *All The President's Men* (New York: Simon and Schuster, 1974), p. 207.
3. Albert G. Pickerell and Michel Lipman, "The Courts and the News Media," *Los Angeles Daily Journal Report,* Office of Criminal Justice Planning, pp. 29–30.
4. Standing Committee on Association Communications, American Bar Association, *Law and the Courts* (Chicago: American Bar Association, 1974), p. 7. Reprinted courtesy of the American Bar Asoociation, © 1980.
5. "Reporting the Criminal Process."
6. Myrna Oliver, *Los Angeles Times* internal memo to vacation relief staff, April 3, 1975, p. 2.
7. "Reporting the Criminal Process."
8. *Law and the Courts,* p. 8.
9. *Ohio Rules of Court* (St. Paul, Minn.: West Publishing Co., 1978), p. 47.

Chapter 8

A TRIAL IS REAL-LIFE DRAMA

As serious as it is, a trial is a stage. It's a football field. It's a political campaign. Participants take their positions, enter on cue, do only that which has been carefully rehearsed, function within the game plan, play according to the rules, accept (although sometimes reluctantly) the decisions of the referee.

Like actors, attorneys seek to project a sense of believability in what they are saying and doing. Like football coaches, they develop strategy but seek to maintain enough flexibility to take advantage of an opponent's weaknesses. Like politicans, they try to persuade certain constituents to vote in a particular way.

In so doing, attorneys—indeed, the whole criminal justice system—are not deliberately trying to protect an individual who is guilty of a crime. They are not saying laws should be violated. They are seeking to protect a system that maintains that an accused person is innocent until proven guilty and that the accused has a right to due process and a fair trial.

At its core, the job of the reporter also is to protect that system. The Sixth Amendment to the Constitution guarantees a speedy, public trial with the idea that full exposure to public view provides the best insurance the system will function as intended. And reporters represent the public in that system. They take full advantage of the fact that court documents, for the most part, are public records and court proceedings usually are open. They observe what happens in the courtroom, provide the public with descriptions of those events, relate individual and institutional actions to public expectations, and, at times, are critical when some aspect of the system strays from the norm.

105

Reporters, however, differ over how they cover the courtroom. For example, David Offer of the *La Crosse* [Wisconsin] *Tribune* says he spends very little time in it.

"Most trials are deadly dull," he says. "None of them is the Perry Mason type. I must have covered, off and on, hundreds of cases, and I have yet to be at an exciting trial. Most witnesses don't sparkle. Most lawyers don't do a great job of examination. I have yet to see anybody break down and confess on the stand. The way to cover trials is to be sure you've talked to all the lawyers, to be there for the opening and closing statements, and, if you can, skip an awful lot of the testimony in between."

Offer stresses, however, that reporters can be this free only if they understand the system, religiously read documents, and keep in close touch with attorneys to be assured of knowing what is going to happen in their absence from the courtroom.

That's the general, day-to-day approach, but there are times when a trial will be of such community concern or legal importance that it merits full-time coverage. The reporter then simply has to adjust priorities or get help to be there.

"In a trial involving a serious matter," says Jeff Watkins of the Charleston, South Carolina, *News* and *Courier*, "I'll make it a point to be there in the morning when they begin and to stay there until they close the courthouse at night. I just think the more I can see and hear myself, the better job I can do. I don't like to rely on other people for information if I don't have to. If I can see it or hear it myself, I'm much better off, and I can write a better story."

Covering a trial, either full time or on a spot basis, involves knowing what kinds of stories are likely to occur during the various parts of the proceedings. Every step can make news. Every step may provide clues to future developments. And reporting these from a trial which may last days or months can help readers, listeners, or viewers understand both what is happening in an individual case and, importantly, more about the criminal justice system.

JURY SELECTION

Specific jurors, composing the trial (or petit) jury, for either a civil or criminal trial are selected from a list of prospects compiled from voter registration lists, tax assessment lists, or some other official listing of citizens. The selection process (voir dire) consists of questions from attorneys and/or judges to determine a prospect's suitability. These questions may seek to determine if the prospect has biases that may affect the decision. They may examine the individual's background or knowledge, which could have a bearing on the decision.

Attorneys, naturally, will seek to eliminate jurors who might be biased against their side. In so doing, they may ask the court to dismiss a prospective juror "for cause" when they discover evidence of an opinion or prejudice that might influence the decision. Or they may use "peremptory challenges," which permit them to excuse a specific number of prospective jurors without stating a reason.

Reporters ordinarily do not cover the jury selection, choosing instead to report simply on the results, usually giving a demographic breakdown of the twelve jurors (and, in some states, the alternates). They would report, for example, that a jury was composed of seven women and five men or that it included four blacks. The basic effort is to provide any information that might be pertinent to the representativeness of the jury. Otherwise the selection process can be time consuming and result in very little solid information for the reader, viewer, or listener. But there are at least two kinds of situations in which being on the scene may be of value.

A good story could result from the answers or lack of answers given by prospects, especially when there is difficulty in seating the jury for a particularly noteworthy trial. Or the story could be broader, perhaps even only indirectly related to the specific trial.

Again, David Offer: "We had a trial in Milwaukee a couple of years ago, in which two members of the American Nazi Party were charged with a misdemeanor for allegedly throwing rocks at or beating up a couple of members of the Jewish Defense League. The question of Nazism became important because obviously you were looking for jurors who wouldn't be so prejudiced against Nazis that they couldn't fairly judge the specifics of the case.

Mike Hardy of the *Norfolk Virginian-Pilot*

(*Virginian-Pilot* photo by Mike Williams)

"I got a page one piece out of it because questioning showed that the possible jurors had almost no knowledge of Nazism. Somebody didn't realize that Hitler was a Nazi. This was a group of people who just didn't link Nazism with the war in Germany. It was an incredible story, and I got it out of knowing what was going on and being there at the right time."

Jury selection also can provide an early opportunity to gain insight into what attorneys think is important to their case. They use questions to guide the thinking of jurors toward the desired decision.

"Lawyers pound away at certain questions, and they try as much as possible to make jurors feel extremely responsible about the case," says Michael Hardy of the Norfolk *Virginian-Pilot*. "And if you keep pursuing a juror, saying, 'You're not going to be prejudiced about x or y or z,' there's always a feeling on the part of most fair-minded men and women who are in a public setting like that to bend over backwards even more in favor of the side propounding that kind of question."

Hardy, who himself has studied law, says the kinds of cases which attract reporters to the jury selection are capital cases or cases in which a political figure might be on trial. But reporters should seek to avoid any automatic categorization of the story value of the voir dire. That decision has to be made on a case-by-case basis.

OPENING STATEMENTS

Attorneys have two opportunities during a trial to move to the center of the stage, command the attention of the whole courtroom, and try to invoke the sympathy of the jurors. In both the opening and closing statements, attorneys may relate more emotionally the facts and law of a case.

The purpose of opening statements—given first by the plaintiff's attorney in a civil case or the prosecution in a criminal case—is to establish what attorneys feel are the facts of the case. This phase sets the scene. It's like reading a program before a play. Reporters learn the characters and the lines of argument.

In some states, defense attorneys will exercise the option to delay their opening statement until just before their presentation of evidence. This is partly because it gives them the opportunity to better set the stage for their witnesses. And it's partly because they see an advantage in waiting until after the prosecution has presented its case. By making an early statement, they sometimes think, they put themselves into the position of needing to prove something to the jury. They would rather leave that burden on the prosecution, where the system places it.

But regardless of when opening statements occur, reporters stress their value as news and as a means of providing specific insights into the arguments of the case.

"You want to see who is going to be the main prosecution witness," says Rita Ciolli of *Newsday*. "It could be something like an eye-witness identification, the neighbor who saw the guy fleeing from the house. You know that's where the defense is going to zero in and try to destroy the person's credibility. Or if all they have is one fingerprint, you can be damn sure the police technician is going to get grilled, and you can build a whole story about how this one fingerprint is going to make the difference.

"And then check the defense to see whether there is an alibi: 'Dentist So-and-so was fixing his teeth at the time.' Or they're going to bring someone to show that there is another suspect the police ignored or didn't bother doing their homework on."

PRESENTING THE EVIDENCE

As usually happens during the trial process, attorneys for the plaintiff or the prosecution are first in presenting evidence. Some evidence is in the form of documents or physical objects (the murder weapon, for example), but most usually comes from witnesses who respond to questions from the attorneys or, in a few instances, the judge.

Reporters take differing points of view about such testimony. Some, like Offer, tend to remain unimpressed with witnesses, preferring to concentrate on documents and out-of-court comments from attorneys. Others, like Shelley Epstein of the Peoria, Illinois, *Journal Star*, feel strongly about the journalistic value of reporting testimony directly from the courtroom, especially in an important case.

"It's my feeling that the copy reads best, and you get the best information by sitting through the testimony," he says. "However, that's the most time consuming, and you have a lot of dead time while doing it. But I really don't see any way of doing it fully and properly without listening to the testimony. On occasion, I have skipped the witnesses and gone in for the closing arguments and gotten somewhat of a synopsis of what was going on. But I find that what the attorneys are saying in the closing arguments is not always what the witnesses are saying from the stand."

That testimony comes in four flavors, as attorneys tug away at the witnesses to make points for their sides. In direct examination, the attorney who calls the witness seeks to present that person's direct experience or expert knowledge about the circumstances or subject matter of the case. The opposing attorney, through cross-examination, then asks questions that seek to lead the jury to doubt the credibility of the witness. Back comes the original attorney, in a redirect examination, to try to repair the damage. The opposing attorney may then conclude the questioning with re-cross-examination.

Most witnesses are restricted in their testimony to fact. They may tell what they experienced directly, or they may identify documents or other physical evidence presented in the trial. They are not permitted to state opinions about those facts, and they often are not allowed to tell what they have heard others say (hearsay).

But one type of witness who may express an opinon is the person with special knowledge, defined as an expert. Because expert testimony often is technical, some reporters tend to gloss over it, a situation that Hardy considers unfortunate.

"My own criticism of journalists is that they tend not to see the differences among, let us say, a fingerprint expert, a voice expert, and a guy who might be able to tell something about locks or evidence like hair samples and mud samples," he says. "They're all thrown into the same pot."

Reporters' glossing over the expert witnesses, presenting little more than a quick summary, he says, may fail to provide readers, viewers, and listeners with an adequate picture of the value of the testimony, either pro or con. Too much emphasis on the term *expert,* for example, may obscure the fact that the findings are not adequately scientific or do not provide an important element of the prosecution's case.

Journalists do not, however, gloss over those witnesses who were directly involved in the incident that led to charges being filed—the victim and the defendant.

"I make a greater attempt to get the testimony or something from the victim than I do, for example, from the officer who investigated the case," Watkins says. "To make the story more readable, I would try to get that firsthand account of what happened and what it meant to the victim or the victim's family. I guess it's kind of a people-oriented approach and that makes better reading."

This coverage applies as well to defendants, who are not required to testify in either a criminal or civil trial. And often they do not appear because their attorneys are reluctant to put them on the stand, where they will be subject to cross-examination. But, if they do testify, reporters make a special effort to be on hand. This, of course, is not only a matter of good reading. It's part of the natural journalistic tendency to provide readers with as much firsthand detail as possible about all sides of an issue.

That leads Hardy to pay considerable attention to the cross-examination. He disagrees with reporters who concentrate on the points witnesses are trying to make rather than attorneys' efforts to question their credibility. One means of achieving balance, he says, is through presentation of cross-examination.

"I at least try to give the reader an idea that, 'Hey, this is one side of the story today, but as you recall the defense attorney said in his opening statement that he's going to try to prove just the opposite or to discredit the witness or to point out that the evidence isn't so strong as to satisfy the beyond-a-reasonable-doubt standard.' "

The effort by the court to see that the presentation of evidence is fair basically is in the hands of the judge, who determines the admissibility. But the opposing attorneys are expected to help keep the system honest by calling to the judge's attention what they think are improper practices or inadmissible evidence. Attorneys for either side of a case may lodge objections, but the stakes are higher for the defense. Often the success of an appeal, or even at times the right of an appeal, hinges upon whether the objection was appropriately made.

Whether journalists emphasize or even mention objections in their coverage depends upon the specific circumstances. Often, the outcome of the trial itself may depend on a judge's decision as to whether particular evidence may be admitted. In those circumstances, naturally, the reporter will provide full details of the evidence, the objection, and the reasons the evidence was admitted or ruled inadmissible.

In all situations the question to ask is: How important is the evidence in terms of the overall guilt or innocence? This applies even to evidence that is excluded.

If, for example, the objection concerns whether the jury will be permitted to hear testimony about an incriminating statement made by the defendant, the jury often will be sent from the room during the discussion. Even if the judge rules out the testimony, most reporters would consider it valuable enough to include it in the story. Their goal would be to inform readers of the fact that the defendant made the statement even though it's not going to be entered into the evidence.

Sometimes debates are conducted in the courtroom after the jury has been dismissed, or the judge and attorneys may go to the judge's chambers. Here, too, the reporter makes every effort to get the full picture.

"If you see the court reporter going into chambers with the judge and the lawyers," Offer advises, "feel free to go in too. It's part of an open court hearing. You might get thrown out, but you haven't lost a lot by trying. We bounce painlessly. Generally speaking, any time the judge goes into chambers with the lawyers, the press, if it is excluded, should howl."

Once the prosecution has completed its case, attention turns to the defense, which follows pretty much the same routine. In some instances, defense attorneys present no evidence, on the grounds that the burden of proof is on the prosecution and that requirement has not been met.

At the conclusion of the defendant's presentation, the plaintiff's or state's attorney may present additional evidence (rebuttal evidence) to refute testimony and evidence offered by the defendant. This is followed by one more opportunity for the defense to refute the rebuttal.

CLOSING ARGUMENTS

This is the last chance for attorneys to present the case as they believe it should be interpreted. First, the attorney for the plaintiff or state, then the defense counsel, will stride to the jury box, summarize from their perspective, sometimes cajole, sometimes plead, sometimes demand that the decision be in favor of their side. The importance of closing arguments is not lost on attorneys or reporters.

"We have some very good what I call country lawyers here who can make a very impassioned plea on somebody's behalf, and I've heard them from both the defense and the state's side," Watkins says. "All the testimony has been given, the cases have been presented, and how the attorneys present their views to the jury, along with the evidence, can make a pretty good story."

Although closing arguments may be freewheeling, attorneys still function under restrictions. They must confine their comments to the facts, evidence presented, and properly drawn inferences of the case. They are not allowed to comment on a defendant's failure to testify in a criminal case. If an attorney gets carried away and goes beyond these boundaries, opposing counsel has the right to object, and the judge will rule on that objection. At the extreme, too much improper argument could result in a mistrial.

Once both sides have concluded, the plaintiff or prosecution gets one final shot at the jury to answer defense arguments.

INSTRUCTIONS TO THE JURY

Although there is potential journalistic value in some situations in the instructions given by the judge to the jury, most reporters find that value limited. Because instructions represent the judge's statement of how the law applies to the facts of the case and provide interpretations and definitions, the point is, of course, that the reporter must understand the case to determine whether to hear them. To the reporter with time, however, the instructions, because they are written by the judge for lay jurors, often can help put a focus on the whole trial.

In some states, although the judge decides which to accept and which to refuse, instructions are based on proposals submitted by attorneys for each side. If an attorney feels that improper instructions were given, he or she lodges an objection for the record, in case of a later appeal.

WAITING FOR THE DECISION

Juries, of course, don't always cooperate with reporters facing deadlines. Once their secret deliberations begin, jurors discuss the evidence in detail and relate that evidence to the possible verdicts given them by the court. In criminal cases, their decision usually must be unanimous. In civil cases, some jurisdictions permit a verdict based on the agreement of nine or ten jurors. If they can't achieve the requirements (a hung jury), the whole trial may be repeated before a new jury.

That rather heavy burden may be taken care of in minutes, but more frequently it requires several hours or even days of deliberation. For reporters, long deliberations can create a void during which they must have the knowledge and initiative to fill editor and reader expectations.

"When the jury is out, I always try to keep a story going," Hardy says. "After all, people wonder what ever happened to that little case out there. I will talk to the defense attorney or prosecutor and, invariably, they have their own theories which are based on hunches at best. I try to talk to the victim or if the victim has been slain, the family of the victim and, of course, the defendant and the family of the defendant."

The reporter also watches the courtroom, in case the jury returns to ask questions of the judge about the instructions. If such an event is missed, a quick check with courtroom personnel, especially court reporters or stenographers, should cover it.

Keeping in touch with courtroom personnel also helps reporters ensure that they will be available when the jury returns with its verdict, which can happen at almost any time. Generally, reporters who cannot wait in the courtroom (and few ever can) will arrange to have an attorney or other courtroom official call when the jury is expected.

INTERVIEWING JURORS

Once the verdict has been announced, and jury members have been dismissed, reporters often will take advantage of the opportunity to get some good inside information.

"It's so important to talk to the jurors afterwards," Ciolli says. "Some of them are very helpful and will give you a whole idea of what happened inside. You can develop so many angles by talking to the jurors. Sometimes, they are nowhere near what the case is about. How good are these jurors, really, in deciding the case? Were they totally influenced by other situations? What about the victim's mother sobbing in the front row? Talking to jurors is a good chance to look at both the strengths and weaknesses of the system."

Whether reporters do talk with them, of course, depends on the type of case it is, how legally important it is, the degree of public interest, or whether the case is out of the ordinary. Reporters will try, certainly, in capital cases and in cases in which persons of some popularity, political standing, or prestige have been on trial.

Although there are no legal ramifications in talking to jurors after the verdict, reporters often have to overcome efforts by some judges to make such interviews difficult. Sometimes, after a noteworthy trial, these judges will tell jurors to avoid reporters. Or they may insist that everyone in the courtroom remain until jurors have left the room. But, for a reporter who has determined that juror interviews are necessary, these efforts should represent little more than minor inconveniences.

MOTIONS AFTER VERDICT

The verdict, once announced, is not official until the judge enters judgment. And, prior to the judgment, the losing attorney may again make motions if he or she thinks some aspect of the process was conducted unfairly. Among the most common of these motions are

Motion for a new trial, which sets out alleged procedural errors and asks the judge to grant a new trial.

Motion in arrest of judgment, which attacks the sufficiency of the indictment or information in a criminal case.

Motion for judgment non obstante veredicto, which requests the judge to enter a judgment contrary to the jury's verdict.[1]

JUDGMENT AND SENTENCING

The judgment of the court determines action to be taken based upon the jury's verdict, subject, of course, to any appellate court decision.

In a civil damage suit, the judgment establishes the amount of damages a guilty defendant must pay. These damages may compensate the plaintiff for losses incurred (compensatory) or be paid as a means of punishment (punitive).

JUDGMENT OF CONVICTION
Judgment

This _____ day of _____, 19____, Defendant came into Court represented by Attorney _____ and the State/City of _____, came represented by _____, defendant having entered a plea of _____ to the charge (s) of _____.

WHEREFORE, the trial began _____, 19____ and on ____ _____, 19____, having heard all the testimony adduced by both parties, the Court/Jury in writing made its

FINDINGS, to wit:

_____ as to _____ (if motions made, so recite, together
guilty/not guilty   charges
with disposition)

Counsel for defendant having been given an opportunity to speak on behalf of defendant, and defendant personally having been given the opportunity to make a statement in his own behalf and present information in mitigation and _____
"no good and sufficient cause" [or] "good and sufficient cause"
being shown to mitigate punishment and nothing said by defendant as to why sentence should not now be imposed, SENTENCE AND JUDGMENT WAS PRONOUNCED AS FOLLOWS:

For the offense(s) of _____, you are sentenced to _____ _____ (etc.)

In a criminal case, the judge generally will set a time for sentencing of a defendant found guilty. During the interim, the judge will seek to determine whether other factors should be considered in establishing the sentence.

This process gives the reporter several story possibilities, the most significant of which is, of course, the sentence itself.

"My own predilection is that sentencing is the most important thing in criminal justice," Hardy says. "Given all the plea bargaining, 90 percent of the cases never get that far. And I think that's a crucial moment, to find out what's going on, how fair the thing is, and what components the judge might have taken into consideration in sentencing someone. In Virginia, also, presentence reports are prepared, and I try to read those even though they're supposed to be sealed. They contain a lot of information."

Again, interviews with the defendant, the lawyers, jurors, family members about their reactions to the sentence can provide good copy in which the human and legal elements come together.

DEALING WITH LEGAL MUMBO JUMBO

The law is complicated. That's enough to make the job of the reporter difficult. But adding to it is the legal profession's use of black-robe, high-ceiling language which few but law school graduates can understand. The law, perhaps more than any other profession, still clings to Latin phrases and rambling discourse. "Certiorari," says the judge. "No exeat," pleads the attorney. "What?" asks the citizen.

Cutting through all this legal mumbo jumbo may be the major task of court reporters. First, they have to wade through the jargon and the concepts and gain understanding themselves. Second, they have to communicate with their audiences, and this means avoiding the terminology and seeking instead lay definitions.

"That's the problem any specialist reporter is going to have to deal with," says Bob Rawitch of the *Los Angeles Times*. "And the longer you cover a specialty, the more you have to guard against letting the terminology slip into your copy. You have to avoid becoming a part of the inner circle. You know what they're talking about in the courtroom with the legal jargon flying from one side of the room to another, but I just don't think you can let it slip into your copy."

GLOSSARY OF LEGAL TERMS

A

abstract of record—A complete history of the case as found in the record, in short abbreviated form.

accumulative sentence—A sentence, additional to others, imposed at the same time for several distinct offenses; one sentence to begin at the expiration of another.

acquittal—A determination after a trial that a defendant in a criminal case is not guilty of the crime charged.

action in personam (in per-sō'nam)—An action against the person, founded on a personal liability.

action in rem (in rem)—An action for a thing; an action for the recovery of a thing possessed by another.

adjudication—Giving or pronouncing a judgment or decree; also the judgment given.

adversary system—The system of trial practice in the U.S. and some other countries in which each of the opposing, or adversary, parties has full opportunity to present and establish its opposing contentions before the court.

allegation—The assertion, declaration, or statement of a party to an action, made in a pleading, setting out what he expects to prove.

amicus curiae (a-mē-kus kur-ē-ī)—A friend of the court; one who interposes and volunteers information upon some matter of law.

ancillary bill or suit (an'si-la-rē)—One growing out of and auxiliary to another action or suit, such as a proceeding for the enforcement of a judgment, or to set aside fraudulent transfers of property.

answer—A pleading by which defendant endeavors to resist the plaintiff's allegation of facts.

appearance—The formal proceeding by which a defendant submits himself to the jurisdiction of the court.

appellant (a-pel'ant)—The party appealing a decision or judgment to a higher court.

appellate court—A court having jurisdiction of appeal and review; not a "trial court."

appellee (ap-e-le')—The party against whom an appeal is taken.

arraignment—In criminal practice, to bring a prisoner to the bar of the court to answer to a criminal charge.

arrest of judgment—The act of staying the effect of a judgment already entered.

at issue—Whenever the parties to a suit come to a point in the pleadings which is affirmed on one side and denied on the other, that point is said to be "at issue."

attachment—A remedy by which plaintiff is enabled to acquire a lien upon property or effects of defendant for satisfaction of judgment which plaintiff may obtain in the future.

attorney of record—Attorney whose name appears in the permanent records or files of a case.

B

bail—To set at liberty a person arrested or imprisoned, on security being taken, for his appearance on a specified day and place.

bail bond—An obligation signed by the accused, with sureties, to secure his presence in court.

bailiff—A court attendant whose duties are to keep order in the courtroom and to have custody of the jury.

banc (bangk)—Bench; the place where a court permanently or regularly sits. A "sitting **en banc** is a meeting of all the judges of a court, as distinguished from the sitting of a single judge.

bench warrant—Process issued by the court itself, or "from the bench," for the attachment or arrest of a person.

best evidence—Primary evidence; the best evidence which is available; any evidence which is available. Any evidence falling short of this standard is secondary; i.e., an original letter is best evidence compared to a copy.

binding instruction—One in which jury members are told if they find certain conditions to be true they must find for the plaintiff, or defendant, as case might be.

bind over—To hold on bail for trial.

brief—A written report or printed document prepared by counsel to file in court, usually setting forth both facts and law in support of his case.

burden of proof—In the law of evidence, the necessity or duty of affirmatively proving a fact or facts in dispute.

C

calling the docket—The public calling of the docket or list of causes at commencement of term of court, for setting a time for trial or entering orders.

caption—The caption of a pleading, or other papers connected with a case in court, is the heading or introductory clause which shows the names of the parties, name of the court, numbers of the case, etc.

cause—A suit, litigation or action—civil or criminal.

certiorare (ser-shē-o-ra'rē)—An original writ commanding judges or officers of inferior courts to certify or to return records of proceedings in a cause for judicial review.

challenge to the array—Questioning the qualifications of an entire jury panel, usually on the grounds of partiality or some fault in the process of summoning the panel.

chambers—Private office or room of a judge.

change of venue—The removal of a suit begun in one county or district, to another, for trial, or from one court to another in the same county or district.

circuit courts—Originally, courts whose jurisdiction extended over several counties or districts, and whose sessions were held in such counties or districts alternately; today, a circuit court may hold all its sessions in one county.

circumstantial evidence—All evidence of indirect nature; the process of decision by which court or jury may reason from circumstances known or proved to establish by inference the principal fact.

code—A collection, compendium or revision of laws systematically arranged into chapters, table of contents and index, and promulgated by legislative authority.

codicil (kod'i-sil)—A supplement or an addition to a will.

commit—To send a person to prison, an asylum, or reformatory by lawful authority.

common law—Law which derives its authority solely from usages and customs of immemorial antiquity, or from the judgments and decrees of courts. Also called "case law."

commutation—The changes of a punishment from a greater degree to a lesser degree, as from death to life imprisonment.

comparative negligence—The doctrine by which acts of the opposing parties are compared in the degrees of "slight," "ordinary" and "gross" negligence.

competency—In the law of evidence, the presence of those characteristics which render a witness legally fit and qualified to give testimony.

complainant—Synonymous with "plaintiff."

complaint—The first initiatory pleading on the part of the complainant, or plaintiff, in a civil action.

concurrent sentence—Sentences for more than one crime in which the time of each is to be served concurrently, rather than successively.

condemnation—The legal process by which real estate of a private owner is taken for public use without his consent, but upon the award and payment of just compensation.

contempt of court—Any act calculated to embarass, hinder, or obstruct a court in the administration of justice, or calculated to lessen its authority or dignity. Contempts are of two kinds: direct and indirect. Direct contempts are those committed in the immediate presence of the court; indirect is the term chiefly used with reference to the failure or refusal to obey a lawful order.

contributory negligence—A legal doctrine that if the plaintiff in a civil action for negligence was also negligent, he cannot recover damages from the defendant for the defendant's negligence.

corpus delicti (kor'pus de-lik'tī)—The body (material substance) upon which a crime has been committed, e.g., the corpse of a murdered man, the charred remains of a burned house.

corroborating evidence—Evidence supplementary to that already given and tending to strengthen or confirm it.

costs—An allowance for expenses in prosecuting or defending a suit. Ordinarily does not include attorney's fees.

counterclaim—A claim presented by a defendant in opposition to the claim of a plaintiff.

court reporter—A person who transcribes by shorthand or stenographically takes down testimony during court proceedings.

courts of record—Those whose proceedings are permanently recorded, and which have the power to fine or imprison for contempt. Courts not of record are those of lesser authority whose proceedings are not permanently recorded.

criminal insanity—Lack of mental capacity to do or abstain from doing a particular act; inability to distinguish right from wrong.

cross-examination—The questioning of a witness in a trial, or in the taking of a deposition, by the party opposed to the one who produced the witness.

cumulative sentence—Separate sentences (each additonal to the other) imposed against a person convicted upon an indictment containing several counts, each charging a different offense. (Same as accumulative sentence.)

D

Damages—Financial compensation which may be recovered in the courts by any person who has suffered loss, detriment, or injury to his person, property, or rights, through the unlawful act or negligence of another.

declaratory judgment—One which declares the rights of the parties or expresses the opinion of the court on a question of law, without ordering anything to be done.

decree—A decision or order of the court. A final decree is one which fully and finally disposes of the litigation; an interlocutory decree is a provisional or preliminary decree which is not final.

default—A "default" in an action of law occurs when a defendant omits to plead within the time allowed or fails to appear at the trial.

demur (de-mer')—To file a pleading (called "a demurrer") admitting the truth of the facts in the complaint, or answer, but contending they are legally insufficient.

de novo (dē nō'vō)—Anew, afresh. A "trial de novo" is the retrial of a case.

deposition—The testimony of a witness not taken in open court but in pursuance of authority given by statute or rule of court to take testimony elsewhere.

directed verdict—An instruction by the judge to the jury to return a specific verdict.

direct evidence—Proof of facts by witnesses who saw acts done or heard words spoken, as distinguished from circumstantial evidence, which is called indirect.

direct examination—The first interrogation of a witness by the party on whose behalf he or she is called.

discovery—A proceeding whereby one party to an action may be informed as to facts known by other parties or witnesses.

dismissal without prejudice—Permits the complainant to sue again on the same cause of action, while dismissal "with prejudice" bars the right to bring or maintain an action on the same claim or cause.

dissent—A term commonly used to denote the disagreement of one or more judges of a court with the decision of the majority.

domicile—That place where a person has his true and permanent home. A person may have several residences, but only one domicile.

double jeopardy—Common-law and constitutional prohibition against more than one prosecution for the same crime, transaction or omission.

due process—Law in its regular course of administration through the courts of justice. The guarantee of due process requires that every person have the protection of a fair trial.

E

embezzlement—The fraudulent appropriation by a person to his own use or benefit of property or money entrusted to him by another.

eminent domain—The power to take private property for public use by condemnation.

enjoin—To require a person, by writ of injunction from a court of equity, to perform, or to abstain or desist from, some act.

entrapment—The act of officers or agents of a government in inducing a person to commit a crime not contemplated by him, for the purpose of instituting a criminal prosecution against him.

equitable action—An action which may be brought for the purpose of restraining the threatened infliction of wrongs or injuries, and the prevention of threatened illegal action. (Remedies not available at common law.)

equity, courts of—Courts which administer remedial justice according to the system of equity, as distinguished from courts of common law. Equity courts are sometimes called courts of chancery.

escheat (es-chēt′)—In American law, the preferable right of the state to an estate to which no one is able to make a valid claim.

escrow (es′krō)—A writing, or deed, delivered by the grantor into the hands of a third person, to be held by the latter until the happening of a contingency or performance of a condition.

estoppel (es-top′el)—A person's own act, or acceptance of facts, which preclude his later making claims to the contrary.

et al.—An abbreviation of **et alii**, meaning "and others."

et seq.—An abbreviation of **et sequentes,** or **et sequentia,** meaning "and the following."

exception—A formal objection to an action of the court, during the trial of a case, in refusing a request or overruling an objection; implying that the party excepting does not acquiesce in the decision of the court, but will seek to procure its reversal.

ex contractu (ex kon-trak′tū)—In both civil and common law, rights and causes of action are divided into two classes: Those arising ex contractu (from a contract) and ex delicto (from a wrong or tort).

ex delicto (ex de-lik′tō)—Rights and causes of action arising from a wrong or "tort."

exhibit—A paper, document or other article produced and exhibited to a court during a trial or hearing.

ex parte (ex par′tē)—By or for one party; done for, in behalf of, or on the application of, one party only.

expert evidence—Testimony given in relation to some scientific, technical, or professional matter by experts, i.e., persons qualified to speak authoritatively by reason of their special training, skill, or familiarity with the subject.

ex post facto (ex pōst fak′tō)—After the fact; an act or fact occurring after some previous act or fact, and relating thereto.

extenuating circumstances—Circumstances which render a crime less aggravated, heinous, or reprehensible than it would otherwise be.

extradition—The surrender by one state to another of an individual accused or convicted of an offense outside its own territory, and within the territorial jurisdiction of the other.

F

fair preponderance—Evidence sufficient, in a civil case, to create in the minds of the triers of fact the belief that the party which bears the burden of proof has established its case.

false arrest—Any unlawful physical restraint of another's liberty, whether in prison or elsewhere.

false pretenses—Designed misrepresentation of existing fact or condition whereby a person obtains another's money or goods.

felony—A crime of a graver nature than a misdemeanor. Generally, an offense punishable by death or imprisonment in a penitentiary.

fiduciary (fi-du′shē-a-rē)—A term derived from the Roman law, meaning a person holding the character of a trustee, in respect to the trust and confidence involved in it and the scrupulous good faith and candor which it requires.

forcible entry and detainer—A summary proceeding for restoring possession of land to one who has been wrongfully deprived of possession.

forgery—The false making or material altering, with intent to defraud, or any writing which, if genuine, might be the foundation of a legal liability.

fraud—An intentional perversion of truth; deceitful practice or device resorted to with intent to deprive another of property or other right, or in some manner to do him injury.

G

garnishee—The person upon whom a garnishment is served, usually a debtor of the defendant in the action; (verb) to institute garnishment proceedings.

garnishment—A proceeding whereby property, money or credits of a debtor, in possession of another (the garnishee), are applied to the debts of the debtor.

general assignment—The voluntary transfer, by a debtor, of all his property to a trustee for the benefit of all of his creditors.

general demurrer—A demurrer which raises the question whether the pleading against which it is directed lacks the definite allegations essential to a cause of action, or defense.

grand jury—(see **jury, grand**)

gratuitous guest—In automobile law, a person riding at the invitation of the owner of a vehicle, or his authorized agent, without payment of a consideration or a fare.

guardian ad litem (ad lī'tem)—A person appointed by a court to look after the interests of a minor whose property is involved in litigation.

H

habeas corpus (hā 'be-as kōr-pus)—"You have the body." The name given a variety of writs whose object is to bring a person before a court or judge. In most common usage, it is directed to the official or person detaining another, commanding him to produce the body of the prisoner or person detained so the court may determine if such person has been denied his liberty without due process of law.

harmless error—In appellate practice, an error committed by a lower court during a trial, but not prejudicial to the rights of the appellant and for which the court will not reverse the judgment.

hearsay—Evidence not proceeding from the personal knowledge of the witness.

holographic will (hōl-ō-graf 'ik)—A testamentary instrument entirely written, dated and signed by the testator in his own handwriting.

hostile witness—A witness who is subject to cross-examination by the party who called him to testify, because of his evident antagonism toward that party as exhibited in his direct examination.

hypothetical question—A combination of facts and circumstances, assumed or proved, stated in such a form as to constitute a coherent state of facts upon which the opinion of an expert can be asked by way of evidence in a trial.

I

impeachment of witness—An attack on the credibility of a witness.

implied contract—A contract in which the promise made by the person obligated is not express, but inferred from his conduct or implied in law.

imputed negligence—Negligence which is not directly attributable to the person himself, but which is the negligence of a person who is in privity with him, and with whose fault he is chargeable.

inadmissible—That which, under the established rules of evidence, cannot be admitted or received.

in camera (in kam´e-ra)—In chambers; in private.

incompetent evidence—Evidence which is not admissible under the established rules of evidence.

indeterminate sentence—An indefinite sentence of "not less than" and "not more than" so many years, the exact term to be served being afterwards determined by parole authorities within the minimum and maximum limits set by the court or by statute.

indictment—An accusation in writing found and presented by a grand jury, charging that a person therein named has done some act, or been guilty of some omission which, by law, is a crime.

inferior court—Any court subordinate to the chief appellate tribunal in a particular judicial system.

information—An accusation for some criminal offense, in the nature of an indictment, but which is presented by a public officer instead of a grand jury.

injunction—A mandatory or prohibitive writ issued by a court.

instruction—A direction given by the judge to the jury concerning the law of the case.

inter alia (in´ter a´lē-a)—Among other things or matters.

inter alios (in´ter a´lē-ōs)—Among other persons; between others.

interlocutory—Provisional; temporary; not final. Refers to orders and decrees of a court.

interrogatories—Written questions propounded by one party and served on an adversary, who must provide written answers thereto under oath.

intervention—A proceeding in a suit or action by which a third person is permitted by the court to make himself a party.

intestate—One who dies without leaving a will.

irrelevant—Evidence not relating or applicable to the matter in issue; not supporting the issue.

J

jurisprudence—The philosophy of law, or the science of the principles of law and legal relations.

jury—A certain number of persons, selected according to law, and sworn to inquire of certain matters of fact, and declare the truth upon evidence laid before them.

grand jury—A jury of inquiry whose duty is to receive complaints and accusations in criminal cases, hear the evidence and find bills of indictment in cases where they are satisfied that there is probable cause that a crime was committed and that a trial ought to be held.

petit jury—The ordinary jury of twelve (or fewer) persons for the trial of a civil or criminal case. So called to distinguish it from the grand jury.

jury commissioner—An officer charged with the duty of selecting the names to be put into a jury wheel, or with selecting the panel of jurors for a particular term of court.

L

leading question—One which instructs a witness how to answer or puts into his mouth words to be echoed back; one which suggests to the witness the answer desired. Prohibited on direct examination.

letters rogatory (rog′a-tō-rē)—A request by one court of another court in an independent jurisdiction that a witness be examined upon interrogatories sent with the request.

levy—A seizure; the obtaining of money by legal process through seizure and sale of property; the raising of the money for which an execution has been issued.

liable—When it is determined that the plaintiff in a civil case has proved his claim against the defendant, the defendant is "liable" (rather than "guilty," as in a criminal case).

libel—A method of defamation expressed by print, writing, pictures, or signs. In its most general sense, any publication that is injurious to the reputation of another.

limitation—A certain time allowed by statute in which litigation must be brought.

lis pendens (lis pen′denz)—A pending suit.

locus delicti (lō′kus de-lik′tī)—The place of the offense.

M

malfeasance (mal-fē′zans)—Evil doing; ill conduct; the commission of some act which is prohibited by law.

malicious prosecution—An action instituted with intention of injuring defendant and without probable cause, and which terminates in favor of the person prosecuted.

mandamus (man-dā′mus)—The name of a writ which issues from a court of superior jurisdiction, directed to an inferior court, commanding the performance of a particular act.

mandate—A judicial command or precept proceeding from a court or judicial officer, directing the proper officer to enforce a judgment, sentence, or decree.

manslaughter—The unlawful killing of another without malice; may be either voluntary, upon a sudden impulse, or involuntary in the commission of some unlawful act.

master in chancery—An officer of a court of chancery who acts as an assistant to the judge.

material evidence—Such as is relevant and goes to the substantial issues in dispute.

mesne (men)—Intermediate; intervening.

misdemeanor—Offenses less than felonies; generally those punishable by fine or imprisonment otherwise than in penitentiaries.

misfeasance—A misdeed or trespass; the improper performance of some act which a person may lawfully do.

mistrial—An erroneous or invalid trial; a trial which cannot stand in law because of lack of jurisdiction, wrong drawing of jurors, or disregard of some other fundamental requisite.

mitigating circumstance—One which does not constitute a justification or excuse for an offense, but which may be considered as reducing the degree of moral culpability.

moot—Unsettled, undecided, A moot point is one not settled by judicial decisions.

moral turpitude—Conduct contrary to honesty, modesty, or good morals.

multiplicity of actions—Numerous and unnecessary attempts to litigate the same right.

municipal courts—In the judicial organization of some states, courts whose territorial authority is confined to the city or community.

murder—The unlawful killing of a human being by another with malice aforethought, either express or implied.

N

ne exeat (nē ek 'sē-at)—A writ forbids the person to whom it is addressed to leave the country, the state, or the jurisdiction of the court.

negligence—The failure to do something which a reasonable person, guided by ordinary considerations, would do; or the doing of something which a reasonable and prudent person would not do.

next friend—One acting for the benefit of a minor or other person without being regularly appointed as guardian.

nisi prius (nī'sī prī'us)—Courts for the initial trial of issues of fact, as distinguished from appellate courts.

no bill—This phrase, endorsed by a grand jury on the indictment, is equivalent to "not found" or "not a true bill." It means that, in the opinion of the jury, evidence was insufficient to warrant the return of a formal charge.

nolle prosequi (nol 'e pros 'e kwī)—A formal entry upon the record by the plaintiff in a civil suit, or the prosecuting officer in a criminal case, by which he declares that he "will no further prosecute" the case.

nolo contendere (no'lo kon-ten 'de-rē)—A pleading, usually used by defendants in criminal cases, which literally means "I will not contest it."

nominal party—One who is joined as a party or defendant merely because the technical rules of pleading require his presence in the record.

non compos mentis (non kom 'pos)—Not of sound mind; insane.

non obstante veredicto (non ob-stan 'tē ve-re-dik 'tō)—Notwithstanding the verdict. A judgment entered by order of court for one party, although there has been a jury verdict against him.

notice to produce—In practice, a notice in writing requiring the opposite party to produce a certain described paper or document at the trial.

O

objection—The act of taking exception to some statement or procedure in trial. Used to call the court's attention to improper evidence or procedure.

of counsel—A phrase commonly applied to counsel employed to assist in the preparation or management of the case, or its presentation on appeal, but who is not the principal attorney of record.

opinion evidence—Evidence of what the witness thinks, believes, or infers in regard to facts in dispute, as distinguished from his personal knowledge of the facts; not admissible except (under certain limitations) in the case of experts.

ordinary—A judicial officer in several of the states, clothed by statute with powers in regard to wills, probate, administration, guardianship.

out of court—One who has no legal status in court is said to be "out of court," *i.e.*, he is not before the court. For example, when a plaintiff, by some act or failure to act, shows that he is unable to maintain his action, he is frequently said to have put himself "out of court."

P

panel—A list of jurors to serve in a particular court, or for the trial of a particular action; denotes either the whole body of persons summoned as jurors for a particular term of court or those selected by the clerk by lot.

parole—The conditional release from prison of a convict before the expiration of his sentence. If he observes the conditions, the parolee need not serve the remainder of his sentence.

parties—The persons who are actively concerned in the prosecution or defense of a legal proceeding.

peremptory challenge—The challenge which the prosecution or defense may use to reject a certain number of prospective jurors without assigning any cause.

plaintiff—A person who brings an action; the party who complains or sues in a personal action and is so named on the record.

plaintiff in error—Appellant party who obtains a writ of error to have a judgment or other proceeding at law reviewed by an appellate court.

pleading—The process by which the parties in a suit or action alternately present written statements of their contentions, each responsive to that which precedes, and each serving to narrow the field of controversy, until there evolves a single point, affirmed on one side and denied on the other, called the "issue" upon which they then go to trial.

polling the jury—A practice whereby the jurors are asked individually whether they assented, and still assent, to the verdict.

power of attorney—An instrument authorizing another to act as one's agent or attorney.

praecipe (pre 'si-pē)—An original writ commanding the defendant to do the thing required; also, an order addressed to the clerk of a court, requesting him to issue a particular writ.

prejudicial error—Synonymous with "reversible error"; an error which warrants the appellate court to reverse the judgment before it.

preliminary hearing—Synonymous with "preliminary examination"; the hearing given a person charged with a crime by a magistrate or judge to determine whether he should be held for trial. Since the Constitution states that a person cannot be accused in secret, a preliminary hearing is open to the public unless the defendant requests that it be closed. The accused person must be present at this hearing and must be accompanied by his attorney.

preponderance of evidence—Greater weight of evidence, or evidence which is more credible and convincing to the mind, not necessarily the greater number of witnesses.

presentment—An informal statement in writing by a grand jury to the court that a public offense has been committed, from their own knowledge or observation, without any bill of indictment laid before them.

presumption of fact—An inference as to the truth or falsity of any proposition of fact, drawn by a process of reasoning in the absence of actual certainty of its truth or falsity, or until such certainty can be ascertained.

presumption of law—A rule of law that courts and judges shall draw a particular inference from a particular fact, or from particular evidence.

probate—The act or process of proving a will.

probation—In modern criminal administration, allowing a person convicted of some minor offense (particularly juvenile offenders) to go at large, under a suspension of sentence, during good behavior, and generally under the supervision or guardianship of a probation officer.

prosecutor—One who instigates the prosecution upon which an accused is arrested or one who brings an accusation against the party whom he suspects to be guilty; also, one who takes charge of a case and performs the function of trial lawyer for the state.

Q

quaere (kwē'rē)—A query; question; doubt.

quash—To overthrow; vacate; to annul or void a summons or indictment.

quasi judicial (kwā'sī)—Authority or discretion vested in an officer, wherein his acts partake of a judicial character.

quid pro quo—What for what; a fair return or consideration.

quotient verdict—A money verdict determined by the following process: Each juror writes down the sum he wishes to award by the verdict. These amounts are added together, and the total is divided by twelve (the number of jurors). The quotient stands as the verdict of the jury by their agreement.

quo warranto (kwō wō-ran'tō)—A writ issuable by the state, through which it demands an individual to show by what right he exercises an authority which can only be exercised through grant or franchise emanating from the state.

R

reasonable doubt—An accused person is entitled to acquittal if, in the minds of the jury, his guilt has not been proved beyond a "reasonable doubt"; that state of the minds of jurors in which they cannot say they feel an abiding conviction as to the truth of the charge.

rebuttal—The introduction of rebutting evidence; the showing that statements of witnesses as to what occurred [are] not true; the stage of a trial at which such evidence may be introduced.

redirect examination—Follows cross-examination and is exercised by the party who first examined the witness.

referee—A person to whom a cause pending in a court is referred by the court to take testimony, hear the parties, and report thereon to the court. He is an officer exercising judicial powers and is an arm of the court for a specific purpose.

removal, order of—An order by a court directing the transfer of a cause to another court.

reply—When a case is tried or argued in court, the argument of the plaintiff in answer to that of the defendant. A pleading in response to an answer.

rest—A party is said to "rest" or "rest his case" when he has presented all the evidence he intends to offer.

retainer—Act of client in employing his attorney or counsel; also denotes the fee which the client pays when he retains the attorney to act for him.

rule nisi, or rule to show cause (nī'sī)—A court order obtained on motion by either party to show cause why the particular relief sought should not be granted.

rule of court—An order made by a court having competent jurisdiction. Rules of court are either general or special: The former are the regulations by which the practice of the court is governed; the latter are special orders made in particular cases.

S

search and seizure, unreasonable—In general, an examination without authority of law of one's premises or person with a view to discovering contraband or illicit property or some evidence of guilt to be used in prosecuting a crime.

search warrant—An order in writing, issued by a justice or magistrate, in the name of the state, directing an officer to search a specified house or other premises for stolen property. Usually required as a condition precedent to a legal search and seizure.

self-defense—The protection of one's person or property against some injury attempted by another. The law of "self-defense" justifies an act done in the reasonable belief of immediate danger. When acting in justifiable self-defense, a person may not be punished criminally nor held responsible for civil damages.

separate maintenance—Allowance granted for support to a married party, and any children, while the party is living apart from the spouse, but not divorce.

separation of witnesses—An order of the court requiring all witnesses to remain outside the courtroom until each is called to testify, except the plaintiff or defendant.

sheriff—An officer of a county, chosen by popular election, whose principal duties are aid of criminal and civil courts; chief preserver of the peace. He serves processes, summons juries, executes judgments and holds judicial sales.

sine qua non (sī'ne kwa non)—An indispensable requisite.

slander—Base and defamatory spoken words tending to harm another's reputation, business or means of livelihood. Both "libel" and "slander" are methods of defamation—the former being expressed by print, writings, pictures or signs; the latter orally.

specific performance—A mandatory order in equity. Where damages would be inadequate compensation for the breach of a contract, the contractor will be compelled to perform specifically what he has agreed to do.

stare decisis (stā're de-sī'sis)—The doctrine that, when a court has once laid down a principle of law as applicable to a certain set of facts, it will adhere to that principle and apply it to future cases where the facts are substantially the same.

state's evidence—Testimony given by an accomplice or participant in a crime, tending to convict others.

statute—The written law in contradistinction to the unwritten law.

stay—A stopping or arresting of a judicial proceeding by order of the court.

stipulation—An agreement by attorneys on opposite sides of a case as to any matter pertaining to the proceedings or trial. It is not binding unless assented to by the parties, and most stipulations must be in writing.

subpoena (su-pē′na)—A process to cause a witness to appear and give testimony before a court or magistrate.

subpoena duces tecum (su-pē′na dū′sez tē′kum)—A process by which the court commands a witness to produce certain documents or records in a trial.

substantive law—The law dealing with rights, duties and liabilities, as distinguished from adjective law, which is the law regulating procedure.

summons—A writ directing the sheriff or other officer to notify the named person that an action has been commenced against him in court and that he is required to appear, on the day named, and answer the complaint in such action.

supersedeas (sū-per-sē′dē-as)—A writ containing a command to stay proceedings at law, such as the enforcement of a judgment pending an appeal.

T

talesman (tālz′man)—A person summoned to act as a juror from among the bystanders in a court.

testimony—Evidence given by a competent witness, under oath; as distinguished from evidence derived from writings and other sources.

tort—An injury or wrong committed, either with or without force, to the person or property of another.

transcript—The official record of proceedings of a trial of hearing.

transitory—Actions are "transitory" when they might have taken place anywhere, and are "local" when they could occur only in some particular place.

traverse—In pleading, traverse signifies a denial. When a defendant denies any material allegation of fact in the plaintiff's declaration, he is said to traverse it.

trial de novo (dē nō′ vō)—A new trial or retrial held in a higher court in which the whole case is gone into as if no trial had been held in a lower court.

true bill—In criminal practice, the endorsement made by a grand jury upon a bill of indictment when it finds sufficient evidence to warrant a criminal charge.

U

undue influence—Whatever destroys free will and causes a person to do something he would not do if left to himself.

unlawful detainer—A withholding of real estate without the consent of the owner or other person entitled to its posession.

usury—The taking of more interest for the use of money than the law allows.

V

venire (ve-ni′rē)—Technically, a writ summoning persons to court to act as jurors; popularly used as meaning the body of names thus summoned.

venire facias de novo (fā 'shē-as dē nō 'vō)—A fresh or new venire, which the court grants when there has been some impropriety or irregularity in returning the jury or where the verdict is so imperfect or ambiguous that no judgment can be given upon it.

veniremen (ve-nē'rē-men)—Members of a panel of jurors.

venue (ven 'ū)—The particular county, city or geographical area in which a court with jurisdiction may hear and determine a case.

verdict—In practice, the formal and unanimous decision or finding made by a jury, reported to the court and accepted by it.

voir dire (vwor dēr)—To speak the truth. The phrase denotes the preliminary examination which the court may make of one presented as a witness or juror, as to his qualifications.

W

waiver of immunity—A means authorized by statutes by which a witness, in advance of giving testimony or producing evidence, may renounce the fundamental right guaranteed by the Constitution that no person shall be compelled to be a witness against himself.

warrant of arrest—A writ issued by a magistrate, justice, or other competent authority, to a sheriff, or other officer, requiring him to arrest a person therein named and bring him before the magistrate or court to answer to a specified charge.

weight of evidence—The balance or preponderance of evidence; the inclination of the greater amount of credible evidence, offered in a trial, to support one side of the issue rather than the other.

willful—A "willful" act is one done intentionally, as distinguished from an act done carelessly or inadvertently.

with prejudice—The term, as applied to judgment of dismissal, is as conclusive of rights of parties as if action had been prosecuted to final adjudication adverse to the plaintiff.

without prejudice—A dismissal "without prejudice" allows a new suit to be brought on the same cause of action.

witness—One who testifies to what he has seen, heard, or otherwise observed.

writ—An order issuing from a court of justice and requiring the performance of a specified act, or giving authority and commission to have it done.

writ of error coram nobis (kō'ram nō'bis)—A common-law writ, the purpose of which is to correct a judgment in the same court in which it was rendered, on the ground of error of fact.

*Source:*Standing Committee on Association Communications, American Bar Association *Law and the Courts*, American Bar Association, Chicago,1980, pp. 28–36. Reprinted courtesy of the American Bar Association.

NOTE

1. Standing Committee on Association Communications, American Bar Association, *Law and the Courts* (Chicago: American Bar Association, 1980), p. 19.

Chapter 9

REPORTING THE COMPLEXITY OF THE STATEHOUSE

Tucked away somewhere in every state capitol in the country is a room or series of rooms in which reporters play what is considered by some to be their most vital function of the democratic system: coverage of state government. Seldom quiet, always cluttered, often unbelievably chaotic, these rooms tend to be characterized mostly by telephones, typewriters, and tons of stacked paper.

In contrast to the governmental officials they cover, statehouse reporters seldom have the opportunity to sit in solitude as they consider their next action. The governor makes a statement, the legislature passes a bill, an agency head announces an investigation, or a special interest group launches a campaign. The reporter gets the information, dashes back to the press room, perhaps getting comments from another official on the way or making a couple of telephone calls, and types the story. Or, if too close to deadline, the reporter dictates the story by telephone. Maybe, just maybe, the reporter will have the chance later for a more detailed follow-up story.

But not now. There's a committee meeting scheduled, the legislature is about to vote, or the editor has insisted on a story from a commission hearing that started fifteen minutes ago.

But sometimes there is a little time. The reporter may work for a larger news organization that has more than one person covering state government. But this usually just creates greater expectations, and all the reporters keep the same pace, producing more copy. Usually, the reporter gambles when he or she takes time to do a depth story that what is missed will be minor.

Consider the near impossibility of covering government in a small state like West Virginia which, exclusive of courts, lists six statewide elected officials, thirty-nine appointed department heads, 116 state boards and commissions, thirty-four state senators, and 100 members of the House of Delegates. Official business generated on these fronts, plus the activities of thousands of employees, is covered for the two capital city newspapers, the *Charleston Gazette* and *Charleston Daily Mail,* by two reporters each.

Even granting that most state officials and employees do not provide much news, it's small wonder that statehouse reporters express frustration over their assignment and that they have had to live with considerable criticism.

Speaking of the forty-eight reporters, representing fifteen daily newspapers, five news services, one weekly, several periodicals, a lone local radio, and one public television station officially covering the New York State Legislature in 1976, attorney Ken Norwick said:

"In theory, the Albany press corps is supposed to cover and report to its readers the activities—both public and concealed—of this entire state government. But it does not really do so. Instead—usually the direct result of staffing and assignment decisions by their editors, and, occasionally, as the result of reporter disinterest—Albany correspondents concentrate their attention almost entirely on what happens inside the Capitol, with barely a glance by most at the agencies and the courts.

"Moreover, even within the Capitol, the members of the Albany press corps often do little more than report what happens right before their eyes—either on the floor of the legislature or as handed to them by press conference, press release or leak. Again due in part to limited resources, they spend comparatively little time investigating the story that may lurk behind the press release or official's 'no comment.' "[1]

The criticism is common and, in fact, is made by many statehouse reporters themselves. But at the same time, most of these correspondents know the importance of what they are doing. Even if imperfect, their coverage of state government is the only source of public knowledge other than that which comes from officials themselves.

Thus, they go about their demanding business with some considerable satisfaction, checking regularly with those offices or individuals most likely to produce copy and with others occasionally. When desirable, they do attend legislative sessions or committee meetings. But more frequently they get those stories by interviewing the person in charge and concentrating on reporting official actions. While meetings and governmental documents result in considerable news, the more fruitful source of information is the interview of public officials, politicians, individuals such as lobbyists, who have a particular interest in a state action, and other special-interest representatives.

In covering state government, these reporters occasionally may have help. Often a news organization will assign additional personnel during times of peak activity, such as when the legislature is in session. Or reporters on other beats may find their way into the statehouse. That could be an education reporter, a business reporter, a science reporter, or anyone whose responsibilities include state government implications. Some news media will depend on a wire service for some coverage so their reporters may concentrate specifically on selected acts or issues.

But coverage assistance goes beyond that, for state government is conducted out of more than one building, often out of more than one city. Many state agencies and commissions are outside the capitol, and some state offices, such as the secretary of state if he or she has responsibility for elections, may have branch offices in key cities throughout the state. So the statehouse reporter is the cog, and other reporters provide the spokes for the total state government coverage.

The division of responsibility among those reporters who regularly cover the statehouse tends to be based on traditional government division of authority— the executive, the legislative, and the judicial, with the latter often falling to the court reporter. The *Denver Post,* for example, during legislative sessions has one reporter in the state senate, another in the house, and a third responsible for the governor, most of the executive branch, and the state budgetary process.

Other news organizations, such as the *Arkansas Gazette* in Little Rock, try to organize more on the basis of the specialties of the available reporters. The *Gazette* will have as many as four or five reporters at the statehouse when the legislature is in session, says Ernie Dumas, who has been covering the Arkansas statehouse since 1965. But three regular reporters on a day-to-day basis cover issues in which they have some special knowledge.

"Carol Griffee's specialties, for example, are pollution and environment and some other technical things," he says. "The same applies to me and our other reporter. But we have tried to avoid just carving all the state government up and saying this is yours, this is mine, and this is somebody else's. Because whoever got the governor's office, for instance, would have a large part of the more interesting news. So we try to share the more exciting sides of the capitol beat."

Regardless of the organization, adequate coverage of state government depends most upon the reporter's knowledge of the people in charge, their responsibilities, how they relate to other officials, and how official governmental actions are interwoven with politics. Without such understanding, the reporter will only get trapped in the maze, accomplishing little.

COVERING THE EXECUTIVE BRANCH

Some reporters may disagree with Ernie Dumas that the more interesting news comes out of the governor's office. Covering a legislative session, with all of its political maneuvering and backroom trade-offs, can be as interesting as any journalistic assignment. But an active governor is involved in every phase of state government, and covering that office can provide a journalistic challenge hard to match. The legislature sets the policy, allocates the funds, and determines the law.

But the executive implements the programs and thus provides year-round, day-in-and-day-out copy for an enterprising reporter.

The Governor Makes News Every Day

A governor wants and needs news coverage. To say "a governor needs us more than we need a governor" is an overstatement. But to say that to be effective, any governor must gain significant news media attention is a truism. That's why a 1976 survey by the National Governors' Association showed that governors spend as much time meeting with the general public, performing publicity-oriented ceremonial functions, and working directly with the news media as any other activity.[2]

That association, in fact, advised in a book for newly elected governors that "a candid and open relationship with the press is the only way to achieve success in clearly portraying the administration to the public. Without that relationship, an administration that is successful in every other way will encounter serious problems."[3]

That is not to say, however, that governors will run into the open arms of reporters. Governors and reporters always will have their differences and that's expected. Even the National Governors' Association admits that any governor will want to earn favorable press coverage, and reporters will see their proper role as informing the public of the facts, whether favorable or unfavorable.

The relationship also depends on individual personalities and experience reporters and governors have had with each other. It is inevitable that at times a governor will be irritated with reporters (and vice versa), and this irritation has been known to reach extremes. Witness, for example, the case of former Tennessee Governor Roy Blanton, who announced in 1978 that he would no longer answer negative questions of reporters unless they also asked him positive questions.

Whatever the relationship, the governor is news and has to be covered. Reporters may choose to ignore an occasional story, but they have little choice but to persist and, if necessary, find alternative sources if shut out.

Governors are unusual in American government because their responsibilities cut through traditional separation of powers. While their principal function is executive, they also have legislative and judicial responsibilities that represent page one or top-of-the-newscast candidates.

As executives, governors appoint and remove many state officials. This gives them political clout and often provides a means of gaining legislative support for programs. They control the overall administration of many of the functions of a long list of state agencies. They are responsible for the law enforcement, including authority over a state police force or state highway patrol. They have military powers as commander-in-chief of the National Guard when it is not in federal service. They have significant financial powers in that, in most states, they draw up and submit a budget to the legislature. Even after the legislature has approved a budget, governors have another means of input through veto power.

Governors also have a wide variety of ceremonial functions that represent vital means of voter relations. Local reporters grumble, but they find themselves following governors to social affairs, dedications of buildings or highways, speeches, welcoming ceremonies for distinguished visitors, and tours to make constituent contact.

The legislative functions of governors are classified under two broad headings: (1) contributing to legislation by proposing or vetoing bills and by delivering special messages to the legislature; (2) calling special sessions of the legislature, sometimes with authority to limit the business of that session to specific matters.

A governor's efforts to obtain legislation are closely watched by reporters because success or failure determines whether the governor lives up to campaign promises or achieves goals set for the administration. The process begins long before specific bills are introduced, starting when the legislature elects its leaders. A governor's success or failure at influencing choice of political leadership in the legislature is important news. It provides an early assessment of potential success when the governor does make specific legislative proposals.

When governors attempt to gain support by sending or delivering messages to legislators, it is often with the intent that such messages be equally for public consumption. They also may meet with legislative leaders and/or members, and they may offer or withhold appointments desired by legislators. If a specific bill has not been passed by the time of adjournment, they may call a special session.

The power, or even the threat, of the veto is an effective weapon of governors in their efforts to control legislation. All governors, except in North Carolina, have the authority to say no to a specific bill and send it back to the legislature. Reporters pay particular attention to the possibility of a veto long before a bill is passed, cover it, and then shift their attention to whether the legislature can muster what usually is a two-thirds vote to override.

In most states, governors may use an item veto to block specific provisions of a bill but allow the remainder to become a law. Often this power is restricted to appropriations bills, although in some states it has broader applications.

Exercise of judicial authority by governors almost always provides good journalistic copy. Governors serve as a final court of appeal in criminal cases involving state laws, and this may result in the granting of pardon, reprieve, commutation, or amnesty to convicted criminals.

Normally, governors delegate these powers to a state board, but they will take personal action at times. These actions merit journalistic attention because of their relative infrequency and because the cases tend to be of public interest, frequently involving capital punishment.

The pace of covering a governor's office is cyclical, ranging from frenzy to relative inactivity. Routine stories about minor appointments, state grants, activities of staff members, visits to cities throughout the state, or any of the ceremonial functions almost always are available.

Reporters make it a habit to check with the governor's office early in the day, get the schedule of activities, talk with aides who are assigned as liaisons for state agencies. In general, they try to keep tabs on what is happening and perhaps get leads on stories to be done then or later.

Major material—developments of state government, activities of state agencies, reaction to legislation, reaction to federal developments, political activities—generally is obtained through news conferences or interviews with governors, major staff members, or other state officials. Just how frequently a governor and the reporters should formally get together for specific questions and answers is a source of frequent disagreement.

Many governors want to hold news conferences, for example, only when they feel they can benefit. If they have a specific announcement to make, an accomplishment to discuss, or some other specific reason to reach the public, they are willing. Former Texas Governor Dolph Briscoe, for example, met with the capitol press corps infrequently because, he said, he didn't want to have news conferences unless there was a specific reason and because he met with journalists in various Texas cities as he traveled around the state. The standard journalistic reaction came from *Houston Chronicle* Austin Bureau Chief Bo Byers:

"Capitol reporters . . . would like to see Briscoe schedule at least weekly news conferences. That would give them the opportunity to question him regularly and fully on the numerous issues of state government and state politics which steadily arise. It is the governor's prerogative to call news conferences as he deems necessary. Regrettably, he does not seem to see much benefit, from a public information viewpoint, in meeting regularly with the press."[4]

Thomas K. Diemer of the Cleveland *Plain Dealer*

(*Plain Dealer* photo)

But even though they want regular gubernatorial news conferences, reporters note that the news conference format has several inherent journalistic problems. It's too easy to control. A governor can structure the content by opening remarks, by giving only friendly reporters an opportunity to ask questions, by informing friendly reporters as to which questions would be welcome, by answering (or not answering) specific questions, and by refusing to recognize follow-up questions.

Another problem for competitive reporters is that everyone gets the same information at the same time. The desire for exclusive material is a vital part of reportorial life. And it's a source of considerable irritation to be forced to function in a structure that does not provide individual rewards for individual initiative. In addition to news conferences, reporters also want personal interviews.

Except for occasional governors who will not cooperate on any consistent basis, these interviews usually are granted, although a news secretary may first attempt to channel the request to a member of the governor's staff. Governors have their own styles, and reporters quickly learn the basis of how to deal with them. Cleveland *Plain Dealer* reporter Tom Diemer, for example, had few problems with Ohio Governor James Rhodes:

"You couldn't just go right into his office, but if he knew you and if he thought your organization was important to him, it usually was possible to at least get him on the telephone to ask him a question. And usually I could call and get an appointment with him the same day. He understood the media very well."

Press Secretaries May Channel or Block

How much value a press secretary (or news secretary, public information officer, director of public affairs, or whatever the title) is to reporters depends, most of all, upon that individual's relation with the governor and his or her understanding of journalism. Some are integral parts of the decision-making apparatus or at least important advisers. Thus, they know what is going on and, at times, may even speak officially for the administration. Others have little contact with policy making, may not know the answer to reporters' questions, or may not be authorized to answer.

Press secretaries, of course, serve two masters: the governor and reporters. In most instances, they serve as a point of contact for reporters who want to see the governor, although, as Tom Diemer points out, once a reporter gets to know the governor well, this step often is eliminated. They also arrange news conferences, prepare news releases, keep the governor informed of news happenings and media reaction to proposed policies. Often they either write governors' speeches or review speech material written by another staff member.

Press secretaries with journalistic background, obviously, are likely to be more helpful. They understand the importance of deadlines, of the differing needs of electronic and print journalists, and of the need for speed in obtaining certain types of information.

A new press secretary very quickly gains a reputation as a knowledgeable straightshooter, as a protective flack, as being removed from policy making and therefore not authoritative, or as an incompetent. How much reporters will rely on the press secretary for information or especially for comment depends upon their assessment of the person, the professional relationship established between the two, and what the story is. Even if a press secretary is trusted and knowledgeable, there are occasions when reporters must insist on going straight to the governor.

For example, if the governor is in a political struggle with other party leaders or if the reporter is doing a story on outside business activities of the governor, only direct comment is acceptable. If the story involves an assessment of the success of a pet project or, indeed, of the administration, that official assessment must come from the top. If the governor is preparing to move in new program directions, he or she must defend the rationale personally (although it may be possible for a press secretary to provide reporters with many of the specific details of implementation).

In general, if reporters seek specific information or background material or even a formal statement of policy, a competent secretary may be a reliable source. But the more personal or more stylistic the information, the more likely the reporters will insist on getting it straight from the person most directly involved.

Other Executive Officials Merit Attention

Governors share executive leadership of a state with several other elected officials who function more or less independently or appointed officials who serve on a group often called the governor's cabinet. Journalistic attention given these individuals depends greatly on their personalities and how they run their offices. But basically, their functions provide the basis for amount and type of coverage.

For a *lieutenant governor,* for example, reporters will be interested in stories related to his or her service as presiding officer of the upper house of the legislature, such as committee appointments or the progress of specific legislation. Occasionally, news media will notice if the lieutenant governor is acting in the temporary absence of the governor or will report on general political matters that involve the lieutenant governor. However, the position varies in importance from state to state. In states where authority is limited, it tends to gain little public attention unless the individual holding the title has a particularly strong personality or has some special assignment from the governor.

Given that the *secretary of state* is the keeper of records and often in charge of state elections and motor vehicle registration, the office can be the source of considerable news material, especially statistical information. In most states, records from the secretary of state provide election results or historic comparisons of the results, comparative or up-to-date statistics on motor vehicle registration, or invaluable material on corporate ownership, leadership, and operation. Indeed, the material is so varied that reporters other than those regularly at the statehouse often find reason to request information.

The *attorney general* is the state's chief legal officer and principal legal adviser to the governor, other state officials, and the legislature. The attorney general may get media attention in his or her capacity as the state's chief prosecutor or as the major representative when the state is involved in litigation. Most stories, however, occur when local officials seek an opinion from the attorney general on major legal questions.

Stories involving state financial matters often include information gained from the state *treasurer* or state *auditor.* The treasurer pays the bills and generally maintains all financial records, while the auditor serves as the watchdog of state funds. No money may be spent until the auditor certifies that the expenditure is legal in all respects, and this function often results in good journalistic copy. Stories on the financial condition of the state, tax collection figures, tax money use, and efforts to raise additional funds (especially through bond issues) certainly will involve one of these offices, probably both.

Administrative Agency Coverage Is Weak

As assistant metropolitan editor of the *New York Times,* Sheldon Binn is frustrated by the problems of trying to provide reasonable coverage of a huge, sprawling system of state agencies that spend millions of dollars on programs of direct public impact.

"I think if there's a weakness in statehouse reporting," he says, "it's the difficulty of covering the administrative side. I think we do, and I think almost everybody does, a good job of covering the legislative process—the fighting which is the legislative process. But covering the administrative part of government, through which most citizens have their contact with the government, is intrinsically very difficult."

Part of the problem is the complexity of state agency organization. For one thing, there are too many of them. The Council of State Governments, essentially a research organization that provides information to and about the governments of all fifty states, lists 100 separate administrative functions in its 1977 directory of state administrative officials.[5] And that is only a partial listing. Reporters also face the problem that state governments have outgrown their original capitol buildings, and state agencies are scattered all over the city and, indeed, all over the state.

STATE ADMINISTRATIVE OFFICIALS, CLASSIFIED BY FUNCTION, 1977

Adjutant General
Administration & Finance
Aeronautics
Aging
Agriculture
Arts Council
Attorney General
Banking
Budget
Business Regulation
Centralized Accounting
Chief Justice

Children & Youth Services
Commerce
Community Affairs
Consumer Protection
Corrections
Court Administration
Criminal Justice Planning
Disaster Preparedness
Drug Abuse
Economic Development
Economic Opportunity
Education (Chief State School Officer)
Elections Administration
Employment Security
Energy Office
Environment
Ethics
Federal-State Relations (Washington Office)
Fire Marshal
Fish & Game
Food & Drugs
Forestry
General Services
Geology
Governor
Health
Higher Education (Executive Officer)
Highways
Historical Preservation
Housing Finance Agency
Human Rights
Informational Systems
Insurance
Juvenile Delinquency
Labor (Arbitration & Mediation)
Labor & Industrial Relations
Library (Law)
Library (State)
Licensing (Business)
Licensing (Occupational/Professional)
Lieutenant Governor
Liquor Control
Lotteries
Manpower
Mass Transit
Medicaid Programs
Mental Health
Mental Retardation
Mining
Motor Vehicle Registration
Natural Resources

Nuclear Energy
Occupational Safety & Health
Oil & Gas Regulation
Ombudsman
Parks
Parole & Probation (Adult)
Parole & Probation (Juvenile)
Personnel
Police & Highway Patrol
Pollution Control (Air)
Pollution Control (Water)
Post Audit
Pre Audit
Public Lands
Public Utility Regulation
Purchasing
Railroads
Secretary of State
Securities
Social Services
Soil & Water Conservation
Solid Waste Management
State Employees Retirement
State-Local Relations
State Planning (Overall)
State Printing
Taxation (Overall Administration)
Tourism
Transportation Department
Treasurer
Veterans Affairs
Veterinarian
Vocational Education
Vocational Rehabilitation
Water Resources Management
Welfare (Overall Administration)
Workmen's Compensation

Source: State Administrative Officials Classified by Functions, Council of State Governments, Lexington, Ky., 1977, p. iii.

In the case of Binn, how the *New York Times* staff can cover that territory in addition to the governor's office, the legislature, and the state supreme court is a puzzle.

"A newspaper is like an army," he says. "It's got limited resorces that it can expend in covering the front. And you can defend the hell out of that front, and then you can say, 'What have I got as a result of all this activity?' Because when you get it, it's hard to write it in an exciting or in a commanding way. How is the welfare department functioning? What is its connection with the people it's supposed to be servicing? See, that's not nearly as dramatic, and when it competes for the space in the paper, it obviously has a harder way to go than the story that says Representative Smith says Representative Jones is a jerk."

But this doesn't mean Binn and his colleagues at other newspapers simply throw up their hands. They know that state agencies spend too much money and have too much direct public impact to be ignored. It is significant that most of the upper echelon officials, even given that they are popularly elected, devote much of their attention to the internal maintenance of state government and have limited contact with the public. At the agency level specific decisions reach directly into the living rooms and kitchens of the state, either through operation of specific programs or through supervision of locally operated programs.

The "people's right to know" is, perhaps, a cliché, but it's one of truth. They do have a right and a need to know about policies and nitty-gritty operational procedures of those agencies responsible for meeting their needs. Utility regulation, as dull a subject as it can be, hits home. Taxation has become an ever growing source of public concern and interest. Public education has always been important. What programs are provided by the state of possible benefit to my children? Are we in serious danger because of what the state is or is not doing about environmental protection? Will we have enough energy? Is the state doing anything to protect the consumer? And what about public health? Human rights? Mass transit?

One aid to reporters in covering agencies is the fact that nearly every one has an information officer whose job it is to gain coverage. These persons provide the routine news. They send out press releases and call reporters about special programs, qualifications, impending deadlines, application procedures, public hearings, and the like. Sometimes, the statehouse reporter serves a clerical function and only passes them along, although ordinarily with some rewriting.

But how a reporter uses the releases depends, of course, on the story, on whether the information officer is trustworthy, on the reporter's competing responsibilities, and on the quality of the releases themselves. Sometimes they should be ignored. Sometimes, on a minor story, the release may be given only a nominal rewriting. Often the reporter will follow up on the release information, interview the proper authorities, and write a more comprehensive story, perhaps with a different angle.

But reporters are nervous about depending on information officers. The very nature of their jobs of such persons—to gain favorable publicity for their agency —means that the reporter has to find the time to make periodic, preferably regular, checks with the agency itself.

"I cover the Arkansas Education Department," says Ernie Dumas of the *Arkansas Gazette.* "Education is not really that big a beat at the state level because it's largely a local issue. Nevertheless, it does furnish considerable news over a year, some of which is pretty important. So, at least once a week, I'll go down the hill and see the commissioner of education, maybe visit for thirty or forty-five minutes. We talk about various issues that I'm aware of, like the education of handicapped children, which is a big issue right now.

"You just try to keep abreast of those kinds of things. Each one of us tries to spend time with each of our agencies. Not just by telephone. And, of course, you have your contacts at the lower level—the handicapped children's director, for example, or the supervisor for special education."

Like Dumas, reporters stress the value of developing sources other than just the department head. Often, the best sources of information are individuals at the second or third level. In most instances, these are the persons who actually supervise each program, and they tend to know more of the specifics of its implementation. The reporter, over a period of time, will learn who to contact for whatever reason within an agency. The reporter and those sources will develop a sense of understanding and trust. In that way, specific facts and verification of claims made by a department head literally are at the reporter's fingertips.

Lower level sources also are valuable because they are much more likely to provide the reporter with tips, both on the agency's official activities and on illegal or improper conduct within the agency. Given time constraints and the work load, the statehouse reporter is less likely to uncover a scandal, for example, unless he or she goes looking specifically for something, usually after having received a tip or a leak. It happens sometimes, but that initial information, in all probability, will not come from the department head. Neither will the document that verifies the information.

In too many instances, a reporter may get very little useful information from department heads, especially those appointed by the governor. Their natural tendency is to shy away from anything but the most positive information, and their job tends to be one of establishing policy rather than implementing a program. The journalistic value of a department head depends upon two things: first, the degree to which that person is secure in the job, which affects how willing he or she will be to speak out, and, second, the degree to which the governor's office permits open discussion by department heads.

An elected official is much more likely to be candid than one who owes allegiance to a governor. There are cases, of course, in which the personality of an appointed official is strong enough to override this, but those instances are rare. Many states have administrative policies that stipulate that reporters, especially those with touchy questions, be referred to the governor's office. And many states have policies that reserve announcements of departmental programs and activities for the governor.

It takes a stable of ready, willing, and trustworthy sources to overcome these circumstances.

But, while such sources are vital, it is risky to depend upon them exclusively. So most reporters maintain a file system in which they store clippings of previous stories, with special attention to those with possible future developments. This may be a notation of a meeting date, a deadline for some governmental action, or perhaps a comment from the director or lower level source about when a certain development is likely to occur.

COVERING THE LEGISLATIVE BRANCH

Get any reporter to sit down and talk about covering the statehouse, and the odds are good that, sooner or later, he or she will say something like: "We normally have two full-time reporters at the capitol, but when the legislature is in session. . . . " That's when journalistic reinforcements join the regulars. Once a year —or in some states, once every two years—the legislators flock in from all parts of the state, and following right behind are lobbyists, representatives of special-interest groups, and numerous others who hope to contribute to the lawmaking process.

Reporters will be trying to keep up with all of these persons, along with related increased activity by members of the state's administration. They will be there to report to the people the degree to which the legislature is satisfying its three general functions, one symbolic and two actual.

The symbolic function is that of representation, of making decisions ostensibly based on what the people want. The news media report back to the people on issues of local importance, paying particular attention to the votes and contributions of local representatives. Second, reporters inform citizens of specific decisions made that affect the people. Thousands of proposals are considered by state legislatures each year, and those passed into law may affect the taxes individuals have to pay, establish or abolish programs of personal impact, or determine how much emphasis will be placed on education, welfare, or employment programs. Third, reporters will watch the legislature's supervision of the state's administrative agencies through its control of the purse strings.

Pressure on Legislators

If the task of reporters were simply to cover legislative debates and votes, the job would be uncomplicated. But it's not. Reporters also must make sense of the very complex pressures placed upon legislators. What individual lawmakers say and how they vote—even what issues come under consideration—may be as much a matter of other forces as the legislators' personal beliefs and ideas. They (and, subsequently, reporters) have to cope with demands and efforts to persuade them from a cadre of well-trained and knowledgeable lobbyists from the private world and from agencies within state government. Political interest groups, consumer organizations, the governor, state agencies, the citizens themselves, local and federal governmental officials all have access to and hope for impact upon the state legislator.

Many major bills are the products of persons or groups outside of the legislative apparatus, most frequently the governor, who in many states is the dominant force of any legislative session. And most governors will put the total force of their administrative and political leadership behind specific bills or legislative programs.

Closely related is the constant pressure most legislators feel from their political party. While the degree of impact may vary with individual personalities and situations, no legislator is immune. The impact may arise out of a particular set of philosophical beliefs; out of the practical benefits of patronage, reelection assistance, or committee assignment; or out of a strong feeling that members of a minority party must stand together.

Reporters note particularly the impact of a party division in state government. Passing legislation is a simple matter when one party controls both the governorship and both houses of the legislature. When party control is divided, however, the process becomes more complex. Often the intent of legislation is to improve the image of one party or to embarrass the other. For example, a Republican-controlled legislature may pass a bill, knowing that the Democratic governor will be forced to veto it and face public outcry.

The role party politics plays in the legislative process is one that has been criticized by those who forget that it provides the very basis of the American governmental system.

"Almost everything has political implications," says Tom Diemer of the Cleveland *Plain Dealer*, "and the reporter has to guard against getting too cynical about that. I guess more than anything since Watergate, the words *political* and *politician* have come to have a negative connotation in many people's minds, and that's bull. Politics is good. Politics is the business of the people. It is true that everything shouldn't be political. Some things should be done out of ethical motivation. But, at the same time, to approach a news story with a negative attitude because it has a political connection, I think, is a big mistake."

One other important source of influence on the legislator is the constituency he or she represents. The impact, of course, will vary. A number of legislators see themselves more or less bound by desires expressed by a majority of citizens in their district. Others feel that they were elected in a broader sense to vote according to their own intelligence and convictions of what is best for their district. But all will be most interested in securing passage of legislation that has direct positive impact in their districts, and all will seek local publicity about how well they are serving the interests of the folks back home.

Legislative Organization

Nowhere is the impact of political parties more evident than in selection of legislative leaders. This is especially true of individuals who will serve as presiding officers of the two houses that make up the legislature in all states except Nebraska, which has one house. In states that have a lieutenant governor, that person usually presides in the senate; otherwise, the senators themselves elect a president pro tempore. All states provide for their lower houses to elect a speaker as presiding officer.

While the specific organization will vary from state to state, like the U.S. Congress, the selection process invariably is political. Often the governor, as party leader, is a dominant influence, or the majority party meets in caucus to make the choice. The floor vote is only a formality.

In principle, the presiding officer of each house has authority over discussion and debate on the floor and thus controls the flow of legislation. And, importantly, the presiding officer appoints committee chairpersons, committee members, and assigns bills to particular committees.

In addition each party has its own floor leaders to coordinate activities within each house. Elected by party members, the majority and minority leaders specifically lead the battle for favored bills or against opposition bills. In most states, each is assisted by a party whip.

Another source of some considerable power in state legislatures, although not as much as in Congress, is those legislators named to chair standing committees. Committees have the responsibility of analyzing bills, perhaps holding public hearings (although these play a much smaller role than at the federal level), perhaps amending them and making recommendations to the senate or the house. Committee jurisdiction in most states is defined in terms of its subject matter. Membership, at least in theory, is based on an individual legislator's expertise in that area.

It is, of course, to a legislator's advantage to earn appointment as chairperson of any committee, although the importance of committees varies considerably. One that is most significant in all states is the committee given responsibility of scheduling legislative business. Called by different names—steering committee, calendar committee, rules committee, for example—this group establishes the formal calendars for floor action and determines the rules that govern consideration of bills. Such control of the agenda may be especially important as adjournment draws near.

**STANDING COMMITTEE OF
THE HOUSE OF REPRESENTATIVES
OF THE 66TH TEXAS LEGISLATURE**

Agriculture and Livestock: agriculture, horticulture, farm husbandry; livestock and the livestock industry

Appropriations: all bills and resolutions appropriating money from the state treasury

Business and Industry: commerce, trade and manufacturing; industry and industrial development; protection of consumers

Calendar (procedural): all matters pertaining to the calendar system, bill assignment, priority determination, rules for floor consideration

Constitutional Amendments: amendments to the Texas Constitution; ratification of pending amendments to the U.S. Constitution

Criminal Jurisprudence: criminal law; criminal court procedure; revision or amendment of the state penal code

Elections: all matters relating to the right of suffrage in Texas and the conduct of elections

Employment Practices: hours, wages, working conditions and welfare of labor and wage earners; collective bargaining; industrial safety; employment and unemployment; workers' compensation

Energy Resources: conservation of energy resources; production, regulation, transportation and development of energy resources

Environmental Affairs: air pollution; state parks; wildlife and fish; hunting and fishing; fish and oyster industries; water pollution

Financial Institutions: banking, the state banking system; savings and loan associations; credit unions; the lending of money

Government Organization: extension of state departments and agencies; organization, powers, regulations, and management of those state departments

Health Services: protection of public health; mental health and mental retardation; nursing homes

Higher Education: education beyond the high school; state colleges and universities

House Administration (procedural): administrative operation of the House and its employees; House funds; property, equipment, and supplies; office space; parking spaces; admissions to the floor; recording or broadcasting of sessions proceedings; all witnesses appearing before the House or any committee

Human Services: welfare programs and their development, administration, and control; programs for veterans, senior citizens, blind, deaf

Insurance: insurance and the insurance industry

Intergovernmental Affairs: cities, municipalities, and town corporations; home-rule cities; counties

Judicial Affairs: civil law; civil court procedure; regulation of private corporations; administrative law

Judiciary: civil law; civil court procedure; regulation of private corporations; administrative law

Liquor Regulation: regulation of the sale of intoxicating beverages and local option control; proposals to revise the Alcoholic Beverage Code

Local and Consent Calendars (procedural): determination of whether bills are, in fact, local or will be uncontested; makes up the calendar for periods designated by the House for consideration of such bills

Natural Resources: conservation of state natural resources; control and development of land and water resources; irrigation; forests and the lumber industry; water supply districts

Public Education: state public schools; programming of elementary and secondary education; changes in school districts

Regions, Compacts, and Districts: legislative districts, both House and Senate; congressional districts; election districts; state-federal relations; state participation in Council of State Governments

Rules (procedural): House rules of procedure; all procedures for expediting House business; nonmember invitations; congratulatory resolutions

Security and Sanctions: Texas Youth Council; Texas Department of Corrections; Board of Pardons and Paroles; Texas Adult Probation Commission; Texas Department of Public Safety; Texas Commission on Jail Standards

State Affairs: questions and matters of state policy; administration of state government; management of state agencies; regulation of public lands and state buildings; state institutions; employee compensation; defense matters

Transportation: commercial motor vehicles; state highway system; drivers' licenses; traffic regulation; railroads; pipelines and pipeline companies; airports; water transportation

Ways and Means: all bills and resolutions proposing to raise revenue; taxes or other fees; changes in the state revenue statute; tax collection

Source: *Rules of Procedure*, House of Representatives, 66th Texas Legislature, pp.18–34. Jurisdiction statements have been edited and represent only a partial listing.

To assist the committees and the legislature as a whole, many states have established legislative reference services to compensate for the fact that state legislators tend not to have large staffs. Often attached to a state library, such services are available to supply information to legislators on subjects such as possible bills. Some states provide bill-drafting services in which legally trained individuals assist in wording and in ensuring that the bills are not contradictory or incomplete.

The difficulties of conducting all necessary business in the time allocated to a legislative session have prompted many states to establish agencies concerned with planning and advanced preparation of bills. Two types of agencies exist for this purpose, one temporary and the other permanent.

In some states, planning is accomplished by interim committees that study proposals on specific subjects and prepare for the coming session. These committees are bipartisan, are made up of legislators, and are responsible for conducting research on their assigned concerns and of reporting to the legislature when it reconvenes. In this way, members can get a running start on complicated issues.

The other major type of planning body is the legislative council, which is similar to an interim committee except that it is permanent and unrestricted in subject matter. Such councils are more likely to have legislative leaders among their membership. Their primary function is to draft a legislative program for the coming session. Unlike interim committees, they usually have full-time research staff and at times carry their assignments as far as the drafting of specific legislation.

The Legislative Process

Failure by many reporters to understand how state government functions and why it functions that way has resulted in considerable criticism from those who feel the public suffers from bad reporting. Milo Dakin, director of communications and public information for the Georgia House of Representatives, for example, echoes the familiar theme:

"Government has become more complex so that even its participants seem confused on occasion. And it has become more difficult, even impossible in some cases, for newspapers, television and radio stations to hire reporters who understand the nuances of the political process, or, if they don't understand, have the energy and ability to learn."[5]

Dakin's comment may be too cynical, but he is correct in stressing that a prerequisite to good legislative reporting is comprehension of all the controls in legislative behavior, the limits on officials' conduct, and both the formal and informal rules that establish those norms.

The process through which legislators propose, consider, and pass bills into law is nearly identical in all states and very similar to that of the federal government. It is a process that is governed by rules, some formal and expressed in writing, some informal and passed along almost as legislative folklore.

The formal regulations—as important to reporters as they are to legislators— generally are outlined in published rules of procedure. The 151-page *Rules of Procedure* of the Texas House of Representatives, for example, contains descriptions of the duties and rights of the speaker; listing of employee responsibilities; outline of the jurisdiction of legislative committees; parliamentary rules governing the conduct of debate, amending, and voting; procedures for reconsideration of a bill; requirements for writing and amending bills; discussions of the procedures for communications from the governor and the Texas Senate; and the work of conference committees.

Understanding such procedural matters, along with standard rules of parliamentary procedure, will get a reporter through some situations that border on the ridiculous. It may not happen frequently, but some reporters will have to cope with the presentation of an amendment which is a substitute for an amendment which is a committee substitute for the orginally proposed constitutional amendment.

But it's not really adequate for a reporter to simply refer to page number in a written manual, for legislatures operate as much by informal rules as formal ones. Tradition plays a large role in the life of state and national legislators, and they must structure their activities in accordance with that tradition. It's much stronger at the national level and at times is a formal rule, but perhaps the best example of such an informal rule is seniority in legislative activities. Likewise, it is often expected in most state legislatures that members will abstain from discussing bills that affect only their sponsor's district, will not criticize or ridicule a member those constituents are visiting the chamber, and will speak on subjects only when technically or politically informed.

Violation of such traditions by a legislator can result in sanctions, and at times the informal sanctions may be most significant. It is possible, for example, that persistent violators may see their proposed legislation get nowhere, or they may not receive a desired committee appointment.

The rules—formal and informal—are applied within the larger context of legislative organization and a more or less standard set of practices through which any bill must pass before it becomes law.

The process begins when any member prepares a proposal in the proper form and submits it to the clerk of his or her house. This may take the form of a bill, which proposes changes in the law, or a resolution, which expresses the feelings of one or both houses. Often such proposals represent more than the desires of a single legislator, and some states have provisions to accommodate joint sponsorship, bills written by committees or bills directly from the administration. In an effort to save time, the bill may be introduced simultaneously in both houses. In any event, the clerk assigns a number to the bill, and it is ready for consideration.

Informal considerations enter the picture even at this early stage, giving some bills greater likelihood of passage. A poorly written or incomplete bill immediately begins losing support. And the legislative reputation of the sponsor comes into play. Especially if the bill does not have a direct impact upon their districts, busy legislators will provide more or less automatic support for a proposal from a respected colleague. Even for a significant bill, questioning may be less severe for a bill sponsored by a respected or important legislator.

In some instances, also, a bill that is part of a governor's package or has received the governor's stamp of approval may move more easily through the process. The opposite, of course, is sometimes true within a political context. A Democratic governor will expect Republican criticism of administration bills, and perhaps even real problems if Republicans control one or both houses of the legislature.

As with local governments, a bill or resolution in most states must pass through three readings (two in some instances) before becoming an official legislative action. These readings, however, usually do not involve a full reading of the text. The first often consists of the clerk of the appropriate house reciting the title of the bill and the number assigned to it.

The presiding officer then assigns the bill to the appropriate standing committee. Many political scientists and journalists consider this stage the most important part of the deliberations, and reporters cover committees and subcommittees as closely as time permits. A bill may die right there. But some states have taken away the power of committees to "pigeonhole" legislation by requiring them to report on all bills referred to them or by establishing a rather easy way (generally majority vote) to call a bill out of committee.

Committee deliberations may mean members simply expressing their opinions, or they may call for additional research or public hearings. The deliberations completed, the committee may recommend passage or rejection or, in some states, it may amend or rewrite the bill. The amendment process will vary. Committees of the Texas House of Representatives, for example, have no power to change a bill. Instead, they recommend amendments to the full house, and these become effective only if approved by a majority.[6]

Having survived the standing committee, a bill must then go through one more step before reaching the floor. This is the committee that sets the specific agenda with a legislative calendar. In most circumstances, this is not a serious hurdle. The committee (Calendar Committee, Rules Committee, Steering Committee) often has the power to kill a bill if it delays placing it on the agenda long enough.

Discussion on the floor of most state legislatures usually is not as complicated as in Congress. Most states do not permit extensive filibustering, although each knowledgeable legislator does have the opportunity to speak. Generally, this discussion and debate is the second reading of the bill, and it is the point at which all members may offer amendments or statements of support or opposition.

As much as possible, reporters will attempt to cover committee meetings and floor debate on issues of importance. Scheduling often makes this impossible, especially for committee meetings, and reporters simply have to determine their priorities, cover the most significant meetings, and get information on others by talking with the chairperson, committee member, or a legislative aide.

With regard to floor debate, reporters know that statements made often are more symbolic than real. The debate often is more for the news media and constituents than for fellow legislators, and it is rare that voting decisions are influenced. To the degree that a legislator does not have a preconceived notion, decisions are much more likely to result from private conversations. And that's also how reporters gain their understanding of the prospects of a particular bill.

The major value for reporters in hearing the debate personally is the opportunity it provides for human interest material. Solid information may be rare, but good direct quotes, color, and anecdotes may be abundant.

The vote, of course, is journalistically important, and reporters may make a special effort to be on hand if the issue is significant and if the deadline is near. The voting stage usually is defined as the third reading. Many states require a roll call vote for final passage or, if a voice vote is used, relative ease in insisting that the roll be called.

With the exception of Nebraska, a successful bill is then passed on to the other house, where the process is repeated. If the same bill was introduced in both houses, then the one passed will simply be substituted for its counterpart at whatever stage it happens to be in. If the two houses do not agree on the substance and wording of a bill, a conference committee of members from both houses is named to work out the differences. The compromise version is then submitted to both houses and generally is accepted.

Once passed by both houses, a bill will be sent to the governor for his or her signature, and it becomes law after passage of a time specified by the state. In the case of a veto, the legislature will enter the picture once more as it considers whether the required number of members (usually two-thirds) will vote to pass the measure over the veto.

Legislative Sources

So where does the information come from? There's nothing unusual about legislative coverage. All of the traditional journalistic methods of collecting information are appropriate. Much comes from observation. Much comes through the journalistic interview. And much—perhaps more than for many other areas of coverage—comes from documents.

For the most part, it's fair to say that legislators want to be interviewed and that they are most likely to cooperate with any request. Of course, there are those who at times will not cooperate, especially if the issue involved is controversial. But with few exceptions, legislators know that their political careers depend, at least in part, upon keeping their names before their constituents. They know that every mention, every picture, every television or radio interview may someday be translated into votes. There are times, in fact, when some are so anxious that reporters have to fight them off.

The most frequently used sources, for understandable reasons, tend to be the legislative leaders in both houses: the presiding officers, majority and minority leaders, the whips, and the committee chairpersons. After all, these are the individuals responsible for guiding legislation through the process. They tend to have a more thorough knowledge and a broader view of the status of a given bill. They tend to be in closer contact with the governor and party leaders. The fact that they have achieved a position of leadership may indicate that they are respected by their colleagues and know how to deal with reporters.

Likewise, administrative leaders who have much at stake in what the legislature does, particularly with regard to funding, are frequent sources of comment. One of the necessities complicating the life of the statehouse reporter is the task of coordinating coverage of the governor's office, for example, with legislative coverage. They are often covered by different reporters who must maintain constant contact with each other to avoid duplication and to ensure coverage of an issue from all important angles.

But, as in all reporting, a problem exists in overemphasis of leadership sources. Statehouse reporters try to develop a diversity of individuals from whom information is gained. For example, it is a mistake to ignore the sponsor of a bill. Presumably, that individual presented the proposal for a reason and, certainly, has knowledge about the bill's progress and opinions about its importance. Likewise, reporters will seek out legislators whose districts will be directly affected by a bill. And, if a bill has statewide implications, an effort is and should be made to reach a cross-section of the legislators, with special effort to avoid overconcentrating on those who simply are most quotable or who have proven themselves dependable in the past.

Legislative aides also can be extremely valuable for factual or background information, particularly for statistics. They are contacted on a formal or informal basis, depending on how touchy the information is. Frequently, a legislative aide can provide the reporter with good behind-the-scenes information if mutual trust has been built. And, although reporters often go to state agencies for material on a legislative issue, often the same information is more readily available through a legislative aide.

Reporters tend to be cautious in two ways, however, when dealing with legislative aides. After all, those people do work for the legislature and are in a good position to provide one-sided or otherwise misleading information. First, reporters make sure the original source of the information is clear. They must know if it comes from a state agency, from staff research, or from private research. It must be perfectly clear whether it is legitimate research or whether it is guess-work. Second, reporters are very cautious about who they deal with, especially when information is being provided on a not-for-attribution basis. Confirmation is important always, but especially so until the reporter learns that a source is dependable and trustworthy.

A related information source often is the very source used by legislators for much of their information. Two research-oriented arms of most state legislatures are the legislative reference services and the legislative councils. It is quite possi-ble, and very desirable, in many states for a reporter to simply request copies of reports and studies so that he or she can deal with the same sources as the legislators.

Lobbyists provide a controversial, but nonetheless often used, source of infor-mation for reporters. Often the most knowledgeable person on a particular bill —perhaps even more than the sponsor—will be the lobbyist who, after all, is in the information business. Some lobbyists don't want to talk to reporters. Most lobbyists shy away from public comment. Many define their business as being a private matter between whomever they represent and the legislator.

In spite of that and the fact that information received from lobbyists will be one-sided, most reporters have few problems in getting background or technical information from them. But they do so with caution.

"I guess I deal with them a fair amount in asking for background information on specific bills," says Margaret Edds, who covers the Virginia legislature for the Norfolk *Virginian-Pilot.* "I deal with them also in terms of coverage of how they might influence particular bills and the controls placed on them as to how far they can go in their persuasion of someone."

Edds and other reporters, such as Tom Diemer of the Cleveland *Plain Dealer,* stress that their dealings with lobbyists have generally been good and profitable, but they make every effort to check information received.

"Usually I turn to a lobbyist only for technical information," Diemer says. "What's in this bill? And this is something that you can easily check by reading the bill line for line. And I want to know his bias, to know where he's coming from. I want to know why the real estate lobby wants this bill. I expect a bias if he's lobbying for a particular cause. I also want the other side—what they don't want."

---

14 Ways to Stop a Bill

Wilmington News Journal

Bruce D. Ralston is one of the most influential lobbyists in Dover. He represents business interests and when he talks legislators listen. His track record makes that obvious.

A few years ago, Ralston recalls, he made a list of bills he was interested in and rated his performance. "We got involved in 130 pieces of legislation," he said matter of factly.

"We got what we wanted done on 125 of them. That scared me."
Following are Ralston's 14 ways to block a bill:

1. Stop the drafting of the bill.
2. Stop introduction of the bill.
3. Kill the bill by committee assignment; by asking the presiding officer to assign it to a friendly committee.
4. Kill the bill in the committee; by talking the chairman into sitting on the bill.
5. Kill the bill in committee by talking the committee members into refusing to vote the bill out of committee.
6. Kill the bill by talking the majority leader into not bringing the bill up to his caucus, or not putting it on the agenda.
7. Kill the bill by talking a majority of legislators into voting against it.
8. Kill the bill by talking the sponsor into not pushing the bill in the other house.
9. Kill the bill by "grabbing the messenger" who takes the bill to the House. Get him to lose the bill and play the can't-find-the-bill game.
10. Kill the bill in the second house by making a deal.
11. Kill the bill in the second house by using all the methods employed in the originating house.
12. Kill the bill in the governor's office by convincing the governor's counsel that it is a bad, illegal or unconstitutional bill.
13. Kill the bill by calling the governor's friends and "those who contributed to his campaign" and getting them to call the governor to tell him how bad, illegal or unconstitutional the bill is.
14. Kill the bill by going directly to the governor.

"All you have to do is win at one of those and you've killed the bill,"
Ralston says.

Source: "14 Ways to Stop a Bill, Inside Legislative Hall, 1977," *Wilmington News-Journal*, p. 17.

Understanding the biases of lobbyists, making those biases clear in news accounts, and accepting the responsibility of checking information can open up a very valuable source of legislative information. Few reporters fear that such information will be inaccurate, although they know it will be one-sided. It's not an unusual journalistic situation, and it's up to the reporters to fill in the gaps by talking to lobbyists with different points of view, by checking with legislators and legislative documents, and by seeking information from state agencies.

FUNCTIONS OF STATE GOVERNMENT COVERAGE

Even though reporters and news organizations will disagree on what their main function might be, few would deny that there are at least three tasks that merit attention. It's easy to express very complicated thoughts in a few words: "To inform the public." "To educate the public." "To serve as a watchdog of government." And it's easy to say reporters should be satisfying all of these important social needs. They should. But reporters face a variety of complications in doing what they feel would be the ideal job of covering state government.

Do they have enough time or space to do it all? No. Even if they could produce the copy, would their editors agree on the importance and give it the play it deserves? Probably not. Does the public want extensive coverage and analysis of everything that is significant about state government? Very doubtful.

And that provides the context in which reporters determine their priorities of coverage. They have to make hard decisions about how to compromise on what, in a practical sense, they can do and what, in an idealistic sense, they would like to do.

Most frequently emphasized is the attempt to provide readers with up-to-date information about what government officials or agencies did or said today. News accounts relate the facts: The governor announced this program. The legislature passed that bill. A state department head made this statement. This approach is based on the assumption that readers and viewers can take the individual pieces of information and put them together into an understanding of what state government is up to.

This, of course, involves some selectivity. There's no way any given newspaper or broadcast reporter can cover everything. But in stressing an informational approach, news organizations generally paint with a rather wide brush, seeking to cover more than just the most significant issues of the day.

"Rather than limit ourselves to just the hot issues of the day," says Carl Miller of the *Denver Post*, "we're also trying to report on increases in drivers' license fees and that kind of thing. A small bill may not be controversial, but we still feel we ought to go out after it, pursue it and get the story in the newspaper in some readable and informative form. Everybody has a driver's license and if fees are going up, you have to let them know about it."

This kind of small-issue, "people approach" to coverage is important to the *Denver Post*, Miller says, adding:

"I think our basic philosophy is that we have an intricate role in the community and, even if the people don't want to read about that stuff, we have an obligation to present it for them and try to make it interesting. I try to approach government and political coverage as a consumer beat. I think that we make it interesting and also meaningful to people. We have to try to find those things in government that a taxpayer can identify with. And so we use the phrase "It's a 'me and you' bill in the legislature. We'll spend more time on that sort of thing, maybe, than on a broader issue."

In legislative coverage, particularly, many newspapers and the wire services may not spend a lot of time or space on a wide variety of issues, but they will provide a quick summary of the status of legislation being considered. Such a daily roundup of legislative activities in bare bones form gives readers a chance to be at least minimally informed on legislation in which they might be interested.

The information approach to coverage is good, however, only if it is supplemented by broader analyses. Occasionally, information-oriented reporters will seek to assist the readers or viewers by doing a "Sunday piece" in which they put the puzzle together into a more comprehensive package. Many wish they had the time to make the idea behind the "Sunday piece" the norm, to make education a function to which they devote major efforts. They would like to do more on how government works, what role it plays in the lives of the people, and, more specifically, what a given piece of legislation or governmental program is likely to mean to specific individuals.

Failure to accomplish this goal has resulted in considerable criticism of statehouse coverage from a wide variety of persons. Three examples:

Richard D. Lamm, Governor of Colorado: "The press corps in Colorado does a great job of covering the day-to-day operations of government. They're aggressive and objective. The only criticism that I would have—and it's one that applies across the board to politics, politicians, and the press—is that we tend to emphasize the immediate rather than the long range. I happen to think that society is on a collision course with some vast, very disturbing trends, and I'd like to see those discussed more."

Cecil Neth of Legis 50: the Center for Legislative Improvement: "How laws are made is equally as important, if not more so, than what laws are made. There must be, in other words, an orderly and open process supported by adequate resources—time, staff, money, et al.,—and a press corps capable of interpreting the process."

Norman Lockman, *Boston Globe* Statehouse Bureau: "The public does care about what the legislature is doing about major issues, and an increasing number of editors are demanding that their statehouse reporters devote more energy to analytically presenting the legislative treatment of those issues. That means the statehouse reporter is having to demand more of his sources: more solid information and less self-serving twaddle."[7]

The implication of these comments is not that day-to-day information is unimportant. Rather, it is that the background, the context, and the implications of daily activities merit greater attention. Efforts to accomplish this may involve something as simple as an extra paragraph or two in the daily material, or they may go as far as concentrating analytically on the broader issues rather than the events themselves.

For example, Douglas Caldwell of WSOL-TV in Charlotte, North Carolina, says it's easy to write stories about government actions from the point of view of the bureaucrat or politician—or from the perception that living all one's working life in a pressroom will provide.

"But that's a disservice to the reader in many cases," he adds, "because it fails to tell up front what a government decision will mean to the citizen. That's why we try for a graf or more high in the story that says, essentially, 'This means . . .'

Often, the graf will start off just this way and go on to explain the government action in lay terms. Of course, care must be taken to avoid oversimplifying a complex topic. But without the effort, the only people who will read the story will be the politicians, other reporters, and those hell bent on being terminally bored."

Or, in a larger sense, the effort means assigning reporters to cover the stories from a larger perspective than today's events. Call it what you like: issue-oriented coverage, trend coverage, depth reporting, or overview coverage. The point is that government does not operate in a vacuum. And reporters need to provide greater continuity to the day's events by concentrating on the reasons for its existence: efforts to solve social problems.

In spite of the rough pace of statehouse reporters' lives, some time must be found to concentrate not only on what government is doing, but why it's doing it and how it works. This may take either of two forms: stories on the process of government or stories on how *well* it works. The latter is the watchdog, the adversarial, function of the media. The job of the reporter is to lay out the facts regardless of whether they make government officials look good or bad, effective or bumbling, honest or dishonest.

Reporters are natural adversaries of government officials. At its minimum, the adversary relationship involves a healthy skepticism by reporters in their dealings with government. It means asking the tough questions and persisting. It means asking for proof. It means insisting on getting the answers.

At its maximum, the adversary relationship is a full-blown investigation of possible scandalous behavior by government officials. It means digging out the facts on misuse of public money. It means discussion of an official's personal problem—alcoholism, for example—which interferes with that person's ability to do the job. It means demonstrating how the governor made a serious mistake that cost the taxpayers money.

But the adversarial relationship must remain constructive. It must be to ensure the proper use of public money, to result in a solution to the alcoholism problem, to prevent the recurrence of the error.

"The adversarial relationship, I think, works in a good way and a bad way," says Todd Engdahl of the *Denver Post*. "It works in a good way if you have some basic level of respect for the person you're covering so that you can keep it sort of clean and objective. It becomes a problem when you really dislike or you really don't respect the person you're covering."

Hanging over Engdahl's desk at the Colorado statehouse is a plaque he received from the governor's staff. The inscription reads: "Todd Engdahl. The Reporter who has given Richard D. Lamm the hardest time during the last 12 months. April 7, 1979."

NOTES

1. Ken Norwick, "Making the News in the Capitol Press Room," *Empire State Report,* June 1976, p. 1972. See also: Hoyt Purvis and Rick Gentry, "News Media Coverage

of Texas Government: The State Capitol Press Corps," *Public Affairs Comment,* February 1976; William T. Gormley Jr., "Coverage of State Government in the Mass Media," *State Government,* Spring 1979, pp. 46–51; Thomas B. Littlewood, "What's Wrong with Statehouse Coverage," *Columbia Journalism Review,* March/April 1972, pp. 39–45.

2. Thad L. Beyle, "The Governor and the Public," *State Government,* Summer 1978, p. 180.

3. *Governing the American States: A Handbook for New Governors* (Washington, D.C.: National Governors' Association, 1977), p. 142.

4. As quoted from the *Houston Chronicle* (Dec. 21, 1975) by Purvis and Gentry, p. 6.

5. Milo Dakin, "The Press: A Healthy Skepticism," *State Legislatures,* November/ December 1978, p. 9.

6. *Rules of Procedure,* House of Representatives, 66th Texas Legislature, p. 53.

7. Norman Lockman, "Needed: Analytic Approach to State House News," *State Legislatures,* November/December 1979, p. 8.

Chapter 10

GETTING THE LOCAL STORY FROM WASHINGTON

From Washington, D.C., it's 2,813 miles to Portland, Oregon, 1,027 miles to Springfield, Missouri, 331 miles to Akron, Ohio, and 263 miles to Raleigh, North Carolina. But it's not stretching the point at all to say that, in practical terms, the home of the federal government is in downtown Portland, Springfield, Akron, and Raleigh.

How rapidly Americans drive to work depends upon the federal government. Their taxes depend largely upon the federal government. The quality of their food, availability of goods, location of factories and jobs, interest paid for loans or received on savings accounts, how well they support themselves in retirement, the quality of their schools—all are influenced by the federal government.

Much of the news from Washington affects every citizen generally. It is national news: The president meets a visiting foreign diplomat, Congress considers a tax program or debates defense spending, or the Supreme Court rules on the right to counsel. No doubt about the importance of such events, and news organizations devote attention to these stories. They also, to an increasing degree, attempt to get ahead of events by surveying broad policy questions and the underlying issues confronting the country. The bigger newspapers and broadcast stations cover such news from themselves; others depend on the wire services and the networks for their copy or feed.

But there's another side of that Washington scene. Much of what happens in Washington has impact on only a particular state or region or even town and can be considered just as local as if it were out of the county courthouse or city hall.

And since the people in Washington must come from somewhere, they're sometimes hometown people.

THE REGIONAL CORRESPONDENT

The more local these stories get, the less likely they will be reported by the news agencies, networks, or big national media. The specific stories are the domain of another type of Washington correspondent, one who seldom gains the celebrity status of his or her national counterparts. Called regional correspondents, or "regionals," these reporters thrive on the Washington story with local importance. They may work in the nation's capital, but their news judgment is not far from Portland, Springfield, Akron, or Raleigh.

Leo Rennert covers Washington for the McClatchy Newspapers and primarily that chain's *Sacramento* [California] *Bee.* He explains:

"You concentrate on covering the Washington news that is of direct immediate interest to the readers of an area of the country. In our case, it's California, and in particular, northern California. We're not there to do the top story of the day on President Reagan or on a Senate filibuster. The wires are going to handle that. What we do go after is the very largely uncovered area of California news which the wires either touch only peripherally or not at all. So 90 percent of our stories are really totally divorced from what's moving on the national lines."

Rennert and his McClatchy colleagues focus on the congressional delegation, and this is a prime source of news for any regional correspondent. These are the folks from back home who must return occasionally to talk with voters and gain permission to return to Washington for another term. The regional reporters' task, especially in a large state such as California, with two senators and 43 members of the House of Representatives, can be massive.

The regionals also cover federal agencies, which supervise programs and often distribute money to local areas or regulate local activities. Rennert himself concentrates on the Department of Agriculture and those farm policies that have to do especially with cotton and wine production, both important to northern California. And when the U.S. Supreme Court makes a decision of particular impact to California, one of the McClatchy reporters is there.

Because of the role Californians play in national politics, Rennert also finds himself dealing with stories of national significance. His beat has included Californians Ronald Reagan and Edmund G. (Jerry) Brown as they pursued the presidency, Senate Majority Whip Alan Cranston, and former important House veteran John Moss.[1]

That diversity is normal. Some few of the larger bureaus provide opportunities for reporters to focus on a particular subject or government agency, to become an expert in one narrow area, but most, and certainly the one-person operations, must spread themselves over a wide range.

"A Washington correspondent for an out-of-town paper in a relatively small bureau, a bureau of fewer than five people, is really nothing but a fairly educated general-assignment reporter," says Arthur Wiese of the *Houston Post.* "Because one day you're covering air pollution, then the next day it's the defense budget, and the next day the hometown congressman's reelection problem, and the next day the farm bill."

The method is similar to that of the city hall or statehouse reporter. It's still a matter of developing sources by maintaining frequent contact, keeping track of what's happening, attending meetings, reviewing documents, and conducting interviews. Even the stories themselves may be the same as they were back home Witness the experience of Miller Bonner, regional correspondent for The Associated Press:

"Although our environments have changed drastically, the job remains basically unchanged. During my stint as correspondent in the Rio Grande Valley (Texas), some of the more prominent stories dealt with the illegal alien problem, striking farmers, narcotic trafficking, and a fraud-infested federally funded jobs program.

"Since arriving in Washington, I have covered Senate hearings on the illegal alien problem, written a Sunday feature on narcotic trafficking, covered numerous 'striking farmer' stories and interviewed Labor Department officials concerning a fraud-infested jobs program in South Texas."[2]

Part of this may be because the correspondents often determine for themselves the stories they will work on. With some exceptions, most get little more than an occasional assignment from editors back home or a request from another reporter for information on the federal component of a story.

Regional reporters do complain, however, about some editors' attitudes toward their Washington offices. At times, this shows up in what the reporters consider ridiculous story assignments, but the attitudes are more likely to emerge in treatment of stories from Washington. The complaint is that some editors view the Washington office as a supplementary wire service, not as an extension of the local staff. This results in downplaying of the regional's Washington copy.

The problem, the correspondents say, is that few editors back home have Washington experience and thus have little understanding of what a regional reporter can and cannot reasonably do. Another complaint is that editors at times are provincial in their approach to news and uninformed about national issues.

But reporters also depend on those editors to help them avoid the Washington trap of losing touch with the rest of the world. It would be very easy, over a period of time, to begin to consider Washington the world and to lose the Portland, Springfield, Akron, or Raleigh perspective.

"I think the selection at the outset of a regional reporter is critical from the newspapers' standpoint," Rennert says. "I think maintaining local interest is almost a direct function of your own background as an individual, your own experiences as an individual your own ties to that area and your professional background and experience in the newspaper field. If you have a regional beat in Washington and you have only peripheral ties to the area you cover, then the temptation to drift away and become part of the Washington scene, the chance to catch the [Potomac] fever is going to be greatly enhanced."

Once on the beat, most reporters return to home base occasionally and call frequently to discuss coverage within the organization and with possible local sources—the mayor, the governor, the heads of state agencies. This helps to retain the local perspective and strengthen understanding of local attitudes and expectations about federal policies and programs.

Maintaining such contacts is particularly important since governments are becoming so much more intertwined. Especially when dealing with federal money for specific purposes, reporters must cope with two or three layers of government. To handle these kinds of stories, they need the full assistance of the home office and contacts with officials in all layers.

PATTERNS OF COVERAGE

Covering the local impact of the federal government involves more than just sending a reporter to Washington. Someone in the home office has to think seriously about the mix of coverage and types of stories needed by the community. Specific coverage patterns seldom are absolutely locked in, but more frequently combine three types of coverage.

One is what may be called the *follow-the-legislation approach*. Stressing the nuts and bolts of congressional action, reporters tell the status of legislation, the positions taken, the roles and votes of hometown members. This type of coverage may result in perhaps three or four 10-paragraph stories daily.

Proponents of this approach say readers, viewers, and listeners are most interested in the day-to-day activities of Congress. They want to be in touch with what's going on. So reporters spend most of their time picking up specific pieces of information and dutifully passing them along. Occasionally, they take a somewhat broader, long-range look and write a longer evaluative story or "think piece."

It's rare that any reporter avoids the requirement of doing some event coverage. The breaking news must be provided even if the focus is more issue-oriented. This second coverage philosophy may be labeled the *project approach*. In it, the idea is that, given some release from event coverage responsibilities, the reporter has more time to study the issues, perhaps even specializing to a degree. This may give wider perspective and more meaning to the news organization's coverage.

At times this approach may assume the appearance of national coverage, but the key lies in careful selection of topics of local interest or value. And, often, the stories get their local flavor through use of examples or sources from back home. Quantity expectations will vary. Some reporters may be expected to provide a major event story once a week, usually in the form of Sunday stories. Others may be given more time to produce a major piece, say, every two to four weeks.

As a kind of hybrid, although journalistically standard, form, some news organizations have particular interest in more *personal* stories about government leaders, that is, variations of the hometown-boy-or-girl-makes-good theme. Senate Democratic Leader Robert C. Byrd, for example, is a strong focus of Geoff O'Gara of States News Service for the Charleston, West Virginia, *Gazette.*

"It [the *Gazette*] is less interested in what Byrd has to say about Panama or his positions on national issues," O'Gara says. "But it is very interested in anything that illustrates his kind of personality and the way he handles his position. So whereas the *Gazette* may not want an issue story on something like the labor law, it does want a Byrd story on how he handles the labor law. He's from the area, and readers like to know how he's doing."

This approach is more than reporting about the personalities of government. It's a methodology which seeks to present federal business in a human way. The stories are about individuals, but they also shine through that individual's role to, say, the legislative process or a particular piece of legislation.

"What I like to do," says Bill Choyke, who does regional coverage for the *Dallas Morning News,* "is take a situation in which an individual is involved in legislation, call several others who have been following that legislation for special interest groups and say, 'How is Joe Hovinchrogin doing? How's he been voting? Has he been on the right side or the wrong side of the issue?' Then I would go to a committee meeting, watch him perform and talk with him about what I've learned.

Bill Choyke of the *Dallas Morning News*

"Too much writing is done, both back at the local level and in Washington, based on just what was said at meetings without making those follow-up phone calls. There's too much ink in terms of what individuals say and not what they do."

SOURCES CLOSE TO CAPITOL HILL

Potomac River water apparently infects people with a fear of being quoted by name, and thus attribution becomes one of the most difficult aspects of dealing with Washington sources. From cabinet secretaries down to the lowest congressional staffer, reporters find individuals who open their conversation with "Don't quote me" or "This is for background only."

Some reporters won't take anything off the record, and others thrive on unattributed quotes and "informed sources" statements. But a reporter just starting to cover Washington, either by phone or in person, must be prepared to deal with the problem. The trouble, of course, is that Washington reporters for too long have let officials dictate interview terms, so that it's difficult for a single reporter to buck the tradition.

The best approach to the problem is the same in Washington as it is back home: Reporters make it clear at the outset of the interview that they want to quote the source. If that source objects, they then try to work out the best possible deal. How much the reporter cooperates depends on how desperate he or she is to obtain the information or comments from that particular source.

COVERING THE CONGRESSIONAL DELEGATION

To concentrate on the Washington news of greatest interest back home, it makes sense to key in on those decision makers who are from back home. In Congress, that's the local delegation. This helps make elected officials more answerable to their public, and it provides a hometown flavor to issues of importance.

News from Washington generally is of decisions made and problems attacked rather than events occurring. And that fact highlights development of sources and contacts. Regional reporters seldom have time regularly to attend floor sessions or committee meetings, and few members of Congress are likely to hold regular news conferences. Thus, the reporter must be familiar with activities: who is responsible for what and which persons are most likely to talk under what circumstances.

Part of this is understanding the system. Another part is deliberate effort to cultivate possible sources of information.

"I probably take somebody to lunch at least three times a month," says Arthur Wiese of the *Houston Post.* "It may be a senator's press secretary. It may be a congressman's administrative assistant. It may be a staff member on a committee.

It may be a visiting politician or a congressional candidate. It's a good business investment. You may not get a story, and you usually don't out of the conversation, but the next time you pick up the phone and you need something fast or, more important, you need someone to level with you, that personal relationship just pays off."

Getting to know members of Congress as possible news sources is not difficult because of the obvious: The information process is a two-way street. Members of the House of Representatives who must face election every two years are especially anxious to get publicity.

"Most members—whether they are senators or house members—are going to be interested in what's going back to their people," says Rep. Clarence Miller of Ohio's mostly rural Tenth District. "And there's a limit to how far the *New York Times* and *Wall Street Journal* can help. It's what's in the newspapers locally that conveys a message about our thinking to the people."

That means the welcome mat *usually* is out for reporters, although the Congress member will attempt to structure the conversation to his or her benefit. And, predictably, there will be times when an individual member will be less likely to want to talk, especially in the face of a possible negative story.

As a general rule, however, reporters find staff members cooperative in discussing factual information and the role of the representative or senator in specific matters. Reporters soon learn the bases upon which staff members will deal, whether information may be attributed, the circumstances under which it is defined as background or off the record. They learn which staff members are capable and with whom they can effectively work.

"I've learned that there are capable and intelligent people on these staffs who are concerned and really try to do a job," says Frank Aukofer of the *Milwaukee Journal.* "Regardless of their politics, and I don't judge politicans by their politics but by how well they present their viewpoints. They all work hard, and they all have a high degree of integrity and do a good job representing where they are coming from. That's all you can ask. They're a good bunch to work with, to trust (which helps), and you soon learn who the people are you can get information from quickly and usably and the people who will bog you down with all sorts of

Frank Aukofer of the *Milwaukee Journal*

(*Milwaukee Journal* photo)

detail you don't need. So after a while, you get your sources, and people begin to call you."

In effect, every member of the staff of a representative or senator has a public relations function. The goal of every employee is to enhance the boss's image. They're therefore willing, and reporters—especially those in small bureaus without clerical or library help—find themselves taking frequent advantage of the opportunities they provide.

An understanding of the PR function of staff members, however, leads good reporters to a wariness about relying on them too heavily or exclusively. They often have vested interests and can steer a reporter to the wrong source or to a source who will merely confirm one point of view. Given an understanding of that fact, reporters can deal effectively with staff members who function under a variety of titles carrying differing responsibilities but are of several basic types:

Administrative assistant. As the Congress member's top aide, the administrative assistant is involved in nearly everything, knows what is going on, performs a variety of direct services, and thus usually is the best staff source of information. Almost always empowered to speak for the record, he or she is readily available to provide background information or to see that the Congress member is available. This is especially true if the information being sought concerns a party political matter. The reporter who develops a working relationship with an administrative assistant seldom needs to look further.

News secretary. All members of Congress do not have a staff person with this title. But all have someone who serves as the liaison with reporters and coordinates production of news releases, columns, and other statements. At times this latter responsibility and answering queries cover the job description. Depending on how much authority news secretaries are given, reporters may depend upon them as much as an administrative assistant or may confine their contact to minor points.

Case worker. In general, this is a person assigned to work on a particular type of issue, especially one which provokes constituent mail. Often a specialist in a problem area such as veterans' affairs or Social Security, the case worker is a good source of specific professional information.

Legislative assistant. This job is used in varied ways, but it generally indicates an individual assigned to work with specific pieces of legislation. Thus, a legislative assistant to the sponsor of a bill, for example, would be a strong source of information on that bill.

Committee staff. Aides who work for congressional committees tend to have stronger educational backgrounds than those who make up Congress members' personal staffs. Many recently graduated lawyers, for example, may use a committee staff position as an entry into government work. They may be more professional than political and thus serve well as sources for specific legislation and other committee work.

Staff willingness to cooperate, of course, is both a blessing and a curse for reporters. It is, on the one hand, valuable to have resources for quick responses to questions. It's helpful to receive reports or even news releases from the Congress member's office as background or starting points for stories. That makes it more possible to cover the territory expected. But there is the very real problem of becoming too dependent on the releases, the reports, and the ready-made comments. Like their counterparts at city hall, county courthouse, or school system office, harried Washington correspondents at times do yield to the temptations of making their tasks easier.

And this, when combined with the fact that most news organizations are not represented in Washington, creates a wide boulevard down which congressional staffs drive with glee.

"Traditionally, political coverage in the district has been a case of self-generated news, the individual candidates or elected representatives going to the news media rather than the news media coming to them," says Bob Reintsema, staff assistant to Rep. Miller. "Principally this is because of the limited size of most of the media operations in southeastern Ohio. The pattern is changing somewhat, given the increasing affiliation of those media operations with state and national news services, but for many of the smaller operations, it's still the standard operating procedure."

That "self-generated news" comes in three standard packages: the news release —and its modern broadcasting equivalent, film, video, and audio tapes—all of which too often are used without indication that they are less-than-true news presentations; the weekly column used, especially by small papers, under the byline of the Congress member; and the visit to news organization offices when the official is back in the district.

Indiscriminate and widespread use of this material across the country worries media critic Ben H. Bagdikian, who thinks most of the print and broadcast news media have permitted themselves to become "propaganda arms" of Congress.

"The news media simply don't tell the folks back home what their member of Congress really does," he says. "Worse than that, most of the media are willing conduits for the highly selective information the member of Congress decides to feed the electorate. This propaganda is sent to newspapers and broadcasting stations, and the vast majority of them pass it off to the voters as professionally collected, written and edited 'news.' "[3]

For example, among the most common stories passed along from congressional offices is that a particular member has sponsored a certain piece of legislation. The fact is that very few members ever sponsor legislation which gets passed, says John Felton of *Congressional Quarterly,* who adds: "Except for those who chair committees, the best most members can do is sponsor an amendment in committee or on the floor. Most bills have half a dozen or so 'cosponsors' who usually are fellow committee members of the true sponsor but who have little to do with actual passage."

John Felton of *Congressional Quarterly* (*Congressional Quarterly* photo)

Yet, when Congress members announce in a news release that they have cosponsored legislation, that message gets passed on with little explanation by news media. That's why Bagdikian's comments strike home, particularly with small newspapers and broadcast stations, but larger news organizations are not immune to the problem.

For those who are there, however, it's a constant battle to meet the demands from back home without falling back on unrestricted use of news releases and other staff-prepared material. The most effective use of news releases, of course, assuming the story is valid, is as a beginning. The reporter who understands the Washington scene may make a few telephone calls and expand a one-sided release into a legitimate, balanced story.

COVERING THE FEDERAL BUREAUCRACY

There's nearly universal agreement on one point: The federal bureaucracy—the complex and confusing maze of agencies, bureaus, commissions, divisions, offices, branches, sections, and units—is undercovered. Reporters who attempt to do it, government officials themselves, and media critics point to thousands of stories, important to the public, which remain buried somewhere in the bureaucracy. A study done at the American University School of Communication in Washington, D.C., for example, concluded:

"A routine presidential briefing may be standing-room-only for Washington reporters, but less than a mile away an administrative policy hearing that could affect the lives of millions of people is often presented to four walls. Dozens of reporters may hang over the edge of the Senate press gallery to catch every word of a heated floor fight on a controversial bill; but who is writing about the federal agency guidelines established to administer the legislation once it becomes law? Further, who will go out in the country to describe how that legislation works —or doesn't?[4]

News attention is most likely to be on an agency during an emergency. The potential disaster at Pennsylvania's Three Mile Island nuclear power plant put the journalistic spotlight on the Nuclear Regulatory Commission. The collapse of a cooling tower in West Virginia vaulted the Occupational Safety and Health Administration into the headlines. There are exceptions, of course. Gaylord Shaw of the *Los Angeles Times* wrote an award-winning two-part series on the nation's unsafe dams with emphasis on the Bureau of Reclamation, Army Corps of Engineers, Federal Power Commission (now the Federal Energy Regulatory Commission), Soil Conservation Service, and other agencies. But, again, it wasn't until the collapse of a dam in Toccoa, Georgia, in the fall of 1977 that attention was paid to Shaw's work and other reporters began to look into the responsible agencies.[5]

Gaylord Shaw of the *Los Angeles Times*

(*Los Angeles Times* photo)

Andrew Alexander of the Dayton *Journal Herald*

(*Journal Herald* photo)

But the journalistic value of governmental agencies is more than regulation and disaster investigation. They represent an almost inexhaustible source of information on almost any subject. Federal agencies are full of experts who are willing to talk about their special subject. The Department of Commerce has experts on the history and technical details of every industry in the country. The Department of Agriculture has experts on every crop. The Department of Education has people who know about the latest research in teaching methods. They're as close as the telephone. They're listed in the directory. But they're seldom called unless some big event captures the attention of journalists.

Reporters know the problem. They know the reasons for it. And they know that many are trying to do something about it. Take, for example, Andrew Alexander of Cox Newspapers:

"An increasing number of regionals, myself included, have begun to give much more emphasis to the agencies. In fact, I would say that at least half of my regular checks are with agencies. That increase reflects the fact that the bureaucracy continues to grow in size and power, with more and more agency officials making decisions which have a direct impact on local jurisdictions.

"I still cover my delegation very closely. But more and more I do it with an eye toward covering the bureaucracy. For example, when I talk to congressional staffers about local issues, I routinely ask if they have been working with any agencies to help with the issues or if any agency has expressed an interest in it."

But in spite of such efforts by Alexander and others, many regional reporters will admit that part of the problem is the desire of some reporters to gain journalistic prominence by covering news which will get front-page or top-of-the-newscast play. They will point out as well that many editors back home want the same kind of coverage and to concentrate on agencies is like saying, "I want all my stories stuck on the obit page."[6]

But they also will list more fundamental journalistic problems. Especially the regional reporters in small bureaus struggle daily with inadequate time to find stories buried in a very complex system. And government bureaucrats, ambitious and concerned with protecting their flanks, often are uncooperative with any but the representatives of the nation's most prestigious news organizations.

"The mentality here is geared to maybe eight or 10 newspapers. And the rest —if it is convenient," says Douglas Lowenstein of Cox Newspapers. "I remember once being in an office and seeing a list. It has Steve Aug of the *Washington Star,* Dave Burnham of the *New York Times,* So-and-so of the *Post,* So-and-so of the Baltimore *Sun* and the *Wall Street Journal.* I wanted to get my name on that list, and I wanted him to call me when he had something. But they never think to call unless, and even this isn't a certainty, they see your delegation as active."

Alexander suggests that one solution to this problem is persistence—to call the official at home and to keep calling, sometimes until very late at night, until he or she comes to the phone.

"I once did that to a guy who worked at the White House," he says, "and finally got him about 11:30 P.M. The next day he called me and said: 'Look, I'll return your calls. Just don't call me at home again. It drives my wife crazy.' From that point on, he's always returned my calls. Promptly."

To the regional reporters' problem of inadequate time there is no real answer except, perhaps, a change in priorities. It may be that additional coverage of the federal bureaucracy would be of more benefit back home than many of the stories being written now. Aside from the problem of finding the time, the answer is good basic journalism. It's overcoming the complexity by putting in the kind of effort and study required to understand the agencies' functions and how they work.

"Reporters only cover a particular segment of what has become a vast and particularly impressive bureaucracy," says Gene Smith of the Topeka, Kansas, *Capital Journal.* "No one individual can even hope to do an in-depth or even decent day-in-and-day-out job of covering all of the federal government. So you have to pick and choose. In addition to that, to do a reasonably competent job of covering a particular branch of government, it takes considerable background and understanding in that field. It takes a couple of years of on-the-job training before reporters can expect to become even reasonably competent."

And it takes sources. On the one hand, there's the top person, who often is more open than "those 9 million people who 'know just what the boss wants,' " Smith says. But, on the other hand, it's deliberate cultivation of the middle-level bureaucrats who do the day-to-day work and therefore know more about the

Reporting on Government Agencies: Four Models

A number of alternative ways of describing the activities of a government agency are available to a journalist. In the most conventional model of reporting on the government the journalist simply describes the changes in the top executives of the agency, changes in its performance as reported by these executives, or charges of misbehavior on the part of members of this agency. This form of reporting simply involves rewriting press releases from the bureau itself—or possibly from other bureaus in the position to criticize it. Most newspaper reporting of the Bureau of Narcotics and Dangerous Drugs and its successors falls into this category.

A second model of government reporting involves chronicling the exploits of a particular agency. In this model the journalist reconstructs a particular operation—the seizure of a large quantity of heroin, the arrest of top figures in a crime ring, or even an adventure story on the part of agents. Journalists who wish to use this form and be critical simply report the excesses of drug agents and the way that they violated the rights of citizens. . . . Public-relations officials at the drug agency would spend considerable time reconstructing the exploits of drug agents for the benefit of reporters interested in publicizing them (the more critical reports usually come from rival agencies interested in discrediting the Office of Drug Abuse Law Enforcement). . . .

A third way of organizing information about a government agency might be called the power-struggle model, and involves the reporter's delineating the various bureaucratic interests which are at stake. . . . It assumes that much of the activity of government agencies results from the actions of those in the organization attempting to maintain their position of power. As is necessary in this mode of reporting, I relied heavily on disgruntled officials in the various drug agencies and their rivals in the government. . . .

Finally, there is a model of reporting which is more difficult to employ in the time frame available to a journalist and which would attempt to correlate the actions of an agency with the changes in the environment in which it exists. This model might be called the natural-history model. It might be possible, for example, to understand the evolution of what began as the Nutt unit in the Alcohol Tax Division into the Bureau of Narcotics and Dangerous Drugs in the Justice Department, and so on, if one could also chart the psychological and political changes in the population to which the government was reacting. There was, no doubt, heightened anxiety over crime in the 1960s, and this was connected to the fear of drugs promoted by a whole range of public officials, police officials, and politicians.

Source: Edward Jay Epstein, "Reporting on Government Agencies: Four Models," reprinted from the *Columbia Journalism Review,* November-December 1977, p. 56. © 1977 *Columbia Journalism Review.*

specific workings of the agency. Only a relationship of trust and respect can overcome their natural inclination to protect themselves through reluctance to make comments to reporters.

Once that trust is established, however, and the reporter knows individuals who can be called at any time, the job of covering the agencies becomes more manageable. It's not possible, or even necessary, to contact every agency every day. It's regularity of contact that helps ensure that individuals will be willing to provide factual information, tips, or sensitive information.

And the more a reporter develops good contacts, the more a reputation for honesty and dependability spreads within an agency. That, in turn, opens up additional avenues. And if the reporter is on good terms with the congressional delegation, a call to a senator or representative also may produce enough pressure on uncooperative agency officials to ensure at least some grudging cooperation.

Sources are more than people. One of the best sources to the federal bureaucracy, at least as a starting point, is the *Federal Register*. Published five days a week, it contains information on regulations, grants, deadlines, hearings, and, in general, progress reports on federal agency activities. Reporters who find the time to monitor the *Federal Register* regularly find good local stories about the federal bureaucracy—more than they can handle.

WASHINGTON COVERAGE BY TELEPHONE

No news coverage by telephone equals having a reporter on the scene. Granted, even reporters in Washington get much of their information by calling sources across town, but only as a supplement to face-to-face conversation or witnessing an event. To be wholly dependent on telephone interviews is to run the constant risk of missing stories and information because the source is not available at the proper time or does not return calls.

If the regional reporter in Washington has a problem getting officials to call back, that would be magnified for the unknown reporter from a distant city. It's difficult to develop the kind of personal relationship, the kind of trust, that leads to sharing of confidential or sensitive information. And, if a reporter from afar is suspicious about information received, confirmation by WATS line is not easy.

But that's not the question. It is obvious that most news organizations will not have a correspondent in Washington. One does not have to agree with the decision to recognize that many publishers and editors are unwilling to pay the $30,000 to $60,000 a year required to support a full-time person or even $100 a week to share an individual.

The question is: What can the reporter back home do to broaden coverage of local news which has federal angles? Why don't reporters provide readers, viewers, and listeners with some federal news? Is it not better to attempt the job, given the alternatives of using wire stories and one-sided news from a Congress member's office?

There's no hesitancy in the answers given by Edmund B. Lambeth of Indiana University and John A. Byrne of Fairchild Publications: "Deficient as it most often is, the practice of covering Washington via Ma Bell is far and away superior to the shabby subterfuge of printing the press releases of local lawmakers verbatim under Washington datelines, leaving the impression that what is printed beneath the headline is bona fide news written by a reporter."[7]

It's simply good reporting. A story with a federal angle should contain information from federal sources. Stories involving varying points of view should utilize several sources, even if some of these sources are miles away. Evaluation of a public official's performance should not be based exclusively on information from that official.

Even home-based reporters for news organizations that have Washington correspondents should form the habit of making their own calls to Washington for the federal information they need. The regional correspondents can provide that service, of course, but a local reporter usually would be better off talking with an agency official rather than having the questions put to the same official secondhand by the correspondent.

Thus, there are a number of circumstances in which local reporters, however small the news organization, should be on the telephone seeking additional information:

When the reporter knows of something scheduled which involves local persons or which could have significant local impact. Such initiation of coverage would be appropriate, for example, if the House of Representatives were scheduled to vote on an important bill or amendment sponsored by the local member or if a federal agency were considering a local application for a grant.

When a news release is received and involves anything more than straight factual information such as the schedule of the Congress member's next visit to town. Follow-up telephone interviews to broaden or change the focus of the story should be routine. This may be a call to the Congress member, to congressional leadership, or to a federal agency.

When a wire service story makes inadequate reference to the local impact of a federal action. It is, of course, possible to contact AP or UPI for a specific story or additional information, but the success of such a request may be spotty or slow. A reporter who personally makes the federal contact has control over the specific questions asked and knows what and when information is avilable.

When a reporter is writing a local story which has a federal component. This may be spot news or issue-oriented. A story on local law enforcement, for example, could be greatly enhanced if the reporter had national statistics with which to make comparisons. A story on local educational expenditures, on the need for a new local sewage treatment plant or a new bridge—all could be more meaningful with material showing how the local situation fits into the national picture.

As initial steps in accomplishing these goals, a news organization must know who the sources are and get to know those sources well enough to have cooperation in telephone coverage. Part of the answer lies in availability of up-to-date reference material, especially directories. It is quite possible to make a blind call to a federal agency, ask for "someone" who could provide information and get a story. But it's at least easier, usually more successful, and certainly quicker to know the right person.

That's a problem. Certainly, over a period of time, a reporter can get to know sources by telephone. Many are successful at it. They have to be. But a news organization dedicated to getting the local story from Washington could reap long-term benefits by sending a reporter for a short stay in the capital. The reporter or editor would then have the opportunity of knowing the individual sources most frequently called and, more important, having them know of the news organization's interest in getting the federal story.

The major alternative, or course, is taking advantage of periodic visits by the federal officials. The most frequent will be by members of Congress and their staffs, and there's no question that they will be interested in taking the time to get to know local reporters. But, occasionally, other federal officials may get into the area, and news organizations should seek time for conversations beyond normal news coverage.

The congressional delegation provides the key to getting local news out of Washington by telephone. Members may have the information readily available. Beyond that, they are in a position to obtain specific information, tell the reporter who the proper source would be, or, on occasion, intercede for the reporter who is having difficulty with other federal sources. Members of Congress, for example, have direct access to the Legislative Reference Service and the Office of Legislative Counsel, whose function is to provide them with information. And, since Congress supervises federal agencies, those officials are less likely to ignore a specific request for cooperation from representatives or senators.

Though hometown reporters depend a great deal on members of Congress, they also seek to develop other sources. Within the legislative branch itself, the best bets are those persons in leadership roles. Persistence may be required to get assistance from high-ranking Senate or House leaders, but it's an effort which could pay off. Some special attention, for example, should go toward those who chair committees on which members of the local delegation sit. While it is unlikely these persons will provide evaluative comments on the role of the local delegates until they know the reporter well, other information may result. Does the bill sponsored by the local senator have any chance of passage? What is the importance of the local representative in obtaining either passage or defeat of a particular bill?

More difficult but certainly worth the effort would be establishing a relationship in which information or comment could be obtained from Senate leaders (president *pro tempore,* majority leader, minority leader, majority whip, or minority whip) or House leaders (speaker, majority and minority leaders, majority and minority whips).

Perhaps the most willing alternative sources would be lobbyists who represent special interest groups in Washington and throughout the country. In Washington, these persons track reporters down to present opinions about legislation and other governmental actions. The local reporter, however, will have little difficulty finding them.

Many are obvious national organizations known to have particular points of view on certain subjects, for example, the American Petroleum Institute on any legislation dealing with oil or the National Education Association on educational issues. Others may be located with a little library work.

Making contact with the proper organization may involve little more than asking the congressional staff which groups have been working on a particular piece of legislation or through contacting local groups which are chapters of national organizations. The National Education Association, for example, has organizations in every state which may provide information or help make contact with its national office. It's certainly helpful to get on the mailing list of such national organizations.

Information obtained from lobbyists tends to be too one-sided to be used alone. But it is precisely the kind of material needed to help balance the equally one-sided information received from the congressional delegation.

One other potentially good source of information, particularly at the agency level, usually is close to home but often forgotten by local reporters. All federal government is not located in Washington. Many federal agencies have regional offices scattered around the country whose function is to facilitate communication and program coordination.

In 1972, the nation was divided into ten standardized federal regions, and most federal agencies now conform with this organizational setup. For example, the Department of Health and Human Services has regional offices located in Boston, New York, Philadelphia, Atlanta, Chicago, Dallas, Kansas City, Denver, San Francisco, and Seattle. The Department of Transportation has offices in the same cities, except that nearby Cambridge, Massachusetts, is substituted for Boston and Fort Worth, Texas, for Dallas.[8]

These offices may not be able to provide the specific answer to a reporter's questions, but they may either get the information or refer the reporter to the proper source. As usual, it's experience with a given regional office through which the reporter learns who is helpful and who is not.

RESOURCES FOR THE FEDERAL GOVERNMENT REPORTER[9]

A host of publications exist which a federal reporter inside or outside of Washington might find useful. Some are easy to obtain. The reporter will want to own some, but a substantial number will be available in the local library, especially if it's a Federal Depository Library. The following is intended to be a list of what is available. Certainly, it is not inclusive of all material a reporter would find helpful. But it is more than most would ever need.

Never-Be-Without Group

Congressional Quarterly, a weekly news journal primarily on congressional activities. 1414 22nd St., NW, Washington, D.C. 20037.

National Journal, a weekly news journal on issues and governmental doings. Expensive, but possibly the best. 1730 M St., NW, Washington, D.C.

Congressional Record, a listing of the day's events in Congress. Presumably a complete and verbatim account of words spoken in the two houses, but doesn't fit that description because members may have material removed or inserted. Printed in three forms: the daily *Record,* paperbound biweekly *Record,* and the permanent bound *Record.* Inexpensive and handy. Superintendent of Documents, Government Printing Office, North Capitol St., Washington, D.C. 20402.

Washington Information Directory, published annually by Congressional Quarterly, has names, responsibilities, and telephone numbers of governmental agencies and associations. 1414 22nd St., NW, Washington, D. C. 20037.

Good-to-Have Group

Federal Register, a publication of what executive agencies are doing. Appearing five days a week, it contains a listing of regulations of all executive agencies. Monthly, quarterly, and annual indexes are issued. May be purchased through Government Printing Office (GPO).

Democratic Study Group Legislative Digest, published by House Democrats, tells what is going on for the week and breaks down the legislation. May be obtained from congressional offices at minimal cost.

House Republican Digest, published by House Republicans to serve the same purposes. May be obtained from congressional offices at minimal cost.

Environmental Study Conference Report, a publication which chronicles the major legislative/environmental issues. May be obtained from congressional offices at minimal cost.

Other Valuable Material

Magazines of major lobbies, ranging in philosophy and issues. May get newsletters from a wide range of such groups from Common Cause to the National Rifle Association. For names and addresses, see *Encyclopedia of Associations* at any library.

Facts on File, a very helpful listing of chronological news summaries.

General Accounting Office monthly publication list. May provide excellent material, or at least a list of monthly reports which reporters can track down. 441 G St., NW, Washington, D.C. 20548.

In addition, there are a number of magazines which a reporter would want to have available. Some are political, such as the *New Republic* or *Progressive* (left) to the *National Review* and *Human Events* (right). There are also some trade publications which might be good depending on the news organization's area. For instance, a region rich in defense contracts should follow *Aviation Week and Space Technology,* a McGraw-Hill publication. A farm area should subscribe to farm publications. Also, news organizations may want to use a service called *Roll Call Report,* published by Rick Thomas of Ohio-Washington News Service, which lists the votes of Congress members.

Congressional Budget Office also does excellent issue papers, called *Background Papers,* not just on budget issues. Available through GPO.

Congressional Research Service, Library of Congress, provides very good reports. Available through the library or GPO.

Monthly Catalog of U.S. Government Publications lists every governmental publication for the month, with index. Available through GPO.

Congressional Information Service, a private firm, has all congressional hearings and reports on microfiche. Indexed and abstracted annually. An extremely useful resource. Available at many libraries.

Every newspaper in the country should subscribe to the *Washington Post, Wall Street Journal,* and *New York Times.*

Reference Materials

The following would be a useful part of any news organization's library and should be on the desk or in the office of any reporter who covers politics and government. The texts will supply both valuable background and information and serve to give quick phone numbers and other details.

Washington area telephone directories.

Executive Department telephone directory, published by the federal government.

Congressional Staff Directory, most useful for staff names and telephone numbers. P.O. Box 62, Mount Vernon, Va. 22121.

Federal Regulatory Directory, also published annually by Congressional Quarterly, lists the who's who of the executive branch regulatory agencies.

Almanac of American Politics, privately published, excellent resource book on legislators and their political history and the history of their districts. E. P. Dutton, New York.

Congressional Directory, provides information relating to Congress and all other branches of the government. Biographical data; congressional session information; lists of executive officials; governors; information on international organizations. Available from GPO.

Braddock's Federal-State-Local Government Directory, compilation of telephone numbers and addresses of the federal government. Published by Braddock Publications, Inc., Washington, D.C.

Washington Lobbyist Guide/Lawyers Directory, written and compiled by Ed Zuckerman of Knight News Service. Excellent to identify lobbyists and public interest groups, particularly for Federal Election Commission reports (campaign financing). Published by American Ward Publications.

National Trade and Professional Association of U.S. and Canada and Labor Unions, published by Columbia Books, Inc., of Washington, D.C.

U.S. Budget, can be obtained from Office of Management and Budget or GPO.

United States Government Manual, specific reference information about all governmental branches. Available through GPO.

General Material

A number of resource materials are available along with other avenues to obtain information easily. Some of these are:

Congressional mailing lists, from a member of either the House or the Senate.

"Think tanks," for example, Brookings, American Enterprise Institute. These groups publish studies, provide transcripts of seminars, etc.

Newsletters and other material provided by special-interest groups. Many are located in Washington and are willing to provide oral and written help. Many monitor public policy and the decision-making process, for example, the National League of Cities, National Education Association, and the National Governors Conference. It would be worthwhile to subscribe to the newsletters of the public interest groups which monitor the activities of the committee on which the local Congress members sit.

Generally, a reporter can make good use of federal depository libraries and regional offices, particularly for grants, investigations, and other developments. Other material which might be helpful can be obtained from the *New York Times Index* and through the Library of Congress Information Service.

NOTES

1. Mick Rood, "Washington's Other Reporters," *Washington Post Magazine,* June 18, 1978, p. 14.
2. Miller Bonner, "Regional Eye on the Capitol," *AP World,* August 1978, pp. 5–6.
3. Ben H. Bagdikian, "Congress and the Media: Partners in Propaganda," *Columbia Journalism Review,* January-February 1974, p. 4.
4. Diane Kielse, June Nicholson, John Henkela, and Geri Fuller-Col, "Washington Neglected," *The Quill,* May 1978, p. 19.
5. "Washington Neglected," p. 25.
6. "Washington Neglected," p. 22.
7. Edmund B. Lambeth and John A. Byrne, "Pipelines from Washington," *Columbia Journalism Review,* May-June 1978, p. 54.
8. *United States Government Manual, 1979–1980.* Washington, D.C.: Office of the Federal Register, 1979, pp. 274 and 440.
9. With special thanks to Bill Choyke of the *Dallas Morning News,* Andrew Alexander of Cox Newspapers, John Felton of *Congressional Quarterly,* and Randy Wynn of Ohio-Washington News Service, who compiled this listing.

Chapter 11

CAMPAIGNS AND OTHER ASSORTED POLITICS

Bob Lancaster has spent more than half his life in journalism. Now associate editor of *Arkansas/A Monthly Portfolio,* a regional magazine published in Little Rock, he labels his one year of college as "very unsuccessful." But he did spend a successful year as a Nieman Fellow at Harvard University, where he studied American intellectual history.

A novelist and biographer of country music star Kenny Rogers, Lancaster has developed a political philosophy from his educational background and his work as columnist for three Arkansas newspapers (*Arkansas Gazette, Arkansas Democrat,* and *Pine Bluff Commercial*) and the *Philadelphia Inquirer.* Not yet 40, his comments about politics and political reporting sound as though they come from a combination scholar and street fighter.

He's right at times. He's dead wrong at times. He's always thoughtful, precise, and provocative. Here's a sample:

What should be the focus of political coverage?

"The more I see of American public life, the more I'm convinced that hardly anything original or worthwhile has happened in American politics since the Jefferson-Hamilton dialogue. Andrew Jackson 'rabbleized' American politics, to coin a word, and that's caused subsequent great deterioration of quality. But insofar as anything valuable going on, . . . well, maybe in the judiciary. Some of the judicial activism is interesting. It's amusing sometimes, but it's not often really innovative."

If there's nothing interesting going on in American politics, why do journalists cover it?

"There's a very practical and disillusioning reason for that. American newspapers historically have been really cheap operations. They wanted to hire people for as little money as possible, and the one thing any dimwit off the street could write about with some conviction was politics. Everybody could understand sleazy political maneuverings. It didn't require any great education or sophistication to understand the crudities of what was going on. So the papers could hire deadbeats to 'write' about it, and pay them very little money and get away with it. I suspect that's how the tradition of exaggerated newspaper attention to politics got started. And, of course, the tradition continues."

Aren't the people interested in politics?

"I think the political tomfoolery we pass off as 'news' interests intelligent people in the same way zoos do. There was something vital and challenging about early American politics, but since the Bill of Rights, it's just been a side-show for the most part. The first-rate minds have turned their attention elsewhere. To borrow an image from Cyril Connolly, journalists writing about politicians now are like jackals snarling over a dried-up well."

Doesn't politics have an impact on the quality of people's lives? On their pocketbooks? Shouldn't journalists be there to report that impact?

"I think it probably does, but that influence has been greatly exaggerated because of the close attention we journalists pay to politics. We don't pay that close attention to religion, for example. Probably the good religion journalists in America you can count on one hand. And yet it seems to me that religion is a much more influential factor than politics in determining the quality of our lives. I think it was Thomas Mann who said the tragedy of modern man is that we can't conceive of any aspect of our lives except in political terms. And we, as journalists, are partly responsible for that because of the exaggerated attention we pay to politics."

Well, you're part of this, too. What's different about your columns?

"Well, all I try to do is to be honest. If something is silly, to say it's silly. If something is evil, to say it's evil. If somebody is a joke as a candidate for public office, to say that. That's not much, and it's considered bad form in some journalistic quarters. It's considered a violation of our standard of 'objectivity.' But it seems objective to me. If something is stupid, calling it stupid seems to me both natural and objective. The concept of the newspaper as a passive conduit of information is a relatively new one, and network television reporting shows just how ghastly an aberration it is."

All right, who declared you god? You say you like Mencken. Who made him god? Or Tom Paine? Why them?

"I think the United States Constitution did. It made us all gods—not just journalists: Everybody. It made a fundamental human right out of free expression of ideas, and it was just a technological accident that newspapers grew up the way they did, and some of us were singled out to practice this right on a larger scale.

But that doesn't give any more substance to my opinion than it does anybody else's. There should be a great diversity of opinion writing and of opinions. And for people to gain some perspective on this blizzard of conflicting opinion, they're going to have to look to somebody with the vision and the time and the patience to put it all together."

In politics, that's the reporter?

"No. We shouldn't look to journalism for that. That's why we have novelists and playwrights and essayists. Those are the great generalists. People should read them more and read newspapers less anyway. The irony sometimes gets me, you know, that there may be 50,000 people reading some garbage that I write when they could be reading something Joseph Conrad wrote which would be more instructive and encouraging and pertinent. And yet they don't do it, and I don't know what to do about that. But journalists can't be everything. We are particularists, detail men and women, like the little studio assistants daubing the beards and the crockery in 'The Last Supper.' And I think that's what we ought to be. We provide specific information about specific events and situations and opinions about those events and situations."

And occasionally some great person comes along who can provide the perspective?

"Yes. We can only hope so. And I can't think of any journalist who's been able to do it. The ones who have tried have not been successful. There's a book that I reviewed not long ago about ... some pretentious title ... it was about Mencken, and it was a book about Mencken as a 'thinker.' Well, it's ridiculous to regard journalists as formal thinkers because what they do is catch-as-catch-can. Every day there's something new and usually something trivial that they have to occupy their minds with. The best journalists are people who know how to get compartmentalized information in an increasingly complex and compartmentalized society."

Don't you think that's simply going to breed confusion?

It depends. In the last decade or so journalism has made some encouraging progress in some ways. There's been a trend to specialized reporting, for example. That is, the reporter who has been extensively educated in the field he or she eventually will write about."

A good political reporter, then, is an intellectual—one who has studied and understands politics?

"It's not necessarily intellectual. You can have a good reporter in auto mechanics, for instance, if he knows the technology and can write adequately. The trick is to have reporters who can express themselves well, who know something about this incredibly complicated English language, who have some kind of specialized education or knowledge, and who are working for an organization that recognizes the need for reporters with proficiencies in both these areas."

You've been labeled an excruciating writer.

"Yeah. It's not easy for me. I do the Flaubert bit. You know, my great dream is to some day be able to write as well as E. B. White, and I know I never will. But it's still something to work toward. I think it was Whitehead who said when you work you don't work for the mass audience out there. You work for a few people that you respect, that you know will care about certain things you do and certain pains you take. And if you can write it so it will satisfy—maybe even delight—those few people, then everything else that happens is just a bonus."

POLITICS IS MORE THAN JUST ELECTIONS

It *may* be that such blasphemy is uttered with Bob Lancaster's tongue planted firmly in his cheek. Or it may not. But his comments are designed not to be ignored. It's difficult to be blasé about someone who so deliberately steps on everyone's toes. The more journalists think about what they're doing and why, the greater the chances that what they are providing the public will be more pertinent and meaningful.

That's the beauty of a Bob Lancaster. In just a few paragraphs, he has assumed the role of extreme critic of political reporting and the American government, sought to guide reporters' efforts to cover the political process, intermarried a new journalistic trend with an age-old philosophical justification, panned much of the conventional wisdom of political coverage, and outlined what he thinks are qualities of good reporting, individually and institutionally. That's a good day's work.

One doesn't have to agree with all the specifics as Lancaster lovingly flogs the institution he serves to see in his comments a number of recurring themes from the pages of media criticism. Questions such as: What is the value of political coverage? How much balance in political coverage is necessary or desirable? Are reporters politically biased? What should be the focus of political coverage?

Reporters will take differing approaches in their answers to these questions, depending, of course, on what they think their jobs are, on how they define politics. Too many reporters seem to function on definitions which are so narrow that coverage is naturally limited to the commonplace. Does politics equal an election campaign? If so, maybe Lancaster is right. Anyone off the street, without education or training, can write about speeches, rallies, and baby kissing. Maybe he's also correct in stating that nothing significant has happened in American politics for years.

One shouldn't deny the importance of campaigns. They do represent breaking news stories which end in necessary reporting of who won and how those persons will attempt to direct government in coming years. But that can't be all that's reported. In a large sense, politics is the basis of everything, from who drives what on which city streets to whether a citizen can buy the preferred food for this evening's dinner to where and in what way athletes participate in "nonpolitical" Olympic games.

And media critics have been calling for an expansion of the traditional definitions. Three examples:

Free-lancer J. Anthony Lukas, Pulitzer Prize winner and former *New York Times* reporter, calls for coverage which emphasizes politics as broad power relationships between different segments of society.[1]

"If you take the Aristotelean notion of what politics is, which was the life of the *polis,* the life of the Greek political body, then politics can be seen as virtually all that is interesting to write about in any society," he adds. "In that sense I do find politics interesting. I do not find politics compelling when it is defined conventionally to mean partisan politics or electoral politics or particularly quadrennial Presidential politics."[2]

Prominent media critic Ben Bagdikian, likewise, notes that politics includes much more than campaigns. It includes public policy, how it evolves and who influences it. Politics includes the state of public need, a condition, he stresses, which is not determined on Capitol Hill or in the White House or in corporate headquarters, but among people.[3]

"Political reporting has to be less concerned with the acting skills of candidates and more concerned with their social policies, less concerned with how they use their hands and more with how they use their minds," Bagdikian says. "To do this, reporters have to get out of that aluminum tube more often and down to earth where people live, less caught up in pre-programmed campaigns run by consultants and more with the issues that press upon most of the population and which are not discovered in airplanes filled with speech-writers and acting coaches."[4]

Among the issues in the late twentieth century have to be the interrelationships among politics and national and local economies. Yet, says *Washington Post* columnist Nicholas von Hoffman, political writers increasingly have tended to see the American system of government as a static structure in which the formalism of law and office are given an attention beyond what they merit. He defines politics as "primarily a matter of government supervision of the society's economic activities" and points out that reporters who ignore political economics as an important part of their coverage are not doing the proper job.[5]

The urgings of Lukas, Bagdikian, von Hoffman, and scores of others are part of a chorus which includes many political writers. Their cry is similar to one heard from other parts of journalism. It's a cry for more understanding of the system, greater depth of reporting, and recognition that politics is a process of complicated dependencies. It's a call for reporting about the fabric instead of the individual threads. And it's a plea for greater emphasis on the citizen's perspective rather than mere one-way communication from the system to the people.

THE IMPACT OF POLITICAL REPORTING

The need for broader coverage does not depend upon one's theory or even proof about the type or degree of impact which political communications have on individual voters. Do the news media directly influence the specific decisions of individual voters? Probably not in most cases. That's more likely to result from interpersonal relationships and deeply held attitudes. What about the impact of information on citizen decision making? A factor, but basically a long-term influence and one, again, which is filtered through significant mediating factors.

But even if they do not directly influence specific decisions, don't the media set the agenda of what subject matter is under public consideration? Yes, but personal considerations again provide a filter, and this may be a chicken-egg question. It may be equally likely that the news media emphasize what already is in the public consciousness more than they place agenda items into that consciousness.

The greatest potential impact is much more subtle than what has been considered by researchers. Though it it yet to be proven, it is conceivable that the quality of political coverage helps establish public attitude and the public mood about the political system. How one covers politics in an age of antipolitics is an important question. But it may be more important to consider the forces behind antipolitical attitudes. It's more than likely that the news media represent one of those forces.

"A society based on the assumption of choice," Bagdikian says, "is not much better off unless the voter is given meaningful knowledge. If the choice is simply one pleasantly wrapped but sealed package over another, voting is worse than meaningless. Such emptiness corrupts the process. It degrades the standing of the democratic process in the minds of people and therefore makes it easier for them to dispense with it.

"For us, election campaigns too often have no systematic presentation of real programs to choose from but offer instead highly slick manipulation of symbols by new technology. This ploy plays Russian roulette with our national fate, twirling the dial of our voting machines in the hope that the candidate with the most skilled television consultant will, by sheer luck, happen to be the best person to lead the country."[6]

The lack of systematic presentation takes several forms, only one of which is the lack of depth in reporting of real programs. Three forms, specifically, merit discussion.

One is what political scientists refer to as *now-ism,*[7] the journalistic tendency to emphasize what happens today as if it were a pattern or a trend, but with inadequate explanation of how today relates to yesterday's activity and how today's news story is part of a larger picture. Worse than the cause of journalistic incompleteness, now-ism often results in journalistic error as reporters hastily and with inadequate thought assume that today's event is a predictor of the future. Examples occur daily, but perhaps the most frequent in politics grow from reporters' early and quick assessments of leading candidates based on the results of a single primary election or, locally, on the results of a party caucus or reception at a public rally.

A second source of public confusion may be said to grow from the news media's *dramatization of apparent political conflict.* Political scientist Richard L. Rubin of Columbia University, for example, charges that reporters treat the strategic conflict of primary contenders as if the conflict were genuinely substantive. Public cynicism may easily be fed by reports of what candidate X said about candidate Y during a primary campaign when those reports are followed by accounts of the two candidates getting together after the primary.

"It is not simply the exposure of intraparty battles that has served to further fragment already unstable conditions," he adds, "but rather the media's relentless dramatizing of the differences between the candidates and their supporters without properly identifying and affirming the substantial common ground shared by many of the candidates. Differences in style rather than substance are exploited for dramatic purposes and 'probes' by the media often serve to make minor differences of degree evolve into apparent 'confrontations' of principle between candidates—who actually share much in common."

Conflict and differences of opinion, of course, must be reported, be they during primary or general campaigns or as politicians seek to perform the duties of their elected positions. They do make good copy, and they represent a significant part of the political process at all levels. But clarity of reporting requires that conflict not be highlighted for dramatic purposes when that conflict is only on the political surface or is only a small part of the circumstance.

The third form of the problem may spring from the greater tendency toward investigative reporting and the subsequent increased number of *negative stories* about politicians which affect public attitude about the political process. Uncovering unethical or illegal behavior by public officials may rank among the greatest achievements of twentieth century journalism. From Watergate to countless similar exposés by local news organizations, journalists have methodically exercised their function as watchdogs of the public. But, as in stories of political conflict, sometimes the tendency goes too far.

In situations which provide possibilities for negative, neutral, or positive stories, reporters have proven themselves anxious for the former and much less enthusiastic otherwise. For example, among the most productive materials available to the political reporter are those campaign finance records kept in state secretary of state offices and by the Federal Election Commission. Use of these public records has declined as Watergate recedes further back into memory. But, of campaign finance stories which are produced, the majority are negative, telling of improper contributions, financial connections between officials and special-interest groups, or improper filing procedures. These are legitimate stories, but one Federal Election Commission official said he considered it a problem that "most" of the stories are negative, "many" are neutral, and "a very small number" are positive.

"Reporters don't seem to want to write the story that says a candidate filed at the proper time and that the contributions received were within the law," he added.

The problem of now-ism, conflict coverage, and negative stories is not that they are with us. They have valuable elements. The problem is that, despite numerous examples to the contrary, too many reporters place too much emphasis on them, distorting overall coverage. Whatever their impact, they are problems with which political reporters have to deal, especially if their goal is to provide the whole truth.

IT'S PROFESSIONAL VERSUS PROFESSIONAL

Reporters are aware of these problems. It's not just in politics that many fail to move beyond the commonplace. And their immediate response is correct, to a degree. To do the kind of job everyone would like to see requires more time than most have available. Campaigns are hectic and complex, and just the simple act of keeping up on specific events can be massive. Covering the politics of public policy is complicated by the need for hours to interview officials and to review piles of documents. And these hours are limited by the fact that many political journalists are expected to double as governmental beat reporters.

What makes the task of political reporters more difficult, however, is the fact that the people they deal with may know as much about the techniques of journalism as they do. If politicians themselves are not at least "semi-pros" in communication, they make it a point to hire professionals and to train carefully others on their staffs in the art of dealing with reporters. Many political press officials are former political reporters. Often they're veterans who know how reporters think and how to use that knowledge to gain what they want.

It's true that reporters may benefit because these former journalists better understand their needs and may even retain some journalistic loyalty. But when push comes to shove, where will the loyalties lie? How long will the former journalist keep his or her job if cooperation with reporters works to the disadvantage of the politician? In most cases, these are rhetorical questions.

Who Manipulates Whom?

The struggle between the professional journalist and the professional political communicator is the basis for the adversarial approach, which is accepted as perhaps necessary but certainly inevitable. And it's double-edged, says Richard D. Cudahy, who has been Wisconsin Democratic party chairman, campaign worker, candidate, and now is a federal judge in Chicago.

"No politician can entirely trust a reporter since the reporter's job is to use the politician as a source or subject of news whether such an end may or may not be in the interest of the politician. Neither can a reporter entirely trust a politician for the politician's objective is to manipulate information (and to project his own conduct) in such a way as to secure favorable publicity from the reporter.

"The basic terms of exchange consist of information or priority access to newsworthy words or acts in exchange for puffery (or at least attention) from the media. To the extent that both parties to the transaction (and, in particular, the reporter) are able to maintain their integrity, intercourse between politicians and reporters produces stimulating and accurate information for the public. The achievement of this result is, of course, the essential public commitment of the mass media."[8]

Cudahy, in a statement unusually frank for a politician, adds that the reporters' duty of maintaining the public interest is paramount to any private relationships they may have with politicians. They are obligated to publish unfavorable news even involving friends among politicians. And, though he admits that politicians may withhold information, he says they have a similar obligation to tell the truth about items they do discuss.

In this regard, he places the burden directly on journalistic shoulders with his opinion that "a strong sense of commitment to the public interest by the journalistic fraternity is the best assurance of relatively ethical politicians and modestly informed voters in a world which would benefit greatly from a larger supply of both."[9]

That's rather strong language, especially since politicians are so image-conscious and painfully aware of every word printed or spoken about them. That sensitivity, in practice, means they would like to control every reference to them, and reporters must be ever mindful of their efforts. Without such awareness, reporters will contribute truth to the charge leveled in one textbook that they "do not reside in an independent fourth branch of government but are, for the most part, handmaidens in each branch, going about the routine, bureaucratic roles of filing stories."[10]

Reporters aware of this relationship consider efforts to manipulate a normal part of political activity. Dana Spitzer of the *St. Louis Post-Dispatch,* for example, points out that very sophisticated politicians realize that the news media have critical need for information. They manipulate reporters by providing good information and, at the same time, seeking to steer news accounts in particular directions.

"There's no reason to resent it," Spitzer says, "but you do have to understand it. You are your own person, and you are a representative of an institution. You have to understand that they look upon you in terms of their self-interest and not

Dana Spitzer of the *St. Louis Post-Dispatch*

(*St. Louis Post-Dispatch* photo)

Frank Sutherland of The Tennessean (*The Tennessean* photo by Billy Easley)

yours. And you must also understand that you look in terms of your self-interest and not theirs. If the two of you know this, you can have a compatible relationship. They may try to use you, and they do, but you must always try to use them. If you can keep ahead of the game, your newspaper probably is pretty good."

It's not a matter of making deals, of you-scratch-my-back-and-I'll-scratch-yours. It's constant, aggressive sparring between two individuals seeking to gain their own goals. The only deals reporters make are those which involve protection of sources. They may not identify a source, or they may not use a story if it endangers the relationship with a good source or places the source in danger. Otherwise, newsworthiness is the only reasonable criterion for any story.

Variations in degree of newsworthiness, however, do give reporters some flexibility which permits them to write stories for the deliberate purpose of cultivating a source. The priority of political reporters is to write the page one or top-of-the-newscast story, but they daily must make decisions of whether to devote time to marginal stories which have less than blockbuster news value.

"There are a lot of stories that you could rightly pass or write," says Frank Sutherland of the *Tennessean* in Nashville. "They have news value, but if you do them they go into the back of the paper. It's a question of whether you take the time. If the same story applied to anybody else, if I was busy that day, I might not do it. If I'm not busy, I might do it. But with a source, if he or she is friendly to me, I would make a point of doing it even if I would have to stay over extra or whatever."

For Immediate Release

Perhaps there's no better example of this give-and-take than the specific efforts of politicians to control media content and coverage direction through production of news releases and taped actualities. Reporters know releases are prepared for one reason: to gain publicity. Releases actually assist reporters in keeping up with day-to-day requirements of their jobs. They need not feel guilty about supplementing their normal coverage with some releases. But they usually try to do some additional research and rewriting.

Some critics charge reporters as a group don't do enough additional research and rewriting. They simply take the releases, perhaps make some perfunctory revisions, and that provides their major coverage of governmental or political activity. That is not the work of professionals. Actually, one can make coverage by release look relatively authentic. The problem is that it places virtually all news judgment into the hands of the politicians. Certainly, it won't uncover a scandal, provide any negative information, or demonstrate less than effective performance by a politician.

Veteran politicians know and new politicians very quickly learn the value of the news release. They learn, especially in more rural areas, that if they're going to get the publicity so valuable to their campaigns, they will have to generate most of it. So reporters will continue to face the necessity of making daily decisions about whether to use the releases with only minor modifications, ignore them, or whether to pick up an idea or two from them and bounce them off other sources as well.

"I think papers depend a lot on political public relations for leads," says Glenn Fowler of the *New York Times.* "Some of them say, 'I don't use anything from a flack. Throw it in the waste basket. It's no good.' That's a mistake. I think we can use them to our advantage in getting leads on stories that we may otherwise never know about. Every reporter uses them to an extent, even though they deny it, because they call the PR staff up for basic information, background information they need."

A political reporter may generate a rather good story, for example, by taking a basic release on a governor's appointment and expanding it with an interview of the appointee about office organization, program goals, procedures, and possibly how mistakes of the previous administration may be overcome. Also, in many instances a handout from a candidate should prompt a nearly automatic call to that person's opponent.

Another way to use releases to the reporter's advantage is as a basis of comparison with what an official is saying in office or during a campaign. A reporter who saves releases has a ready record of what has been said in the past, of campaign promises or statements of opinion.

In short, news releases can represent a source of some factual information on minor stories, of the beginnings of major stories, of a means of allowing busy reporters to expand the scope of coverage. Problems occur when reporters get too busy or lack the initiative to dig up their own stories and prefer instead to wait for the latest handout.

Gaining the Advantage

All reporters are manipulated. Their need for information is so great that they cannot avoid being used to political advantage by those who control that information. That does not mean, however, that reporters must just sit back and accept it. It sounds like standard and stale advice, but it's true that the degree to which a reporter avoids being overly manipulated is the degree to which he or she is aggressive.

And that means more than just fighting back. Defensive journalists do little more than just hold their own. It means being on the offensive, aggressively seeking the story behind or beyond the facts or comments provided. It means seeking, searching, pushing, testing, asking. The reporter who can do that effectively is one with a full knowledge of the political and governmental systems and one with the kind of personal drive which prohibits passivity.

It's the kind of drive which makes reporting more than just a conduit. It's a learning experience which, says Pulitzer Prize winner Walter Mears of The Associated Press, must be constant.

Walter Mears of The Associated Press

"If you wake up one morning and think you didn't learn anything yesterday as a political reporter, then you probably are a lousy reporter and should go do something else," Mears says. "The effectiveness of any reporter depends on whether there's still a creative process or an educational process in what that reporter does."

Reporters stress that learning is a combination of formal education and on-the-job experience. Textbooks are helpful in establishing the structure, but only battle scars provide the wisdom to apply that knowledge. Politics functions within a structure, and reporters need both political knowledge and political instinct to give it meaningful perspective. Continuous learning comes from insatiable reading, particularly of documents, current newspapers, and magazines. The instinct grows from political interest, ego involvement, and commonsensical use of powers of observation, says Meg Greenfield, editorial page editor of the *Washington Post* and *Newsweek* columnist.

"All of us—press and politicians and voters—insist on complicating the process unnecessarily," she says, "and trusting everything but the evidence of our senses and the strong beat of our own impulses. Not trusting our own observations, we incline to elaborate theatrical theories instead."[11]

Combining knowledge and good instinct into political wisdom makes possible the best use of standard journalistic techniques to diminish control by those who would use the reporter.

Principal among these techniques is development of a wide variety of sources. The American press was developed originally on the notion that a multiplicity of voices is needed if citizens are to discover truth. Effective political reporters today function on the same notion. The best balance of voices that cry in behalf of special political interest comes from other voices, other viewpoints, other alternatives. Therefore, numbers and variety of sources are important. And deliberate efforts need be made to cultivate at least four types of persons from whom information may be sought:

Inside sources, persons within the party or government organization. The most obvious is party leaders at the appropriate levels: local, county, state, or national. These may include legislative party leaders or individuals who have been selected to chair party organizations in efforts to select candidates and coordinate campaigns. But reporters also must go beyond political leadership to the workers within party organizations—either professionals or volunteers—who are veterans of political conflict.

"Enemy" sources, persons from the opposition who usually are quite willing to comment upon activities, programs, or statements by government officials or party leaders. Again, this may be the leadership of the "loyal opposition," individual legislators, former government officials, or other individuals who have specialized knowledge. The effort partly is one of gaining alternative comment, but, predictably, it also is in the hope of receiving tips which could develop into investigative or depth pieces about wrongdoing, bad decisions or program plans of significant public impact.

Special-interest sources, individuals who are close to the political scene but not directly involved in party or governmental activities. Some may be lobbyists, but others may function in more informal ways. They may be business executives or labor leaders or scientists or simply individuals who are part of a cause, advocating or opposing certain types of governmental programs.

Grapevine sources, persons with their ears to the political ground, perhaps lower level governmental workers with whom reporters become familiar. As Sutherland says, "It's almost automatic. The reporter stops in and says, 'Hi, what's going on today?' They stop and think. 'What's going on? I heard out in the hall. . . .' That's where you get most of your stories. They come from a source who works there. They're not some secret documents that are supposed to be hidden away. Governmental employees like to talk, and if you like to talk and are patient, talk to them, then it happens naturally."

Sources beget sources. A reporter who needs information but doesn't have an automatic line should be able to make a call and say, "I need to know such-and-such. Where can I get it?" But it doesn't all happen on the telephone. Personal contact develops the kind of trust which produces information, especially confidential information, on a regular basis. The key, actually, is regularity. A reporter doesn't have to see a source daily, but the contact must be regular enough that the source is comfortable talking about sensitive issues.

"You develop a kind of sense, whether you are covering a village or a police department, a political campaign or anything else," says Dave Allbaugh of the Dayton, Ohio, *Daily News.* "After a while there is something that crops up in your inner ear, and it says, 'Gee, I haven't talked with John so-and-so for three weeks. Something ought to be brewing there.' Sure, you keep calendars and reminders, but you do develop a sense about an area you have been covering."

And part of the contact may be in social settings. Political and governmental reporters usually try to attend as many receptions as possible even though the practice does contain dangers. The main purpose is to get to know the political figures in a more informal setting. Occasionally, something will be heard which results in a story, but it is seldom that reporters can run immediately to their typewriters as the result of a social encounter. One reporter, for example, has a personal rule that after three drinks everything is off the record until he can contact the source the following day for confirmation and additional conversation.

Socializing, while necessary, also provides the potential for relationship between the reporter and the source to become too close. It doesn't have to be in a social setting. It could result from strictly on-the-job contact. But it's axiomatic that friendship can erode the necessary professional relationship between reporter and source. It's a fine line between friendship that produces professional trust and friendship that chips away at the independence of the reporter.

Cutting Through Rhetorical Fog

Developing sources may help political reporters add depth and perhaps even more truth to their reports. But that does not solve what may be an even bigger problem. Ben Bagdikian asks the question as well as anyone: "What can the news media do if the candidate will not speak clearly of his plans? If questions are answered only with platitudes and slogans? What if official press conferences increasingly produce glittering generalities and misleading trivia?"[12] At least two answers may be presented for Bagdikian's question, and it's best if they can be accomplished together.

One is that the news media need to get candidates more into structured situations, involving, perhaps, only a single subject, in which they are interviewed by persons with background in that subject. Especially television, through programs such as *Meet the Press, Face the Nation,* and *Issues and Answers,* perhaps with even more structure, could put candidates into situations where ducking would be more difficult or, at least, more obvious.

More structured news conferences, debates, or panel discussions likewise place politicians into situations which should force more direct answers. Newspapers, especially, need more opportunities to ask the candidate to respond to direct questions.

"Such access does indeed mean that the press is allowing itself to be 'used' to some extent," says media critic Edwin Diamond, commentator for the *Post-Newsweek* stations and lecturer in political science at MIT. "But more air time and more print space for the candidates, and for lively scrutiny of the issues, is the kind of use the voters need in political campaigns. The challenge for the press is to get Ronald Reagan and the other candidates out of the snowbanks and housing sites and into television studios, where they can make their points and answer questions."[13]

But even if such expanded opportunities for direct talk are available, they will be meaningless if the reporter/interviewers ask broad questions and accept soft answers. Direct answers only will come through tough, direct questions from reporters who know as much or more about the political process as the candidates. Why so many reporters persist in their failure to ask specific questions is a question asked by many, including Jeff Greenfield, who approaches the matter from both sides as a freelance writer and political consultant.

"The most puzzling omission in political coverage, at least to my thinking," he says, "is the press's inability to penetrate the rhetorical fog of campaigns and to draw from a candidate's public statements and record the substantive heart of his effort. The most important question about a candidate is *what would be different*—in our lives, in the public policy of the community—if that candidate were given power. And it is that question that the press seems least willing, or least able, to answer."[14]

Direct answers result from specific subject matter and structured wording. The most frequent questions reporters ask tend to be "What do you think about . . ." or "Would you want to comment on . . ." Even if the subject matter is precise, these kinds of questions leave open the door to indirect answers. They simply provide too many avenues of answer. In contrast, "Where would the funds come from?" or "How much would that program cost? or "In what direct ways would individuals gain from such a program?" make vague answers much more difficult, especially if the reporter is ready with a specific follow-up question.

CANDIDATES AND CAMPAIGNS

Covering a political campaign is frustrating hurry-up-go-get-'em-meet-a-dead-line-dash-to-the-next-event journalism. Reporters chase candidates. Candidates chase reporters. It's confusion with a capital C. It's tiring. It's often boring. But it's gratifying and ego building. Reporters get to know the leaders of the community, state, or nation on a first-name basis. As the campaign progresses, they know they are writing the top news of the day. They know they're being read.

Maybe that's why the job of covering politics is the most sought on any staff.

But being up front has its drawbacks. It's being on the firing line for critics. It may be the most public of all reporting. Candidates and citizens alike consider political news fair game for criticism, comments, and complaints. Most of all, it means dealing with individual candidates who may understand journalistic goals but seldom agree with them. And it means sorting out candidates who have varying motives, personal characteristics, and qualifications for the jobs they are seeking.

Distinguishing the Candidates

If citizens are to have bases upon which to decide which candidates merit their votes, they need first to understand how one differs from another. And they should know, as the basis of that sorting process, who these candidates are, why they want the office, and what they propose to do with the position if it is obtained. Perhaps the more cynical would say voters don't use that kind of information. But there is more evidence of voter sophistication than such cynics are willing to accept. And, anyway, if reporters operated under that assumption, they would be thinking themselves out of a job. So, they must assume that the democratic process functions with vitality and, therefore, accept three major responsibilities in their campaign coverage.

They must find means of effectively determining which candidates are true contenders for the office; they must place considerable focus on how candidates differ from each other; they must seek authenticity instead of the imagery preferred by most candidates.

None of these tasks is easy. They're all impossible unless the reporter has a thorough understanding of politics and is willing to do the legwork necessary to overcome efforts of politicians and their staffs.

There are those who regret that the news media have the function of determining the relative significance of any candidate in a campaign. Among them are some reporters. But it is a fact of journalistic life that reporters' impressions, when translated to copy, can make a big difference in how seriously a candidate is considered.

"One must start with the proposition that an individual does not exist for political purposes until he becomes known to the media and thereby enters the public consciousness," says politician Richard D. Cudahy.[15]

How to do this effectively is a dilemma. Political history is full of examples of candidates at all levels who have surprised reporters and done well even though they were, in effect, written off early in the campaign. Part of the answer must be observation. How well is a relatively unknown candidate received in public situations? What is the reaction of citizens who come into contact with this person? Another part must be based on consideration of how well the person fits into current controversial issues. Another must grow from assessment of the strength of the candidate's financial support, political organization, and who his or her primary supporters are.

But politics is full of surprises, and it is most important for reporters to maintain their flexibility, constantly alert to apparent shifts of political opinion. The biggest mistake a reporter can make is to develop such a strong opinion about a candidate that there is an unwillingness or inability to recognize change in public mood.

On the other hand, while it is crucial that every serious candidate gain news media attention, that no candidate be virtually ignored, reporters do have to ration their limited column inches or minutes of air time. And they are especially wary of making a person a candidate he or she is not capable of being.

Another fact of political life that affects reporters is that most candidates, regardless of their political philosophy, will make every effort to avoid offending voters. The effort is based on the notion that candidates will automatically get a substantial portion of the votes from members of their party and that their major need is to gain the uncommitted votes of independents and some persons in the other party. Often, this is translated into an avoid-the-negative rather than say-the-positive approach. And often it means avoiding the specifics and concentrating on broad philosophical statements and image making.

It leads to the kind of political strategy admitted in one instance by one of California Governor Edmund G. (Jerry) Brown's top campaign aides:

"If there was a strategy in the campaign, it was to try to keep out of trouble and not get involved with issues like the death penalty or victimless crimes or marijuana. . . . We were very careful. . . . The issues we picked were obscure and boring and dull. . . . The press coverage never bothered us. It was as adequate as we wanted it to be. It was our feeling that the less coverage the better. . . . The duller the race the better. We wanted this dull, dull campaign."[16]

Such a situation means conservative Republicans and liberal Democrats all begin sounding like moderates. Everybody is moving toward the center to get the vote, and it becomes the political reporter's job to get candidates to say something significant, different, or controversial.

In the absence of such an effort, it's little wonder many voters make their choice on the basis of perceived personalities or uninformed expectations. That's why reporters need to step back from the day-to-day campaign and assess what they're doing. Is there a need to work harder to force candidates out into the open? Should they take the campaign disclosure route? What specific questions should be asked at every opportunity—with news accounts if the candidates didn't answer the questions—until they are forced to come up with specific answers?

It's standard textbook lore to say reporters seek truth, but there's no way to avoid it. "Everyone" knew, when Joe McGinniss wrote in *The Selling of a President 1968*[17] that candidates were being merchandised on the basis of an image which may or may not have related to their true character or beliefs. Today, that's a much discussed situation, and to reporters it's a circumstance with which they must deal daily.

They can go along and provide, as Jerry Brown's campaign aide said, coverage which is as adequate as the candidates want. Or they can put their efforts into ducking the imagery and trying to highlight the authentic person, issue, or relationship within a campaign. They can, in short, ask the tough question, make the tough observation, discuss the tough conclusion.

"As political and other institutional decision makers become more adept in their efforts to structure and manipulate public opinions," says John P. Robinson of Cleveland State University, "the press needs to become more adept at labeling clearly for its audience those pseudo-events, trial balloons and other public relations puffery that often pass for news. By so drawing voters closer into the realities of the political process, voters will get more from their exchanges with the press. In the long run, both the press and the voter should derive more from their exchanges with institutions that serve the public."[18]

Candidate Mistakes, Inconsistencies, Naivete

Part of the truth about candidates is that they don't always say or do the right thing. They are overworked during a campaign. Political newcomers may have problems because they have not learned how to handle reporter or citizen questions or because in their enthusiasm they talk about subjects on which they are inadequately informed. But even the most seasoned veteran will blunder from time to time, and reporters will be faced with how to deal with it.

Reporter reaction, of course, will depend on the nature of the occasion and the significance of the mistake in terms of the overall campaign. A slip of the tongue in a private conversation probably will be ignored unless its significance is worthy of follow-up. A public misstatement, perhaps before thousands at the scene or on television, must be dealt with. If the mistake is relatively minor, the reporter may give the candidate an opportunity to clarify it and then determine whether to ignore it or cover it with the clarification.

For major misstatements, however, the general attitude of reporters would be to use the story, giving opportunities for comment to the candidate, the candidate's party officials, and representatives of the other party.

Reporters must avoid creating a bigger issue than the error deserves or leaving the impression that they are unfairly taking advantage of a situation. Noting one instance in which he thinks a candidate ultimately was driven out of a race by reporters, Dave Allbaugh of the Dayton, Ohio, *Daily News* says:

"It was just like a bunch of little kids ganging up in the schoolyard and poking fun and yelling and nicknaming a guy until he is reduced to tears."

One type of "mistake" for which reporters must remain alert is inconsistency of statement by candidates. Persons legitimately change their minds, especially over long periods of time. But reporters are alert to the possibility that the changes represent an effort to tailor remarks to the attitudes of particular audiences.

This practice was more prevalent in earlier years of American politics, when speeches remained more local. While it's not as easy for them to get away with it today, candidates nevertheless may make the attempt.

"It's up to reporters to catch it if what a candidate says today is different from what he said yesterday and that is different from what he said two years ago," says the AP's Walter Mears. "It's important for people to know about such things. And you do it the same way you do anything else. You study, talk, and read as much as possible to find out where the candidate has been and what he said when he was out of your hearing."

This involves careful record keeping, a file of clips or news releases, and periodic comparisons. Usually, however, it is the type of thing that only good solid homework before the campaign can uncover. In the heat of a campaign, reporters seldom have the time to review past materials unless memory lights a spark. If the inconsistency represents a legitimate change of opinion, a good story may result from a candidate's explanation of that change.

Charges of wrongdoing in a campaign also represent a challenge to reporters seeking to be fair to all parties. They're common, and they vary in degree of severity from statements that the opposition candidate is being inconsistent or vague to charges that campaign or other laws have been violated. In too many instances, such charges are little more than efforts to degrade the opposition. But they are legitimate and necessary stories, and reporters must cover them—with caution.

"Usually something like this will unfold and you say, 'Okay, you make this charge. Give me your explanation.' Then you give the other guy a chance to answer, which is usually the first day's work on that," says Dotty Griffith of the *Dallas Morning News.* "Then, after that, you try to ascertain the situation or the law as much as possible by using documents or interviewing experts. But you have to be careful. It's not our job to try a case. Our job is to report the news responsibly. Some of these things are off the wall and totally unfounded, but I don't feel the obligation to go out and prove somebody right or wrong before I put in print that the charge has been made."

Dotty Griffith of the *Dallas Morning News*

(*Dallas Morning News* photo)

Griffith does, however, urge follow-up. She notes that too frequently news will break that a candidate has been charged with some improper to illegal activity, and the story will end right there, especially if legal authorities do not get involved. It's unfair to the candidate and to the citizens if reporters do not follow up with the story that no action was taken on the charge. If the lack of official action results from the influence of persons in positions of importance, that is a story. If the inaction is because the charge lacks validity, that is a story. Allegations of wrongdoing are too important to allow them to simply fade from the scene.

The Incumbent Advantage

Reporters have limited control over the fact that the incumbent is in a position to use them as election time draws near. Sophisticated incumbents know how to structure activities or statements from their office so that reporters cannot avoid providing them the publicity they seek. They have too many "nonpolitical" circumstances at their disposal which are legitimate news.

The mayor proposes changes in the city's budget, the president visits a poverty-stricken area, the legislator criticizes a state agency, the county commissioner seeks federal funds to build a new jail. It's news, and the fact that those individuals are involved in battles to keep their positions is almost journalistically irrelevant.

Incumbents know the reporters with whom they are dealing. They control valuable information. They control when that information is made available and to whom. The advantage is stronger for administrators, who can make actual decisions about programs or governmental activities and who speak officially for the state or community. Journalists tend to look with greater skepticism at a legislator's proposal, which may or may not become fact.

Nonincumbents, on the other hand, have little valuable official information, and their public activities can only be defined as part of their efforts to gain office. Unless they held office before and are known to reporters and the public, they carry an automatic burden into any campaign. It's possible thay they may turn their lack of incumbency into an asset because they have more time to spend in the district among the voters. Often, their efforts to overcome the burden and attract news media attention come through aggressiveness, use of wild charges, or taking extreme positions on public issues.

Reporters, for the most part, rely on their political instinct to reduce at least the excessive publicity which an incumbent may gain. Many do not define the incumbent advantage as a problem, for example, until an election draws near. They know most incumbents will increase their efforts to gain full benefit only within, say, two or three weeks of the actual election. And as that effort intensifies, reporters begin to be more skeptical about what is being said and done. Especially when the incumbent has only nominal competition, reporters may ignore or give only minor coverage to activities of limited news value and obviously political.

Reporters also go to great lengths to include the nonincumbent opponent into the story. This is difficult, of course, if the item is a legitimate, perhaps routine, act of government. But, to the degree that the item involves public policy, legislative proposals, or any version of campaign promise, reporters may seek to assure their stories are politically balanced.

In extreme cases in which a story must be written, but it obviously is designed to gain political publicity, reporters will make a point of mentioning that fact. Citizens understand politics. They know the purpose of politicians' activities at election time. And they are most likely to appreciate such honesty by reporters.

An incumbent has a voting record or performance record and must be held accountable for it. Reporters who have done their homework can relate those records to statements made during the campaign. This kind of coverage is difficult and involves homework, but incumbents cannot be allowed to act as if their political campaign and their performance are separate entities.

Playing Favorites?

Reporters are human. They like some people better than others. In politics, they spend a lot of time with candidates, and it is inevitable that they are going to develop preferences. Sometimes, this is just a personal decision. Other times it results from on-the-job treatment received from candidates. Or a combination of the two.

That raises the obvious question: To what degree does this human characteristic influence a reporter's coverage of campaigns or individual candidates? One can find evidence for answers all the way from "a lot" to "very little." Certainly, some reporters and news organizations have taken it upon themselves deliberately to help a candidate win an election, using whatever power they have. This will be almost universally criticized. Whatever one's notions about the possibility of being truly objective, very few will condone the practice of becoming an integral part of a candidate's effort to gain office.

Most reporters will place themselves at the other end of the continuum. "Very little," they say, not because they don't like one candidate more than another, but because they take calculated—sometimes extreme—precautions to be fair. Most, for example, make a point of not developing close personal relationships with politicians, both to avoid temptation and to avoid the appearance of a relationship that is too close.

"It's a conscious decision for me," says Tom Price of the Dayton, Ohio, *Journal Herald.* "I have no close friends among the politicians. I don't socialize with them beyond what is expected. I may go to dinner with someone or have a beer, but it's all in the context of the job I'm expected to do."

Tom Price of the Dayton *Journal Herald*

(*Journal Herald* photo)

The extreme form of such an effort to be fair could be a system in which column inches or air minutes are compared to assure that candidates are receiving at least equal quantitative attention. Or it may involve deliberate tombstoning of headlines so that stories about individual candidates run side by side.

It is more common, however, that reporters trust their own judgment and journalistic instincts to provide coverage. They stress accuracy and legitimate news information rather than quantitative measures. Campaign coverage thus becomes a matter of providing candidates with breaking news coverage of specific events, asking specific and detailed questions and looking for contradictions or inconsistencies.

The play given any event depends on its value. Price points out that his paper tends to cover most political activities. But whether that event gets one inch or twenty inches depends upon whether it had substance or consisted of another round of political platitudes.

Providing coverage which goes beyond the individuals is another strong link in a reporter's efforts to do the job well. Rather than giving wall-to-wall coverage of individual activities, the reporter will create packages which include the candidates' views on issues. This could, for example, concentrate on one subject, such as education. Or it could be a story which provides a general lead, then segments the candidates' comments compartmentally on several issues.

PAINTING THE WHOLE PICTURE

An artist who paints only half a picture seldom wins acclaim. But an incomplete picture is often the result of American political coverage.

Most journalists are sincere and professional, despite those who suspect their motives. Criticism that does crop up mostly grows from the sheer complexity of a campaign and the lack of time to provide the kind of comprehensive coverage reporters would prefer.

It's difficult to discuss fully the relationships between individual candidates and the campaign issues when one has countless day-to-day duties. It's difficult to find time to sit back and think about or investigate the larger picture of a campaign when reporters must deal with editors' expectations of daily stories. To be on the road is a dream of young reporters, but it's tiring and mind numbing. Too many reporters do find it easier either to rely on the candidates themselves to establish the focus of the coverage or to join the pack and follow the leads of their fellow campaign journalists.

That's not to make excuses. Less than adequate coverage does create misimpressions, does fail to inform voters, and does tarnish the reputation of political reporters in general. And quality coverage is not impossible. Many good journalists have served their readers, listeners, and viewers with distinction, and they have done so with a combination of knowledge and sheer hustle. They have provided comprehensive coverage because they have taken a comprehensive approach. And that means they have accepted the difficult responsibility of covering all elements of a campaign—the candidates, the issues, the strategies, the support, the events, and all those broader social factors which play parts in any election.

No individual reporter, of course, can do it all. Even local elections require teamwork. And successful news organizations have organized their efforts to deal with some combination of at least seven types of campaign stories. None of these stories is adequate alone, and the balance among them will vary according to local circumstances, the personality of a campaign, and news media preferences. But each has something to offer which is difficult to ignore.

Breaking News Is Essential

In spite of the overall requirements, breaking news remains the backbone of campaign coverage. Candidates make appearances, they speak, they answer questions, they relate to voters in specific ways. Their activities must be given straightforward coverage. Reporters tire of hearing speeches and attending meetings, but only by being on the scene can they provide the raw material which citizens need.

This raw material consists mostly of what the candidates have to say, but there's more. It includes how the candidate is received, the level of audience enthusiasm, and how the candidate handles questions and complaints. A reporter may get an early indication of the constituency of a candidate by observing his or her relationships with voters of a given background or voters who live in a particular part of the community, state, or country.

In spite of efforts by candidates to structure the content of their campaign and in spite of ideas about the news media's agenda-setting function, human beings have their own ideas about what is important to them. And the perceptive reporter on the scene can develop greater insight on campaign issues from what citizens say and ask when given the opportunity.

Breaking news accounts of campaign activities also provide the foundation of more detailed and analytical coverage of a campaign. Failure to observe the candidate in specific situations creates a disadvantage when reporters want to discuss the issues, a candidate's political philosophy, or the possibilities of election success. Without such observation, reporters must depend on interviews and are subject to being manipulated.

The Issues Are the Context

"The basic job of reporters," says the AP's Walter Mears, "is to give the guy who votes some idea of what he will get. If you can't put over some picture of what the future will be like, the campaign is a futile exercise."[19]

And that provides the rationale, if one is needed, for going beyond the events and the personalities involved in a campaign. Candidates become public officials, and public officials have ideas of what is important and what should be done. Is it therefore necessary to say that the voter deserves to know about these directions while time remains to influence the decisions? The responsibility of reporters to the public, says Ben Bagdikian, is to report not only what the candidate says, which obviously is important, but "to give as well the fairest and most careful possible description of what it means, and where it fits into the present and the past, especially the past performance and words of the candidate."[20]

Bagdikian's comment represents the need for more serious news media discussion of the issues of a campaign. It's providing broader perspective of how candidates relate to an issue, how that relationship varies during the campaign season, and how they are likely to govern with respect to it. This also involves deciding the subjects that will be placed in the journalistic spotlight.

Who determines the issues? On the surface, the answer must be the reporters. They decide what stories to write. But that answer is incomplete. Reporters look to others for cues. And, increasingly, the tendency is to look less to the candidates themselves and more to the public. Such an act has broad implications. By giving the public more weight in the process, reporters are reinforcing the democratic process. And, if political scientist David E. RePass of the University of Connecticut, Storrs, is correct, they are at the same time broadening the personal impact of campaign coverage.

"Most voters . . . display a definite concern for specific issues and these issue concerns have a considerable impact on electoral choice," he says. "When we allow the voters to name the issue of greatest importance to themselves, rather than presenting them with a list of pre-formulated issue questions as most pollsters do, we can learn which issues are really on people's minds and are thus salient enough to affect voting decisions.

"But the diversity of issues mentioned suggests that the public is making its own selection of issues—the ones that are important to them. Most issue concerns of the public seem to derive 1) from actual events or conditions (i.e., Vietnam, inflation, campus disturbances, etc.), 2) from government programs or activities (i.e., test ban treaty in 1962, Civil Rights Act of 1964, detente with Russia, etc.), or 3) from personal interests and concerns (i.e., inadequate schools, job discrimination, decline of moral and religious standards, etc.). Again, there is little in the data to suggest that people's concerns are channeled by special attention given to certain issues by the candidates or the media."[21]

Concentration on political issues important to citizens raises three significant journalistic requirements, the first of which is political knowledge and instinct on which to base judgments. Often, the public's perception of important issues is discovered through news-media-sponsored surveys. At other times, the choice depends upon the abilities of reporters to understand and identify individual and collective public concerns. Both methods require more than casual understanding of the political process.

The second requirement is one of time and space. It simply takes more time to analyze a political issue than it does to cover a campaign speech. It takes more digging. And when the result of that effort appears, it usually requires more column inches or air time, something that will be provided only if news organizations are dedicated to fulfilling the need for greater depth of campaign coverage.

Third, unless people are emphasized, stories may be dull, dull, dull. The problem grows out of an attitude which emphasizes things over human beings. Inflation as an abstract concept is deadly. But inflation has direct local impact on the lives of individuals. It is an issue of local political concern. Stories which relate that point and in which candidates are required to address themselves will capture citizens' interest.

"What readers generally wind up with are endless stories based on quotes and speeches plus some mood stories designed to give the feel of a campaign and a few gossipy articles," says Alvin P. Sanoff of the Dayton, Ohio, *Journal Herald.*

"But stories about how candidates would cope with unemployment and inflation, how they would handle tax reform, what their plans are for dealing with energy problems are badly needed if the public is going to penetrate the campaign facade."[22]

Campaigning Shows Character

Speaking of the 1980 New Hampshire presidential primary, Meg Greenfield of the *Washington Post* and *Newsweek,* presented what she called a "way out theory" of why candidates Ronald Reagan and Jimmy Carter won: They looked better—more reasonable, competent, and authentic—to their parties' voters than the other guys did.[23]

It is significant that Greenfield's thoughtful discussion of the fictions and illusions of political campaigns concludes on that personality note. Under all that candidate play acting, there are real persons who have feelings and emotions, who live real lives and have real families, who work and play like everyone else and who have very human strengths and weaknesses. What kind of public officials they will become depends in part on these personal qualities. That's one reason citizens are interested and why they expect reporters will devote at least some attention to personal qualities of those seeking office.

On another occasion, Greenfield, a Pulitzer Prize winner for editorial writing, discussed this very question, pointing out: "People are more than their opinions and intentions. Of their stands on the issues themselves it is essential to ask, first, how they reached these stands, and, second, whether the stand has any relevance to the way things will turn out—i.e., whether they have a gift for making things happen in a political environment—or for knowing when to go down in flames for a principle."[24]

The discussions of personal characteristics may be beneficial or detrimental to candidates. But this is not the journalistic point. The task of the reporter is to provide the full picture and allow individuals to assess candidate character traits.

Providing that information requires much more than a single interview or perhaps listening to a speech. It's not the sort of material that is likely to be the subject of a news release. The reporter has to take the time to get to know the candidate well and to seek understanding of personal as well as political motivations.

But *Washington Post* Pulitzer Prize winner David Broder, although saying he would like to see more reports on the character of candidates, is concerned about turning loose "a bunch of amateur psychiatrist-journalists." And he urges that such stories be approached from the perspective of the candidate's public life.

"I don't think we have to go around the back door, the bedroom door or the barroom door as a way into that kind of story," he says.[25]

The danger that such character stories may border on gossip does worry journalists. But the sensitive reporter truly interested in serving voters a slice of the candidates' personalities for no motive other than to fill in the complete picture can deal with the problem. This must involve, first, a concentration on known facts rather than speculation. Even trained psychiatrists cannot tell with assurance what motives or thoughts lie deep within a human being. It is quite possible to learn much about a person's character by concentrating on what that person has said and done and on what others say. It's mostly a matter of taking a personal focus with traditional journalistic techniques.

Second, this kind of story must involve very careful use of the language and all the writing skills the reporter possesses. Meaningful character presentations are not really possible unless the writer has the skill to focus the facts more deeply on the personality rather than taking the usual journalistic approach.

Assessing the Impact of Big Bucks

The early 1970s spawned a wave of reform throughout the United States, the aim of which was to make governmental activities more open. Not the least of the results was action making political candidates more accountable for the money they handle during the campaign. Especially from big contributors.

Until 1971, it was almost impossible for reporters to cover campaign finances. Archaic laws applying to them were easily circumvented. Then Congress passed the Federal Election Campaign Act of 1971, and the rules of the game changed. In many instances, so did the score, as reporters flocked to study and report on records federal candidates were required to make available.

That law has been amended several times, but it still serves the same functions: It establishes contribution limits and spending limits, it regulates public financing of presidential campaigns, and, importantly for journalists, it provides for disclosure of all records filed with the Federal Election Commission.

Federal action provided strong impetus for the states to act. According to Herbert E. Alexander, director of the Citizens' Research Foundation and professor of political science at the University of Southern California, from 1972 to 1976, 49 states improved their laws regulating political money. And, by 1979, 17 states had enacted varying forms of public funding.[26] These actions brought many state candidates under the disclosure umbrella, generally through the secretary of state or other election regulatory agency.

Such opening of campaign financial records is important to reporters because it gives them opportunities to assess possible influences upon the governmental process.

"It's important for reporters to be examining the sources of contributions to candidates in their areas. They should be determining how heavily candidates are relying on special-interest groups for their money and whether it's getting to the point where they're relying more on Washington lobbyists and Washington-based political action committees than they are on their own districts," says Steve Dornfeld, Washington reporter for Knight-Ridder newspapers.

Dornfeld points out that before passage of contribution limits, 502 special-interest groups had political action committees, the vehicle through which contri-

Steven Dornfeld of Knight-Ridder Newspapers

(Knight-Ridder photo)

butions are channeled into campaigns. By 1980, that figure had grown in excess of 2,000. Similarly, the amounts of money contributed to campaigns had jumped from $8.5 million in 1972 to $35.2 million in 1978.

This trend is particularly important at the congressional level because candidates are relying more on the special-interest groups for funds, and the relationship can affect how they're voting on legislation or whether they're paying attention to the folks back home or the special-interest groups in Washington.

And that emphasizes the importance of another type of financial story: examination of the relationships between contributions and votes on legislation, especially bills being supported by special-interest groups.

"In the states that have disclosure laws, reporters can do the same thing at the state level," Dornfeld says. "In the years that I covered the Minnesota legislature, I always tried to make such a comparison when there was a bill that obviously was being pushed by a special-interest group. Very often there was a strong correlation between votes in committee and on the floor and the pattern of contributions by that special-interest group."

With the increasing availability of the necessary records, reporters have only internal problems to overcome in their efforts to cover campaign finances. Often they contend with a news organization that does not provide enough time to study properly the thousands of pages of available records. And they have to deal with the complexity of the records themselves.

The latter can only be overcome when reporters are willing to devote time to a careful study of federal and state campaign financing laws to keep abreast of reporting requirements and available information.[27] Probably more than most other journalistic efforts, campaign finances stories come from documents. Dornfeld, for example, estimates that about 95 percent of all his political stories are based on or spurred by information from financial records.

"A lot of the stories," he says, "are just laying out the sources of money and letting people draw their own conclusions. In a heavy labor district, for example, the fact that a particular member of congress draws 50 percent of his or her support from organized labor may not concern people. But if that same member from a heavy labor district was drawing the bulk of the support from, say, the oil companies, people might wonder.

"You're not always talking about something illegal or sinister, but if you lay out the information, people can draw their own conclusions. And it's important to give that information at the time they're able to act on it—when they go to the polls and vote."

The Strategy of Political Strategy

Individuals who discuss journalistic coverage of political campaigns love analogies. They have referred to the political race as being, among others, like a horse race, a football game, and a military operation. Each comparison, in its own way, makes a point, but perhaps it is equally significant that the analogies have two common points with political campaigns which reporters consider part of their responsibilities: the victory or loss at the end and the fact that conduct of each depends to a large degree on preconceived strategy.

The emphasis reporters place on campaign strategy, of course, depends upon individual circumstances: closeness of the race, relative importance of specific actions, significance of the strategic element in the campaign. Strategy should not be the essential point of coverage. One study of a congressional election, for example, found that campaign strategies received more than three times as much attention as political philosophies. Also, the candidates' campaign "moves" or "plays" were 23 percent more likely to be reported than their personal or professional backgrounds.[28]

But that does not mean campaign strategy should be ignored. Citizens need assessments of why campaigns take certain directions as much as they need reports on specific actions. Understanding the kinds of strategies a politician uses helps citizens better anticipate the governing style of that individual. The conclusion may be that the candidate uses all available techniques to move toward specific accomplishments. Or it can suggest the candidate uses the system to avoid responsibility.

Taking the Pulse of the Public

Conducting political surveys is tough. Most political reporters have neither the expertise nor the desire to do it. But, especially in larger news organizations, they often find themselves working with others more capable to gain information on the public's attitude. Perhaps the most significant contribution of what has come to be called precision journalism is that it has opened up another avenue of public communication. It has given citizens another voice and has expanded the opportunities of journalists to broaden the scope of political coverage.

News organizations use surveys for a number of reasons, including marketing and public feedback. But it's around election time that the pollsters appear most prominently on the journalistic scene. They may want to assess the relative strength of candidates in a primary or general election. They may seek information on why an election went a particular way. Or the purpose may be broader:

What are the criteria citizens are using in making their voting choice? What are the issues of greatest importance?

It's a relatively new and exciting brand of journalism, representing the marriage of social science techniques and the more traditional journalistic effort. Perhaps it is true, as many observe, that the veteran political reporter, through intuition and the traditional interview, can produce the desired results. But the public emphasis and the scientific methodology of the survey have increased the legitimacy of information gained. The formal structure, on the surface at least, increases the neutrality of the information and adds to the credibility of resulting stories.

Granted, the term "precision journalism" may be somewhat off the mark. One can find too many examples in which hindsight has proven pollsters wrong. Perhaps there is truth to charges that survey results reduce the momentum of the trailing candidate by discouraging campaign workers and slowing the flow of campaign contributions. Perhaps there is a bandwagon effect in which persons leap to the support of the leader.

And, worse, there are instances in which news organizations overemphasize surveys and give their coverage the flavor of a horse race. Who's ahead? Who's behind? Who's catching up? What are the odds? That's a real temptation because such coverage catches the attention of the citizens. And it feeds the collective ego of the news organization which calls the shots correctly. Media critic Edwin Diamond is correct in his condemnation of coverage which "substitutes counting noses for examining ideas."[29]

But the criticism is no worse for news organization polling efforts than for other aspects of political coverage. Journalistic survey technique may lack maturity. It's certainly not perfect. But it adds two significant elements to campaign coverage which merit considerable emphasis. The addition of a new set of information-gathering techniques, in concert with the more traditional means, has broadened the scope of political reporting. And growth of the use of surveys may represent history's most extensive effort to make news sources of individuals who hold no high offices and have no fancy titles: the voters. And that's what it's all about.

From the Inside Out: The Media Story

From candidates' perspective, the road to political success is paved with publicity. And that means, in the words of Richard Cudahy, that they "must say things and do things that are news." But that's not enough. There's no political point to a good idea unless reporters pick up that idea and give it widespread exposure. Thus, candidates also must "through press releases, personal conversation, the supplying of tapes or whatever may be required make it easy and personally rewarding for even the laziest and most incompetent reporters and correspondents to report the news" which they create.[30]

That's strong stuff. Forget all the fancy definitions of news. Forget all the theory about the democratic process. Much of what candidates do depends upon whether there happens to be a reporter around to see or hear it. They're called "media events." Sure, the goal still is reaching the voter. But the techniques of today are dramatically different from those of yesteryear. In politics more than any other aspect of society, the mass media, especially television, have had a direct impact upon the rules of the game. We're told the presence of the modern media has resulted in changes in the nature of candidates' personalities, the selection process, the way campaigns are run, and the conduct of candidates upon achieving public office.

Back to the traditional definition of news. If the media have had an impact on the way campaigns are run, it would be reasonable to consider that fact as an integral part of campaign coverage. Journalists traditionally have been reluctant to write about themselves. But more news organizations have come around to the idea that their role in political campaigns is too important to ignore.

"The day of the *Boys on the Bus*[31] has passed us," says Knight-Ridder's Steve Dornfeld. "Reporters who spend a lot of their time on the bus with the candidates are not seeing the campaign that 95 percent of their readers or viewers are seeing. They're seeing the campaign as it unfolds on television. I definitely think we should be spending more time covering the media as they cover politics."

And that coverage, as a supplement to the standard reporting of who says what, etc., would necessarily include discussions of the staging of media events, with at least some labeling of the purpose of such activities. It also would include presentations of the campaign as it unfolds in television advertising, which many candidates use as a means of ducking situations in which they must give public answers to difficult questions. And it would include discussions of how citizens seem to react to campaign polls.

Much of this has been done over the years. But not enough. Candidates for president, Congress, governor, state legislature, mayor, or city council are using very sophisticated media techniques. Reporting of those techniques needs to be equally sophisticated. And that, too, will be the task of those who seek to cover American politics professionally.

NOTES

1. J. Anthony Lukas, "Covering the *Real* Politics," *Nieman Reports,* summer 1978, p. 11.
2. "Covering the *Real* Politics," p. 9.
3. Ben H. Bagdikian, "Failure, Frustrations and the Future of Reporting American Politics," *Bagdikian On,* by permission of The Texas Christian University Press, Fort Worth, Texas, 1977, p. 9.
4. "Failure, Frustrations and the Future of Reporting American Politics," p. 12.
5. Nicholas von Hoffman, "Covering Politics: The Economic Connection," *Columbia Journalism Review,* January-February 1975, pp. 25–26.
6. "Failure, Frustrations and the Future of Reporting American Politics," p. 4.

7. See, for example, Dan Nimmo and James E. Combs, *Subliminal Politics* (Englewood Cliffs, N.J.: Prentice Hall, 1980), pp. 158–188. (This chapter provides a provocative assessment of the relationships between journalists and politicians.)
8. Richard D. Cudahy, "Politics and the Press," *Two Perspectives on Politics and the Press,* 1973, pp. 18–19, with permission of the American Institute for Political Communication, c/o Edward M. Glick, Washington, D.C.
9. "Politics and the Press," pp. 19–20.
10. *Subliminal Politics,* p. 184.
11. Meg Greenfield, "Politics and Play-Acting," *Newsweek,* March 10, 1980, p. 108.
12. "Failure, Frustrations and the Future of Reporting American Politics," p. 3.
13. Edwin Diamond, "The New Campaign Journalism," *Columbia Journalism Review,* March-April 1976, p. 11.
14. Jeff Greenfield, "Campaign Reporting: Advice from a 'Double Agent,'" *Columbia Journalism Review,* July-August 1975, p. 37.
15. "Politics and the Press," p. 1.
16. Mary Ellen Leary, "California 1974: The Browning of Campaign Coverage," *Columbia Journalism Review,* July-August 1976, p. 18.
17. Joe McGinniss, *The Selling of a President 1968* (New York: Trident Press, 1969).
18. John P. Robinson, "The Press and the Voter," *Annals of the American Academy of Political and Social Science,* September 1976, p. 103.
19. Jane Levere, "Reporters Defend Press' Election News Play," *Editor & Publisher,* November 20, 1976, p. 15.
20. "Failure, Frustrations and the Future of Reporting American Politics," p. 7.
21. David E. RePass, "The Audience for Political Reporting," *Columbia Journalism Monograph No. 2* (New York: Graduate School of Journalism, Columbia University, 1976), pp. 9–10.
22. Alvin P. Sanoff, "The Pack Is Back on the Campaign Trail," *The Quill,* February 1976, p. 28.
23. "Politics and Play-Acting," p. 108.
24. Meg Greenfield, "Character Does Matter," *Newsweek,* April 7, 1980, p. 100.
25. Michael Mayhan, "Will the 'Boys' Board the Bus in '76?," *The Quill,* December 1975, p. 21.
26. Herbert E. Alexander, "Election Reform and National Politics," Smithsonian Institution Lecture, April 23, 1980.
27. At the federal level, for example, reporters should be well acquainted with three Federal Election Commission publications: *Campaign Guide for Congressional Candidates and Their Committees; Federal Election Commission Annual Report;* and *Federal Election Campaign Laws.* Similar background materials often are available in some states, usually through the office of the secretary of state.
28. "Political Campaigns and the News Media," *Society,* July-August 1976, p. 7.
29. "The New Campaign Journalism," p. 14.
30. "Politics and the Press," p. 3.
31. Dornfeld's reference is to Timothy Crouse's excellent book, *The Boys on the Bus,* in which he analyzes the activities and problems of the campaign press corps (New York: Ballantine Books, 1973).

Chapter 12

EDUCATION MIRRORS THE COMMUNITY

No social institution approximates the day-to-day impact of education upon citizens. Even those who would define themselves as nonpolitical or nonreligious cannot use the same label with regard to education. Public attitudes fluctuate, and the early 1980s represents a period of general disillusionment. And yet, in the eyes of Fred M. Hechinger of the *New York Times,* even this does not tarnish the deeper attitudes about education.

"The public may veer this way and that under momentary political or financial pressures," he says. "But the people viewed as individuals—as parents or as children—have not really changed their basic view of school and college. In selfishly reactionary moments (and we are living through one such period now) they may ... make some headway with the case against college for those other children. But there is no change in the people's perception of education's crucial role in the lives of their own children and grandchildren."[1]

It is for these reasons that, since colonial days, education has remained a focus of American journalism. Even if public attitudes have fluctuated, reporters have consistently chronicled the role of schools as a social and personal force. In modern times, education reporting gained impetus from three happenings which propelled the nation's centers of learning to the front of public consciousness.

The 1954 U.S. Supreme Court decision in *Brown* v. *Topeka Board of Education* began the long string of school desegregation events which may represent the top news story of the century. When the Russians marked human entry into the space age with the launching of Sputnik I in 1957, American education went into a frenzy of scientific emphasis in an effort to overcome the seeming technological gap between the two countries. And when college campuses erupted with violence and social uproar in the late 1960s and early 1970s, the nation again turned its collective eye toward educational institutions.

It may be that journalistic coverage in all three cases has contributed to the ups and downs of public attitude. There is no question that reporters covered education in numbers. Their coverage was extensive, and it reflected and perhaps magnified feelings which stimulated and resulted from these important stories of American history.

That twenty-year period represented perhaps the high point of journalism's dependence on the education reporter. However, Hechinger points out, the excitement has gone out of the education story. He says the calm after the flamboyant 1960s has persuaded too many news organizations that education deserves little space or time. And this fact has tended to widen the gap between educators and the public they serve.

"And yet, I am firmly convinced that those who write education off as a matter of low public priority are dead wrong," he says. "The politicians who overlook education as an issue and the editors and radio/TV programmers who think the public has turned away from education are ignorant of some of the strongest currents that have affected American society and have not lost their force today."[2]

Journalistic emphasis or lack of emphasis on education seems to result from confusion over the seeming contradiction between public and personal attitudes about schools and their programs. If education as a social institution is a source of distrust and therefore lack of interest in the early 1980s, the specific impact of a school on a young person remains a subject of intense concern to parents. And, as much as anything, this may reflect upon the kind of coverage being provided by news organizations.

These are days in which all forms of social bigness are suspect. An institutional approach to journalistic coverage of education, concentrating on national policies and governmental actions, will not strike home. A personal approach emphasizing individual circumstances in local situations, on the other hand, will not be ignored by those human beings whose lives are most directly affected.

CRITICISM OF EDUCATION REPORTING

Complaints follow journalism. And education reporters get their share, perhaps more than their share, because they are dealing with subject matter everyone knows something about. Validity of the criticism depends upon the situation. Much of it is valid; some is patently unfair. But its persistence must provide at least some clues to education reporters about what is expected of them by the public and by the educators with whom they work.

The manner in which reporters react to specific criticism depends upon their news judgment and upon their sense of fair play. In no way can they go as far as most educators would like and become propaganda arms of the system. But, at the same time, they must remember that they, like all reporters, bear the burden of providing complete and representative coverage, whether that coverage has positive or negative impact. Within that context, then, reaction to criticism becomes an if-the-shoe-fits-wear-it proposition. But recognition of at least three general themes of criticism should help provide the background to the total efforts of education reporters.

"Too Much Education Reporting Is Dull"

In response to the suggestion that education reporting is boring, reporters say it's because too much education is dull and because educators themselves are seldom flamboyant. That's valid sometimes, but it's doubtful that educators have a monopoly on dullness. Reporters can't pass the buck on this one. It's not the responsibility of educators to be interesting. It is the responsibility of reporters to present significant material—whatever its dullness quotient—in as meaningful and interesting a way as possible.

The *Oakland Press* in Pontiac, Michigan, in a policy booklet for its staffers, takes note of this responsibility and identifies one major way it—and other news organizations—can be dull in education coverage.

"We can do it by writing, not about the schools, which interest him [the reader] very much, but about the school board, which likely interests him not at all. And we have done this. Just as we have assumed that the township board is the township, we have assumed that school news is whatever—and only what—turns up on the school board agenda.

"As an example of how board-oriented we are, consider our treatment of the nonpublic school. It does not have a board that holds formal public meetings every week or two, and so we ignore the school almost entirely. We define news to mean that which official bodies do in meetings, and when we do that, we wander away from our reader."[3]

Coverage of the school board is important, but it is not an end in itself. Schools are teachers, young people, and programs—not policies, resolutions, formal discussions, and debates. Maintaining that perspective provides automatic human interest to news coverage without ignoring the value of official decisions.

Likewise, such a perspective will help overcome what is a fairly routine relative sameness to education coverage across time and news media. Too much education coverage for years has involved the same subjects, used the same approaches, and often reached the same conclusions. Such a lack of imagination, which results in established patterns of coverage, is not likely to whet the citizen's appetite for education news. It's true that school programs run in cycles. Certain events occur regularly every year. The need for annual "back-to-school" coverage, to be read or seen by the same audience, places a burden upon the news media to develop fresh and meaningful ways of highlighting this important part of the school year.

But reporters also must look wider and dig deeper to discover the meaningful stories that have not received coverage over the years. Very few news organizations can boast of having done a thorough job of explaining what citizens need to know about curriculum development and meaning. This may be because reporters don't understand curriculum or because they define curriculum as inevitably dull or because they don't have time to uncover these stories. Whatever the reason, the result has been the virtual ignoring of the mission of education and that part of the story which has most direct impact upon the people involved.

"Education Reporting Overemphasizes Controversy"

A second criticism, that education reporting dwells on conflict, sounds like a contradiction. How can education reporting be both dull and overemphasize controversy? The answer is that education reporting too often is a matter of extremes. Noncontroversial, day-by-day coverage often is routine and not given prominent play. Much of it may be very positive, and there may be a lot of it. But it's hardly conspicuous or attention grabbing.

When controversy erupts—and it's inevitable given the political nature and personal feelings involved in education—the stories move to the front. Parental complaints about textbooks, official efforts to reduce extracurricular activities for financial reasons, complaints that Johnny or Jane can't read, concern over violence in schools—these are the stories which get widespread attention. And, regretably, their very polemic nature make them easier to write in an arresting manner.[4]

So, does education reporting emphasize the controversial? In some cases, no, even though it looks that way, especially to sensitive educators in the midst of those controversies. In other cases, yes, when reporters find a competitive story which gives them the opportunity to move to page one or to the top of the newscast.

But such explanations don't really provide solutions. It's big news when something goes wrong in a social institution as important as education. It's time-honored that citizens must know of disagreements, mistakes, and problems. To what degree does this very natural journalistic effort become overemphasis? There are, of course, several answers. Educators—especially those with administrative responsibilities—will be quick to draw the line. Journalists will stress flexibility within an overall context of balanced coverage.

And therein lies part of an answer: traditional journalistic technique. The news organization satisfied that it gives citizens the bigger picture of school life and accomplishments over time will simply say "not so" when such charges arise. The reporter whose efforts include board coverage, features, trend analysis, and the day-to-day grind of educational activity can be comfortable in the face of complaints. Coverage of negative stories is justifiable when school officials have ample opportunity to present their side.

This will not stop the flow of complaints. It shouldn't. But it will assure reporters and editors a means of knowing they have done their jobs. And that's important.

"Education Reporters Are Not Aggressive"

Perhaps the most damning of all is the criticism that education reporters often do not demonstrate the aggressive drive of their counterparts in other specialties. At the extreme, this raises the specter of the very antithesis of good journalism: proeducation, pliable, overly accepting, nonquestioning, unimaginative. Few critics intend such an extreme, and most admit to countless exceptions, but the comments persist.

To the degree that the charge contains truth, it is the result of three interwoven factors which say something about the education reporters themselves and about their news organizations.

First, in the face of many years of massive public support for education and the fact that news organizations generally want to be supportive of the needs of schools, education journalism probably has been slower to assume the adversarial stance. It's not an absolute requirement that investigative reporting be negative, but it usually is. And, in general, it has been more difficult for reporters to be critical of individuals whose function is to help children prepare for their lives. There's a big difference between public attitudes about politicians, for example, and public attitudes about educators.

Second, education is much more complex than the concept of "covering the schools" would indicate. Understanding it involves psychological theory as well as familiarity with a wide range of specific subject matter and the processes of political interaction. While many reporters have taken political science courses, for example, few will have set foot in an education class. Thus, most reporters who move into the education specialty face a rather massive task of developing the background expertise in the field. It can be learned on the job, but few ever have the time or the opportunity to do it properly.

Third, many editors, as a result of their own attitudes about education reporting, have affected the long-range value of their organization's coverage. Perhaps there are signs that these attitudes are changing, but all too frequently editors have placed low priority on education coverage. And this has been reflected in their assignments.

"It's generally been viewed in most papers as a place to put beginners," says Gene Maeroff of the *New York Times.* "It's seen by the editors and by the reporters themselves merely as a steppingstone. There hasn't been enough concern with getting very good, experienced reporters into this beat—people with an interest in the subject, who really want to cover it and who want to stay with it

Gene Maeroff of the *New York Times*

(*New York Times* photo)

for a number of years. If that attitude could be changed, it would be a very important step toward improving education coverage generally."

IT REQUIRES BACKGROUND, EXPERIENCE, DESIRE

The requirements for providing comprehensive education coverage are the same as for any other journalistic specialty. The news organization must be committed to providing a setting in which reporters may develop and effectively use understanding of educational dynamics. The background expertise may come, in part, from classroom training, but it's better in coordination with general reporting experience.

Further, any person moving into education reporting must feel an obligation to read and study extensively, with particular concentration on law, political science, the budget process, and education methodology. In many ways, the requirement of keeping abreast of the field is more stringent for reporters than for the educators themselves. The reporter seldom has the luxury of concentrating on a single education specialty; rather, he or she must be prepared to deal with a broad spectrum of education-related information.

For example, Steve Adams of the Dayton, Ohio, *Journal Herald* stresses the value of government reporting experience for the education reporter. He says once a reporter has covered a basic unit of government—whether it be township trustees, city council, county commission, or state agencies—that person can better understand how an elected body works with an administrative staff.

And most education reporters list education finances as the most difficult story with which they must cope regularly. An understanding of the budgetary process, accounting principles, and financial terminology is necessary, whether it's from formal training or from on-the-job dealings with school financial officers.

Also useful is regular reading of publications which pay particular attention to educational trends. A must on the list of any reporter concerned with higher education would be the *Chronicle of Higher Education,* a weekly tabloid newspaper devoted to tracking trends on college and university campuses. *Phi Delta*

Steve Adams of the Dayton *Journal Herald*

(*Journal Herald* photo)

Kappan is often mentioned as an excellent source of elementary and secondary school information. The *NEA Journal,* published by the National Education Association, provides general information from the perspective of the nation's largest professional organization.

Reporters also attempt to read newspapers and magazines which regularly provide education material, particularly the *New York Times,* the *Los Angeles Times,* and the three national newsmagazines. This diet is supplemented further with local newspapers, student newspapers, and newsletters published by professional education associations.

As in all of journalism, the purpose of reading education materials and talking with educators is not always to gain information for a specific story. At times, a national story may have local application. Or the reporter may gain the name of a new source. But the real point is development of a general expertise which provides substance to any reporter's overall coverage of education. Without such background, the reporter loses a valuable weapon in the constant fight to maintain control of coverage.

A STRUCTURAL APPROACH TO EDUCATION SOURCES

It was a rather exaggerated episode of television's Lou Grant. Book burning evolved into television set burning. Scissors cut into library books. Censorship reached school textbooks. In an early part of the show, a teacher who eventually lost her job because she refused to discontinue use of a banned book was confronted by the principal and told, "Marilyn, you're really forcing my hand. The board made the decision. I'm to enforce the policy. If you persist in this, you'll have only yourself to blame for how it turns out."

Educators believe in such delegation of authority, and the organization of most school systems proves it. It is a precise hierarchy based on categorical job descriptions which tightly constrict the functions of everyone in the system. These boundaries are carefully maintained, especially in dealings with reporters. It is not uncommon that deliberate efforts are made to box reporters into using a limited number of sources at the top of the structure. Educators seem to be more successful at that than other government officials.

The most generally accessible person in any school system usually is the superintendent at the top of the heap. Accessibility often declines dramatically as one moves down the hierarchy.

It's unfair to generalize, of course, but reporters seem to agree that even those at the top often are hesitant at best in their dealings with the news media. Even when seeking to be cooperative, the average educator may be cautious in answering direct questions. Perhaps it represents an extreme, but it is very noticeable, especially to journalists, when a major education journal advises new school board members when facing television cameras and microphones to "smile and spew forth a few sweet nothings." The author assures the new board members that they will develop a style for dealing with reporters, but "until then, have a set of remarks at hand that will ensure your elusiveness and unpenetrability."[5]

Perhaps the advice (which later included a circumstance in which the author advocated lying to reporters) may be discounted as one which most educators would ignore. What may be most instructive, however, is that the *American School Board Journal* was willing to run the article.

The point is not that educators consistently seek to deceive reporters or that they deliberately withhold information or seek to cover up questionable activities. Most educators are honest, dedicated people and probably are less self-serving in what they say and do than many other categories of public officials. But, as a group, they are difficult for reporters. The jargon they use to communicate with each other is natural to them, but a curse to journalists. Their use of qualified remarks and complex philosophical explanations is not for a general audience. Their desire to see only good news spread before the public seems to have greater intensity than that of other news sources. And they sincerely believe what they often tell reporters: "If you print that, you'll hurt the schools and the kids."

But such generalizations may not be fair. Some educators are more gregarious and naturally more open. Some have better understanding of journalism and thus less fear about dealing directly with journalists. Some simply believe more strongly in the value of publicity and are willing to take their chances that the good will outweigh the bad. Some have had bad experiences and thus have resolved to avoid situations in which they may be burned. Some have developed a trusting and cooperative relationship with journalists.

The subject matter often makes the difference. It's not uncommon that the greater the controversy, the greater the reluctance. And it makes a difference whether the questioning is about programs or policy. Educators like to talk about programs, but they reserve discussions of policy matters for the very few. That's hierarchy again.

"They're easy to talk to as long as you don't talk policy," says Margo Pope of the *Florida Times-Union* in Jacksonville. "When you start talking policy, no one wants to talk. They want you to go to the board chairman and the superintendent. The board sets the policy, and the superintendent administers it. And if he tells an assistant superintendent, 'I want the school closed every night,' even though it's supposed to be a community school which is open from 8 in the

Margo Pope of the *Florida Times-Union*

(*Florida Times-Union* photo by Bob Donaldson)

morning until 11 at night, that assistant has to do it. And that's when you come in and really have to have some experience in dealing with people."

And, as in all of journalism, dealing with educators means deliberate efforts to cultivate them as sources: spending time with them in discussions which may not produce immediate stories, getting to know them and demonstrating interest in their jobs and their lives, doing homework so that questions asked will reflect both knowledge and interest. This kind of investment of time will reap a considerable return when the reporter must ask about problems or must call at night for a quick response on a breaking story.

When she became an education reporter for the *Chicago Tribune,* Meg O'Conner was worried about developing sources, especially the kind she could deal with on a confidential basis. Her assumption was that such a relationship grew only from manipulation, and she had little confidence in her ability to accomplish that.

"I proceeded not to do anything except just relate to people as you relate to people, to laugh and joke with them, have lunch with them because there's a break in the meeting, just normal interaction," she says. "All of a sudden, I discovered that all these people wanted to tell me everything. That was a wonderful thing to find out—that all you have to do is just talk to people. You don't have to meet them in dark alleys and try to persuade them to spill their guts. If they know you, if they trust you, they want to talk."

Meg O'Connor of the *Chicago Tribune*

(*Chicago Tribune* photo)

But the basis upon which they want to talk and subjects on which they are willing to make public comments may depend upon their place in the education bureaucracy. The reporter who understands the structure of education and knows the functions of persons within it will not waste time questioning the wrong official and will gain stronger, more precise information.

The First Authority: State Government

In spite of the tradition of local control, education is a state function. The U.S. Constitution makes no direct reference to education, and most state constitutions stipulate establishment and maintenance of a system of free public schools. Even though local officials are permitted to make most specific operational decisions at home, the states establish the rules of the game. And reporters covering education locally will find it necessary to be in touch with political and/or educational leaders in the state capital.

That means, first, the governor and state legislators. The legislature passes the laws which set educational standards and, perhaps even more important, rules on the budget which determines how much money will be available. The governor proposes that budget, is a strong political force in how much emphasis education will receive, and often appoints the state board of education which supervises and regulates local programs.

All states have a supervisory body for education, with the most frequent organization being an appointed lay group which names the state superintendent of schools (or public instruction). In some instances, the board or superintendent or both may be elected. Reporters also will have to deal with a state department of education, which may have thousands of employees, as the professional complement to the superintendent and the board.

Major functions of board members are to establish, within legal and constitutional boundaries, standards of instruction and program development; provide broad leadership and direction to their counterparts on the local level; regulate when necessary; and provide educational resources through planning, research, and evaluation. For the most part, it is expected that local superintendents and boards will run their systems in compliance with state requirements without involvement of state or federal officials. And the system, over the years, has tended to work that way.

But in many areas of the country that process has been changing. The state and, to some degree, the federal government are assuming more and more authority in how local programs are run. There are several reasons for this, but it's mostly a financial matter. As school programs have grown, local financial resources for education (principally property taxes) have proven inadequate. Thus, local officials have been forced to turn to state and national governments for financial assistance. And that sort of situation, over time, is bound to have impact on the decision-making process. Indeed, it has.

It is most likely that education reporters in the coming years will find that covering local school programs involves greater attention to state government. Local control is not a thing of the past, but local officials now have much more active partners in the decisions they make about neighborhood schools. It's going to be more necessary that reporters trace those strings from the local board to the state capital or Washington, D.C.

Board of Education: Lay Control

At the top of the local hierarchy is the board of education, and it is here that reporters devote a high percentage of their attention. This is for two reasons, one good and one not so good. First, board members, legally agents of the state, are responsible for directing the local program within state law. Reporters must carefully follow decisions because they represent directions local schools will take. Second, boards, for the most part, operate as a group and thus have very convenient meetings which usually are subject to open meeting laws and make it easy for reporters to get needed information.

In some states, board members are elected, usually on a nonpartisan basis. In other states, they are appointed, often by the mayor with council approval. But in either event, their function is to set the educational policy of the school system and thus serve the fundamental American concept that schools should be locally controlled.

The resulting political activities must capture the attention of journalists. Local control means citizens should be made aware of the degree to which the board is representing their educational interests. And it means citizens must have information to evaluate a board's internal management of the school system. Since schools are such an essential part of any community, educational decisions often have broad repercussions.

More and more, the society, through court decisions, seems to expect the schools to serve as the focal point of social change. In desegrating schools, for example, boards of education have been forced to serve as the most visible— sometimes the only—aspect of efforts to cope with a serious social dilemma.

Thus, reporters will be on hand as boards select the system's administrative leadership, allocate its financial resources, plan school construction programs, hire teachers, establish attendance areas, determine which federally funded programs to implement, and seek to abide by court decisions. Reporters will inform citizens not only of the decisions made but also the process and considerations involved.

Much of this information will be gained from meetings, although it always will be supplemented by interviews with board members and other school officials. This means that education reporters occasionally may have to face traditional battles against executive (closed) sessions to ensure that the process remains open to the public eye.[6] It means they must understand what often is very complex educational and legal material.

And it means they must fully comprehend the power structure of a board and school system. Legally, all board members are equal. But that's legal fiction. As is usually the case, practical realities are that some—because of the force of their personalities, their place in the community, or their longevity on the board—have greater influence than others. Board members also may form coalitions representing educational philosophies, desire to gain political power, or efforts to represent specific community groups.

The relationship between members and superintendents is an essential part of any analysis of school board politics. While board members hold legal authority and technically cannot delegate that authority to anyone, many serve as little more than rubber stamps for a forceful administrator. In almost all cases, the superintendent recommends and the board determines. But the process is distorted when a superintendent's recommendations are accepted automatically. Such a circumstance, of course, will dictate to reporters that they spend more time in conversation with the administrator and then rather matter-of-factly report the board's official decisions.

But even a board which maintains its legal authority does not function in a social or political vacuum. Members are subject to countless pressures from individuals and groups within and without the school system. American society has become increasingly pluralistic, and this is reflected by those who desire to influence directions a school system takes. A survey commissioned by the National Education Association in 1978 determined that only 58 percent of those citizens questioned expressed confidence in school boards.[7] And the more people become disillusioned with their education system, the more likely they are to attempt to bring changes to that system.

Therefore, reporters will have to monitor internal efforts of such teachers' organizations as the National Education Association and the American Federation of Teachers. They also will give attention to numerous external groups which include educational change as part of their reason for existence. Among others, this would include minority, ethnic, and women's groups; taxpayer organizations; broad-based community groups; and citizens who form special organizations for specific curricular or other educational purposes.

The Professional Administrators

When reporters are after specific information about school programs and problems, they must deal primarily with those whose day-to-day duties are to run those programs. Most school districts—even the smallest ones—have a central office which is responsible for dotting the *i*'s and crossing the *t*'s of school board policy. They implement. And no reporter who wants more than generalities can afford to ignore them.

In a sense, there are two kinds of school system administrators: generalists whose responsibilities are system-wide and specialists who deal with more narrow components of the program. It is fair to say that the lower one moves on the system hierarchy, the more likely one is to deal with specialists whose major journalistic value grows from their expertise in specific types of educational activity.

Superintendents, for example, must be generalists. The larger the school system, the more general their knowledge is likely to be. They fit the pieces of the system puzzle into place. Like the school board, they provide direction and can be expected to have broad understanding, if not specific knowledge, about given programs or schools within the system. In contrast, directors of curriculum are valuable as sources only when reporters are after that kind of information. That sounds simple enough, but is a principle too many reporters ignore by devoting the bulk of their attention to the top of the educational hierarchy.

Reporters need large numbers of administrative sources, first, because of the differing levels of expertise, and second, because of the extreme sensitivity to publicity characteristic of many educators. They need individual experts to give depth to their coverage, and they need trusted alternative sources when traditional paths to information are blocked. This means conscious cultivation of sources at three levels of the administrative organization.

Without question, *the superintendent* will be the major source of administrative information. As chief executive officer, he or she is in charge, and it's only natural that reporters maintain constant contact. If the board of education is close to a major decision, comments from the superintendent may influence that decision. If a citizens' group is complaining about education quality or about an individual program, the superintendent must be first to answer the questions. If staff specialists are working on a new program, their action comes only on the superintendent's direction, and the reasons for that direction should be made public.

But superintendents do more than maintain the internal organization and provide educational direction. Theirs is a political job as much as it is educational. Local school systems gain their financial support through public action. The success of any school system depends upon public support. And this is a major responsibility to which superintendents devote large amounts of time.

How the effort is structured depends on the style of the superintendent. It may be through numerous public appearances before citizens' groups, parents, and local government bodies. It may involve remaining constantly in the public eye and developing personal trust or even charisma. Or it may be sought through quiet circulation and attempts to cultivate lay leadership. There are limitations, but a superintendent can be less conspicuous if the school system is publicly supported by respected individuals in the community.

Whatever a superintendent's style, reporters will watch the effort to maintain educational support. The public component of that effort is easy to follow, and journalists simply make day-to-day decisions about whether to report on a specific speech or panel discussion. Quiet leadership is more difficult to follow, but it is a story which requires the effort.

A superintendent's leadership, internally and externally, is extended by a central staff which may include several *assistant superintendents.* Depending on local organization, some of these assistants may have general functions and therefore do some of the superintendent's legwork, or they may have responsibilities for specific components of the operation, such as assistant superintendent for pupil personnel services, instruction, or business. Reporters, naturally, will at times work with these individuals, but the nature of their positions is such that they often are reluctant to speak on the record. Reporters seeking information will be told, "You'd better see the superintendent about that" or "Here's the information, but be sure to talk with the superintendent before you publish it."

At times, the assistants or the superintendent may refer reporters to *staff specialists* who direct specific parts of the school system's program. Given varying titles—director, supervisor, or consultant—these individuals usually are trained professionals in an educational program. As such, they advise the board and the superintendent on the areas of their expertise and supervise programs in the schools.

The number of such specialists available to school administrators and reporters will vary according to school district size, but among them could be directors of elementary education; secondary education; curriculum; special education; adult education; instructional materials; audiovisual education; publications and information; planning; research; evaluation; finance; buildings and grounds; health services; cafeteria services; transportation; elementary, music, art, or physical education supervisors; or mathematics, science, and foreign language consultants.[8]

It's difficult, especially when dealing with a large school system, for reporters to maintain frequent contact with the number of persons who serve as staff specialists. It's not necessary to see them as frequently as board members or the superintendent. But special efforts should be made to become acquainted with them so that, when a need arises, both the reporter and the source will be on familiar ground and know how to deal with one another.

Another source of assistance will be the school system's office responsible for *public relations* or *public information.* Pick up any education journal and browse through it. Chances are you'll find an article titled something like "Competencies and Skills for an Effective School Public Relations Program"[9] or "Blast Your Critics with Education's Good News."[10] Educators are interested in good public relations, and school systems typically devote considerable attention to gaining favorable publicity about their activities and programs. Someone in the system will have that responsibility even if there is no formal office devoted to the cause.

Dealing with school public relations personnel is like dealing with them in business or government. They will produce news releases and provide information, but their chief journalistic value is in suggesting story ideas and making school system personnel available to reporters. They can provide factual information and background material, but should seldom be depended upon as the sole source.

The Action Is in the Schools

Sports reporters go to the ballpark. Government reporters go to city hall. Court reporters go to the courthouse. How strange it is that many education reporters spend so little time in schools. "Don't have time," they say, and that's true as long as news organizations cling to the idea that education can be covered at board meetings and from the superintendent's office. But education is schools. That's where the action is, and that's where many of the most important stories are. Not only during times of crisis, but daily.

It's in the schools that programs succeed and fail. It's in the schools that thousands of feature stories—not just the "cutesys," but real, meaningful human drama—literally walk the halls. It's in the schools that value is gained or lost from the millions of dollars invested annually in education. And it's in the schools that some of the very best sources of information sit unnoticed by reporters who pass through those doors infrequently. Principals, teachers, and the students themselves may know more about a school system's education program than anyone in the central office or board room. It may not always be easy to get access to them, but there certainly is no hope until they're approached.

Most *principals* are conscientious and nice people. Many are good administrators. Some are excellent educators. But as a group they have perhaps the worst reputation for cooperation with reporters in any school system, even among their colleagues. Witness, for example, the attitude of Robert P. Hilldrup of the Richmond, Virginia, public schools as he advises school PR directors on how to deal with school violence:

"Be prepared for some empty answers when working with principals. Ask them what they'd do if a student got knifed. Don't be surprised if the answer deals solely with calling an ambulance, ignoring the news media and public response aspect entirely. Remember, a serious school incident can't be covered up in today's climate. The sooner administrators, principals particularly, understand this, the more receptive they will be to proper planning and the easier it will be for you to deal with disaster when it comes."[11]

This lack of sensitivity to the need for informing the public probably is the result of some combination of three separate explanations. One, expressed by Thomas Baultmann, himself a principal in Jefferson City, Missouri, is that "too many teachers and principals work on the ludicrous premise that their job is to simply stay in the building and 'teach' the children."[12]

Also true is that in too many situations principals are not expected by those with whom they work to be up front in public situations. Principals should not rock the boat. Surveys of superintendents and teachers demonstrate this attitude, and one leading textbook concluded from one piece of research: "One gets the feeling from these data that superintendents and teachers cherish principals who 'keep the lid on,' who do not have too many 'fool notions,' and who keep things running smoothly."[13]

And perhaps a third component is that principals have been ignored by reporters so universally that few have had the opportunity to develop journalistic understanding. They fear what they don't understand, especially when it is their perception that stepping out of line could cost them their jobs.

The answer to the dilemma is easy to state and difficult to accomplish. Principals have the same relationships within their schools as superintendents have within the system. They are generalists responsible for direction and coordination of the staff toward established goals. Thus, they have potentially great journalistic value. For the reporter, that means long-term cultivation, frequent contact, coverage of successes as well as failures. Reporters must not allow principals' reluctance to overcome determined efforts to develop the kind of trusting relationship which leads to more complete coverage.

And the same logic applies to *teachers*. That relationship may be hampered if their immediate superior is the principal who is perceived as reluctant or if the teachers have direct orders to be silent. In some instances, reporters must get the permission of the superintendent and/or the principal to interview teachers.

But the flip side of the teacher situation is courage gained from peer support in the form of the increasing openness of various teachers' organizations. Especially on certain issues, such as teachers' salaries and working conditions, teachers —most likely younger ones who have not developed overly protective attitudes about their schools or the system—are more inclined to make statements for publication. This can make good copy and can help balance out what too often is top heavy coverage.

Aside from controversy, teachers represent potentially the most valuable resources for reporters interested in discussing a school program or curriculum or even a successful graduate. Only teachers are in the classroom regularly. They're the first to know if the system has problems. They know more about young people than many parents. Whatever the burden, they shoulder it; whatever the success, they share it.

What about those young people, the *students* themselves? Are they too inexperienced to speak on something as serious as their education? The answer is no, not if they are given the right kind of opportunity. Reporters, of course, must be cautious with statements made by young people, especially those at the elementary level. Questions must be asked carefully, and answers must be evaluated. But, like teachers, students are very close to education, and often their perspective is a significant addition to a news story.

Take, for example, a story run in the *Florida Times-Union* of Jacksonville. The school board had decided to put the question of air conditioning of schools before the public in a referendum. The administration compiled information packets and brochures. Representatives made television appearances to gain support for the vote.

"It would have been very easy to cover that situation by just using information provided by the administration," says reporter Margo Pope. "But the better stories are the ones which result when you go out into the schools and you ask the kids in the middle of May when it's 82 degrees and the air isn't moving in the classroom how they feel about school that day. Our job is not necessarily to support school board requests, but the kids will tell you, and they did, when air conditioning or anything else is needed."

In addition, opportunities for features stories about students are great for the reporter who spends time in the schools. Some of these, of course, will be of limited substance. Their chief value will grow from humor or their quality of "kids say and do the darnedest things." There's a need for that kind of story. But that's not all. Young people represent a microcosm of the community at large. They have successes and failures. They struggle to overcome problems. They make tough decisions. They react in very honest ways to their environment. Both the strengths and weaknesses of society will be reflected in the school hallways, and reporters can capture those reflections.

There is, of course, a potential access problem for reporters who want to talk with students. Superintendents, principals, and teachers naturally are wary of anything which may disrupt the flow of school activities. They also are nervous about what young people will say to a reporter. But, surely, sensitive journalists and educators can overcome such concerns.

It is possible for the determined journalist to talk with young people (and teachers) outside the school, and there are occasions when that is the best course of action. But, unless there are reasons for going outside the school, the same atmosphere of understanding and trust which applies across the journalistic spectrum should be developed with school officials. Interviews, even with cameras and microphones, can be organized in a manner that will not disrupt a school program. And, while school officials can in no way be granted control over the content of the interviews, their fears can be reduced by the understanding reporter whose approach to any story—positive or negative—is honest, accurate, and well balanced.

CAMPUS SOURCES TEND TO BE MORE OPEN

Problems faced by reporters of getting information in elementary and secondary schools are duplicated on college and university campuses, although they usually are not as severe. The very nature of higher education is that academic debate is encouraged or at least tolerated. And this means campus administrators and faculty are more accustomed to answering questions, presenting points of view, and, when necessary, dealing with dissent.

"There's more of a mutual respect when you get into higher education," says Victor Volland of the *St. Louis Post-Dispatch,* "and, consequently, there's a little more openness. Faculty members talk much more freely than those in high school or grade school. But, still, when you are dealing with administrative officials, they can be guarded, at least on the record."

Victor Volland of the *St. Louis Post-Dispatch*

(*St. Louis Post Dispatch* photo)

One helpful characteristic of college faculty members is that, even when at odds, they're more likely to respect each other's viewpoints and often will lead reporters to individuals with whom they disagree. And this openness on the part of faculty members—perhaps tenured and thus more secure in their positions— is a circumstance which reporters such as Don Speich of the *Los Angeles Times* use to gain insight into possible campus stories.

Don Speich of the *Los Angeles Times*

(*Los Angeles Times* photo)

Especially when he is on a relatively unfamiliar campus, Speich seeks first to determine which faculty members are in positions of power. Often these are leaders of such organizations as an academic senate or a faculty union. Talks with these persons may help him gain an understanding of issues on the campus.

"After finding out what the issues are and getting a reasonable knowledge of the faculty viewpoint, I talk to the president about them," he says. "Otherwise, all you're going to find out is that 'Things are reasonably well, although they could be better.' That'll be it. It's not that they're being devious, but if you don't know the questions to ask, an administrator's not going to volunteer information that might be harmful."

College and university presidents, on the other hand, are more likely than their counterparts at other levels to put themselves into positions in which they must deal with reporters. They may hold formal news conferences or informal briefing sessions. They may make more effective use of public relations offices in informing reporters of possible news stories and in providing background information. And they may more readily submit to one-on-one interviews.

This is not to imply that they always greet reporters with open arms. They can be as mum as they can be open. It's partly a matter of individual personality and administrative style. It's partly a matter of their position. Vice presidents, for example, often are less than open because of fear of jeopardizing their positions. As in government and corporate structure, the person at the top is more likely to speak candidly. Or, a reporter may assume that if the person at the top will not speak candidly, it's not likely any other loyal administrator will.

Like faculty members, college students also represent an alternative source or a means of gaining fresh perspective. Perhaps the best are individuals involved in student governing bodies, although many reporters will make the campus newspaper their first stop. The goal is to find students who have a campus-wide perspective and who may reasonably be assumed to be informed. Often, higher education reporters will make it a practice to read student newspapers to gain story and source ideas.

THEY'LL PUT IT IN WRITING

Educators at all levels love to write reports and memos. Some seem to believe that an explanation is not valid until it's in writing. The same applies to requests. This can be helpful to the reporter. Invariably, a reporter seeking information for a story will walk out of a superintendent's office with an armload of written material, some of which may be extremely valuable as background, verification, or quotation. Many good stories, in fact, are tucked away in file cabinets awaiting discovery.

But the reporter dealing with such reports—or their counterparts produced by public or corporate officials—must be cautious. Each of those reports represents a potentially incomplete, misleading, or even inaccurate news story. The problems are not unique to the written word. The same dangers exist in the normal interview. But there's something about a piece of writing which grants it an almost automatic validity and may lull the reader into nonthinking acceptance.

Specifically, reporters must cope with three major problems: tendency for reports to be written in educational jargon; ease with which pertinent points may be obscured; and complexity of the psychological, statistical, or specialized subject matter which often is the subject of such reports.

California school teacher Mary H. Thompson has complained that the language of educators is more than a cause of misunderstanding. It is, rather, a cause of alienation which drives wedges between parents and educators and between students and their teachers. She suggests that this alienation is enhanced when educators seek a sense of superiority through use of such words as *underachiever, overachiever, severe normal violator, hyperactive,* or the vague term *average.* And a report card, she says, which uses the phrase *academic achievement not commensurate with individual ability* (meaning "the student can do better") obviously is not designed to facilitate communication with parents.[14]

Reporters face the same problems. The degree to which they let their educational sources dictate the language used in stories is the degree of risk that readers and viewers will not understand the message. And they run the same risk of alienation. The problem is double-edged: the inexperienced or nonaggressive reporter may copy the language out of lack of understanding and fear to attempt translation; the experienced reporter may become so comfortable with educational jargon that its use seems natural.

The easily stated solution, once again, comes from the *Oakland Press* in Pontiac, Michigan:

"Eschew obfuscation. Educators are in the grip of an irresistible impulse to use five-pound words of their own invention to prove they are smarter than everyone else. Our impulse must lead us in exactly the opposite direction. Their vapid verbiage is changed from time to time, but some recent examples we could have done without include facilitate, parameters, interface, contingency, implementation, utilization factors, cocurricular, needs validation, conceptualization and prioritize. A learning research center is a library, we believe. If you don't know what an educator is saying, ask him. See if he knows."[15]

Although jargon adds unnecessary complexity to stories, there are some stories of legitimate complexity. Dealing with children is an awesome responsibility, and understanding the techniques requires study. Reporters run a big risk if they do not have the background, don't take the time to equip themselves, or don't work carefully with the experts. Psychological or statistical information is easy to misinterpret or interpret inadequately.

Consider, for example, one of the most controversial educational issues of the early 1980s: standardized testing. Critics charge that educators and reporters alike are doing great public disservice through their use and misuse of test scores. First, there is considerable debate over whether IQ tests, the Scholastic Aptitude Tests (the SATs), or American College Test (ACT) actually provide the kind of information they are designed to produce. There is equal debate over indiscriminate usage by colleges of such test scores. And much concern as expressed over the fact that news organizations present such test scores without proper analysis or explanation.

Journalists do a better job of reporting the debate over standardized testing than they do of solving their contribution to the problem.[16] Like hundreds of other subjects, it's difficult. It's not the kind of material that can be presented on the basis of a single interview or use of the report presented by the testers.

The kind of understanding which makes it possible for reporters to handle such complex stories also is required to ensure that they will know when pertinent information is missing. It's too easy to overlook what is absent from an impressively detailed report. This is not necessarily deliberate deception, although it may be. Often it's a problem that grows out of the fact that reporters don't have opportunities or the desire to follow a story as it is being developed. And, even if they had the opportunity, it is questionable that many reporters could afford the time to sit through hours of planning sessions. But they must have knowledge and the perception to fulfill the responsibility of finding the whole story.

FOLLOWING THE EDUCATIONAL DOLLAR

Reporters follow the educational dollar carefully. They know that how funds are obtained and spent is a major factor in the quality of public or private education. It's a subject in which citizens are intensely interested, and it's especially important because those citizens provide most of those funds and usually have a strong voice in the amount of money made available.

Generally, funding for public schools comes from three main sources, with the federal dollar representing an important contribution, although a relatively small one in comparison with state and local funds. The typical federal contribution represents about 8 percent of the total budget, usually allocated for such specific programs as special education and school lunches. It is likely, given the fiscal mood in Washington these days, that even this amount will be reduced in the coming years.

Some state funds also are earmarked for specific programs. But the biggest proportion is provided for general support, meaning that local school boards may allocate the funds for whatever use they deem appropriate and necessary.

On the local level, property taxes are the biggest single source of income for public school systems, and this provides some financial problems. In many instances, property tax systems are outdated and inequitable and do not produce adequate revenues. Often taxation rates must be submitted for a public vote, and the public mood in recent years has not been to support increases or even continuation of present rates.

Nevertheless, school systems remain dependent upon the property taxes which are calculated on the assessed value of property within the school district. The unit of taxation is called a mill, with 1 mill being equal to 0.1 cent (1/10 cent). In some states, tax millage is based on the full assessed property value, while in others it is calculated on a percentage of assessed property value.

If taxable property in a school system, for example, is assessed at $8 million and the system needs an additional $80,000, it will ask for an increase in property taxes of 10 mills, which translates into 1 cent on every dollar of the assessed property value. The formula for calculating mill levies is

$$\text{Mill levy} = \frac{\text{additional taxes to be collected}}{\text{total assessed property value of the district}}$$

The importance of whether a district uses the total assessed value or a percentage of that value is thus clear. Property owners with holdings valued at $40,000, paying 10 mills on the full assessed value of that property, will owe $400 in property tax. If the system is based on, say, 50 percent of the assessed value, the amount will be $200.

Thus, while millage rates are important, reporters also must be aware of how much of the assessed property value is used in the tax calculations. The calculations can become even more complicated because of the existence of rollbacks which, for one reason or another, reduce the amount of millage authorized. For example, senior citizens may be granted a rollback which reduces the amount of property taxes they pay. Or a state may use a rollback to limit the total amount which may be collected, especially in times of high inflation when property values are soaring.

The need for such mill levies to produce additional operating funds is one major instance in which many school systems call for a public vote. A related form occurs when the systems want additional income for capital outlays—expansion or renovation of present facilities or the building of new facilities. These are termed *bond issues* and usually are limited to a time period which will allow production of the funds needed to accomplish the stated capital goals.

An equally important side of the budgetary picture, of course, is how the available funds are spent. By far, the largest proportion of school expenditures comes under the heading of "personnel" (generally from 65 to 85 percent of the total). Other spending categories of perhaps greater immediate interest to readers, viewers, and listeners would include administrative expenses, teaching supplies such as textbooks and audiovisual materials, transportation expenses, provisions for student health care, and maintenance costs.

Whatever the expenditure category, however, the point to remember is that the budgetary figures mean little by themselves. The dollars are spent for people—students, teachers, administrators, and other necessary personnel—and have meaning only when related in human terms. Specific line items in a school system budget are best translated into how they result in curriculum, other services, or, in general, the quality of instruction.

Thus, while the documents themselves may be available to reporters, interviews with school officials or visits to the individual schools are needed to put meaning into the figures. It's not enough, but possibly the earliest opportunity for reporters to make these connections grows from the fact that most states require public budget hearings. Such hearings give reporters the chance to hear discussion by board members and any residents who attend or to interview the officials themselves.

And there's one other major function for the reporter following the education budget. It's probably true that school systems provide fewer instances of fraud or conflict of interest than other public bodies. But they do handle millions of dollars, and it's inevitable that cases will occur in which some officials yield to temptation. Contracts will be awarded in ways which will financially benefit board members, or officials may seek other ways to benefit personally from their professional decisions. And the large number of requirements increases the chances that legal improprieties—even though they may be honest mistakes—will occur.

Reporters will watch carefully for these situations. They recognize that, in spite of the relatively good record educational officials have attained, the journalistic watchdog functions are no less necessary. Reporters must understand the law and the budgetary process. That's the only way to ensure that the public will know its money is being properly handled.

THE BROAD CHALLENGE OF EDUCATION REPORTING

Done properly, education reporting is like taking on the whole society. While the focus may be the school program, the stories represent the total community. What happens in the schools reflects what is happening on the streets of town. And the attitudes of the citizens are more than reflected—they are magnified—

in the offices and hallways of school buildings. The community's major social problems, in fact, may surface first among the young, who are not quite so adept at hiding their feelings.

Some of the most significant educational stories of the twentieth century have not been educational stories at all. They have been social stories which, for only circumstantial reasons, occurred in educational settings. Desegregation, for example, the top education story, is the most visible particle of a massive civil rights movement which has permeated every corner of this society. And it will continue in coming years to absorb the attention of education reporters as this society persists in its efforts to use its schools as a means of solving its problem of human inequality.

Others can be added to that list: problems of violence and vandalism; efforts to expand social and economic opportunities of whole classes of people—women, minority groups, the handicapped, the gifted, the poor; creeping control of local lives by federal government; coping with massive problems created by the exodus of millions to the suburbs.

The nation's financial problems—inflation, taxpayer revolts, dwindling local resources, inequitable taxation formulas, fluctuating abilities of state and federal governments—all have their educational components. Boards of education have only the authority to ask taxpayers to raise their own taxes voluntarily, and that's not a popular request these days. The quality of an educational program depends from the beginning on availability of funds to meet minimum needs or to develop innovative programs. And this should make the budget one of the education reporter's most dog-eared documents.

Internal money battles, especially those between teachers and boards of education, often erupt into the streets and become volatile community issues. Growing strength of teachers' unions, inexperience of most school board members in collective bargaining, and lack of financial abundance represent a combination which makes journalistic attention inevitable. And it's more than money. Often the teachers are fighting for more control over the programs of which they are a part or for guarantees that the atmosphere in which they work will be improved.

This latter category provides news organizations with stories about school discipline, attendance, and transportation, and about the physical environment in which students and teachers have to work and the resources available to them. It provides a focus on activities which create special learning opportunities or just enjoyment or on meals provided. Popular community-oriented activities such as athletics or adult education merit attention, as does the impact of the energy crisis upon the nation's schools.

But perhaps in the long run the most significant story will be of classroom learning opportunities. In spite of the often mentioned public disillusionment about education, the belief continues that education provides the key to improvement of one's life. And the validity of that belief rests squarely upon what is being taught and how well that teaching is accomplished. It's a paradox that, except for occasional bursts of enthusiasm when a curricular matter somehow leaps into the public's mind, curriculum perhaps represents the weakest component of education coverage. If there is a back-to-basics movement these days, if there is concern over why Johnny or Jane can't read, it's curricular trends of previous years which led to that situation. One wonders, therefore, what today's curricular trends will give us tomorrow.

Reporters themselves admit to the weakness. Doing the curriculum story properly requires extensive use of every skill education writers are supposed to possess. Unless the reporter understands the subject matter and knows how to deal with education specialists, understands research and has the writing skill to make educational theory come to life, the chances are good that the story about curricular innovation will be deadly dull.

But if contemporary discussions of why young people can't read or write have captured the public's interest, it makes sense that these same discussions could be even more valuable if done before the controversy arises. It's not just the reporters who must understand this. If educators dislike the negative publicity they occasionally receive, they, too, must look ahead. And many of them must adjust their thinking in terms of dealing with reporters.

Education mirrors the community. It's certainly the most pervasive social institution and probably the object of the most natural social interest. This is what makes the tasks of the education reporter interesting, and this is what provides the greatest challenge.

NOTES

1. Fred M. Hechinger, "The Public Perception of Education," *College Board Review*, No. 102, Winter 1976–77, p. 15.
2. "The Public Perception of Education," p. 15.
3. *Covering Government: A New Testament to Newswriting* (Pontiac, Mich.: The Oakland Press), p. 25.
4. For a discussion of educators' views on the media role in controversy, see, for example, Bill Armer, Charles Yeargan, and Mary Elizabeth Hannah, "Community Polarization Over Educational Programs Can Be Avoided," *Psychology in the Schools,* January 1977, pp. 54–61.
5. Helen Clara Lee, "For New (and Some Old) School Board Members: How to Seem Smarter Than You Really May Be," *American School Board Journal,* April 1976, p. 41.
6. For a good discussion of access to school board information, see Kurt Rogers and Patricia Murphy, Freedom of Information Center Report No. 312: *Access to School Boards* (Columbia, Mo.: University of Missouri School of Journalism, 1973).
7. News release distributed by the National Education Association at its annual meeting in Dallas, Texas, July 1–6, 1978, p. 2. The survey was designed and analyzed by Cantril Research Inc., Washington, D.C., with field work and tabulation by the Roper Organization.

8. Ronald F. Cambell, Luvern L. Cunningham, Raphael O. Mystrand, and Michael D. Usdan, *The Organization and Control of American Schools* (Columbus, Ohio: Charles E. Merrill Publishing Co., 1975), pp. 225–226.
9. D. C. Swedmark, "Competencies and Skills for an Effective School Public Relations Program," *NASSP Bulletin,* December 1979, pp. 61–62+.
10. B. Parker, "Blast Your Critics with Education's Good News," *American School Board Journal,* June 1980, pp. 19–22.
11. Robert P. Hilldrup, "The PR Aspects of School Violence," *Journal of Educational Communication,* September–October 1975, p. 9.
12. Thomas Baultmann,"Public Relations for a Reputable Profession,"*School and Community,* May 1977, p. 34.
13. *The Organization and Control of American Schools,* p. 213.
14. Mary H. Thompson, "We Use Words that Alienate Others," *Instructor,* December 1975, p. 24.
15. *Covering Government,* p. 25.
16. For a good discussion of the debate, see Gil Sewall, "Tests: How Good? How Fair?," *Newsweek,* February 18, 1980, pp. 97–104.

Chapter 13

BUSINESS AND THE ECONOMY

The speaker was Jack Busby, chairman of the board and chief executive officer of Pennsylvania Power and Light Co. His address was to a group of journalists, and he set the tone for a program on business reporting this way:

"It's hard for me to believe that I'm with a group of journalists. First of all, you look so friendly, and also you just demonstrated that you have warm hearts. In trying to prepare myself a little for this, I undertook to do some research. I tried to run through all the nice and thoughtful and kind things businessmen have said about the media. That didn't take very long. Then, I took a shot at researching in detail all the thoughtful and kind things the media have said about business. And that didn't take long. So maybe that's how the subject got on the program."

Busby's remarks underscore the fact that the jury is still out on the case of American business versus American journalism. The testimony is vitriolic. The arguments by the "attorneys" are both emotional and factual. The pretrial publicity is intense, and the debate has spread from the courtroom to the streets. The subject matter—the state of the economy and how American institutions are coping—is a subject of intense public concern.

"People are looking for understanding," Busby adds, "but understanding is very complex. One of the areas that is particularly complex has to do with economics and finance. I don't suggest that life is just a matter of economics and finance. It's only one of the focal subject areas of importance that a journalist has to cope with.

"But the breadth of economics, of course, affects what we do in terms of energy, transportation, automobiles, health care, poverty problems, taxes, redistribution of income, how we deal with the young, how we deal with the aged, how we deal with education. With all of these, we're really struggling . . . to come to grips with the idea of how we get our resources. That's what economics is all about."[1]

SATISFYING TWO PUBLICS

The desire for information on economics today exists not because economics has greater impact, but because citizens are more aware of that impact. They're learning that the stock market affects their return on investments, pension plans, and insurance policies. They are employees, producers, members of labor unions, and taxpayers. It boils down to how much they have in their pockets or whether they are able to buy what they need or want.

As long as the United States functioned with an economy of plenty, the public had limited interest in the cornucopia that spilled forth the good life. When the flow subsided and national economic problems hit home, the interest grew. Inflation. Recession. Tariff. Federal monetary policies. Trade balance. Just words before, but in the 1970s they became subjects of heated conversation on Main Street.

Economic journalism made its move toward respectability when reporters and editors realized they had two publics with which they were expected to deal. Reporters had for years dealt with and catered to the business specialist—executives, brokers, big investers, manufacturers—who understood the language and the process. It was a relatively closed circle. The business section of American newspapers gained the reputation of dullness, puffery, and inside information.

Now business and economic reporters have general readers—consumers—who may not go to the business section but want information on how the economy or governmental economic decisions have impact on their lives. That changes the rules of the game. With the broadened interest, business and economic news is more frequently seen on the front page and more conspicuous on the evening news. This developing public appetite has to be satisfied.

"Although as mystical as ever, economics is no longer the private preserve of the elite," says Dom Bonafede, chief political correspondent for the *National Journal* and senior writer for *Washington Journalism Review.* "With prominent exceptions, many academic and professional practitioners, assisted by autocratic, backward-looking business executives, fight a rear-guard action to ward off the barbaric invaders daring to confront them without exhibiting either a Ph.D. or an M.B.A. Nevertheless, economics today is everybody's game, including consumers, public interest advocates, environmentalists, middle-class home owners, trade unionists and small investers. A reporter who understands, and, moreover, can explain in journalistic language, the Laffer Curve is worth his weight in gold agate type."[2]

The journalistic requirements of understanding and ability to explain economics have thus moved to center stage. They were less necessary when the function of journalists was to transmit information from one set of experts to another. But with the growth of public interest, discontent, confusion, perplexity, and anger, reporters find it much more necessary to engage in what Dan Cordtz of ABC News refers to as "instant anthropology," helping people understand the society they live in, with the economy ranking among the most important factors.

Accomplishing this, Cordtz points out, is not easy. The typical citizen doesn't have the basic facts about economics to enable him or her to judge how much to trust the prescriptions of the experts. When people are asked to guess what the average profit margin of American companies is, they usually are dramatically incorrect on the high side. They don't know what the gross national product is or what the consumer price index measures or who's included or not included in the monthly unemployment figures.

Wordsworth Was a Good Businessman

BY JOHN CUNNIFF

AP Business Analyst

Nearly two million words of *Business Mirror* have appeared under this byline during the past dozen years, but there remain three observations that have urgently sought but always been denied expression.

Daringly, I have just reduced the number to two: I have used the first person singular.

The second aspiration, coming after 1½ decades in business writing, is the desire to ask: What is business news?

Third is to introduce to *Business Mirror* a poet, and perhaps thereby to misapply his words, written in appreciation of nature and most certainly not in defense of business.

But William Wordsworth, perceptive man, did say as concisely as possible just what business is: "getting and spending."

In fairness to Wordsworth, we must show the surrounding words, even though they do not support our cause:

"The world is too much with us; late and soon,

"Getting and spending, we lay waste our powers ... "

So you see that while Wordsworth described business, he didn't really support it, romanticist and naturalist and philosopher that he was.

Getting and spending, the businessman would object, enhances our powers, and he might defer to the "noted economist," as he often is called, to convince us that all the getting and spending at Christmas made the economy expand.

So few writers ever stop to consider that business news is little more than how people acquire and spend their assets—their education and training and skills and jobs; their economic desires and how they fulfill them.

Various institutions, banks, corporations and stock exchanges especially, have been structured to help us in that getting and spending, but in themselves they do not make business news. People, using them, do.

People, getting and spending, collectively and singularly. If there was one business story in 1977 that didn't fit that category it does not make itself immediately apparent.

It includes the federal budget and the household budget, the entrepreneur and the corporation, the regulator and the regulated. The dollar, inflation, interest rates, poverty, jobs, wages, travel. It is all human activity; it is the human condition.

Business news is whatever people are doing, because you can't do much without spending, and if you manage to do so, then that is news too.

Since it is, there is no dearth of good business stories, although we must admit that the presence of good stories does not mean they will be reported. Sometimes they aren't spotted; they aren't recognized without a dollar sign attached.

And recognition of a good story doesn't mean either that it will be presented well. In economic stories especially there is a pitfall: to write in abstractions, forgetting that behind all those dancing statistics there are human beings, getting and spending.

Also, we sometimes fail to spot business stories because we wait for them to be announced instead of applying our own instincts, insights and knowledge to correlate what might appear to be a diverse set of circumstances.

But the biggest pitfall is the failure to recognize that business is people, and that people like to read about people.

Wordsworth might be correct in his entire statement; I wouldn't know, although I'd be inclined to think what he says is worth listening to.

I feel certain, though, that he describes business as succinctly as it can be described, and so broadly that within those boundaries is a good deal of the entire human drama.

Source: John Cunniff, "Wordsworth Was a Good Businessman," *AP Log,* December 26, 1977–January 2, 1978, p. 7. Reprinted with permission of The Associated Press.

"It does no good," Cordtz continues, "to wring our hands about how the schools have failed in their responsibility, and I contend that it's a mistake for us to shrug and say it's not our job as journalists to conduct remedial education. It is part of our job, and it's a part we haven't performed. The failure is particularly glaring and particularly unfortunate where television is concerned."[3]

"MEMO TO THE PRESS: THEY HATE YOU OUT THERE"

And therein lies the crux of Jack Busby's comment about his effort to find all the nice and thoughtful and kind things business executives have said about journalists. Simply put, the business world does not like much of the new attention it is getting from the nation's news media. This was perhaps epitomized when Louis Banks, a former managing editor of *Fortune* magazine and later of the faculty of the Sloan School, Massachusetts Institute of Technology, wrote: "Memo to the Press: They Hate You Out There."

Banks says he thinks it's time news organizations listen to the complaints of economists and business executives, and he pinpoints three distinct levels of antagonism. The first involves everyday operational relationships in the form of specific reactions to specific encounters in which the business executive or the company has been involved. The second is attitudinal: a business executive's conviction that the great power of the media is used selectively to sour the body politic on corporate product, profit, and practice. The third is societal: a gut feeling that, behind a facade of constitutional righteousness, First Amendment guarantees are being misused at the expense of other institutional rights no less basic, with a net loss to the American system.[4]

Others write and speak on the same subject. Business executives take every advantage to run through their litany of complaints. But journalists themselves often join in, and scholars intone their research results to the same tune. Few agree with every comment, but the resulting chorus can be summarized with a half dozen points.[5]

Too many reporters themselves are economic illiterates who know little about economic theory and history and who therefore have inadequate perspective in which to place specific current events. Perhaps even worse, they are ignorant of corporate practice and thus distort the role of decisions made and of the individuals who comment on these decisions.

Journalistic coverage of business is inadequate, overly simplistic, dramatizes the superficial, and too often misses significant points of stories done and, in fact, misses too many of the important stories.

Reporters themselves often are antibusiness, and too much of their work contains flagrant bias and outright slanting of the facts. They tend to regard business as guilty until proven innocent.

Extreme overkill is characteristic of much journalistic coverage, with sensationalizing of environmental hazards, exaggeration of marketplace ripoffs, and overplay of problems with governmental regulatory bodies.

In the extreme, journalists are undermining this society's economy by destroying public confidence in the free enterprise system. Inordinate emphasis of negative news and exploitation of economic anxiety are helping to create a "doom boom" which magnifies public reactions.[6]

News organizations are providing a forum for irresponsible politicians and interest groups who base their charges on emotion and political convenience rather than knowledge of the facts.

Many within the business and journalistic communities nod affirmatively as such charges are being ticked off, but they then quickly admit the exaggerations. The complaints often are legitimate, but journalism does provide reporters whose coverage is exceptional. And the complaints often are exaggerated by corporate executives who rule in their world, are not accustomed to being thus questioned, and are most uncomfortable with their new visibility. They don't understand the scrutiny they are receiving, and they don't feel it's justified.

"We're trying to enter a new era of business coverage," says Phil Moeller of the Louisville *Courier-Journal,* "in which reporters approach business just like they would government. The community of people you're dealing with is not used to this, and it's not entirely their fault. Politicians and bureaucrats have been dealing with reporters for a long time, but the business community has not been dealing with a vigorous business press in most areas. There's been a lot of aggressive reporting recently which doesn't jibe with what business executives have tended to expect."

And these business officials who complain so loudly often ignore the fact that much of the news media attention they receive is positive, at times too positive. While Moeller and his colleagues are willing to admit that journalists have their problems in covering business, they are quick to point out that nothing they do will satisfy the official who expects—and sometimes gets—unqualified support, known in the trade as "boosterism." But while it's not often so extreme, overall coverage is not as negative as charged.

It's fact, as A. Kent MacDougall of the *Los Angeles Times* points out, that newspaper editorial writers generally support business positions. And the news media publish a considerable amount of fluff supplied by businesses promoting food, fashion, travel, real estate, sports, and stocks.[7]

Much of what is perceived as bias or antibusiness is little more than reporters' efforts to follow the lead of the general public, specific interest groups, and, indeed, the government in efforts to spotlight a corner of society which is not accustomed to such attention.

"If the media are questioning with greater intensity the methods and motives of business," says Ralph Otwell of the *Chicago Sun-Times,* "it is only because the reading and viewing public, out of their own needs and anxieties, are prompting the questions and prodding the newsmen to seek out the answers.

"Consumerism, environmentalists, conservationists, public-interest law firms, and a host of other active, sometimes militant and always vocal, citizen groups have entered the American stage in recent years. They are challenging the business community, and often with dramatic success, to change the old methods and seek out newer, safer ways to operate."[8]

Business coverage may at times be negative, but that is not the most worrisome problem. Business journalism has improved dramatically in the past decade, especially with regard to the reporting of events and decision making. There are mistakes and occasional sloppiness as reporters struggle to meet deadlines. But those instances are declining. Reporters have their major problems when they seek to go below events and decisions, when they attempt to inform themselves and the public about the process of economic change that creates events and compels decisions.

"How do we capture this slow process of change, both past and prospective, when the language of journalism and politics emphasizes the immediacy of events, causes and consequences?" asks Robert Samuelson of the *National Journal* in Washington, D.C.

"Because we find this virtually impossible, we distort economic news. We like shape to our stories. We like concrete happenings, conflicts and distinctive personalities. But economic change is often shapeless, involving new technology, evolving institutions and public attitudes. So, mostly, we are the mouthpieces for what others say about the economy. And we project a highly simplified vision of how the economy works and what government can do to change things."[9]

Overcoming that is the major challenge of business reporters.

SEARCHING FOR GOOD ECONOMICS SOURCES

Developing sources—the key to quality of any reporter's work—is somewhat more complicated for the economic journalist. The techniques are the same as those of other areas of journalistic concern, but the problems, while similar, are intensified by both the legal status and the basic attitudes of the business community.

It is obvious that those in business who dislike or distrust reporters are less likely to cooperate. But the attitude impact goes further. Unlike politicians, who tend to be outgoing and gregarious, many business executives are uncomfortable dealing with reporters. Some feel little sense of public obligation to lead them to share the internal workings of their business. They define their business as private and often resent efforts by reporters to get beyond superficial public announcements, particularly if the information sought could have negative impact.

And, unlike the government reporter, economic journalists cannot call upon a Freedom of Information Act to pry open corporate file cabinets. It is true that there are laws requiring financial disclosure, but no laws say the public has a right to know about the internal decision-making process.

At the same time, however, the ingredients for an effective mix of sources are there. The reporter has to dig them out with patience, persistence, and demonstrated professionalism. The economic community is large, its occupants are varied in their interests, and the system functions, internally as well as externally, on competition. And when that competitive spirit is joined with the natural desires of human beings to see their names in print or their faces on the screen, the possibilities are broadened that someone will answer persistent reporters' questions.

"Reporters can get the information," says Tom Walker of the Atlanta *Journal.* "In many instances, especially if you're dealing with top management, and it's a publicly held company—one that sells stock to the public—it's no problem. They know what they've got to tell you legally to meet government regulations, and sometimes if you get to know them personally they will go beyond what they have to tell you. They'll give you a lot of information, although not always for quotation. I've been more often surprised at how much executives would tell me rather than having a problem with how little."

Tom Walker of the Atlanta *Journal*

(Atlanta *Journal* photo)

Such success, however, depends upon the reporter's efforts, the personality of the source, and the location of that person within the firm's hierarchy.

It May Be Refreshing at the Top

Economics journalists, like their counterparts, usually are wary of seeking information, especially sensitive information, from persons low in the business hierarchy. They know that too often middle- or low-level executives either won't say anything useful or will want to provide their conservative ideas of what the boss wants. That's why it's usually best to start with the person at the top, if possible. As Walker indicates, reporters often are surprised at how candid these executives can be.

Not always, of course. Chief executive officers and company presidents vary in their willingness. Some answer their own telephones if the reporter gains access to their direct lines. Some never grant interviews, preferring to delegate responsibility to specific lower executives or public relations personnel.

Part of the problem is executive egocentricity. Reporters occasionally find the attitude that answering questions is beneath the importance of an executive or the belief that public relations departments exist to control the flow of information. And there's the executive who believes that news media content can be controlled through economic power, specifically through the granting or withdrawing of advertising dollars. It is not likely that reporters will get much cooperation from these persons.

Egocentricity, however, can work to journalistic advantage. Executives who feel the company is so dependent upon them that no one else can effectively speak for it may not be tolerant of seeing lower executives' names in the paper or on television. It certainly enhances one's self-image to have reporters knocking at the door.

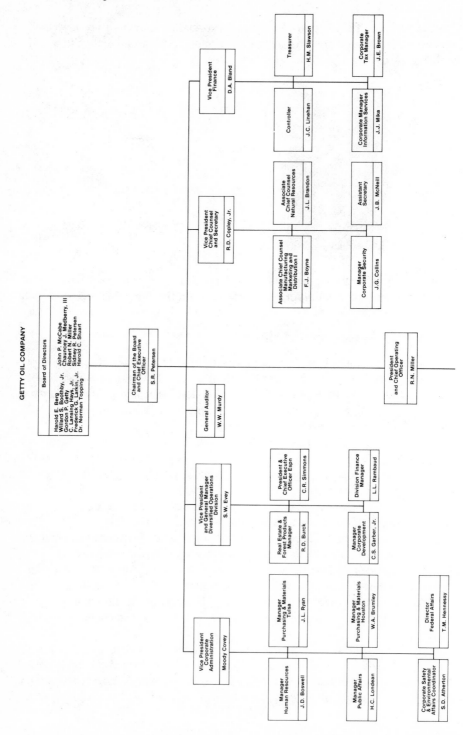

GETTY OIL COMPANY

Board of Directors

Harold E. Berg
Willard S. Boothby, Jr.
Gordon P. Getty
C. Lansing Hays, Jr.
Frederick G. Larkin, Jr.
Dr. Norman Topping

John P. McCabe
Chauncey J. Medberry, III
Robert N. Miller
Sidney R. Petersen
Harold C. Stuart

Chairman of the Board
and Chief Executive
Officer

S.R. Petersen

President
and Chief Operating
Officer

R.N. Miller

Vice President
Finance

D.A. Bland

Treasurer

H.M. Slawson

Controller

J.C. Linehan

Corporate
Tax Manager

J.E. Brown

Corporate Manager
Information Services

J.J. Mika

Vice President
Chief Counsel
and Secretary

R.D. Copley, Jr.

Associate
Chief Counsel
Natural Resources

J.L. Brandon

Associate Chief Counsel
Manufacturing
Marketing and
Distribution I

F.J. Boyne

Assistant
Secretary

J.B. McNeill

Manager
Corporate Security

J.G. Collins

General Auditor

W.W. Murdy

Vice President
and General Manager
Diversified Operations
Division

S.W. Evey

President &
Chief Executive
Officer Espn

C.R. Simmons

Division Finance
Manager

L.L. Rambaud

Real Estate &
Forest Products
Manager

R.D. Burck

Manager
Corporate
Development

C.S. Garber, Jr.

Vice President
Corporate
Administration

Moody Covey

Manager
Purchasing & Materials
Tulsa

J.L. Ryan

Manager
Purchasing & Materials
Houston

W.A. Brumley

Director
Federal Affairs

T.M. Hennessy

Manager
Human Resources

J.D. Boswell

Manager
Public Affairs

H.C. Londean

Corporate Safety
& Environmental
Affairs Coordinator

S.D. Atherton

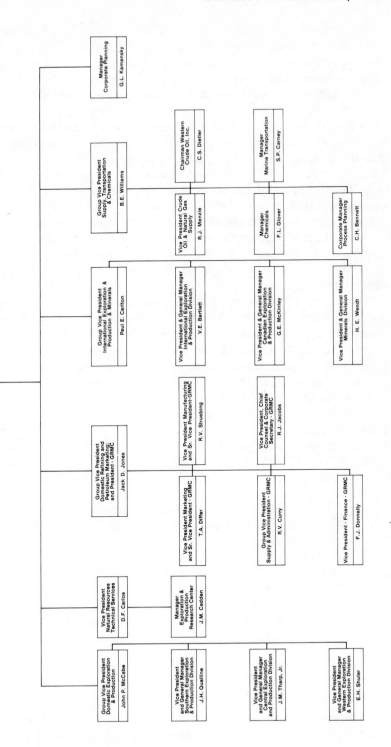

"Maybe it won't surprise you," says ABC's Dan Cordtz, "but I've been amazed at the way successful businessmen lust after getting their faces on the tube. They're afraid of being made to look foolish, of course, but on the other hand they really like having their colleagues . . . and kids and grandchildren see them. I consider that legitimate repayment if you can get the guy to say something of value."[10]

It's not just ego stroking that gets reporters into the executive suite. Much depends on whether a given journalist has demonstrated fairness, professionalism, understanding, and the ability to accurately reproduce the sometimes complex comments and information received. Executives are sensitive to reporters' knowledge. Once that has been demonstrated, many executives are hungry to talk with someone who understands what is going on.

Reporters have a similar requirement of executives to whom they pay greatest attention. It's not common to expect the official to have command of all the technical details, especially in a large corporation. Some executives demonstrate a great deal of knowledge of the intricacies of their operations, but their importance is greatest in providing the broader picture.

"They're savvy, not just about their company but about the whole economy and their industry in general," says Anne Swardson of the *Dallas Morning News*. "You don't get to be a company president or chairman without being a smart person. These big executives usually have a global view that's worth knowing. They can see things from worthwhile perspectives, maybe because they also tend to serve on boards of other business, governmental, and social organizations."

Lower executives are less likely to have that global view, but some are in positions from which they can be of benefit to reporters. Most companies are divided, at least, into the financial side and the operations side, with individuals in charge of each; most have a whole series of vice presidents and others with specific responsibilities for various corporate divisions. These people are potential sources of information for whatever company policy dictates to be their role with reporters.

Journalists do concentrate at the top of the business hierarchy, but they find at least three circumstances in which they may deal with lower level executives. The first, they say, almost flippantly, is "when they're the only ones who can be reached at deadline time." Second, a reporter often is referred to or seeks out lower level executives whose knowledge is appropriately specific to provide detailed elaboration. And, if for no other reason, executives below the top should be cultivated as sources because it is they who are most likely to provide tips. Many are close enough to the top to be aware, and circumstances do arise in which they may be willing to share their inside knowledge with trustworthy reporters.

The Many Roles of PR

The typical corporate public relations operation does not exist. Given many titles —public relations, public affairs, public information, corporate affairs, corporate communication—the roles of the personnel in this office depend upon the philosophy of the firm's top management.

In some instances, the top public relations personnel are involved in most aspects of planning, sit in on strategy sessions, understand philosophy and operation, and are in positions to speak officially. In other instances, they serve as expediters for those, including reporters, seeking information. They know their way around the organization, understand its policy in general, and open doors to individuals who can answer reporters' questions. Some serve only as roadblocks, defining their jobs as protecting corporate executives by placing their bodies in front of the targets of reporter interest. They may be little more than clerical publicists who dutifully type news releases and prepare brochures based on information provided by management and then submit their work to officials for editing.

The first job of any reporter is to determine which role or combination of roles particular public relations personnel have. Some reporters will avoid PR offices at almost any cost, and others will take advantage of some of the services they provide. The most frequent uses are for background or organizational facts, for story ideas, and for persons who know enough about corporation structure to recommend specific persons to answer specific questions.

"Flacks are not useless," Swardson says. "They're worth taking out to lunch and cultivating. Sometimes they can get disaffected, just like any other employee, and they'll tell you things that are about to happen in the company. Or, on a less aggressive level, flacks are worth cultivating just because when a time comes and you have to have something from the company, you want somebody who knows you and who likes you to be there to give it to you."

Governments Have a Say

Cries often are heard from business leaders, some economists, and politicians that government meddles too much into the affairs of business. Without arguing that point, journalists can see that the governmental role provides countless possibilities for information. That role itself must be covered. Reporters will want to talk to corporate and government officials about rules, regulations, standards, enforcement, requests, loans, and all the other economic subjects involving the government.

Virtually every aspect of business is subject to some form of regulation by local, state, and federal governments. Local governments, for example, often inspect gasoline pumps and restaurant kitchens; state governments regulate telephone and electricity rates and examine dairies and the books of state-chartered banks; and the federal government regulates the activities of broadcast stations, chemical plants, and stock exchanges.

Aside from the direct connection, a byproduct of government's role in American business is its record-keeping and statistics-generating function. While not always easy to find, statistics and other background information are available to broaden almost any story, to relate, for example, how the specifics of the local economy compare with other areas or fit into the national picture.

At the federal level, the possibilities are enormous for reporters who have the patience to sort through available paperwork. Once the proper agency has been discovered, both human and paper resources await. Among agencies which deserve attention would be the Securities and Exchange Commission, to whom public corporations report financial data, the Bureau of Labor Statistics and the Commerce Department, the Census Bureau, and the Small Business Administration. The Joint Economic Committee of Congress puts out a monthly booklet called *Economic Indicators* which could serve as a general reference on national statistics. And among the most valuable resources would be *Statistical Abstracts of the United States* and its companion, *Historical Abstracts of the United States.*

State and local governments, although not as systematically as the federal government, also provide information which could help the reporter in analyses of how the local economy fits into the larger picture. State agencies, often attached to a university, make available monthly employment figures, state law enforcement personnel can talk about regulatory actions and investigations, and states have agencies assigned to monitor and regulate utilities and transportation.

Whatever it may be called, states have bodies which would perform the function of a Department of Commerce and would include numerous experts on economic matters. In most instances, records kept by the secretary of state could provide reporters with information on corporations, including owners and members of the boards of directors.

Often, such information is available, but not systematically distributed to news organizations. It is the responsibility of reporters to find out what's there, to request what is pertinent, to evaluate it, and to use that information within the context of coverage philosophy. At times, governmental agencies will send reports or releases to journalists who have demonstrated interest. Such releases may be valuable, but, again, should be used as the starting point for stories about the local economic situation.

Bankers Have a Big Interest

The nation's major financial institutions do not have offices in every town. But practically every town in the country has a reasonable substitute in the form of bankers whose job it is to understand the local economy. Such persons will not automatically share their knowledge with reporters, and they certainly will not divulge specific information about the financial condition of local individuals or corporations.

Bankers are not always correct in their assessments of the local economy, but they do have the background and usually have seriously done their homework. They're in a better position than most to make educated guesses. Some of the larger ones even have economic analyses which could be of journalistic benefit.

Reporters will not succeed with bankers if they simply burst through the door with pointed questions. It must be a continuing process, involving constant

FEDERAL REGULATORY AGENCIES

Although most federal agencies have their headquarters in Washington, many have regional offices that often can supply information to reporters on policies and actions regarding specific businesses. Each of the following agencies falls into that category.

More detailed information on all federal regulatory agencies, including names and telephone numbers of contacts, may be found in the *Federal Regulatory Directory,* published annually by Congressional Quarterly in Washington (about $25, but available at most public libraries).

Consumer Product Safety Commission. The commission establishes mandatory safety standards for the design, construction, contents, performance, and labeling of consumer products. It has the authority to ban the sale of items that do not meet established standards.

Environmental Protection Agency. The EPA has the authority to set and enforce national standards for air and water quality and for handling of hazardous solid wastes and pesticides. It supervises state and local compliance with national standards.

Federal Communications Commission. The FCC regulates radio, television, telegraph, cable, and satellite communications. Its most important function is to license and assign frequencies to individual stations.

Federal Deposit Insurance Corporation. The FDIC insures bank deposits and regulates state-chartered banks that are not members of the Federal Reserve System. It requires periodic reports on the financial condition of banks under its supervision.

Federal Energy Regulatory Commission. An independent agency within the Energy Department, the commission regulates electric utilities and the interstate transportation and pricing of natural gas and electricity.

Federal Trade Commission. The FTC acts to prevent price fixing, unfair competition, false and deceptive advertising, and monopolistic practices by businesses engaged in interstate commerce.

Food and Drug Administration. An agency within the Department of Health and Human Services, the FDA is responsible for testing and setting standards for foods, household products, drugs, and other medical items.

National Highway Traffic Safety Administration. An agency within the Transportation Department, this body sets safety and mileage standards for automobiles and trucks and has the authority to order recalls of vehicles that do not meet the standards.

National Labor Relations Board. The main functions of the NLRB are to prevent employers and unions alike from engaging in unfair labor practices and to conduct elections to determine whether employees want to be represented by a union.

Occupational Safety and Health Administration. An agency within the Labor Department, OSHA sets and enforces on-the-job safety and health standards. It requires employers to file reports on job-related injuries and illnesses and inspects work sites for safety problems.

Securities and Exchange Commission. An independent agency, the SEC regulates the trading of stocks and bonds at national exchanges and over-the-counter markets. It requires public disclosure of financial and other information by companies whose securities are traded on the national exchanges.

cultivation, getting to know each other, and proving that reporters understand and know how to use the information they get.

The Academic Approach

"I guess I'm just an academic kind of person," says Pamela Meyer of the *St. Louis Post-Dispatch,* "but I do a lot of academic work. When something becomes of interest to business executives or is obviously important, I more often than not seek out a university business professor and use that resource and also ask him or her to point me to other resources and things to read."

Pam Meyer of the *St. Louis Post-Dispatch*

(*St. Louis Post-Dispatch* photo)

That's another potentially strong source of broad understanding and specific analysis that is just as close as the nearest college or university. Almost all have some type of economics program, and if a reporter is especially lucky, he or she may uncover a scholar of the local economy. But value may be gained by developing sources who can explain economic trends and impact in general.

Even if those sources never appear in print or on the air—and some prefer it that way—they can help on issues with which the reporter is not familiar. Some economists have made names for themselves because of frequent appearances in the news media, but, more important than that, their understanding provides scope to an economics story and contributes to its authenticity.

They tend to be cooperative, at times even excited, when asked to explain issues to a reporter. It's another opportunity to teach and to talk about what probably is their favorite conversational subject. But they seldom walk uninvited into the newsroom. They must be invited; they must be called; they must be asked.

Professional Industry Watchers

Security analysts are professional gatherers of business information, and that alone makes them candidates for a reporter's questions. But their journalistic value goes further in that their livelihood depends upon the objectivity of their analyses and the quality of their judgments.

Usually attached to brokerage houses, security analysts provide the evaluations upon which decisions are made about the purchase and sale of stocks. They are specialists, concentrating on specific industries, often have inside sources, collect detailed financial information, make it their business to understand the impact of broad economic or political decisions, and pay constant attention to trends which may provide clues to future developments.

"Akron is the home of the rubber industry, and we try to have as many analysts who know the rubber industry as we can on our list," says Doug Oplinger of the *Akron Beacon Journal.* "Most of them are in New York, but some are in this area. But wherever they may be, we give them a call, especially when earnings reports come out, and ask them what they think all this means. And you can do that with any industry. Canton has a lot of steel mills, so we also use a lot of steel security analysts."

Such individuals are not surprised when they get telephone calls from reporters. That's not their business, but they know the importance of their information to news organizations, and they tend to be cooperative. While the heaviest concentration is in the nation's financial centers, most large brokerage houses have offices scattered in cities around the country which can serve, at least, as points of initial contact.

Labor Does Its Homework

Another group of persons with understanding of what's going on in the corporate world consists of labor union officials. They have to have good information at their fingertips. Collective bargaining negotiations must consist of more than educated guesswork. Officials need a clear picture of company finances, an assessment of its place in the industry, future possibilities, policies, and personalities of corporate executives.

To gain much of this, today's more sophisticated labor unions maintain economists and accountants on staff to review the results of various companies with which they do business. They may even issue their own reports or critiques of financial reports of those companies.

And they usually are willing to talk with reporters they trust. In a sense, labor unions represent what in a political context could be called the "loyal opposition." They are interested in future development and growth of their industry, but their ideas on how to accomplish this may differ from those of corporate officials. And, because they are constantly doing their collective bargaining homework, they can be very good sources of specific information about the corporation.

But union officials do have their axes to grind. Their constant goal is to achieve some desired end, and what they say often will be within that context. Thus, they are approached by reporters with the same skepticism as any other source who has something to gain.

Organizations for Every Viewpoint

This is a free country. Citizens have a right to express their opinions. And they have a right to express their opinions collectively. That particular piece of American philosophy has been used extensively in the past quarter century. And business is part of the forum. Trade associations, intraindustry organizations, and chambers of commerce see their function as one of support for business. Consumer groups see themselves not so much antibusiness as proconsumer. Sometimes, antibusiness groups oppose, almost on principle, anything that comes out of corporate headquarters.

A common ingredient among all these groups is the attention they desire and often receive from the news media. It's not easy for the reporter to pick the thoughtful comments from the din of boosterism and degradation. The temptation is to listen to the loudest cries and follow the heaviest footsteps. That has caused problems, and journalists such as Ralph Otwell of the *Chicago Sun-Times* admit it.

"Some groups of anti-business, anti-establishment militants have achieved influence and impact not because their cause was great and their case was good, but because they achieved prominence and attention through the media all out of proportion to their value and significance," Otwell says. "Often, there is a corrective force that takes hold—something akin to 'overkill': eventually, the militants who cling to the spotlight and hog the limelight meet the fate of the moth that is drawn to the light bulb—they wither and die of overexposure.

"But journalism has a professional challenge in finding other ways to screen out the kooks and the charlatans without denying access to the many with legitimate complaints and valid protests. And I suspect that a society that would try to suppress the views of the John Gardners, the Ralph Naders, the Barry Commoners—as much as we might disagree with them from time to time—is a society which neither businessmen nor their customers would long enjoy, nor prosper in."[11]

And on a less controversial level, the activities of such local organizations as a home builders' association or a car dealers' association merit attention. As with chambers of commerce, material gained from them is likely to be one-sided. That does not mean they should be ignored; it means the other sides, if they exist, should be sought. Perhaps the most significant contribution of such groups is in the form of statistics—a demonstration of business activity—and political action designed to gain or maintain special privilege or stall the latest controlling legislation.

VOLUMES OF WRITTEN MATERIAL

Nothing adequately substitutes for general familiarity with business and economics that comes from careful, day-by-day attention. That means extensive reading. Dozens of individuals and organizations are sources for material. Governments require and issue report after report. Corporations prepare statements for share-holders and the public. Business publications analyze industries and economic trends. Special-interest groups write letters and articles and produce brochures, newsletters, and special studies.

Many of these documents are sent unsolicited to journalists. Others are sought for specific purposes, at times against the will of the producer. Somebody has to read this material to extract facts of local value and to be informed about national economic trends with local impact.

The sources include newspapers considered to contain the best business news coverage, including the *Wall Street Journal* and the *New York Times,* and economics-oriented magazines such as *Business Week, Fortune,* and *Forbes.* All three news magazines devote major attention to business. The reporter also may want more specific materials: government newsletters such as housing market reports; industrial publications such as *Dollars and Cents of Shopping Centers* from the Urban Land Institute; and informational and advisory newsletters such as the *Goodkin Report* on real estate matters, published by the Sanford R. Goodkin Research Corp.

Much more is available in the local library, says economist Richard Vedder of Ohio University: "There are a lot of data sources that reporters ought to learn to use. Two good sources published by the U.S. Bureau of the Census are *City and County Data Book* (published every five years) and *County Business Patterns,* published monthly. Another source is Sales Management Magazine's annual *Survey of Buying Power.* Most state employment services have much useful information. The Ohio Employment Service, for example, publishes data on a county-by-county and on a metropolitan area basis. There's a lot of material that the average reporter simply does not know exists. But it's right there in the library.

Annual Report to Shareholders

Information on specific corporations likewise is available, even from firms which may be less than enthusiastic about dealing with reporters. Public corporations are required by the federal government to report routinely on their financial status. These reports take several forms. The monthly financial reports to share-holders (generally issued near the end of the following month to allow time for closing the company's books) cover activity, sales, and expenses. Every three months, companies are required to submit quarterly reports, which in fact are both monthly reports and cumulative reports of the two previous months.

At the end of the year, this information is put together in an annual report, often in a slick magazine format which may reach 100 pages. In the past, compa-nies regarded the reports as a bother, something saddled on them by a med-dlesome government. But now they attach considerable importance to them, says *Financial World,* which sponsors yearly annual report awards. They are regarded as top priority means of corporate communication—not only with shareholders, but with a host of other constituencies ranging from financial analysts and customers to politicians and social activists. Now, too, companies put major effort into interim shareholder reports, postannual meeting reports, security analyst yearbooks, and public issue campaigns.[12]

"The annual report today is used as a marketing tool, recruiting tool, public relations tool, and it has a variety of other functions," says Franklin J. Parisi of Getty Oil Co. "Since compilation of facts and figures is required by law, companies decided years ago to use the required information and add to it additional information not required but of interest to current or potential stockholders, potential employees, and a variety of other publics.

"A good parallel example is the function served by flight attendants on airplanes. Flight attendants originally were required to be on airplanes to provide first aid. They're still required as a safety element. Since these individuals were going to be on board anyway, the companies decided they might as well put them to work doing other things, such as serving dinner. So it is with the annual reports. Since we are required to put out the essential financial information anyway, we might as well do that in as presentable a form as possible."

Reporters are not unanimous in assessments of the journalistic value of these annual reports. They are concerned about the fluff and puffery. They recognize that a corporation has enough flexibility, even in the face of governmental requirements, to make persuasion a focus of the reports. Reporters are uncomfortable with information gained in this kind of situation. It's also true that the annual reports seldom contain new information but represent new packages for material originally published elsewhere, perhaps in monthly or quarterly reports.

Nevertheless, reporters who understand how to use the reports may benefit from them, at least in general ways. They are part of the message a company wants to present. A company having financial problems may make the report look spartan to support claims being made in the copy that everything possible is being done to control costs. And the annual reports of rapidly growing companies may be designed to project the image of unlimited expansion and almost guaranteed success.

This certainly was the case for Warner Communications, winner of *Financial World's* 1979 top prize for annual reports. The firm celebrated the tenth anniversary of its creation—out of the July 1969 acquisition of Warner-Seven Arts by Kinney Services Inc. Since then it's grown into a highly profitable, billion dollar plus entertainment company.

"So Warner decided to pull out all the stops in preparing its 1979 annual report," the magazine says. "The end product is an extremely attractive, highly readable, information-packed report running no less than 92 pages that will tell anybody just about anything they want to know about the company. It helped, of course, that Warner Communications has a happy story to tell these days— one of rising revenues and rising earnings. When there is only bad news to report, companies often don't devote much extra effort to their annual reports—beyond trying to gloss over the unhappy results."[13]

Inside the reports, among matters to which reporters pay attention are the "bottom line" figures. These figures provide the news of a particular company, often expressed in the amount of profit or loss, the percentage of increase or decrease from the previous year, and the per share impact on shareholders.

Trends may be isolated from the reports, perhaps with regard to profit patterns over time or something more specific. For example, if a company shows a substantial improvement in its financial picture because of a specific product which may be manufactured locally, that could indicate possible expansion of local industry. The full story, of course, will not be in the annual report, but observant reporters may find the beginnings of several stories to be pursued.

Professional accountants and experienced journalists alike may moan over the growth of annual reports over the years, pointing out that the significant (and legally required) information generally is found among footnotes and/or tabular information in the back of the book. Footnotes represent exceptions, unusual occurrences which must be noted. It's in the footnotes, for example, that reporters may discover major changes in the chief executive officer's salary. Or they may get the best perspective on lawsuits and active litigation which could have major impact on a company's overall performance.

It may be that the major journalistic value of annual reports is not in the specific information. They do, however, give broad perspectives and provide opportunities to analyze formal statements from corporate executives about the past year's experiences and plans and expectations for the future. And a collection of them gives a chance for comparison—either one company with other companies in an industry, or one company over several years.

Form 10-K

The most significant of all financial reports is form 10-K, the annual report required of all publicly held corporations by the Securities and Exchange Commission. Similar to the annual report to shareholders, but much less grandiose,

---

New Data in Annual Reports

BY STEVE LOHR

The annual reports that corporations send to their shareholders next year will have a decidedly different if bewildering look.

Harold M. Williams, chairman of the Securities and Exchange Commission, was in New York yesterday to discuss the new approach. It is a result of efforts by the accounting profession and the S.E.C. to make financial reports reflect the modern, inflation-ridden world.

According to members of the commission's staff, accounting firm partners and Wall Street analysts, the campaign will drastically alter not only the appearance but also the focus of annual reports. Financial reporting will increasingly be "more subjective and less precise than has been traditional," Mr. Williams said in addressing a conference sponsored by the New York State Society of Certified Public Accountants.

Annual reports will also include more supplemental data. This extra information will concentrate largely on cash flow and liquidity—the financial fuel needed to keep a corporation going—and not so much on net income, the traditional gauge of corporate performance. Wall Street already tends to be more interested in liquidity and cash flow than earnings, or at least earnings figured by the traditional method.

Scarcity of Information

"Professionals don't base investment decisions on the annual report," said Lee J. Seidler, a professor of accounting at the New York University graduate business school and an analyst at Bear, Stearns & Company. The traditional annual report just doesn't tell you very much."

The overall thrust of the coming changes in financial reporting will be to give investors and the public a clearer picture of a corporation's ability to operate in an environment of chronic inflation.

On Aug. 21, the S.E.C. approved a change in the required management commentary portion of the annual report, calling for information on cash flow and liquidity. This will appear in the 1980 annual reports of all larger publicly held corporations.

Adjusting for Inflation

Also appearing next year—since the reports for 1980 will not come out until 1981—will be financial statements that are adjusted for inflation by two methods: constant dollar and current cost. In 1979, larger corporations were required only to show constant dollar numbers, in addition to the traditional historical cost method.

"But next year," said Edmund Coulson, assistant chief accountant of the S.E.C., "we'll see three methods of figuring the financial statement in each annual report."

Simply put, historical cost accounting values the raw materials, inventory and other assets at their original cost. The constant-dollar method takes a single price index (based on 1967) and adjusts accordingly for all assets and all companies. It is a kind of broadside inflation adjustment.

The current-cost approach is a more tailored approach to inflation adjustment. It attempts to take into account the specific situations affecting costs within each company.

Indeed, some type of inflation-adjusted accounting may someday replace the historical cost method as the primary financial statement of corporations, Thomas L. Holton, chairman of Peat, Marwick, Mitchell & Co., said yesterday at the accountants' meeting.

Mr. Williams addressed the group later. Asked about Mr. Holton's remarks, the S.E.C. chairman said he did not forsee such a development by the mid-1980's, but "possibly further down the road."

form 10-K describes in rather intimate detail what businesses do, how much they make, who runs them, and legal problems they may be having. Failure to properly report the information required by the SEC in this form could result in criminal charges against senior officers or the board of directors.

Reporters may obtain copies of a company's form 10-K from the firm itself or from the Securities and Exchange Commission in Washington. As with the annual report to shareholders, companies are not required to share 10-K with journalists, but since the documents are made available routinely to so many persons, it's relatively easy for reporters to obtain copies. The major advantage of 10-K is that its information is in straight, proscribed form without the gloss and puffery of the annual report to shareholders.

Getty Oil Co., for example, produced a fifty-eight-page form 10-K document for 1979 which included the following:

Prose and tabular overview of the firm's operations, including sales of crude oil, condensate, and refined products; description of the firm's relationships with regulatory agencies; discussion of competitive conditions and risks; and presentation of estimated capital expenditures for environmental control facilities.

Detailed material on the firm's property, including oil and gas reserves; discussion of why and how this estimate may differ from estimates filed with federal authorities; crude oil and natural gas net production; average sales price and average production cost; gross and net producing acreage and productive wells; exploratory efforts and listing of undeveloped acreage around the world; transportation, storage, manufacture, refining, and marketing facilities; subsidiaries (including companies involved in chemicals and petrochemicals, nuclear fuels, synthetic fuels, forest products, real estate, and the Entertainment and Sports Programming Network, Inc.).

Detailed discussions of legal proceedings in which Getty Oil was involved.

Increases and decreases in outstanding securities, number of equity security holders.

Financial statements, listing of executive officers.

Appended was a complete copy of the firm's sixty-four-page 1979 annual report to shareholders.

But form 10-K is just the beginning of materials provided through federal government disclosure requirements. The SEC alone uses some 180 different forms to cover the broad range of business activities regulated by the agency.[14] For example:

Proxy statement.   A detailed meeting notice to shareholders, of special value to journalists because the SEC presumes that management includes financial information. Among the most useful information is the salaries of directors and top officers who make more than $40,000 a year. It also includes an agenda for the company's annual meeting, which may give reporters additional insight.

Prospectus.   A document produced when the firm is preparing for the sale of new stock. Prepared for potential buyers, the prospectus includes detailed information about the company, its activities and properties, financial condition, subsidiaries, and plans for the future. Availability of such information opens up numerous avenues for reporters, typified by a *Business Week* story written by Dallas Bureau Chief Andy Wilson:

> Braniff Airways Inc., far and away the most aggressive major airline in its approach to deregulation, is suddenly looking very wobbly. Hit first with surging prices for jet fuel, and now facing a deepening recession and soaring interest rates, the nation's seventh largest airline is in financial straits.
>
> The net income of Braniff International Corp.—99% of which is accounted for by Braniff Airways—dropped 21% in the second quarter, to $8.8 million, even though total revenues were up 47%, to $346 million. Since then, things have gone from bad to worse, as is made starkly clear in a preliminary prospectus, dated Sept. 21, for a proposed issue of preferred stock—estimated at $75 million—by Braniff International. The prospectus reveals that Braniff lost a total of nearly $2 million in July and August and was headed for a net loss of $4.4 million or more in September. "Absent a reversal of the earnings trends of recent interim periods," the document notes— underscoring the point with italics—Braniff may be unable to pay dividends on any of its stock, including the proposed new issue.[15]

Form 8-K.   A document which describes any shift in who controls the company, bankruptcy, and the hiring of new auditors. Such personnel changes often result from major policy changes or from mismanagement of the company. Thus, familiarity with form 8-K, which must be filed within fifteen days after any significant change in operations or finances, may give a reporter a running start on major news.

Schedule 13D.   A document that must be filed when any individual or company buys more than 5 percent of the stock in a company. Included is information on the amount of stock bought, date of the purchase, and source of the buyer's funds.

Availability of these documents and hundreds of others is important to reporters. Companies have the legal responsibility to report any matter of significance which could affect, either positively or negatively, their financial performance. This can range from labor strife to new inventions to the resignation of the chief executive officer to legal battles to new ownership. Often, companies are not likely to call news conferences to make formal announcements.

Thus, the first obligation of reporters is to know what is available, where it may be obtained, and when it must be filed. Some reports, such as form 10-K, are filed at prescribed times. Others, however, are sent to the SEC only when circumstances dictate, and that represents a special challenge. Keeping track of them requires that reporters know what's happening within a company well enough to anticipate such filings and/or that they maintain regular contact with the SEC in Washington.

Tracking Privately Owned Companies

Obtaining information about a company which does not sell stock to the public is more difficult. No Freedom of Information Act applies. No disclosure laws apply. The owners control the degree of cooperation they may extend. In the absence of such cooperation, reporters are on their own. But means to some information do exist.

For one thing, there are financial services which serve the total business world by making information available. While reports from such companies as Dun & Bradstreet and Standard and Poor's Corp. are not designed for media use, they nevertheless may be obtained and can provide usable information about privately owned companies and how they relate to the industry as a whole. Such reports may be obtained by a news organization's business department, through a stock broker or any cooperative business executive.

One of the best sources is the union which represents the company's workers. Officers of labor organizations usually have data and an understanding of the operations of a company and its future plans.

Legal documents may be available as well. A trip to the local courthouse to browse through the public records involving suits and judgments perhaps is a fishing expedition, but could be valuable in getting reporters started on potentially good stories.

But, more than anything, the need is for good, basic reporting. In lieu of documents and as a complement to documents, reporters conduct interviews. They talk to people—hundreds of people—and see what they can piece together. Officials of both public and private businesses must deal with others, and that makes it inevitable that a reporter's enterprise can turn up usable information.

A GLOSSARY OF ECONOMIC TERMS

absolute advantage   The ability of a producer to produce a higher absolute quantity of a good with the productive resources available.

abundance   A term that applies when individuals can obtain all the goods they want without cost. If a good is abundant, it is free.

accelerator   The causal relationship between changes in consumption and changes in investment.

activist fiscal policy   Use of the federal government's taxing, spending, and borrowing powers in order to stimulate economic growth and employment.

actual turnover   The number of times individuals actually spend their average money holdings over a given period of time. Actual turnover is determined by the proportion of income that people receive and actually retain as money balances over a given period of time.

assets   What a person or business owns.

bank balance sheet   A bank's financial position at a given time. The bank balance sheet shows assets, liabilities, and net worth.

capital   The existing stock of productive resources, such as machines and buildings, that have been produced.

capitalist economies   Economies which use market determined prices to guide people's choices about the production and distribution of goods; these economies generally have productive resources which are privately owned.

change in demand   A shift in the entire demand curve so that at any given price people will want to buy a different amount. A change in demand is caused by some change other than a change in the good's price.

change in quantity demanded   Movement up or down a given demand curve caused only by a change in the good's price.

civilian labor force   All persons over the age of sixteen who are not in the armed forces or institutionalized and who are either employed or unemployed.

common property resources   Resources for which there are no clearly defined property rights.

comparative advantage   The ability of a producer to produce a good at a lower marginal cost than other producers; marginal cost in the sacrifice of some other good compared to the amount of a good obtained.

competition   Rivalry among individuals in order to acquire more of something that is scarce.

consumer price index   (CPI) A measure of changes in the price of hundreds of consumer goods.

corn laws   Tariffs which England placed on grain imports form 1815 to 1846. By restricting the supply of grain in England, these laws raised the price of grain in England and increased the value (rent) of English farmland.

cost   The most valuable opportunity forsaken when a choice is made.

cost-push inflation   A term that applies when increases in the price level are caused by increases in cost.

Council of Economic Advisors   Three persons who act as the President's chief economic advisers.

currency   Paper money issued by the government.

cybernetic system   A system which adjusts to changes in its environment by means of feedback information.

deficit spending   A term which refers to the situation wherein the government spends more than it receives in taxes.

demand   The maximum quantities of some good that people will choose (or buy) at different prices. An identical definition is the relative value of the marginal unit of some good when different quantities of that good are available.

demand deposits   Checking accounts in commercial banks. These banks are obliged to pay out funds when depositors write checks on those numbers. Checking accounts are not cash—they are numbers recorded in banks.

demand-pull inflation   A term used when an increase in aggregate demand occurs which cannot be offset by a corresponding increase in real supply, causing an increase in the price level (inflation).

derived value   The consumers' value of an additional unit of the productive services of a resource, such as labor. Derived value is the product of a resource's marginal productivity and the consumer's relative value of that productivity.

desired turnover The number of times individuals want to spend their average money holdings over a given period of time. Desired turnover is determined by the proportion of income that people receive and want to retain as money balances over a given period of time.

diminishing relative value The principle that if all other factors remain constant, an individual's relative value of a good will decline as more of that good is obtained. Accordingly, the relative value of a good will increase, other factors remaining constant, as an individual gives up more of that good.

diminishing returns As more and more of a productive resource is added to a given amount of other productive resources, additions to output will eventually diminish, other factors, such as technology and the degree of specialization, remaining constant.

discretionary fiscal policy Changes in a fiscal (tax or spending) program initiated by the government in order to change aggregate demand.

disposable income The amount of an individual's income that remains after the deduction of income taxes.

efficiency The allocation of goods to their uses of highest relative value.

elastic demand A term used when the percentage change in quantity demanded is larger than the percentage change in price.

equation of exchange (M X T = P X Q) This equation tells us that the money supply (M) multiplied by the number of times that money supply turns over (T) will equal the price level (P) multiplied by real output (Q).

equilibrium The amount of output supplied is equal to the amount demanded.

equity A distribution of goods that is judged to be fair by some ethical standard. The method of distributing those goods as well as the final distribution are dimensions of equity.

exchange The voluntary transfer of rights to use goods.

excess reserves That portion of a commercial bank's reserves in excess of its legal reserves.

external costs Costs involuntarily borne by people other than the individual who creates those costs.

fascist economies Economies characterized by overwhelming government control of economy; usually that control is vested in one individual or in a small group.

financial investment Those investments which do not represent purchases of final products.

fiscal drag A term that applies when the federal government's taxing and spending policies result in federal budget surpluses at full employment (which at times tend to inhibit economic growth and employment).

fiscal policy The federal government's attempts to change aggregate demand through tax and expenditure (spending) changes.

free good A good which is abundant and costless.

full employment budget The amount the federal government would spend and receive in taxes if labor resources were fully (highly) employed.

gains of exchange The difference between the relative values of a good to the buyer and the seller. How this difference is divided between the buyer and seller will depend upon the price of the good. Exchange will not occur unless both the buyer and the seller expect to receive some of this gain.

good   Anthing that anyone wants. All options or alternatives are goods. Goods can be tangible or intangible.

GNP   The sum of the prices of all the final goods and services produced in a given time period.

GNP per capita   The amount of a nation's total production available to each individual.

$$\text{per capita GNP} = \frac{\text{GNP}}{\text{population}}$$

gross national product deflator index   A measure of changes in the prices of goods counted in the GNP total.

highest-valued uses   All uses of a good which have relative values that are not less than the market clearing price.

income statement   An annual summary of income and expenses of a given business in order to determine the net income of that business.

inelastic demand   A term used when the percentage change in quantity demanded is smaller than the percentage change in price.

inflation   A decrease in the value of money.

interest   The annual earnings that are sacrificed when wealth is invested in a given asset or business. The interest sacrificed by investing in a given business is often called the cost of capital.

inter-industry concentration   The proportion of assets, sales, etc. in many industries that are owned by the biggest producers.

intra-industry concentration   The proportion of assets, sales, etc. in a given industry that are owned by the biggest producers.

inventory   A stock of goods or resources held by a buyer or seller in order to reduce the cost of exchange or production.

Keynesians   A group of economists who emphasize an activist governmental role in economic affairs through planned changes in the federal government's expenditures and taxes.

labor supply   The maximum quantities of labor services that will be offered by workers at different wages, other factors remaining constant. An identical interpretation is the workers' marginal cost of time spent working when different quantities of labor services are offered.

legal reserves   That percentage of a bank's demand deposits that must legally be held as reserves and that may not be loaned.

leisure   All uses of time in which one's labor services are not exchanged for money. The uses of everyone's time can be divided between employment and leisure.

liabilities   The debts of a person or business.

lorenz curve   A graph which visually presents a measure of the inequality of a nation's income distribution.

lowest cost uses   The highest-valued uses of a good.

marginal   The additional or extra quantity of something. If one drinks six sodas in a day, the marginal soda would be the sixth soda—the one on the margin. If your total points on the next (marginal) exam equal twenty, your marginal points are twenty.

marginal productivity   The additional output obtained by adding an additional unit of a productive resource, such as labor. More precisely, marginal productivity is the change in total output divided by the change in the amount of the productive resource employed:

$$\text{marginal productivity} = \frac{\text{change in total output}}{\text{change in amount of productive resource}}$$

marginal propensity to consume (MPC) The percentage of new or added income that is consumed.

marginal propensity to save (MPS) The percentage of new or added income that is saved.

marginal revenue The change in total revenue obtained by selling one additional unit of a good. More precisely, marginal revenue is the change in total revenue divided by the change in quantity sold:

$$MR = \frac{\text{change in total revenue}}{\text{change in quantity}}$$

market clearing price A price which rations the supply of a good among competing consumers so that the quantity of the good demanded is equal to the quantity supplied.

market concentration doctrine The belief that greater degrees of intra-industry concentration cause more collusion, resulting in higher profit rates and inflexible prices.

minimum wage A wage below which employers may not legally pay employees for specific kinds of employment.

monetarists A group of economists who emphasize mcney supply changes as a central cause of price and output (income) changes in our economy.

monetary assets Assets whose money values do not change as inflation occurs.

monetary liabilities Liabilities (debts) whose money values do not change as inflation occurs.

monetary policy The federal government's attempt to change aggregate demand through money supply changes.

money Any good which is generally used as a medium of exchange and as a common denominator for prices of other goods.

money multiplier The process by which excess reserves create new demand deposits or money; for example, with a 10% legal reserve requirement, $10 of excess reserves may be used to create $100 of new demand deposits or money.

monopoly A market in which there is only one seller of a given good.

monopoly power The ability of a seller to charge a higher price without having sales fall to zero. Monopoly power is more precisely called market power. All sellers who have downward sloping demand curves have some market power.

monopsonist A single buyer of any commodity in any given market.

multiplier The number of times new investment spending will be re-spent to produce a certain amount of new income.

natural rate of unemployment The amount of civilian unemployment the economy tends to produce even when the supply and demand for labor are equal. The natural rate is determined by the percentage of the civilian labor force unemployed at one time or another during any given year multiplied by the average time people spend searching for jobs.

near monies Assets which are not directly exchangeable for goods and services but which may be readily converted into money. A savings account is an example.

need   A specific quantity of a specific good for which an individual would pay any price. Need denies the existence of choice, for a need means that a person would not choose more of one good for less of another. Instead, a need means that a person will give up all of everything else rather than reduce consumption of a good by even small quantities.

net monetary creditor   A person who owns more monetary assets than liabilities.

net monetary debtor   A person who owns more monetary liabilities than monetary assets.

net worth   The difference between the assets and liabilities of a person or business.

New Deal   Programs initiated in the 1930s that were characterized by significantly increased government aid to various economic groups and equally significant increases in government involvement in the economy.

nominal GNP   The GNP of any year measured in that year's prices.

nominal wage   One's wage not adjusted for inflation.

oligopoly   A market in which most of the sales of a given good are accounted for by a few firms.

open inflation   An increase in the general level of money prices when market prices rise to new market clearing levels.

open market operations   The purchase or sale of government bonds by the Federal Reserve in order to change commercial banks' reserves.

option   Anything that anyone wants. In economics, options (alternatives) are also called goods.

Organization of Petroleum Exporting Countries (OPEC)   A group of nations that produce most of the world's oil and control most of the world's oil exports.

parity   A government guarantee that the ratio of prices now received by farmers to prices now paid by farmers will equal the same ratio that existed during the years 1910–1914.

political economy   Policies that emphasize the interaction between politics and economics and that have political and economic effects.

poverty income level   The minimum amount of yearly money income estimated by the government for an urban family of four. In 1976 that minimum was $5,050.

price   The amount of some other good(s) that one must offer in exchange to acquire a unit of a good. Compare this definition of price to the definition of relative value. Also note that the cost of a good to the consumer can be more than its price if there are additional exchange costs, such as waiting in line, that are borne by the consumer but not transferred to the seller.

price elasticity of demand   A measure of the responsiveness of the quantity demanded of a good to changes in that good's price.

price index   A tool to measure price changes. All price indexes compare the value of goods in a current year to the value of those same goods in a different (base) year.

price searcher   A seller who has a downward sloping demand curve and who must search for the best price to charge for a good.

profit   The excess of income over all costs, including the interest (capital) cost of the wealth invested. The net income of a business is not an accurate measure of its profit.

progressive tax   A tax which takes a higher percentage of income as income rises.

public goods   Goods whose consumption by one individual does not diminish the amount available of that good for other individuals.

pure fiscal policy   A fiscal policy that is effected without any change in the money supply.

real GNP   The GNP of any year measured in the prices of a base year. Real GNP is nominal GNP adjusted for inflation.

real investment   Those investments which represent purchases of new final products.

real wage   One's wage adjusted for inflation.

relative value   The maximum amount of some good(s) that one will offer in exchange to obtain one more unit of some other good. An identical definition is the minimum amount of some good(s) one would accept to give up one more unit of some other good.

repressed inflation   A term that applies when public officials control prices and keep them from rising to new market clearing levels. Resulting shortages cause the value of money to decline.

reserves   Cash held by commercial banks in their vaults or number deposits with the Federal Reserve Banks.

Scandinavian Socialism   A brand of socialism, characterized by abundant government welfare and planning; practiced by Sweden, Denmark, Finland and Norway.

scarce good   A good which people want more of and which is costly to obtain.

scarcity   A term used when the quantity of a good demanded exceeds the quantity supplied at the existing price.

Socialist economies   Economies that are characterized by government ownership of productive resources, significant government planning, and attempts to redistribute national income more equally.

specialization   The act of producing more of a good than one consumes, the rest of that good being exchanged.

supply   The maximum amounts of a good that producers will choose to produce and sell at different prices, other factors remaining constant. An identical definition is the marginal costs of producing a good when different quantities of that good are produced, other factors remaining constant.

surplus   A term used when the quantity of a good supplied exceeds the quantity demanded at the existing price.

survival traits   The characteristics of individuals which permit them to compete successfully.

T account   An account which summarized changes in the assets and liabilities of a person or business.

vault cash   Cash held in commercial bank vaults. This cash is not money.

waste   When the relative value of a good is different from that good's marginal cost of production, waste occurs. Goods or resources are wasted when they are allocated to uses which are not the most valuable.

wealth   The value of the existing stock of goods (assets); those goods may be tangible or intangible.

wholesale price index (WPI) A measure of changes in the prices of goods at the wholesale level, particularly those goods sold between businesses.

Source: Reproduced by permission from *Choice & Change, An Introduction to Economics,* by Dickneider and Kaplan, West Publishing Co., St. Paul, Minn., 1978.

NOTES

1. Jack Busby, remarks made at the Region 1 Conference, Society of Professional Journalists, Sigma Delta Chi, Hershey, Pa., April 22, 1978.
2. Dom Bonafede, "The Bull Market in Business/Economics Reporting," *Washington Journalism Review,* July–August 1980, p. 24.
3. Dan Cordtz, remarks made at the Region 1 Conference, Society of Professional Journalists, Sigma Delta Chi, Hershey, Pa., April 22, 1978.
4. Louis Banks, "Memo to the Press: They Hate You Out There," *The Atlantic,* April 1978, p. 37.
5. See, for example, Herbert Stein, "Media Distortions: A Former Official's View," *Columbia Journalism Review,* March–April 1975, pp. 37–41; "Economists on Reporting," *Washington Journalism Review,* July–August 1980, pp. 32–34; Walter Cowan, "Business Executives Say What They Think of Media," *APME News,* August 1979, p. 8; James L. Ferguson, "Business and the News Media: Can We Find a Better Channel?," *Editor & Publisher,* October 23, 1976; A. Kent MacDougall, "Flaws in Press Coverage Plus Business Sensitivity Stir Bitter Debate," *Los Angeles Times,* February 3, 1980, Part V, pp. 1+ (adapted and reproduced as "A Business Problem: Bull Market in Bad News," *Washington Journalism Review,* July–August 1980, pp. 32–34); S. Prakash Sethi, "Business and the News Media: The Paradox of Informed Misunderstanding," *California Management Review,* Spring 1977, pp. 52–62; William H. Miller, "The Media: Friend or Foe?," *Industry Week,* July 21, 1980, pp. 38–43.
6. Jeff Greenfield, "Selling the Depression," *Columbia Journalism Review,* March–April 1975, pp. 42–43.
7. "Flaws in Press Coverage Plus Business Sensitivity Stir Bitter Debate," p. 4.
8. Ralph Otwell, "Big, Bad Business in the Hands of the Devil Press," *The Quill,* April 1977, p. 17. Courtesy of *The Quill,* published by The Society of Professional Journalists, Sigma Delta Chi.
9. "Reporters on Economics," *Washington Journalism Review,* July–August 1980, p. 31.
10. Dan Cordtz, remarks made at Better Business Reporting Seminar, Russell, Ky., April 25, 1978.
11. "Big, Bad Business in the Hands of the Devil Press," pp. 17–18.
12. "The 40th Annual Report Awards," *Financial World,* October 15, 1980, p. 63.
13. "The 40th Annual Report Awards," p. 63.
14. Steve Woodward, *Public Files of the SEC* (Columbia, Mo.: Freedom of Information Center, August 1979), p. 1. This Freedom of Information Center Report No. 408 is a very good overview of SEC documents of value to reporters. A complete list of forms used by the SEC is available in Title 17 (Commodities and Securities Exchange) of

the Code of Federal Regulations. The SEC publishes another source of general information, titled *Manual of General Record Information.*

15. Reprinted from the October 29, 1979, issue of *Business Week,* "Indigestion Brings Financial Woe to Braniff," by special permission, © 1979 by McGraw-Hill, Inc., New York, N.Y. 10020. All rights reserved.

Chapter 14

ECONOMICS COVERAGE: THE STANDARD-OF-LIVING BEATS

If public interest in economic matters has increased, you can bet it's not in cosmic questions about the economy. Public discussion of abstract economic theory provides almost as good an opportunity as commercials to dash to the kitchen. Fortunately, journalists have begun to learn that. People may be vaguely interested in the gross national product, but their chief concern is the local economy. Their attitude will always be: "That's interesting, but how does it affect me, my family, or my neighbor?"

The economy is not difficult to relate in such local and personal terms. The corner market is part of the economy. So is the factory on the edge of town. Farmers, too. And plumbers.

Dan Cordtz of ABC News may have put the whole approach to economics coverage into its best perspective in a 1978 speech. Despite his position as a network correspondent, which forces him to deal with national issues, Cordtz pushes local and personal coverage of the economy.

> The starting point is what I regard as the proper definition of economics—and that's anything that has anything to do with your viewers' material standard of living. What's more, that's an area that neither ABC nor the other networks will ever cover adequately. We'll leave you all kinds of room to move around in.
>
> For that reason, you can probably—if you want to—even do the sort of explanatory stories about national statistics or trends that we occasionally do on the Evening News. Certainly you can do big-picture stories about what's happening to your local

Dan Cordtz of ABC News

(Photo by J. P. Forsthoffer)

economy. Are you gaining jobs? Losing jobs? Are wages and retail sales and savings and consumer debt and delinquencies and bankruptcies rising as much as they are nationally? More? Less? How come?

What about local companies? Are they doing well? Sales up? Profits up? Enough? Are they expanding, modernizing, turning out new products, breaking new technological ground, trying new approaches to working conditions or employee relations? I recently ran into some stuff on the large number of companies that are into big programs of remedial economic education for their workers. It may be pure propaganda, but even that's interesting.

Take a look at the economic aspects of local institutions. If you have a college in your area, I'll bet tuition and costs are skyrocketing, and I'll bet a lot of people are disturbed and wonder why. And I'll bet that not even you actually know why. A good story, and one that the networks have only given a once-over-lightly.

The economy of local government is a huge subject that I personally have never seen done well on the air. And that's going to be a bigger story every year. Is your city making the same mistakes that New York made? How much has the payroll grown? Why? Is it really doing that much more? Is the local government trying to boost productivity, trim costs, cut services, contract out more work? How about government employees' wages? How do they compare with the private sector? Even if they're low, what's happened to fringe benefits . . .?

Taxes—my god, taxes! Not only are taxes the only thing besides death that's certain, they probably make most of your viewers mad as hell. And unless your city is a rare exception, your viewers probably have a lot to be mad about. Network television pays a fair amount of attention to federal income taxes, but my guess is that they annoy people a lot less than local taxes—especially property taxes. And the property tax structure across much of the country is an inconsistent, inequitable scandal. In most communities, you can find certain organizations and companies given special treatment.

Just the comparison of your local tax structure with that of the statistically average American city may be revealing and interesting. A number of cities have a fantastic percentage of their property entirely off the tax rolls, because it's owned by churches or educational or charitable institutions. One fascinating and important aspect of taxes is what the property tax can do for development. If undeveloped property is taxed at low rates, as it is most places, it encourages speculation and urban sprawl. I know of a couple of places where a drastic shift in tax policy resulted in a miraculous development. . . .

But a better subject for economic stories than any of those things is people. Even the other story ideas I mentioned obviously need to be handled in a way that relates them directly to your viewers. But I contend that viewers are interested in other people almost as much as they are in themselves. And there's absolutely nothing that most people would rather do than peek in the keyhole of somebody else's house— especially to find out just how they live and spend their money. . . .

You can do stories about rich folks, poor folks, the always-disgruntled middle class, young marrieds, swinging singles, blacks, ethnics, divorced parents, you name the category—all of them centered around how these people cope with the economic situation.

I can see this sort of thing spinning off into stories about how people earn their living in interesting, different—or even typical—ways. Especially working women. What kinds of jobs are they getting, how are they doing, what are the problems and complications involved? Teen-agers—why can't they get jobs? Does it really matter to anyone but them? Retirees—do they moonlight to pad out the Social Security? Do they want to work, but can't find anything? The whole business of moonlighting, and families with more than one person working is an important phenomenon with a lot of implications, and it's something to which people must relate, sympathetically or otherwise.

Finally, there's the obvious field of consumerism, and I won't even bother to go into that—but it's clearly a part of the same beat as business and economics.[1]

JOURNALISM'S DIVERSIFIED APPROACH

It takes teamwork and diversification for news organizations to cover the economy. No single individual can know all there is to know, cover the territory, and write even the most necessary stories. The organizational chart may not show it clearly, but newspapers, magazines, and some broadcast facilities will have several—if not several dozen—reporters directly responsible for news and analysis of the factors having economic impact: corporations and smaller businesses, financial news, real estate, transportation, labor, consumers, energy and the environment, agriculture, government. And they may be supplemented by an individual or team focusing investigative skills on economic activities.

Through such diversification, news organizations are reaching into many corners of the economic world. This has greatly improved coverage, of course, but there's room for more.

COVERING THE ENVIRONMENT AND ENERGY

The environment is not a new journalistic subject. Wildlife writers, natural resources writers, conservation writers have been on the scene for years. But it was not until the mid-twentieth century that the subject gained the kind of public interest that attracted and held journalistic attention. Specialized magazines such as *Field and Stream, National Wildlife,* and *American Forest* were examining broader conservation issues in the 1940s. General-circulation magazines began discussing air and water pollution in the 1950s.

"Not in their wildest dreams, however, did pioneer environmentalists anticipate that all the big general-circulation magazines would ever devote virtually simultaneous whole issues to ecology," says Clay Schoenfeld of the University of Wisconsin. "Yet that is exactly what happened in late 1969 and early 1970. Triggered by Earth Day, *Time, Life, Newsweek, Look, Fortune, Saturday Review* again, *Sports Illustrated, Esquire, National Geographic,* and others joined the bandwagon."[2]

Earth Day generally is considered the breakthrough—April 22, 1970, a national day of ecological awareness and consciousness raising. An estimated 20 million Americans took part, including students at more than 2,000 colleges and 10,000 high schools and grade schools.

Reporters covered the observances, and many of them continued on, becoming part of a new breed of journalist. Environmental protection became a political movement. It merited attention, with most of the early focus being on water pollution, air pollution, and urban sprawl.

There were horror stories about the possible destruction of a planet. Environmentalists persuaded more and more people that unchallenged and uncontrolled growth was a major cause of the problems. They pointed particularly to development of what they considered dangerous systems for producing energy, the rate at which natural fuels were being consumed, and pollution caused by the burning of these fuels, especially in automobiles.

Then came the Arab oil embargo of 1973. For the first time in American history, energy was not plentiful. That cemented energy's importance in the public mind and gave environmental journalists another focus.

"I started on this beat in 1967, and it has changed considerably since then," says Casey Bukro of the *Chicago Tribune.* "It still deals with air pollution, water pollution, noise, land usage, population trends. And then energy came along and since the environment people were covering power companies and steel mills anyway and had the contacts, we began to get into oil and gas and nuclear power and coal technology. Of course, you tend to stay with the hot topics, and right now energy is hot. I spend about half my time on energy, although I get back to environment as often as I can."

Casey Bukro of the *Chicago Tribune*

(*Chicago Tribune* photo)

Reporters responsible for covering environment and energy face special challenges which make their tasks simultaneously more difficult and more interesting. The assignment represents a blend of science, business, and government, with a dash of human rights. It can be approached from each angle, depending on a given story, the reporter's preferences, or news organization policy.

The business component is twofold. This country, for many years, operated under the assumption that industrial growth and increasing production could continue forever, that raw materials were infinite. The resultant rapid commercial expansion has affected the environment and energy resources. The rather natural second business element is in efforts to find solutions. How much will they cost? Who must bear the financial burden? What efforts must be made to develop alternative approaches at reasonable cost? What is the role of commercial enterprises and of government?

Certainly, the problems are scientific. They fall under the headings of chemistry, engineering, and biology. And if naivete about the long-range impact of galloping technology is the source of the problem, then most Americans feel it will be the sophistication of technology which provides the solutions. It will be scientific research which produces the alternatives and provides means of returning balance to natural forces. Providing realistic assessments of the validity of this belief, scientifically and economically, is a major journalistic assignment.

But there's another element, one emphasized by Paul Andrews of the *Seattle Times.*

"You have to have the business element in most environmental stories," he says. "But I think more and more it's almost a human rights kind of situation. The environment affects everyday lives and life styles and—particularly in the northwest where people are sensitive about it—people feel they have a right to live a certain way without being infringed on by industry, air pollution, or even noise pollution. It becomes a personal type of issue, a human issue."

The correct answer to an examination question on this subject would be "all of the above." Reporters may prefer a certain approach, but their coverage cannot be exclusive. While there will be regional differences which correlate with public interest and specific problems, it's the job of the environment writer to put it all together.

"Too often, stories are written with one point of view or a limited set of facts," Bukro says. "I'd like to think that environmental writers in the future, whatever we call them, will spend more time trying to show how things relate to each other. It sounds trite, I know, because we've heard since the early days of the environment crusade that everything is related to everything else. A nice slogan, but how often do we see these relationships explored by the media? I'd like to see more 'Big Picture' reporting—the kind that follows chains of events so that the reader can understand, for example, why the snail darter is more than a three-inch fish and represents some larger issues."[3]

White Hats and Black Hats

Getting at those larger issues places the environment and energy reporter into a journalistically unusual situation. Environmentalism sprang from a perceived set of problems. If there were no reasons for concern, there would be no need for a crusade or extensive journalistic coverage. Once the decision has been made that the problems exist, reporters must take sides, not in terms of joining individuals or groups against other individuals and groups, but in terms of seeking to overcome the problems.

"I have strong feelings for environmental advocacy, and I'm not ashamed to express them in any kind of audience, including those who have suffered under the politics of environmental advocacy," says Paul Hayes of the *Milwaukee Journal*. "In the last analysis, everybody is an environmental advocate. What we are after in this life is an environment that is comfortable and reinforcing and inspirational to us all. And that includes the paper mill president as well as the Sierra Club president. Everybody is after clean air and clean water, some living room, and an environment that is immediately healthful."

No one opposes a proper environment, although there are differences on the definition of "proper," on how the goal is to be achieved, how rapidly, and who is to foot the bill. The environment these days is a battleground which has many sides. Reporters utilize traditional skepticism and give the opposing forces equal chances to prove their points. Digging for full information, confirming comments,

Paul Hayes of the *Milwaukee Journal*

(*Milwaukee Journal* photo by Dale Guldan)

and fairly representing opposing attitudes must not be ignored out of a sense of commitment to "the cause."

Much of the environmental movement's early coverage emphasized criticism, with horror stories about rampant destruction by seemingly uncaring people. The criticism included elements of truth, but it often was exaggerated and based too much on emotion rather than scientific evidence. The coverage caught the attention of the public, but it represented a period in which naive journalists were used. An unfortunate legacy of that time is a characteristic negativism that pervades much of environmental reporting.

Part of that negative tone, then and now, grows from the tendency to look at controversy as a dichotomy. The participants are viewed in white hats and black hats. Environmental groups and the Environmental Protection Agency appear as the good guys, and industry and other governmental agencies emerge as the bad guys.

Herb Schmertz of Mobil Corporation is among those who have criticized what he feels is the tendency of reporters to assign such roles to participants. One of the business community's most outspoken critics of energy coverage, Schmertz defines four stereotypes: *liberal politician,* defender of consumer interests and environmental protection; *conservative politician,* in the pocket of big business; *social activist,* a "public interest" representative; *oil executive,* motivated by greed for more profits, unwilling to put the country's good ahead of the company's good.[4]

"The failure of American journalism," he says, "is this: it has felt free to report the gossip and recriminations but has done little to expose the political motivations that give rise to them. Herein lies the information gap. The fact is that the real energy story has been the political manipulation and prostitution of the energy issue. The press has simply ignored this story."[5]

In the early days, the relative newness of the beat and complexity of the issues explained the reporters' failings. First-generation reporters had little tradition and often inadequate backgrounds to help them cope. They have learned and matured since then, but the complexity remains. It's still a government, science, and business story. Reporters still must present information in nontechnical form. They still must deal with debate over the viability of solutions.

Day-by-day breaking news must be covered, but reporters are beginning to pay more attention to long-range coverage. Too many in the past have concentrated on symptoms instead of causes. The problems were decades in the making and may be decades in the solving. The solutions will involve alternatives, not just rehashing of the problems or inordinate enthusiasm over one possible answer.

In short, advises George W. O'Connor, president of Montana Power Co., all participants must look more to the total environment.

"What all this boils down to," he says, "is the fact that we have not always considered the total environment before we took action on specific environmental matters. We have failed to give full consideration to the human environment and the socio-economic environment when we have taken action on other environmental fronts.

"This may be a basic fault in the democratic system. Certainly it is a fault on all our parts—from government to business to education to the media. And I'm not certain anyone has all the answers. I am convinced that part of the solution does lie in your [reporters'] definition of the environmental story, and I believe that definition must attempt to encompass every conceivable part of the environment before you can end the story."[6]

Sources of Information

The mechanics of getting information are largely the same as those for any reporter: interviews and documents. Especially when the issue is controversial, reporters say, persons representing all points of view may line up to be interviewed. Or they present papers, testify, and write articles. The problem for the reporter, frequently, is making sense out of conflicting information and opinion.

Citizens' organizations, especially locally, continue to be a primary source of information, although they probably don't have the clout they once had. Reporters devote more time to balancing charges and responses, and they are more cautious about devoting major attention to highly emotional charges and doomsday predictions.

Larger citizens' organizations are more sophisticated in their discussions and professional in their research. They often have staff or volunteer scientists on whose research and conclusions many of the arguments are based. That helps, but it doesn't mean that local groups, without access to scientists, should be ignored. Their points in an environmental debate deserve attention, and not only because they have the right to speak out. They know the local situation, and that's a perspective which merits journalistic attention.

"You have to be careful not to interpose yourself as some kind of final judge," says Jon Sawyer of the *St. Louis Post-Dispatch.* "You have to make decisions, but you must be careful of too quickly saying, 'Well, this isn't worth a story' or 'This obviously is ludicrous.' Maybe it is distorted and maybe it is overstated, but there may be some truth in it. Part of the function of a newspaper is to let the charges get out and let the countercharges follow and work your way toward some kind of resolution."

Jon Sawyer of the *St. Louis Post-Dispatch*

(*St. Louis Post-Dispatch* photo)

Among those organizations which have achieved national prominence as sources of environmental and energy information are the Friends of the Earth and the Sierra Club, both based in San Francisco; the Environmental Defense Fund and National Audubon Society of New York City; and the Union of Concerned Scientists of Cambridge, Massachusetts. These and other organizations generally have both legal and scientific sources available. They publish books, magazines, newsletters, pamphlets, and other forms of information and tend to be more than willing to work with reporters.

The relationships of business sources with reporters depend upon those sources' attitudes toward news organizations and their past experience with journalists. A common tendency is to refer requests to public relations personnel, a tendency most reporters resist. Utility companies, especially, are criticized by reporters for being less than cooperative during these days of heated controversy.

But industry sources can be developed by reporters, either for quotation or not for attribution. They are becoming more accustomed to dealing with news organizations, they are learning what to expect, and some have gained appreciation for the long-range value of openness. Over a period of time, says Paul Hayes of the *Milwaukee Journal,* industry representatives tend to become more professional in getting information out "if they have professional reporters to deal with."

The industry perspective, like that of ecology groups, is pushed by a number of organizations, some of which have gained some national attention. For example, it's advocated in California by an organization that calls itself Californians for an Environment of Excellence, Full Employment and a Strong Economy Through Planned Development. On a larger scale, the American Petroleum Institute of Washington, D.C., is perhaps the major representative of the oil industry in the national debate. The Atomic Industrial Forum of New York City is the trade association of the nuclear power industry.

As the environmental movement has grown to encompass larger circles of American society, government's role at all levels has become increasingly important to the journalist. The range of activity is great and involves all three branches of government. It includes legislation, regulation, land and resource management, statistical and background information, and educational programs.

The business of state legislatures and Congress provides reporters with countless information possibilities in the form of speeches, hearings on specific acts or general problems, debates, and a long list of sources who are willing, even anxious, to speak on environmental concerns. Court decisions, as always, are of value because they represent settlement of disputes or potentially significant legal interpretations.

It is the executive branch—federal, state, and local—which usually attracts the greatest attention, however, because it is responsible for government's regulatory activities.

"Perhaps nothing has so changed the face of environment coverage in the mass media as has the requirement of the National Environmental Policy Act for the development of environmental impact statements on federally funded projects, accompanied by related requirements in many states," says Clay Schoenfeld of the University of Wisconsin. "The . . . statements have automatically provided

---

One Danger in Nuclear Accidents Is the Fib Fallout

BY CASEY BUKRO

Chicago Tribune environment editor

The confusion and the hysteria over the Three Mile Island nuclear power plant accident last March are often blamed these days on a sensation-mongering press.

The President's Commission on the Accident at Three Mile Island will, let us hope, set the record straight when it issues a report due Oct. 25.

Let's also hope that the report will focus on a fundamental question in reporting and in the issue of nuclear safety: Who's responsible for the truth?

Pennsylvania's Gov. Richard Thornburgh once said: "I came to appreciate the problems news reporters were facing.

"The nuclear trade jargon, the clamor of competing experts, and the garble gap between Harrisburg and Washington, all made it quite easy to understand how five different stories could come out of a single press conference, through no fault of the reporters involved."

It was more than a difference in interpreting the facts. The so-called experts being quoted by the press at the time later proved to be wrong, sometimes drawing attention away from matters that were important in a potentially dangerous situation.

For example, the *Chicago Tribune* disclosed recently that there never was any chance of a hydrogen bubble explosion in the reactor. Yet the experts spent days talking about the potential for such an explosion, which in turn could have triggered a nuclear disaster.

Conflicting statements by Metropolitan Edison Co., operators of the nuclear station, and the Nuclear Regulatory Commission (NRC) were commonplace.

During the course of the accident, the utility said releases of radioactive gas were intentional, "to relieve pressure." The other said they were accidental (which they were). One said "the crisis is over" a few days after the accident started. The other said it was not over.

The arrival of Harold Denton, the NRC's director of nuclear reactor regulation, was intended to solve it. Denton was sent at the request of Gov. Thornburgh. Plagued by disagreeing "experts," the governor asked President Carter to send someone who could speak with authority without adding to the confusion.

About the same time, Met Ed spokesmen said they were being gagged by the NRC. In answer to questions, they said they were barred from giving any answers. Said one:

"As of this moment, we are under strict orders not to say a thing." Asked who gave those orders, he replied: "I don't know. We have an agreement with the NRC."

The NRC officially denies such a gag-order, although Denton made all announcements about the accident from then on. Some segments of the press dubbed him the "Hero of Harrisburg," presumably because he was giving out information when nobody else would.

Met Ed would not issue statements without NRC approval. The NRC said its approval was not needed, leaving reporters with a Catch-22 that hindered their efforts.

Today, nobody will admit that such an agreement existed.

"I'm not aware of it, or I've forgotten," said Robert Arnold, Met Ed's vice president. But he and others often praise the Denton single-voice approach as one that cured the Harrisburg garble.

It is likely to be the strategy used in any future nuclear accident. It was considered convenient and did away with conflicting statements.

But does it serve the truth and public safety? Nobody has explained by what authority, formally or informally, a federal agency can gag a utility supposedly in charge of a potentially disastrous accident. Critics might argue that more voices are needed in such perilous times, not fewer.

What if the single voice is wrong?

Source: Casey Bukro, "One Danger in Nuclear Accidents is the Fib Fallout," *Chicago Tribune*, September 25, 1979, p. 5F. Copyright ©, *Chicago Tribune*. Used with permission.

two basic news ingredients—they are events that are happening now, and they have a high component of conflict. So they have become grist for the media mills. When they have prompted court suits and counter-suits, they have doubled and quadrupled both the quantity and the quality of media coverage.

"Before NEPA, the environmental reporter was like a sports writer restricted largely to 'think pieces' because there were very few 'games' actually to cover. With NEPA, the environmental reporter has a vastly escalated number of points of entry to his running story on environmental issues and actions. It is unlikely that any other single federal act has had such an inadvertent yet nonetheless profound impact on the flow of news on a particular aspect of public affairs."[7]

At the federal level, this trend has made the Environmental Protection Agency the principal source of environmental information. And states usually have a similar organization, often with the same name or perhaps called something such as the Air Conservation Commission or Clean Water Commission. These groups have the authority to enforce standards for air and water quality and often for handling hazardous solid wastes and pesticides. That makes good copy.

But governmental involvement with the environment goes well beyond regulation and the Environmental Protection Agency. Numerous other groups devote attention to environmental protection. The U.S. Forest Service and Soil Conservation Service, for example, have worked for years to preserve natural resources. The Army Corps of Engineers deals with water resources; the National Institute of Environmental Health Sciences is concerned with the impact on health. Then there's the Bureau of Land Management, the Bureau of Outdoor Recreation, the Bureau of Reclamation, and the National Park Service, all of which function as part of the U.S. Department of the Interior for specific conservation purposes.

Another relatively new kid on the block is the Federal Energy Administration, which has responsibility for fuel allocation and for energy conservation programs. Importantly for reporters, this body also operates its own information source, the National Energy Information Center.

Most states also have groups assigned the task of regulating and supervising utility companies. These groups usually are called something similar to Public Utilities Commission, and, properly developed, their personnel may be good news sources.

Among the major needs of the environment and energy reporter are sources who do not have axes to grind and who are not representing specific points of view. For example:

"I think oil companies are very good at telling the press what they want them to know," says Carol Curtis of *Business Week.* "And at keeping from the press what they don't want them to know. What I like to do when I'm writing an oil story is, after checking with the oil companies and getting their response, to call as many other sources as I possibly can—private economists, people in universities, consultants—and see if I can't get some kind of consensus, which I know goes a lot deeper than the oil-company line."[8]

College campuses represent a potential pool of such sources. The environmental movement historically gained some of its strongest support on the nation's campuses, and it probably is there that interest continues at its highest level. New classes, research, books, and continuing education programs all add up to a wealth of information. Major universities have outreach programs with personnel who could be helpful to local reporters. Land grant institutions have agricultural extension services, represented by county agricultural agents, as sources on conservation.

The lack of direct affiliation with a corporation or environmental group does not necessarily ensure that a scientist or economist will be neutral. The debates over the environment and energy involve personal philosophy as much as organizational representation. The job of the reporter is to find scientific and economic sources who speak plainly about their discipline and let the political chips fall where they may.

It's a Human Story

Environment and energy reporters have begun devoting greater attention to providing long-range information in a way that makes it pertinent to immediacy-conscious citizens. Again, this is best accomplished by telling the story in human terms.

"It's strange," Burkro says, "that the environment beat—whose essence is the welfare of living things—is so often explained in terms of technology and legal rulings. The human element tends to get lost as we deal in 'things.' People tend to relate to other people. So we in this business have spent too much time talking about the nuts and bolts. We in environment reporting have come to realize that unless you can relate technology to human needs, there is very little interest in what you're writing. You have to show human concern or interest, both of which are emotions."

But that does not mean going overboard. It's important to know the difference between stories that are inherently emotion-ridden and stories that are sensationalized. Some of the old-time tear jerkers were ordinary events made to look dramatic. That is sensationalism. It makes something look bigger than it is.

In contrast, when Bukro and the *Tribune* did a "Save Our Lake" series on water pollution in the Great Lakes, they decided to let the story tell itself. Although what was reported was factual, it drew charges of sensationalism.

"I thought," he says, "that the situation as it existed was sensational, and needed nothing from me to further dramatize it. So we walked a fine line, just describing what any individual could see or smell if they were at the water's edge, as I was. It's just a matter of giving an accurate and factual account. That's the key—an accurate and factual account—so that you can say to anybody who accuses you of sensationalism: 'You look at what I saw, and tell me if you could describe it any other way.' "

Such natural emotion is not put into a story. It's pulled from that story by writers of talent. Human beings deal with real environmental situations, and reporters miss a bet if they don't key in on that relationship. Is there real danger? Inconvenience? Who suffers? How do environment and energy problems affect life? What's the economic impact? The aesthetic impact? This does not deny the value of technology, legal rulings, and history. It provides a perspective with feeling, one which clarifies the circumstance in terms of their real meaning.

COVERING CONSUMER AFFAIRS

In her college days at Syracuse University, Nancy Webman was a campus activist. Those were the days of protests. The war in Vietnam. Cambodia. Kent State. She couldn't sit back and watch it all happen without expressing her opinion. She had strong beliefs and firm dedication to fairness. As an activist, she sought to live up to that sense of fair play.

Nancy Webman of the *Ft. Worth Star Telegram*

(*Ft. Worth Star Telegram* photo)

"There were two newspapers on campus at the time," she says. "One was extremely radical and presented only the point of view of the students and never the university or the government. The other paper was an administration newspaper. A handful of us got together and started another newspaper called *Dialogue* because the other two papers were monologues. We wanted to give the students something balanced to read."

Her situation is different these days, but Nancy Webman hasn't changed much. She's a consumer reporter for the *Fort Worth Star-Telegram* and still driven by the ideals of her college days. She labels herself a civil libertarian and feminist. Her superiors refer to her as the conscience of the newsroom.

"I like working within the system to change the system," she says. "Our city hall reporters work within the system to report the system. They make no effort to present a problem and a solution, which is my favorite thing to do. Just reporting what happened is boring to me. The business section, rightly or wrongly, takes a business advocacy position. I take a consumer advocacy position. In a way, that's ridiculous because every story's supposed to present both sides. That's what newspapers are all about. So even though I feel like I have to represent the consumer, I bend over backwards to give both sides a chance because, dammit, I'm a newspaper person first."

Types of Consumer Reporting

Webman is thus representative of a new breed of reporters, emphasizing the needs of citizens who historically have had little journalistic attention. Consumer reporting is a twentieth century development which goes hand in hand with environmental reporting in gaining much of its impetus from ordinary citizens. That provides several approaches to the subject matter.

The most common could be labeled the *how-to* story—how to do a more effective job of purchasing, how to save money in the supermarket or buying insurance, how to determine quality. The emphasis is on helping consumers understand the process and on giving them information they can put to use. Often seasonal, it may involve comparison shopping and informing the audience of the best price or the best buy in terms of quality and price. Or it may consist of explanations, for example, of income tax deductions or what the consumer price index means in everyday life.

A second approach is reporting on *regulatory action.* One of the paradoxes of modern journalism is the way it often joins forces with government in efforts to correct practices which are detrimental to citizens. Some would say governmental efforts have been inadequate, but it is fact that in recent years, American government has taken a stronger consumerism approach through its regulatory agencies. Investigations and decisions of such groups often provide the stories which reporters follow or often represent the starting point for deeper journalistic analysis.

Providing information about *citizen-consumer-neighborhood-community action groups* represents a third concentraton. Citizens do not sit still and calmly accept everything these days. Spurred on by leaders of the consumerism movement and even governmental agencies, they organize, protest, request funds to set up and run self-improvement programs. Journalists fan these local blazes by providing the encouragement of publicity and by helping document the concerns for which solutions are sought.

Among the most complex of journalistic consumer-reporting efforts is the reporting of *corporate power* and corporate activities with direct—perhaps negative—impact on the community and its citizens. This may be as simple as reporting on corporate policies on employment or as complex as analyzing the political economy in terms of consumer issues, for example, whether campaign contributions influence votes in legislative bodies.

And there is the *investigative* approach. Reporters define the problem, ascertain the need, conduct their inquiries, and spread the word. Investigative reporting, more than anything, represents a willingness to take the initiative and devote time to finding explanations for social circumstances. This may be reporting of deliberate consumer fraud. It may involve questionable practices—perhaps inadvertent —which raise prices, lower quality, or create health or safety problems. It may be an explanation of a local situation which has affected prices, such as shop owners' increasing prices to compensate for losses to shoplifting.

Few journalists fit exclusively into a single mode of consumer reporting, nor should they. A news organization will establish policies about emphasis, of course, but the best coverage involves all these levels. An expose may be more exciting journalistically than discussing how to select a good cut of meat at the best price but, overall, the value of consumer journalists will depend on how well they cover the spectrum.

The quality of their performance is a subject of some disagreement these days, especially among those such as consumer advocate Ralph Nader, who says the journalistic effort has improved but remains inadequate.

"It's better than it was 15 years ago," he says. "First of all, media are now willing to name brand names in the context of critical stories. Second, the media are willing to report citizen research and commentary more than before when it was primarily official-source journalism. Third, more newspapers and TV stations are devoting resources to having full-time consumer reporters.

"Having said that, however, one must keep in mind that there's a long way to go, that the local department stores and local drug chains and local factories carry a lot of implicit opportunity for self-censorship by newspapers, and the coverage of Main Street USA is not very good. Many reporters will report a dangerous drug finding by a national drug company, but they won't report a local chemical waste dump hazard by a local company that is an economic force in the community."

Nader is particularly critical of journalism's efforts to report the impact of the political system on the consumer. This, he says, is the broadest and most important type of journalism, but it's the most poorly done because the more consumer news focuses on point of sale, the less opportunity it has to provide public information directed toward prevention of the problem in the first place.

"For example, you say, 'Well, here's how you choose different cuts of meat,' but there's very little reporting on the meat plant, on sanitary standards, on U.S. Department of Agriculture regulations. Under those circumstances, the light of public information which might lead to change at the source of the problem far removed from the point of sale in the store, is minimized."

Others, without denying the importance of the larger perspective advocated by Nader, take a different approach, criticizing reporters for overemphasis on stories about business versus the consumer. They say too much consumer news is after-the-fact reporting, and greater attention should be placed on helping the consumer in the marketplace.[9]

Bringing It Home

Whatever the approach, the essential ingredient of consumer reporting is its emphasis on people. The term itself is the clue. It's a broad concept, made up of anything that affects people, the way they spend their money, who has the money, where it comes from, what products and services are available, and any possible health or safety hazards involved.

"My approach is a pragmatic one," says Louise Cook, The Associated Press' award-winning consumer reporter. Business news would tend to look more at the causes of inflation, for example, and what can be done to lower the inflation rate. I tend to say, 'OK, it's happened. It's fine to know why it happened, but here's what you can do to deal with it to minimize its impact on your life—how you can cope.' "

Louise Cook of The Associated Press

Cook stresses the balance between providing such information and advice and conducting an investigation to uncover the deeper causes of the problem. She notes a series of stories about Firestone tires as an example. It was consumer reporting to publicize that the tires had been found to have defects. It was consumer reporting to cover all the lawsuits, the efforts by Firestone to resist a recall, and the efforts by various groups to have a recall. It is equally consumer reporting to answer the questions of the reader who sees all this material and wonders whether it's safe to drive on the tires. And it's consumer reporting to look into why the problem arose in the first place.

When one takes such an approach, story ideas come from everywhere. Here is one advantage the consumer reporter has over other journalists. The political reporter is not a politician. The education reporter is not an educator. But the consumer reporter *is* a consumer and can uncover stories just by being observant during normal day-to-day living. Webman, for example, says that, much to her husband's chagrin, she allows every fast-talking salesperson who comes to her door to come inside. And she gets a story, she says, from about 20 percent of these encounters.

The best consumer reporters also stress that the human approach involves more than writing about consumers and to consumers. It means using consumers as sources in the story. It has been stated, probably correctly, that average citizens were aware of this nation's economic problems in the late 1970s before the professional economists were. They knew it because they experienced it. And they tend to be willing to talk about it. Consumers intuitively know that their problems will not be solved unless public discussion is stimulated. They know public discussion results from publicity. And maybe that's why they're so willing to open up and talk about private financial problems.

For all its value, using consumers as sources also adds a burden to reporters —a burden which necessitates going to economic and/or governmental experts. Individuals who are having problems, as well as consumer groups organized to fight such problems, often are emotional and have a right to be. They're dealing with an emotional subject. Reporters usually find it necessary to consult others who have broader or deeper knowledge, have access to specific facts, and can be objective.

That's why the advocacy role of consumer reporting may pose problems. It is true that the consumer reporter is an advocate in the sense that he or she may represent the consumer. But that is not an excuse for one-sided coverage. The consumer needs a full report, the country needs a full report. It is well that consumers have journalists who are interested in what they say and need. But, as Webman says, "Dammit, I'm a newspaper person first."

COVERING LABOR AND WORK

It's difficult to avoid the conclusion that American journalism has taken an elephant's tail approach to coverage of labor. The attention reporters give to unions in the name of labor reporting simply ignores the size of the animal they should be dealing with. In excess of 100 million persons are employed in this country, with perhaps one-quarter of them involved with labor unions. Yet, by far, coverage has and continues to focus mainly on organized labor.

Even the news devoted to unions has been narrow. In many instances, it has represented only coverage of unions on strike. A "work stoppage," as it is now being called, is only part of the process of collective bargaining. Union and management representatives negotiate, the union makes a proposal, the company responds with a counteroffer, they go back and forth, perhaps there is a strike, perhaps not, an agreement is reached, ratified, and put into effect, has specific impact on the workers and the company, has broader impact on the community at large. Each stage represents a component of the total process. Each merits journalistic attention.

Three other aspects of organized labor have been covered but deserve more coverage. Unions don't come into being at the time of a strike. They exist, elect officers, develop philosophies, and implement programs. Coverage of these operations might help eliminate some of the surprise and anger when conflict does arise. Union leaders have considerable authority and often handle millions of dollars in union funds. Occasionally they get into trouble with legal authorities. Reporters have paid only periodic attention to these matters.

And politics. Union leaders—themselves politicians who depend on votes to maintain their positions—more often take stands on political issues, particularly those which have to do with social welfare. News organizations have noted that the leaders of the nation's largest labor unions have endorsed a political candidate or spoken for or against specific legislation.

But such coverage has not been prevalent on the local level in spite of the fact that almost all labor unions from time to time act as lobbying organizations, support candidates, and contribute campaign funds. Political activities may be concentrated in state capitals or in Washington, D.C., and thus may be covered by statehouse or federal reporters. But they must be an essential part of a news organization's coverage of labor.

It is much easier to cover the organized portion of the nation's work force than the amorphous and far-flung portion which consists of millions of individual workers without a centralized philosophy or method of communication. But labor reporting must be bigger. It must be categorized as both union and nonunion. Perhaps the *New York Time*'s Jerry Flint puts it best when he describes his beat as "labor and work." Or Ira Fine of the *Arizona Republic* in Phoenix, who once covered labor in Pittsburgh and says a labor reporter is a person who covers "news of the working person—those who belong to the unions and those who do not. Anyone who works for a living falls under my beat."

It's the nonunion coverage, other than the periodic presentation of employment statistics, that is most likely to be ignored. Most people who work don't belong to any type of union. But they provide good—although admittedly difficult—opportunities for reporters who want to feel the pulse of the nation and its economy.

"The country is changing," Flint says. "It's changing at an enormous pace, and work is how people spend more of their waking time than any other single activity. So it should be a good way to make some sense out of what's going on. Find how they're working, and you know a lot about them. That's where they make their bread, that's where they meet their friends. If they're dissatisfied with life, it's usually because of their work. But it's tough. Everybody's interested in

---

Labor Is Also Unhappy About Media Coverage

BY A. KENT MACDOUGALL
Los Angeles Times

Labor doesn't like its press coverage either.

AFL-CIO public relations director Albert J. Zack complains that the news media slight the 98% of collective bargaining that ends in peaceful settlements, while often sensationalizing the 2% that results in work stoppages. As a consequence, "most people who read newspapers would never know that the amount of time lost to strikes is less than time lost to the common cold."

Zack and other union officials complain that stories on contract negotiations typically refer to company "offers," implying generosity, while calling union requests "demands."

They say strike stories play up disruption and hardship to the public, while ignoring the hardships that impel workers to go on strike. Strike stories also play up lost sales to local merchants, while slighting the benefits to these same merchants and other businesses from wage settlements that put more disposable income in workers' pockets.

But what rankles many union leaders most is that the media devote considerably more attention to corporate suites than to factory floors, to executives than to workers, to affluent suburbs than to working-class neighborhoods. The *Chicago Tribune* used to have a twice-weekly "Blue Collar Views" column, but Mike LaVelle, the common laborer who wrote the column, gave it up last summer. And few, if any, other dailies have anything similar.

Source: A. Kent MacDougall, "Labor Is Also Unhappy About Media Coverage," *Los Angeles Times,* February 3, 1980, part V, p. 2. Copyright 1980, *Los Angeles Times.* Reprinted by permission.

---

a strike, but many of these other movements tend to be small, and they creep along, and they start here, and it's a little thin there.

"You don't know what has real meaning. There are lots of women working at that new shopping center, but they're working only four hours a day. What does that mean? You don't know what it means. It could mean anything, or maybe nothing. Is it part of some vast new movement? It's harder to understand. It's harder to get other people interested. It's a lot harder to find out what's going on.

"But it's got to be done."

Even reporters who have attempted to provide such comprehensive coverage admit the record is spotty. They find themselves forced to agree, at least in part, with critics such as Thomas R. Donahue, assistant to the president of the AFL-CIO, who complains that too many labor assignments are opened to untrained reporters "with one course in economics and three pages in a history text about the formation of the CIO as their background in labor-management relations."[10]

Labor has not been treated historically as a true journalistic specialty. Granted, some reporters gained a degree of understanding through years of on-the-job experience, but that background is likely to be in labor strategy, particularly strikes, rather than a broad knowledge of the contributions of labor to the economic system and society as a whole. During the economic problems of recent decades, however, the assignment shifted somewhat to journalists who understand economics, labor relations, and the history of the labor movement.

On and Beyond the Picket Line

In spite of the call for broader coverage of labor, journalists will continue detailed strike coverage. When persons are out of work, a community business is shut down or its operations hampered, picket lines are conspicuous on the streets, violence occurs, citizens are affected and interested. Strikes may represent one of a community's most significant breaking stories.

Following that action poses the same kinds of problems any journalist faces when confronted with a relatively widespread, action-oriented news event. But a strike is more than an event. It's part of the collective bargaining process. Specific actions, while of value in themselves, must be understood within the total context.

Covering the collective bargaining process is not done by sitting through long negotiation sessions. The participants seldom will allow that, and reporters don't especially want it anyway.

"Many in collective bargaining . . . often appear to believe that the media, lusting for those news scoops so popular in the old movies about the Fourth Estate, want to hide in every bargaining room closet or lurk near the open transom of every negotiating room," says Edmund Kelly of the *Buffalo* [New York] *Evening News.* "Not so. The truth is that the media are not interested in covering a great deal that goes on in bargaining today. Much of it is too technical, boring or trivial to interest an editor or reporter, much less a reader."[11]

Collective bargaining is a process, and the actual sessions represent the culmination of developments that have been happening piecemeal and long term. It's a process of negotiating. What one side demands, it.may not really expect to get.

So reporters don't always want the intricate details. They want the outline of offers, counteroffers, compromises, and, importantly, factors which influence decisions. How do the latest offers fit in with today's economic facts of life? What is the relative strength of the parties involved in the negotiations? Who are the individuals? Those are people sitting across the bargaining table. They may or may not make mistakes. They're representing others who may have thoughts to express.

Reporters won't necessarily get that information by witnessing the bargaining session. It's a matter of sources. Gaining depth is more than passing along the rhetoric of the day. Reporting rhetoric only is the best way for reporters to become part of the process, to be used by negotiators seeking public support or floating an idea which may or may not be a serious discussion point. To avoid such manipulation, reporters must understand the process and have access to individuals who, perhaps quietly, will provide the full meaning rather than just today's strategy.

That's especially important in efforts to gain the company perspective because corporation officials generally will avoid talking to news media representatives.

"Most of them maintain a very low profile and speak only when spoken to and then not much," Fine says. "For example, we had a strike that lasted for eight months. I called the company people, wanting to do a story from their standpoint. I'd done stories on how the union could get along, and I wanted to do a story on how the company could get along without having production for eight months. And they preferred not having me come up. They just said no. I think it would have been an interesting story as well as presenting their side, but they refused."

Ira Fine of the *Arizona Republic*

(*Arizona Republic* photo)

Union representatives usually are more willing to talk, but they also want to control the content. And it still requires missionary work by reporters to establish a trusting relationship with union sources. In the past, labor unions in this country did not have a good press. It's true that many news organizations were blatantly promanagement. That has changed somewhat in recent years, but the leaders have long memories. They consider their unions sacrosanct and are quick to bristle over the slightest indication of a negative attitude.

Presenting balanced coverage is difficult when the parties are unequal in their willingness to discuss the issues or the progress of the negotiations. But even when they will talk, their comments often are polemic. Their statements often don't square. Their explanations differ. Their analyses are contradictory.

"It's one thing to present each side's viewpoint, but you don't want to put half truths or even untruths in the paper," says Jim Smith of the Toledo, Ohio, *Blade.* "You have to decide whether the parties are telling you the whole truth, and that's often where the mediators can be helpful. They have to be neutral. They usually are privileged to more facts than you are, and even if they are in a position where they just cannot be specific, they might be able to steer you in the right direction."

It also makes sense to talk with the strikers themselves as a means of blending coverage. They're standing out in the weather for a purpose and often will articulate that purpose more directly than union leaders, who have an eye on strategy. But in spite of the potential value, that, too, involves journalistic risk.

West Virginia coal miner Jim Rogers, for example, has seen his share of strikes and is not pleased with how reporters sometimes go about getting strikers' viewpoints.

"Radicals. You're always going to find some guy who won't keep his mouth shut, and those are the ones they always want to interview," he says. "What makes me mad is that every time you see an interview, especially on television, they stereotype the coal miner as a loudmouthed, noneducated drunkard. They always interview in bars, very rarely at home. And you're sitting there watching the national news and they show some guy with a beer in his hand: 'Wal, I ain't goin' back to work' and all this nonsense. You'd be surprised at how many college graduates there are in the mines."

Rogers also is concerned about what he perceives as the news media's excessive emphasis on violence in strike situations:

"Sure, it's a story. The media have a job to do. But the object of the story too often is violence, something that's forceful. A few years back, some guys from the southern part of the state came up here and said they were going to bust heads and burn cars if we worked. You better believe it was covered. Pictures. Yeah, boy, that made news. You're always going to have that in the coal fields, but that's not the point of the whole thing. It's just part of the picture."

Many reporters would disagree with Rogers, perhaps justifiably in countless instances, but the complaint is not uncommon. It stands as a constant reminder of the need for providing readers, viewers, and listeners with broader perspective on the exciting events of the day.

COVERING AGRICULTURE

Agriculture is a paradox in this country, somewhat akin to Charles Dickens's opening line in *A Tale of Two Cities:* "It was the best of times, it was the worst of times. . . ." It's confusing. The American people are aware of the importance of food production, but they also must know that 2 percent of the population feeds the rest, and the number of producers has declined rapidly as farmers migrate from rural areas in search of better opportunities.

Americans believe that farmers take pride in their independence and show disdain for welfare and other types of public support. But, at the same time, society provides special assistance so that farmers can survive on the farm. We say agriculture is basic to the American economy, providing the force which has made this country great and holding the key to development of other countries. Yet the impression that farmers are not sharing in economic gains also is strong.

The problem is that farmers do not speak with one voice. The message changes with time and geography. Urban America believes there is a category of concern called "agriculture," but that may mean anything from the farmer through the retail grocer.

"Even when we talk only about farmers," says James F. Evans of the University of Illinois, "we are hard-pressed to find a 'story' that all can tell with one voice. Yes, they may be able to agree on a general story line that emphasizes how hard they work—how efficient, important and underrewarded they are. But how many specific rural-urban problems will those generalizations solve? Precious few, it seems to me, and for the very reason which explains why there is no one story for agriculture, or for farmers. Farmers themselves have difficulty in finding common grounds because they have many differing points of view."[12]

This confusing picture has been reflected by American journalism. The confusion has been fed historically by news organizations concentrating on breaking news, events, and stories which report what another agricultural expert had to say on some subject. Such a policy reflects the many messages regarding agriculture without providing the context which urban America needs to understand those messages.

It is not possible or desirable for news organizations to adopt a uniform coverage philosophy. They serve different audiences with different needs. Journalists in metropolitan areas have correctly assumed that their audiences have little need for or interest in the kind of agricultural news which emphasizes the how-to aspect of farming, technological developments, or discussions of the latest pesticide. They leave that kind of coverage to their colleagues in smaller towns or rural areas which serve audiences that do need it.

Even there, the focus of coverage depends on local agricultural activity, on what types of products are grown. An Iowa newspaper would provide little news about cotton production. Audiences in Maine would have little need for information on the latest techniques for citrus crops.

Agriculture as a business and as a major force in the nation's economy, however, is a subject of interest in both Iowa and Maine as well as metropolitan centers across the country. When bad weather damages the citrus crop, that means the price of oranges will be higher. When corn blight hits the nation's midsection, market prices will be affected. Then when beef producers cut back on the size of their herds because of the high cost of feed, urban residents will feel the pinch.

And those kinds of stories exemplify the broader treatment journalism is giving to agricultural issues. News organizations continue to provide announcements and to break news pertinent to the area, but they are more likely now to see themselves serving a general audience of consumers which includes farmers.

"We take a broad issue-oriented approach to covering agriculture and try not to get stuck in the situation of being consumed by day-to-day happenings," says Gay Cook, now assistant city editor of the *Denver Post.* "We cover each state agriculture department and the major general farm organizations, both at the state and national levels. We periodically take a look at what's happening in agricultural education.

Gay Cook of the *Denver Post*

(*Denver Post* photo by Duane Howell)

"Another thing we do that is becoming more important is to try to translate farm policy and farm economics into what that means for the consumer. The best example of that right now is skyrocketing beef prices. How has it come to pass that within just a matter of months beef prices have in some cases almost doubled? So we have to give both the farmer and the consumer point of view on that and try to put it into perspective so that it makes sense to the consumer."

Getting to the Issues

The general consumer approach to coverage of agriculture requires integration of subject matter and sources. It means the agriculture reporter must be more than someone who was reared on a farm. It dictates detailed knowledge and understanding of economic and political activity. It requires a reporter who reads broadly and who at the same time understands the thinking and the problems of the agricultural community.

Without such a combination of a broad and specific perspective, the reporter will be forced into continued passing along of superficial and often contradictory points of view from various representatives of agriculture. To succeed at an issue approach without such background would not be possible.

The journalist's goal is to explain the place of agriculture in important social issues. What has public impact? Why? What are alternative courses of action? What can influence decisions?

Evans has urged a similar approach from the perspective of agriculturalists who see a need for public dialogue: "If our goal is to help solve rural-urban problems (not just air them), then we must deal with them on the basis of specifics and in a framework that builds upon the many levels of organization within agriculture. There's a difference between that goal and the more narrow goal of 'telling agriculture's story.' One goal invites give-and-take among competing interests and powers; the other invites emotional barking at the moon."[13]

Once the commitment has been made to issue analysis, there must be decisions as to what those issues are. Issues will vary as social circumstances change. But for the 1980s, chances are good the issues will remain relatively constant. For example:

The Price of Food. Inflation is the biggest economic story today, and the role and problems of agriculture are integral parts of that story. The American people generally do not blame farmers for the rapid increases in food costs. However, they are suspicious of the dealers between farmers and retail grocers. And they have nagging doubts about the grocers. What is the full story? Is there any hope that rising costs can be stopped? What is the role of exports?

Health and Safety. Americans in recent years have become increasingly interested in the quality and healthfulness of their food. Many are skeptical about freshness, nutritional value, purity, and flavor. They seek alternatives. Likewise, there has been an increase in questions about effects on people of herbicides and pesticides used in agriculture.

Government's Role. The role of government in agriculture merits constant journalistic attention. The impact is large and not publicly understood. Farm subsidies as a means of controlling production remain controversial. Buying and selling by governmental agencies is puzzling. What role does government regulation play in health and safety? To what degree are regulatory activity and farm subsidies political footballs? Is government adequately dedicated to agricultural research as a means to some solutions to recurring concerns?

Land Use Planning. As urban sprawl continues and more land is consumed for residential and industrial purposes, the question remains as to whether land needed for agriculture will be available. Legislation on this question is considered and passed from time to time at all levels, but the public has demonstrated little concern. This is a subject, then, that opens up the avenue for journalistic leadership.

Financial Concerns. The public generally is aware that huge investments are required by those who farm on a large scale, and it has been told that the profit margin is slight. Therefore, as in every area of journalistic concern, finances must remain a major consideration. What are the problems of small farming units? Can they survive? Should they survive? What are the long-range implications of a situation in which only the very large can operate effectively? What impact are financial problems having on the farm family and on such social necessities as education in predominantly rural areas?

Such considerations will lead reporters into analysis of the very structure of agriculture. The issues are complex, but the questions must be answered. Much discussion will be necessary about such subjects as foreign ownership of American farmland, the movement of large corporations into farming, and preservation of the family farm.

Local Parallels. If these issues are national in scope, they also have local parallels. News organizations seeking to serve hometown audiences will not ignore such important issues as zoning decisions when public usage of land (airports, for example) would remove farmland from production; public decisions involved in renovation and restoration of strip-mined land; hunting rights; predator control debates over such matters as the sheep producer's need to control losses versus the conservationist's concern about coyotes.

This listing is not comprehensive. The agenda will include other issues, other unanswered questions, other needs for public understanding. What about food import-export policies which touch on the question of using food as a political weapon? What about alternative energy sources, such as gasohol, which use farm products as a substitute for imported petroleum? If solutions are found, one of the requirements will be continued comprehensive journalistic attention.

The Commodity Markets

One point at which breaking news coverage and issue coverage coincide is the point of sale. Today's prices are breaking news, and today's prices are part of long-term financial trends. And perhaps the most conspicuous point of sale for agricultural products is in commodity markets scattered across the country. Buyers and sellers come together; action is concentrated, giving experts and journalists ready opportunities for analysis.

Commodities are not exclusively agricultural. However, the oldest and most extensively covered markets are those involved with grain and livestock trading. And the number of products getting attention is increasing. The Associated Press, for example, recently expanded its Chicago Board of Trade coverage of coffee, orange juice, cotton, copper, silver, gold, lumber, eggs, potatoes, money futures, U.S. Treasury bills, and U.S. Treasury bonds.[14]

The major coverage attention on the commodities markets usually is on products of most local interest and, at times, on general summaries of price trends. This involves both what is called the spot market (real goods for immediate delivery) and the futures market (providing for delivery at a future date).

But coverage involves more, says John Prestbo of the *Wall Street Journal,* even for a relatively small news organization.

"I don't think it is sufficient to just dutifully report the local prices at the grain elevator or the auction ring," he says. "We need to give readers the bigger picture of what's going on in that market. To give some balance to the local scene by explaining what the worldwide supply of whatever commodity is and why that is affecting the price here in Kansas or wherever.

"In that regard I suggest reporters become familiar with the trade publications. Each commodity has one or even several. That's a way of getting the big picture and also a way of spotting potential sources."

Sources and Resources

When Gay Cook joined the *Denver Post* as a general-assignment reporter, she had an undergraduate degree in journalism and graduate work in specialized urban affairs, hardly the background one would expect for an agriculture reporter. But when the opportunity came, she took it, and she made the transition, finding that her background gave her much of what she needed. The agricultural part was up to her.

"People not familiar with agriculture don't realize how much politics and government and economics are involved, and I've had solid backgrounds in all those areas," she says. "So it was just a matter of doing some intensive reading and preparation for that—agricultural history, agricultural finance, agricultural economics, that kind of thing—which I did on my own. Getting plugged into publications relevant to agriculture."

That means broad and specific publications, she says, including the *Wall Street Journal,* the *New York Times,* general-circulation magazines, and both business and agricultural trade journals.

It's more than reading. It's also development of an extensive list of sources who can be called upon for specific information or general explanation. It's government officials, agricultural agents, college or university faculty members, grain elevator and livestock market operators, farm organization leaders, weather experts, and farmers themselves.

"For most of the issue stories we do," Cook says, "in additon to giving the government angle and the policy angle, we probably get farmers' reactions in eight cases out of ten. I've developed an extensive list of farmers who are good contacts for me throughout Colorado, which is important because the agricultural economy in this state is highly diversified."

COVERING FINANCIAL DEALINGS

Few news organizations have the resources, desire, or even the need to provide comprehensive coverage of the stock market. Most rely on the wire services—United Press International, Associated Press, Dow Jones, or Reuters—to meet their needs, principally meaning information from the New York Stock Exchange and the American Stock Exchange. Most newspapers carry the daily market report, which shows changes in stock prices, and broadcast outlets, the daily summaries. And that makes the stock market the most widely covered business story in the nation.

"Day in and day out, it is the only business news regularly carried on the prime-time radio and TV stations," says Arlene Hershman in *Dun's Review.* "And no matter how dull the day's action on Broad and Wall, hundreds of newspapers across the country feature the stock market report as their lead and sometimes only financial story. The stock market is uniquely important news because it is the most consistent indicator of business and economic sentiment."[15]

But even if it's not necessary for local news organizations to provide their own daily coverage of the stock market, there are needs which only they can meet. The wire services will not hit the local angles, except by accident. National averages and stock prices have their value in any community, but some citizens need more specific coverage. Some 25 million Americans own stock.[16] They follow the averages with more than casual interest. And their concentration in a particular community provides incentive for news organizations to give them more discussion of trends and developments.

Certain areas of the country, for example, have large senior citizen populations, which might indicate a sizable number of stockholders or people whose pensions are vested in stocks. If a specific company is in trouble, it may mean a reduction in the dividends it pays. This would affect those in the community who depend upon those dividends.

For example, a fairly large number of the retirees who have settled in Lakeland, Florida, are from the Detroit area. The chances are good that they carry stock portfolios and pensions which are tied to the fortunes of major automobile manufacturers. This opens an opportunity for special efforts to provide news from Detroit even though it is hundreds of miles away.

Of course, the presence of a local plant or office of a major firm also broadens community interest in news about the industry it is involved in. The reader or viewer may work there or may simply be aware of the economic importance of that firm to the community. The local news organizations should therefore cast eyes toward the financial centers for information in addition to what is gained from local sources.

So there are situations in which news organizations—however small they might be—should attempt to develop a ready list of sources who can be called when something unusual occurs or for periodic status reports. These sources are there, principally in New York, and accustomed to being called. But it does require some advance effort, says Tim Metz of the *Wall Street Journal.*

"Ideally, the person ought to come to New York and spend a little time wandering around for no other reason than to get face-to-face contact with some people he or she would be dealing with regularly on the telephone," Metz says. "Those people would certainly be representatives of the major stock exchanges and market analysts for some of the major investment houses. The market strategists, the people in charge of investment policy for some of these big firms, can be very helpful about broadmarket influences, and fast telephone calls to some of them can provide rather meaningful insights into what's going on."

NOTES

1. Dan Cordtz, remarks made at Better Business Reporting Seminar, Russell, Ky., sponsored by Ohio Valley-Kanawha Chapter, Society of Professional Journalists, Sigma Delta Chi, April 25, 1978.
2. Clay Schoenfeld, *The Environmental I&E Ecosystem Yesterday, Today and Tomorrow* (Madison, Wisc.: Center for Environmental Communications and Education Studies, University of Wisconsin-Madison, undated), p. 4. Reprinted by permission.
3. Casey Bukro, letter to Clay Schoenfeld, chairman of the Center for Environmental Communications and Education Studies, University of Wisconsin-Madison, July 10, 1978, p. 3.
4. Herb Schmertz, "An Energy Story the Press Hasn't Told," *Fortune,* November 5, 1979, p. 153.
5. "An Energy Story the Press Hasn't Told," p. 153.
6. George W. O'Connor, "Problems in News Coverage," *Montana Journalism Review,* 1975, pp. 20–21.
7. *The Environmental I&E Econsystem Yesterday, Today and Tomorrow,* p. 6.
8. "Coping With a Crisis," *Columbia Journaism Review,* September-October 1979, p. 40.
9. See, for example, Mitchel Benson, "The Trouble Is . . . ," *The Quill,* January 1976, p. 26.
10. "Labor Leader-Reporters Fault Labor Coverage," *Editor & Publisher,* August 25, 1979, p. 13.
11. "Labor Leader-Reporters Fault Labor Coverage," p. 25.
12. James F. Evans, "Sorting Out the Rural-Urban Scene," remarks made to the Midwest chapter of the National Agri-Marketing Association, Chicago, Ill., March 25, 1974.
13. "Sorting Out the Rural-Urban Scene."
14. "Market Expands for Commodities Writer," *AP Log,* April 3, 1978, p. 1.
15. Arlene Hershman, "Reporting the Stock Market," *Dun's Review,* July 1977, p. 37.
16. "Reporting the Stock Market," p. 36.

Chapter 15

TRACKING THE UPS AND DOWNS OF SCIENCE

A few years ago, it was only in the context of science fiction that we could think of a man walking on the moon. Human beings were confined to a world in which 50,000 persons, mostly children, died annually of polio. Only in movies did physicians successfully transplant human organs. And farmers, at the mercy of nature, suffered plagues which destroyed their crops.

But science attacked these problems. The results provided new drugs, new methods of treatment, new forms of transportation, satellites, television. Without question, the twentieth century has been history's greatest era of scientific discovery and technological development.

To a great degree, the general public knows about such achievements because journalists are there to witness, record, and pass along accounts of what they see. Journalists such as Alton Blakeslee, who retired in 1979 after 22 years as science writer for The Associated Press, are thankful for the opportunities they have had.

"I think one of the rewards of dealing with science and medicine is that you're dealing usually with constructive news and events, adding to human welfare rather than the troubles, the problems. You get into the problem-solving kind of story," he says. "I don't think newspapers are being very smart by not trying to see that they have on page one every day a story about people who are solving problems."[1]

Journalists have been there to record the deficiencies too. Billions of dollars have been pumped into an unwon "war on cancer." Technology has not been able to develop economically feasible alternative sources of energy to replace our finite supply of fossil fuels.

Alton Blakeslee of The Associated Press

The wins, the losses, the gains, the discoveries, the applications, the relationships to society, the long- and short-term impacts of science on individual human
beings—these are all the domain of the science reporter. It's such a big task that
part of it has been delegated to "environmental" reporters, "energy" reporters,
"consumer affairs" reporters, and "medical" reporters.

Says Victor Cohn of the *Washington Post:*

"Science, to the science reporter, is the man working in his laboratory. It is the
search for truth—about people, about microbes, about atoms, about man. It is
a beautiful and inspiring sight and a joy to write about.

"But science is more. If it were only a search for truth, there probably would
not be many of us writing about it. It is also the search to know for man's use.
It is the applied scientist and technologist, the engineer, the doctor, seeking to
know to achieve practical goals: man's welfare, better crops, health, and long life.
This is exciting too, and important to write about—more important every day,
for we are living in a time unlike any other man has known."[2]

Cohn speaks of covering psychology, sociology, medicine, agriculture, physics,
chemistry, biology, oceanography, engineering, electronics, automation, space,
astronomy and the universe and adds:

"It is our job to put this knowledge together, plainly, coherently and effectively,
so that the people can understand what is happening in science and technology

and respond to preserve our democratic governments, our society, our jobs, our families and our lives."[3]

When he retired, Blakeslee looked back and saw two things he would have done differently.

"I would have liked to have done more about the relationship between science, society and politics," he said. "Also, I don't think we've made the public understand the importance of basic research. They just think of research scientists as people goofing off. The thing about basic research is that nobody can predict what will come of it. But all applied sciences come from it, and if they cut it off, this will dry up the well."[4]

Blakeslee thus puts his finger on four types of stories which science reporters face regularly: (1) about basic research, (2) about the application of research findings, (3) about social effects of science and technology, and (4) about the relationships between science and public policy.

SEEKING THE POINT OF ABSTRACT RESEARCH

It's difficult for journalists to handle seemingly obscure scientific research because they want to show its meaning. They want a broader personal or social context. They hesitate to write stories on research when there's little direct application.

But there isn't always that solid news peg, that direct application, that definitive impact because science is a slow, sometimes tedious, step-by-step process to which each individual component may have only peripheral connection. It's a process in which each piece of the puzzle is developed independently. Perhaps later someone fits those pieces together. To report on research which may or may not have some relationship to a human problem, which may or may not be important in the long run, is difficult for journalism.

Ron Kotulak of the *Chicago Tribune* says even scientists themselves don't really know what is going to happen or how much of a practical contribution will be made by their research.

"Most of the stuff we take for granted today, the technological developments, are due to basic discoveries which, at the time of discovery, were thought to have

Ron Kotulak of the *Chicago Tribune*

(*Chicago Tribune* photo)

no practical value—transistors, TV, all that sort of stuff goes back to very esoteric, isolated discoveries which nobody had any use for at the time. Well, we recognize this as the way things are because when you discover something new, you don't have an application for it right away. In time, there may be."

Take cancer, for example. Americans keep looking for the cure. They expect the announcement. But it hasn't come, and it may be a long time before it does. As researchers work toward the cure, however, journalists will be required to attempt regular coverage, and that means they will consistently deal with esoteric developments, little insights which may or may not have significance in the overall effort.

Jane E. Brody of the *New York Times* was a biology major in college and learned what it means to do controlled studies, what statistical significance represents, to look into all the possible contingencies that could influence the outcome of an experiment. That background, she says, has improved her reporting abilities.

"What is more important than actually knowing medicine, or knowing the particular subject you cover, is to have a feel for and a true understanding of the rules that govern the game you're playing," Brody says. "The attitude and understanding of the nature of science, how it's done, why it's done the way it's done, and a feeling for how scientists work and how doctors operate and how medicine is practiced is probably more important than the specific information."

It's not required, of course, that reporters be biology majors, but they should understand scientific technique. Failure to do so may cause a reporter to view basic research as being pointless. This affects both news judgment and clarity of reporting. Only reporters who understand scientific technique have the tools to make stories about research meaningful to readers, viewers, and listeners who are skeptical about scientific work which appears valueless.

Likewise, they will be more able to evaluate the research, to know, for example, when a researcher tries to draw conclusions from very preliminary information. And, equally as important, they will be in a position to develop as sources other scientists working in the same area or, at least, to know how to find them. Asking questions of the experts still is among the best ways to confirm any journalistic information.

Unless citizens are to be surprised consistently by public announcements of major discoveries, the long grind of basic research must be reported. It may come to nothing. It may never bear fruit. But until that day when the results are known, it must be considered part of the scientific mosaic.

MORE PEOPLE, BETTER BRIDGES, LONGER LIVES

Even when research does produce the kind of practical result which solves problems or improves living standards, reporters' coverage may be lacking. For example, Carl Sagan of Cornell University complains that the media and the public do not understand the overwhelming direct contributions science has made. He says the major message conveyed by the media, especially television drama, is that science is dangerous.

"The applications of science, of course, can be dangerous, and virtually every major technological advance in the history of the human species—back to the invention of stone tools and the domestication of fire—has been ethically ambiguous. These advances can be used by ignorant or evil people for evil purposes or by wise and good people for the benefit of the human species. But only one side of the ambiguity ever seems to be presented."

Though Sagan admits that this criticism of television is based mostly on dramatic presentations, he hastens to add that news coverage is not much better: "Most of the news reporting that touches on science is actually about engineering (for example, a test flight of the Shuttle Orbiter) or medicine. It is extremely rare that any discovery in pure science is announced and much more rare that it is adequately explained."[5]

Sagan's charges do contain a germ of truth. Reporters admit the difficulty of covering pure science. And they do concentrate on medicine and engineering in their science coverage. But Sagan may not have given enough credit where it is due. Saving of lives is good copy. And even if Sagan doesn't, many health-related individuals applaud such journalistic attention.

For example, American Cancer Society officials were jubilant over coverage given to the breast cancer surgeries of Happy Rockefeller and Betty Ford. The extensive stories on the disease had tremendous impact on women of this country, says Marv Munro, director of public information of the New York City Division of the American Cancer Society.

"The newspapers were marvelous," she says. "Women all had their consciousness raised. And the press did a fantastic job and was very accurate in all of the information it disseminated. The coverage has contributed substantially in motivating women in getting examinations—the key to curing breast cancer."[6]

In fact, stories about treatment provide *Milwaukee Journal* medicine writer Neil Rosenberg with the greatest satisfaction of his job. The son and brother of physicians, he says he entered medical reporting because of his interest in treatment.

"Now this might mean stories on new research, new tests, new treatments, screening programs, public health measures. Things that are not only interesting to write about but to read," he says. "And I guess I always hope the stories might improve things, by informing people of these things and helping them avail themselves of useful services."

An example is the story he did on a new treatment for rectal cancer. He wrote a cautious report because the treatment was new and could be used in only a minority of the cases. "But it may help a lot of people who will get rid of this cancer without having to undergo surgery," he says, adding that the treatment is considerably less expensive than the surgery.

Neil Rosenberg of the *Milwaukee Journal*

(*Milwaukee Journal* photo by Dale Guldan)

Another example was a story about a premature infant for whom doctors had to scramble to get a rare piece of equipment to save her life: "I wrote right up front in the story, 'This is a story of what good technology does. You've read a lot of the high cost of technology which isn't really working. You've heard about the bad things. Now here's a good story about medicine.'"

On the other hand, the practical problems of applied science, the not-so-good news, merit coverage which is equally as determined. For example, reporters have prominently displayed the public controversy over the failure of the much-ballyhooed war on cancer. Now, physicians and hospitals are criticized for being too quick to place an individual in an expensive hospital bed and prepare automatically for surgery. And much debate exists over whether a radical mastectomy is necessary for women with breast cancer.

This kind of coverage allowed B. D. Colen of *Newsday* to define himself as having a specialty within a specialty. His focus is medical ethics, "decision-making within the medical context—who's going to live, who's going to die, who decides and how they decide it." Colen says he's interested in the type of questions which arose in the case of Karen Ann Quinlan, whose parents wanted to allow her to die and whose doctors would not stop treatment.

University of Minnesota researchers point out that science reporters are becoming more inclined to write critical stories about scientists of all types. In the past, the tendency was to translate science uncritically to the public, they say.

Now there is a greater likelihood journalists will use multiple sources and actually challenge scientific pronouncements.[7]

Of course, at times such critical coverage has little to do with the attitudes of reporters. Witness, for example, the extremely negative period for science and technology in mid-1979 when three separate incidents occurred within months of each other, shaking the faith of citizens in American technology: the fall of Skylab, the structural problems with engine mounts on DC-10 airplanes, and the nuclear accident at Three Mile Island in Pennsylvania.

ASSESSING SECOND-GENERATION IMPACT

Such controversies have become so publicly pervasive that reporters find themselves more frequently covering the broader implications of science and technology, paying attention to the long-term public impact of technological advancements. What happens later?

"Would supersonic transports destroy ozone in the upper atmosphere, or wouldn't they?" asks Phillip J. Tichenor of the University of Minnesota. "Does radiation from a nuclear power plant increase the risk of leukemia in nearby cities, or doesn't it? Does it make sense to use results from experimental feeding of megadoses of saccharin to rats as a basis for banning saccharin in human foods?"[8]

These kinds of questions represent the potential second-generation problems of technological application of scientific findings. Americans did not anticipate the problems of air pollution from automobiles, and it's going to take more knowledge to find the solution. The painful awareness that dangers lurk in the midst of great achievements has developed slowly. The potential problems were not analyzed. Most Americans, including reporters, had little understanding of the risks of technology and, significantly, this failure seems to have become an inherent part of the American character.

"Whatever you do, there is a risk to it," says Jean McCann, a medical freelance writer, "and it's the same way [for example] with taking drugs. One reason for malpractice suits is that we want results. We're very results oriented. Right now, or tomorrow, at least. I think it's part of our American culture. We have to realize that life is not perfect, and drugs are not perfect."[9]

Too frequently, journalists have not conveyed what McCann calls the "risk-versus-benefit ratio." Contrary to what Sagan might say, they and the scientists themselves have tended to overplay successes without adequately discussing (or worse, without even looking into) the possible side effects. They traditionally have accepted announcements without probing for future implications.

It's not simply a negative matter. Future impact of a discovery may be positive; in the long run, there may be hope for solving another human problem. The point is that even though many researchers are reluctant to look beyond the moment of a research project, it's the reporter's task to pry some of that information loose.

Scientists do not work in vacuums. They don't do research without some sort of an idea of where it fits or what it might mean.

"Human nature wants to know reasons," Kotulak says. "So it is very essential to ask, 'Why are you working on this? What do you hope to accomplish by it?'."

SCIENCE IS A POLITICAL ISSUE

Assessing the future implications of scientific developments involves more than scientific understanding, for the role of science and technology as a national priority is as political as it is technical. This places additional responsibilities on journalists, who must be acutely aware of how science fits into the whole fabric of society and how the distribution of power influences that fit.

Expert coverage of the politics of science, Tichenor adds, requires familiarity with legislative bodies at the local, state, and national levels; with agency procedures for establishing regulations for food and drugs; with organization of health delivery agencies; with court procedures and organization of pressure groups generally.[10]

Many of these elements meshed, for example, in former President Jimmy Carter's proposal for a national health insurance program, Senator Edward Kennedy's alternative proposals, congressional and medical reaction to both, and thousands of comments and countersuggestions. As an issue of immense importance to the public, health insurance—indeed, any topic related to the cost of medicine—is a topic of almost automatic reader interest.

"The major issue facing medicine, the most political and highly debatable issue, is the high cost of medical care," Rosenberg says. "How much does a hospital bed cost? How much does a hospital stay cost? Cost enters into the decision of whether a doctor can give a patient a high-priced x-ray treatment, whether a hospital can buy a high-cost piece of equipment. Is the money available? Is the cost worth the benefit?"

It's possible to argue that these kinds of stories fall into the domain of the political reporter or the economic reporter or the consumer reporter. But many will argue for the science reporter, stressing the background in dealing with medical sources. A science writer covering this brand of politics understands how to talk to scientists and how scientists think.

On a national level, such important agencies as the National Institutes of Health, the National Aeronautics and Space Administration, the National Science Foundation, and the National Academy of Science are public institutions run by scientists. The political implications of the fact that such groups control vast amounts of funds cannot be ignored.

"The manner in which these funds are distributed can raise overnight an entirely new research component of American science, or it can destroy it. It is quite important to know how to cover these people," says Byron Scott of Ohio University, former president of the American Medical Writers Association.

He specifically mentions the massive national commitment to cancer research as a program which has had significant impact on the careers of innumerable scientists, on the national economy, and on public attitudes. Many critics charge that the media have provided very weak coverage of that effort. They charge that the public has been seriously misled into believing that this dreaded disease would soon be overcome. And, they charge, the media have been duped by scientists who are interested mostly in getting grants.

Tom Lee, former reporter turned physician, says the media's coverage of cancer has had a double-barreled negative impact.

"A suspicion is growing that the influence of the press on the cancer program is complex and dubious—that sensationalized, intensely personal stories about the disease and its victims have resulted in an exaggeration of cancer's importance in the country's overall biomedical research, and thrown the emphasis on possibly futile attempts to cure it rather than trying to understand it and reduce its environmental causes," he says.

Lee points out that one byproduct of popular interest and public money is an extraordinary pressure on researchers to come up with the kind of findings that will make headlines, please politicians, placate voters, and bring in more funds.

"The nuts and bolts of science appear in the professional journals," he says, "but a researcher who can get his work and his institution covered by the *New York Times* is nevertheless a valuable commodity. Having 'star quality' depends on more than IQ, and researchers know that their work must have obvious clinical implications to draw attention and support. Winning grants often seems a more consuming goal than whipping cancer."[11]

A similar theme is presented by Daniel S. Greenberg, publisher of a Washington-based newsletter, *Science & Government Report,* and author of *The Politics of Pure Science.*

Greenberg points out that U.S. scientists have been depicting science as being in a crisis stemming from public hostility and media indifference. And it has such side effects as diminishing federal support for research, declining student enrollments in science and technology, unemployment among scientists and engineers, jeopardy to the international scientific standing of the country, and delay in the progress of science itself.

"And the chosen cure," he says, "is persuasion of the public—through the media—that science is good but suffering. But as one who once swallowed the 'crisis' theory and occasionally regurgitated it intact in alarmist writings, I now wonder whether our colleagues in the scientific community haven't been using the press for their own self-serving purposes."[12]

Greenberg admits that science has declined from the days of the 1960s when it was perhaps the nation's most powerful and prestigious political force. But he says the change is from riches and power down only to "mere prosperity and moderate influence." It is understandable, he says, that the elders of science are possessed by visions of doom and have taken to the well-trodden route of stumping in the media to recoup their fortunes.

"There is no excuse, however, for the press to become their uncritical instrument. At present, the view that science is in critical condition has become an article of faith in much of the media and is often echoed without the skepticism that would routinely be applied to other matters."[13]

Thus, the cycle continues. Some scientists are determined to use the media as political tools to gain a larger share of public funds and political power. To the degree that they succeed, those are funds and power which will not be available to other parts of society. Public decisions about who gets what portion of available financial resources must be based on comprehensive discussion. If the critics are correct to any degree, if the media are being duped and therefore have not provided the full story, traditional good journalism must provide the solution. This implies knowledge and sources and digging, as well as comparing charges and countercharges. It also implies careful study of politics and straightforward presentation of the results of that study.

DAY-TO-DAY CHALLENGES

Covering individuals and institutions that are among the nation's elite, dealing with material which literally represents life or death to some in the audience, and coping with some of the most complex information available places continuous demands upon science reporters. Their successes at meeting the demands, of course, will vary. But all will face daily challenges which must be overcome.

Dealing with Scientists as Sources

Unlike the political reporter—courted, invited, visited, and assisted by politicians who know they need the media—science reporters often have to deal with individuals who neither know how nor care to deal with them. It's true that more and more scientists are learning the value of the news media, but it's also true that at times reporters face lack of cooperation or outright censorship, sometimes prompted by local medical society codes.

Many scientists do not know how to cope with an individual who insists on simple nonscientific explanations of complex scientific subjects, who writes in what many regard as a frenzied and incomplete manner and pays little regard to the subtleties of science and technology. Others have a basic distrust of reporters because they have been burned by journalistic misinterpretation or exaggeration. Very few reporters have good technical background from which to write, and this creates an awkward situation when one is dealing with highly trained scientists.

The problem is inevitable, but reporters such as Bob Peirce, who was a medicine and environment reporter in St. Louis before he joined the Louisville *Courier-Journal,* know it can be overcome: "The way of establishing beats and developing sources, I think, is the same regardless of what specialty you're in. Probably in medicine it's more important than in other areas that the stories you do are accurate because there's no reason a doctor should necessarily talk to a reporter, where, say, in politics it's very important for the politician to do so."

When a doctor or scientist discovers that the reporter is a specialist, he adds, a degree of trust begins to develop. And this trust matures over time. It's a matter of convincing the scientists that stories will be as accurate as the available facts, that omissions will not be deliberate, that confidences will be protected.

"I think the first interview is the worst," says Linda Little of the *Dallas Morning News.* "Part of the opening up is just convincing one doctor at a time that the story's going to come out accurately, and that it's going to help somebody. As soon as they see that, then I think they're persuaded."

Linda Little of the *Dallas Morning News*

(*Dallas Morning News* photo)

Science reporters are not different from other journalists. They use a variety of sources in their work and find those sources in different places. University of Minnesota research of metropolitan newspapers in 1978 showed the variety: government agencies, 26.4 percent; university researchers, 29.4 percent; private research, 9.7 percent; public interest groups and citizen organizations, 9.6 percent; professional societies, 8.6 percent; secondary sources such as journals, scholarly and professional papers, 10 percent; and other (including individual nonexpert citizens, physicians, hospitals, and the like), 6 percent.[14]

Sources of information are everywhere, from the smallest town to the largest city. And science reporters must avoid the twin problems of ignoring good local sources or of not reaching far enough. Locally, every rural area has county agricultural agents and high school science teachers; most have nearby university science staffs and industrial scientists. Reading scientific literature and even the popular media will provide long lists of names for the enterprising reporter. And then reaching these sources is simple.

"Just use the telephone," advises Bryan Sullivan, AP science writer. "You get on the telephone, and if you know someone even remotely connected with a field, call him up and ask, 'Who is a good source? Who's a good person to talk to about this subject? Who knows about this field?' If this person doesn't know of anyone, call up someone else. Eventually, you'll come up with three or five names."

These sources may be from a nearby university or medical school or clear across the country. Granted, source willingness to cooperate varies dramatically, especially if the reporter represents a smaller news organization. But the effort will pay off more often than not, and the reporter will find more information and more names of persons to call.

Such reaching out produces more comprehensive stories, and it also is the strongest safeguard against superficiality and the possibility that reporters will be misled or used as a mouthpiece for particular points of view. That failure to seek a diversity of sources was a major problem, for example, in coverage of the 1976 swine flu innoculation program was confirmed in research by David M. Rubin of New York University.

Rubin stresses that there is a direct correlation between the quality of coverage in a news medium and the number of sources cited in the coverage: "Despite the many hundreds of experts who might have been asked by the press for comment on the deaths, the same group of government authorities was quoted to the virtual exclusion of everyone else. Why this emphasis on such a small group? In a complex or potentially volatile area, an uncertain reporter is comfortable dealing with 'official' sources. It is the safe approach to composing a story."

Then he advises: "If reporters want to avoid becoming captives of 'official' public-health sources, they must cultivate other sources from among local physicians. While journalists must often rely on doctors in official positions with government or university, local physicians can supply background and a perspective often missing in handouts and briefings."[15]

A related question which reporters must answer for themselves based on the specific circumstances is how willing they are to use material from public relations sources.

Dependence upon a PR person relates directly to the role that individual plays in the overall organization, and B. D. Colen of *Newsday* puts the general attitude succinctly: "If I know the person is really plugged in, then fine, but if it's a flack, I'm not interested."

At times, the "PR person" will not be a staff member, but a scientist or doctor, sophisticated in public relations techniques, who seeks to advance a personal reputation. The person may be an individual with a large ego who thrives on publicity or someone seeking to take advantage of human misfortune to make a fast buck. Again, news media attention depends, most of all, on what reporters know of the qualifications and records of such persons. Delores Frederick of the *Pittsburgh Press* stresses standard journalistic practice as the solution: "Check the person's credentials. Talk with medical authorities. Get a second and third opinion."

A similar red flag is raised by Rae Goodell of Massachusetts Institute of Technology over "visible scientists." Such individuals as Linus Pauling, Margaret Mead, B. F. Skinner, and Barry Commoner, she notes, are not best known for their contributions to science, but for their involvement in public debate over science-related issues: overpopulation, drugs, genetic engineering, nuclear power, pollution, genetics and IQ, food shortages, energy shortages, and arms control.[16]

In the scientific community, these individuals frequently are defined as outsiders, Goodell notes. And even if that's a rather harsh generalization, the other scientists at times do express concern over media attention to these most famed among their number.

For example, William Divale of City University of New York complains of the lack of media attention to anthropologists, especially as sources of stories. He points out that results of a content analysis of newspaper coverage of anthropology contained a category classified as "Margaret Mead."

"What is interesting," he says, "is that the articles' main focus was on Dr. Mead and not the topic she was commenting on. To the general public, anthropology means two things: archeology (something to do with bones) and Margaret Mead."[17]

It's almost impossible to avoid writing a story about these individuals when they come to town and speak to hundreds or thousands of concerned persons on a topic of social importance. Journalists will express their reluctance, but they will be on the scene.

Hill Williams of the *Seattle Times*, for example, admits that if a nationally prominent scientist spoke in Seattle, he would attend the program, seek an interview, and write a story. But, he says, he would concentrate on controlling the content of that story.

Hill Williams of the *Seattle Times*

(*Seattle Times* photo copyright © Seattle Times Co.)

"I would interview Dr. Spock about raising babies, but not about wars," he says. "Or Linus Pauling about chemistry, but not about vitamin C."

Reporters also warn against too much reliance on any scientist. To become addicted to a single source, even if that individual consistently provides what the reporter needs, is a companion problem to permitting personal friendships to influence coverage.

"I'm the last one to pretend that we are all superobjective people," says Jane E. Brody of the *New York Times.* "We all have opinions, we all either like or dislike doctors or like some doctors and dislike others, and I am included in that pot. But I do not have any vested interest group that I represent in any way."

She points out the natural tendency to develop personal allegiances, but warns that reporters must base judgments on the specific circumstances of a given story.

"And you have to be prepared to abandon people when the need arises," she says. "This did in fact come up with a physician whom I had long admired. He became head of an institution where there was a horrendous scandal for which he was directly responsible. It would have been wrong for me to say, 'Look, he's a friend of mine. I can't write that.' You have to be very careful about that sort of thing."

Parlez-Vous Science?

Reporters usually are not scientists themselves. They don't have advanced degrees. Yet they find themselves daily serving as the link between scientists who speak a virtual foreign language and a public that needs translation and critiques, not parroting. There is, of course, no journalistic secret. The point is not to know all about nuclear physics, astronomy, or psychology, though any background knowledge is helpful. The real talent is to ask intelligent questions and to feel no embarrassment over saying: "Let's try that one again. I don't understand."

Take, for example, the problems of covering the nation's worst nuclear accident, at Three Mile Island in Pennsylvania, a situation which Susan Q. Stranahan of the *Philadelphia Inquirer* calls "perhaps the most technical breaking story ever to occur."

Stressing that she and many of her fellow reporters who covered the accident had limited backgrounds in nuclear generation, Stranahan says they gained the story through use of standard reporting techniques.

"I am of the firm belief that expertise in the field of nuclear power was less critical to proper coverage than basic journalistic skills," she says. "The experts in nuclear physics and engineering were themselves in the dark and confused about the events occurring hour by hour. Hence, aside from some basic familiarity with simple chemistry and physics, a reporter's most valuable specialized knowledge was searching out facts and clearly reporting them."[18]

A similar theme is presented by Joseph M. Higgins, president of station WHP in Harrisburg, Pennsylvania, who says reporters found means of coping with concepts and terminology of nuclear power. They turned to the dictionary, to employees, and to experts. Higgins also noted that soon after the accident a radiological physicist was brought in to aid CBS-TV reporters and correspondents with language and correct descriptions of radiation and its effect on people.[19]

However, even though reporters feel they coped with the technical problems of the Three Mile Island incident, an official for Metropolitan Edison Co. reiterated a complaint commonly heard from scientists who deal with reporters.

"There were among the national press representatives some very knowledgeable science, business and industry writers," says Blaine F. Fabian, manager-communication services for Met-Ed. "Likewise, there were many with little understanding of nuclear energy. Finding a remedy to the situation poses quite a dilemma. Very few busy people will take the time in advance to become knowledgeable about any given subject as a matter of preparedness unless they are specifically assigned to that technical field as a regular news beat."[20]

The question of how much background reporters should have, therefore, is likely to receive the response of "as much as possible." Reporters generally suggest a variety of basic science courses in the context of a broad liberal arts education. Studies show that modern science reporters have considerably more science background than their predecessors and certainly more than the average reader.[21] But, given a general and basic background, they tend to feel they can learn on the job through use of reportorial techniques.

Such knowledge helps understanding, but it should not be substituted for persistent questioning.

"I still refuse today to act as a dictionary for a doctor," says Linda Little of the *Dallas Morning News.* "If I don't understand it in perfectly clear English, then he's going to have to repeat it, and he's going to have to get it down to the level where they're going to understand. Because if I do the explaining, even though it might be medically accurate, it might not be what he intended."

Little adds that physicians who have treated patients should be able to speak in lay terms, and most can if prodded by reporters.

Once stories have been written, if time allows, some science reporters permit sources to read copies, with the firm understanding that they are to comment only on the accuracy of the technical information and that the reporter, not the source, determines whether changes are to be made.

"Obviously, a medical or science writer cannot be a physicist, microbiologist, brain surgeon, general practitioner, and all that," says Delores Frederick of the *Pittsburgh Press.* "But when I write about microsurgery, and I want to explain a new technique, it doesn't hurt my pride to let the source read the story, and it doesn't give the source any control. The goal, after all, is to impart accurate knowledge in everyday language."

Working with sources carefully should assist journalists in overcoming the kinds of errors which research has shown appear most frequently in science stories. For example, a West Virginia University researcher asked 242 scientists to identify errors from stories in which they were cited. The errors most frequently listed were omission, overemphasis, and exaggeration.[22] While lack of space can account for many of these instances, it is also logical to assume that they may occur through failure by the reporter to ask follow-up questions.

How far this translation should be carried, however, is something reporters need to consider. While clarity, completeness, and simplicity of style are the goals, Percy H. Tannenbaum of the University of Wisconsin, as far back as 1963, warned against the use of "standardized, shopworn phrases"—"major breakthrough" and "giant step forward"—which distort any discussion of theory and experimentation.

Furthermore, Tannenbaum wondered if science reporters weren't underestimating audiences. In other specialized fields, such as sports, stock market reports, and election results, reporters use the language of the field and readers understand it.

"In the case of science writing, on the other hand, there seems to be a leaning-over-backward to cater to the individual who is not a reader to begin with, perhaps at the expense of the regular reader," he said.[23]

Tannenbaum may have a point, but reporters themselves are much more likely to note with satisfaction what they see as trends in loosening up of writing and coverage—emphasis on lighter, consumer-oriented stories, including case studies and stories about everyday people to explain and give human dimension to major science issues.[24]

But perhaps the best perspective comes from Alton Blakeslee, whose father also was an AP science writer and whose daughter Sandra is a science writer for the *Los Angeles Times:*

"Regard your total audience out there as not ignorant of your subject, but innocent of it. What does an astronomer understand about heart disease? He may not know any of these things, and vice versa, so you're writing for all those people, specialists as well as people in any kind of occupation.

"It helps very much to have the background, but your purpose is to communicate with other people, and you do this, I think, in language as clear and simple as you can. That's what the writer has to do to be fair and effective to a whole great diverse audience out there."[25]

Public Panic or False Hope

It's true in all reporting, of course, but medical reporters particularly face the rather frightening prospect that what they write has direct impact on the very life or death of readers, listeners, and viewers. On the one hand, those who suffer are apt to see any discovery as a miracle cure. Or some may suffer unnecessarily from, say, polio, because parents were lulled by reports that modern science had conquered this dreaded killer of children. Or, thousands may experience needless trauma because of exaggerations of a possible serious epidemic.

The media are not necessarily the sole cause of these problems—public panic and false hope—but reporters must be painfully aware of the need for moderation, caution, and constant explanation in their writing.

That's why medical reporters often run counter to tradition and use disclaimers and qualifications. Like the scientist, they must stress that what is being reported is not necessarily a "cure," but rather another scientific step in a process that by nature zigzags and reverses courses.

Likewise, they must explain fully to avoid creating confusion or panic with reports of potential problems. People are confused these days over threatening discussions of the dangers of saccharin and sodium nitrite. They don't know if they can eat cranberries, drink coffee or diet soft drinks, watch color television, or take birth control pills. Scientists and the news media have not presented the full stories, and they share the responsibility for the communication failure.

A related problem is typified by a plea from T. Gerald Delaney, director of public affairs of the Memorial Sloan-Kettering Cancer Center. He asks journalists to exercise restraint in their use of statistics, especially long-term survival figures.

He uses the illness of the late Senator Hubert Humphrey of Minnesota as an example, saying news reports that the senator had a 20 percent chance of survival from his cancer provide an example of the statistical fallacy of predicting the fate of an individual on the basis of a group.

"Although a picture of group behavior is derived from many individual cases," Delaney says, "a picture of individual behavior cannot be accurately derived from the group."

Likewise important is the fact that Humphrey read these stories and, according to his doctors, was visibly shaken by them, Delaney says. There also is a strong possibility that these same news stories may adversely affect the attitudes of those people linked to the patient as well as others who may improperly relate the published information to their own cases.

"Bear in mind the imperfect state of medical knowledge, the uncertainty of every prognosis, and the ambiguity of statistical information," he advises. "Then it is more fitting to exercise restraint in using potentially painful information by qualifying the numbers, by pointing out the importance of mitigating factors, and by affirming the singularity of individual destiny."[26]

MOVING TOWARD MATURITY

Science writing always has been part of American journalism. But it was not until the two great world wars in the twentieth century that the media came to recognize the essential value of covering scientific developments in detail. And it was not until the Russians launched Sputnik 1 in 1958 that science reporting became a genuine specialty. Hundreds of journalistic "science experts" covered the subsequent space race.

Perhaps the quantitative peak of science journalism came in 1969 when the National Aeronautics and Space Administration accredited 3,597 media personnel for the Apollo 11 liftoff to the moon.[27] But, as the twentieth century progresses, perhaps science journalism is reaching maturity. Reporters seem to be much less anxious for what one called the "gee-whiz, Buck Rogers stuff" and more determined to chronicle scientific and technological developments from the perspective of their role in social development, be that role positive or negative.

And that maturity could be reflected in development of four trends which demonstrate changes in science writing and portend future developments.

Less Breaking News, More Interpretation

Meetings of scientific organizations, news conferences by leading scientists, specific technological developments, and technological accidents always will receive journalistic attention. They deserve it. But these reports don't always give a more sophisticated audience what it wants or needs. Reporters are paying and must continue to pay greater attention to the background, broader implications, and meaning of scientific developments.

Reporters are more likely to be evaluative, at times more critical, of scientists and technologists, their work, and the social implications of their efforts. To accomplish this, reporters themselves are becoming more knowledgeable and using more alternative sources in their stories, especially scientists, but also government officials and other citizens.

Focus on Audience Perspective

Science journalism, in spite of notable exceptions, has tended in the past to echo the journalistic practice of presenting news from the official source to the general audience. It has passed along "the word" from the experts. But many readers, viewers, and listeners are becoming too sophisticated to simply swallow what they are told. Some are becoming more vocal about what they want from science and what they want from journalism.

Science reporters are aware of this need, and they are responding. In medicine, they are writing more from the perspective of the patient; in all of science, they are placing greater emphasis on the social consequences of science and technology. A greater tendency toward consumer orientation to science coverage is apparent. And the traditional flow of news has been made a two-way street. Journalism is seeking to inform government, corporate scientists, and officials of public attitudes about what they are doing.

It Doesn't Have to Be Dull

Most high school students, perhaps for good reason, have the attitude that science is dull. Too many reporters—even some of those who write about science—have carried that attitude into their professional lives. But while science may be complex, many reporters and, indeed, many scientists stress that it is among the most naturally dramatic fields of inquiry. Many reporters simply have not been taking advantage of this.

A change is reflected in efforts to use writing styles which highlight this natural drama and which attempt to humanize the potentially cold facts of scientific developments. This is not simply translating scientific terminology, although that is important. It's writing as though science has a direct impact upon the person reading the magazine or newspaper, watching television, or listening to the radio. It does. And this must be reflected in a professional style which avoids sensationalism for its own sake but stresses the human, the personal, and sometimes even the lighter side of science news.

The Spotlight Is on Health

The American public probably is more interested these days in the state of its general health than it has ever been in history. Persons of all ages jog along highways, country roads, and formal running paths. Local recreation programs are booming as more individuals seek physical activity. But more than exercise is involved. People are interested in their health and in the health of others. And when people are interested, it's reasonable to assume that authors and journalists will provide them with ways to feed that interest.

This journalistic spotlight will focus on more than news accounts of efforts to find a cure for cancer, research into the causes of birth defects, the cost of medical care. These and other health-related topics will always be important. But medical writers also have rediscovered the how-to format, and they are providing more and more information of practical usefulness to those in the audience.

Human beings, being human beings, don't always live according to the health advice they receive. But their interest is enough of a spark for journalists to continue to emphasize health.

That could save lives, and that's reward enough.

NOTES

1. "Covering Science and Medicine," panel discussion during Ohio University's Communication Week, May 4, 1978.
2. Victor Cohn, "Are We Really Telling the People About Science?" *Science*, May 1965, p. 750.
3. "Are We Really Telling the People About Science?," p. 750.
4. Sibby Christensen, "The Blakeslee story (to be continued)," *AP World*, April 1978, p. 25.
5. Carl Sagan, "There's No Hint of the Joys of Science," *TV Guide*, p. 6.
6. Cara Marie Rupp, "Breast Cancer Studies Have News Interest," *Editor & Publisher*, October 26, 1974, p. 22.

7. Everette E. Dennis and James McCartney, "Science Journalists and Metropolitan Dailies: Methods, Values and Perceptions of Their Work," unpublished paper presented to a Symposium on Teaching Science and Environmental Writing, Association for Education in Journalism, Seattle, Wash., August 13, 1978, p. 13.
8. Phillip J. Tichenor, "Teaching and the 'Journalism of Uncertainty,' " unpublished paper presented to Symposium on Teaching Science and Environmental Writing, Association for Education in Journalism, Seattle, Wash., August 13, 1978, p. 1.
9. "Covering Science and Medicine."
10. "Teaching and the 'Journal of Uncertainty,' " p. 6.
11. Tom Lee, "Cancer's Front-Page Treatment," *The Nation,* September 18, 1976, pp. 237–238.
12. Daniel S. Greenberg, "Let's Hear It for Science," *Columbia Journalism Review,* July–August 1974, p. 17.
13. "Let's Hear It for Science," p. 23.
14. "Science Journalists and Metropolitan Dailies," p. 5.
15. David M. Rubin, "Remember Swine Flu?" *Columbia Journalism Review,* July–August 1977, pp. 43, 46.
16. Rae Goodell, *The Visible Scientists* (Boston: Little, Brown and Co., 1977), p. 4.
17. William Divale, "Newspapers: Some Guidelines for Communicating Anthropology," *Human Organization,* summer 1976, p. 189.
18. Susan Q. Stranahan, letter to Neil Nemeth of Ohio University, May 8, 1979.
19. Joseph M. Higgins, letter to Neil Nemeth of Ohio University, May 11, 1979.
20. Blaine F. Fabian, letter to Neil Nemeth of Ohio University, May 22, 1979.
21. See, for example, "Science Journalists and Metropolitan Dailies," pp. 9–10.
22. Michael Ryan, "A Factor Analytic Study of Scientists' Responses to Errors," *Journalism Quarterly,* summer 1975, p. 336.
23. Percy H. Tannenbaum, "Communication of Science Information," *Science,* May 10, 1963, p. 581.
24. "Science Journalists and Metropolitan Dailies," p. 13.
25. "Covering Science and Medicine."
26. T. Gerald Delaney, "The Human Impact of Cancer News Stories," *Columbia Journalism Review,* March–April 1977, pp. 30–32.
27. As quoted from *Editor & Publisher,* February 13, 1971, by Hillier Kriegbaum, "Perspectives on Science Writing," unpublished paper prepared for distribution at the Symposium on Teaching Science and Environmental Writing, Association for Education in Journalism, Seattle, Wash., August 12, 1978, p. 4.

Chapter 16

COPING WITH DISCRIMINATION

The American people seldom have been so surprised, shocked, and bewildered as in the summer of 1967 when violence erupted on the streets of twenty-three of the nation's cities. Blacks mostly—ghetto blacks—sought to overcome their frustrations and vent their rage by striking back at the system which they felt had betrayed them. This predominantly white society was not ready for such rage. Then a year later came another shock: The blame was placed on white society.

"White racism," said the National Advisory Commission on Civil Disorders, the group appointed by President Lyndon B. Johnson to study the riots, "is essentially responsible for the explosive mixture which has been accumulating in our cities since the end of World War II."[1]

About halfway through its report, the group, popularly known as the Kerner Commission, had another surprise, this for those involved with the nation's news organizations. The news media, it said, shared the responsibility for creating the circumstances which ultimately led to the eruption.

"The news media have failed to analyze and report adequately on racial problems in the United States," the commission said, "and, as a related matter, to meet the Negro's legitimate expectations in journalism. By and large, news organizations have failed to communicate to both their black and white audiences a sense of the problems America faces and the sources of potential solutions.

"The media report and write from the standpoint of a white man's world. The ills of the ghetto, the difficulties of life there, the Negro's burning sense of grievance, are seldom conveyed. Slights and indignities are part of the Negro's

daily life, and many of them come from what he now calls 'the white press'—
a press that repeatedly, if unconsciously, reflects the biases, the paternalism, the
indifference of white America. This may be understandable, but it is not excusable
in an institution that has the mission to inform and educate the whole of our
society."[2]

It's been quite a few years since the Kerner Commission issued its indictments.
But few since then have stated the need more precisely or with greater authority.
Few have been so extensively quoted. The specific recommendations of the commission have provided the benchmarks for evaluation of news media coverage of
race and race relations. Among those recommendations were:

> Expand coverage of the black community and of race problems through permanent
> assignment of reporters familiar with urban and racial affairs and through estab-
> lishment of more and better links with the black community.
> Integrate blacks and black activities into all aspects of coverage and content, includ-
> ing newspaper articles and television programming. The news media must publish
> newspapers and produce programs that recognize the existence and activities of
> blacks as a group within the community and as a part of the larger community.
> Recruit more blacks into journalism and broadcasting and promote those who are
> qualified to positions of significant responsibility.
> Accelerate efforts to ensure accurate and responsible reporting of racial news through
> adoption by all news-gathering organizations of stringent internal staff guidelines.[3]

IT'S MORE THAN BLACK AND WHITE

Debate over journalism's response continues into the 1980s. Some people stress
significant improvement and cite examples to prove it. Others shake their heads
that so little has been accomplished. No one, however, says the problem has been
solved. In many respects, progress made has been swallowed up by the magnitude
of the problem and by the manifestation of the problem beyond the black community.

The Kerner Commission described frustrations of one social group, but the
themes it presented were applied more broadly in the 1970s. The civil rights
struggle sprang up among other groups, who also complained about media coverage. Other ethnic groups—particularly Hispanics and American Indians—
echoed the outrage. Women, too, charged that journalism either ignored them or
took a paternalistic approach.

But the awakening went beyond that. Handicapped persons began to demand
full access, physically and socially, to the means of livelihood. They pointed to
a lack of general awareness of the problems they face in coping with a society
structured for those without disabilities. They blamed the media, in part, for this
lack of awareness and strongly suggested that their needs deserved attention.

"You should realize that handicapped people are involved in a civil rights
movement," Siggy Shapiro of WWDB-FM in Philadelphia told a convention of

the Society of Professional Journalists, Sigma Delta Chi. "And I think that it's important that you realize that there's a great need for information about the rights of people with disabilities. The media, as you know, can do an enormous amount to change attitudes."[4]

The elderly, likewise, expressed dissatisfaction over their insignificant status in society and in the media. Some organized, called themselves the Gray Panthers, and began a struggle to move from the confinement of rest homes. At the other end of the age spectrum, some persons began to speak of the rights of children to media attention other than in crisis circumstances.

The situations about which all these groups and individuals complain, while perhaps not identical, are similar. And their suggestions to the news media run parallel to those of the Kerner Commission.

They question traditional news judgment when much legitimate news about them, their activities, and their needs is ignored, treated in stereotypical fashion, relegated to insignificance through placement, or given once-over-lightly, often "cutesy," treatment. They question journalism's collective intent when the tone of news inevitably appears negative. They doubt journalism's role as protector of citizens when they seldom hear the investigative whistle blow on what they perceive as serious social injustices. And they see little evidence that news media are attempting seriously to solve these problems by making their staffs more representative of the total population.

Perhaps the charges are exaggerated and overly emotional. A general social consciousness truly has swept through American newsrooms. There is more attention to a larger variety of social groups. Statistics and examples also would show that news media recruiters are actively seeking individuals who will help broaden journalism's overall perspective. But is it enough? The answer, even from most journalists, is a resounding "no."

"I do not think it too much to suggest that we have come this far by fear, fear of physical danger in a riot, fear of being beaten by that other news organization with a black staff member who might edge us out on a racial story," says Robert C. Maynard of the *Oakland* [California] *Tribune* and director of the Berkeley Summer Program for Minority Journalists. "The question is whether such inauspicious beginnings can be transformed into concerted effort to be as fully representative of the total society as we possibly can be."[5]

RACISM, SEXISM, AGEISM

The Kerner Commission is hardly alone in charging that deep-rooted attitudes are at the core of many of this society's most serious problems and affect news judgment. Asked once if he felt the media had improved their coverage of black life, civil rights leader the Rev. Ralph Abernathy was blunt in his reply:

"I certainly do not. I don't think there has been a marked improvement at all. I think that's simply because of racism on the part of those who make up the press. The roots of racism are so terribly deep that it is impossible to separate one from his background in the white community—whether he lives in Georgia or Alabama or New York or California or Michigan. That is, in any particular walk of life, if a person comes out of a racist background, he takes that racist feeling and attitude into that chosen field. And, unfortunately, those who control the news media in our country are from the white community."

The charge: racism. The automatic response is defensiveness. But the truth is that it is extremely difficult for any person to overcome those factors which provide the basic perspectives of life. And the attitudes are not always racial. They may concern gender, for those who control the news media also tend to be men. They tend to be less than elderly or to have gained their positions and wealth in their younger years. They seldom are physically handicapped. And what they are naturally will be reflected in the decisions they make.

It is not that journalists, as individuals, make their decisions on the basis of race or sex or age. Perhaps some do, but the majority fall into the trap somewhere along a continuum which is made up of what scholars consider three types of attitudes.

Expressed in racial terms, the lowest rung of the ladder is *individual racism,* which could be labeled individual sexism or ageism as well. This represents action based on the belief that one's own race is superior. When individuals transfer that attitude to social institutions and consciously manipulate those institutions to achieve superiority, the label is *institutional racism.* To the degree that persons do make such conscious use of their news positions, they are a disgrace to journalism. But they are small in number and usually are taken care of by the system. The most far-reaching and evasive problem is that which grows from cultural bias, termed *cultural racism.*

"[Such] cultural racism exists when cultural differences demonstrated by certain members of the society are negatively reinforced by those in power and when the cultural contributions of an entire group or race are overlooked," says author Andrea L. Rich.[6]

And that sounds very much like the statements of the Kerner Commission, women, the handicapped, and the elderly.

If it were simply a matter of attitudes which create coverage voids, the problem, though continuously difficult, would be easier to handle. Journalists could resolve to do better and then institute a program of pointed coverage. But it is more complex. Even when attention is paid to a group, there is the danger that it may be equally negative. The attention may take the form of colonialism, which is degrading because it implies authority and the need to help those who cannot help themselves. Yet another form, equally degrading, is paternalism, in which the subjects are looked down upon and overly patronized.

The historic journalistic result of such cultural racism, sexism, or ageism is that most news has been about, by, and for white males who are part of the central order. In most cases, this has not resulted from deliberate decisions to degrade or ignore any section of the population. Journalists are aware of their responsibilities to the total community. But they must make judgments about what news is important and what is significant to society. And these judgments are based on the perspectives of the decision makers.

Much of the blame for the skewed coverage may have to go to unconscious neglect.

"First of all, there's the news selection and the perception of what's important," says Mary Gardner of Michigan State University, former national president of the Association for Education in Journalism. "We have to be very honest that one of the reasons there's so much news about male activities is that males do control the budget and have attained higher positions and therefore are more newsworthy in general. But I get impatient, particularly in this day and age, because men who make journalistic decisions should be making more effort. They have been socialized, though, and it doesn't occur to them that anything a woman says could be important. They tend not to think about it."

But journalists must think about it, in two ways. First, as Abernathy says, "They have to overcome themselves, and they have to be aware of the fact that they have been molded by a certain type of society." But that would not be sufficient. Witness the number of reporters whose interest in providing solid coverage of the total community has been stifled by institutional traditions or unyielding editors. Journalism is moving into a new era, one in which the traditional patterns of news must be modified institutionally.

"Empathy is perhaps the key to overcoming the shackles of our own belief and value systems," Rich advises. "We must try in interracial settings to step outside ourselves in order to gain an understanding of the reality of others."[7]

GETTING TO THE ROOTS OF UNDERSTANDING

Gaining an understanding of the "reality of others" is one of the challenges for reporters who find themselves covering ethnic and other social groups. Journalists long ago accepted the fact that the successful science writer is one who understands science. That means knowing how science developed as well as contemporary work. The greatest political reporting comes from individuals who know the political system and who have developed political instinct based on study and observation.

The same requirements must be applied to those who cover the lives and activities of this nation's social groupings. Without such knowledge and understanding, reporters are doomed to continue their superficial coverage.

Cultural values are learned best through personal contact. Reading textbooks and scholarly analyses and talking with experts are activities the conscientious reporter must find time to accomplish. They provide the background and help establish the proper questions to ask. But another necessary requirement is to be on the streets, visit the reservations, the black or Hispanic neighborhoods. Too much journalistic information comes from the power structure, from government or law enforcement officials. This is information from an outsider's perspective. It is, at best, marginally helpful, and sometimes it is just plain wrong.

"I don't think we're really even getting at the people out there who are the frustrated masses, the concerned, the people who feel that nobody gives a damn," says Ben Burns of the *Detroit News*. "I don't think we're really acquainted with these people."[8]

Without an understanding, for example, of the nonindustrial life styles of American Indians, it would be too easy for a reporter to be appalled at life on the reservation and to miss important stories. The Associated Press's Howard Graves, who has covered Indians in the Southwest, believes strongly that reporters have to spend time on a reservation to fully appreciate their life style preferences.

Howard Graves of The Associated Press

"They have been exploited by the white man for so many years that they don't care to be exploited again," says Graves, former national president of the Society of Professional Journalists, Sigma Delta Chi. "They've had anthropologists and sociologists come on the reservation to get them into some kind of a program, and they're turned off by that. They don't like tourists coming and going and asking them to pose for pictures, and they don't like tourists driving through their holy grounds or their living areas and seeing all the debris that is around—old furniture, old car bodies, trash.

"That's the way they want to live, and they don't care how the white person feels about it. They don't want their life style disturbed. If they wanted to live in the white man's world, they would move into the white man's town. A lot of them have never had any dealings with the media unless they are Indian government officials who have been off the reservation or have been involved with the police. The reporter has to know these things to deal with Indians effectively and to do the kind of job that needs to be done."

THE PERSPECTIVE OF AN INDIAN TRIBAL CHAIRMAN

(EXCERPTS OF REMARKS BY PETER MACDONALD, NAVAJO TRIBAL CHAIRMAN)

If this panel was set up as some sort of enemy to The Associated Press or the news media, let me say this. You are not my enemy or the enemy of the Indian peoples. As a matter of fact, you are our friend and our ally. I may criticize you, but I decline to attack you or heap abuse on you. I have great respect for the press for the critical role it plays in preserving a democratic society. We need you. The native American peoples need you if we are to have any hope of surviving the growing backlash against Indians for daring to wish to survive as separate peoples and separate nations within the United States.

I respect your professionalism, your moral courage, your willingness to expose corruption and scandal and betrayals of trust in high places. You are idealists, even if you sound cynical. You really believe in free speech, a free press, the power of truth, and a democratic process. You have my highest respect.

If the question is: Is your record perfect? Can you improve? Have you sometimes failed? Are there recurring problems? the answer, of course, is yes, and I wish to talk about these. But I do not wish you to believe that these criticisms and comments cancel out my respect, my trust, and my gratitude for the job you have done.

Peter MacDonald, Navajo tribal chairman

First, the truth is not always bad. Not everything that happens in this world is a scandal or a tragedy even though it is a major item in a newspaper or makes headlines. Investigative reporting is a dominant fashion today for many papers, but some papers and some TV programs, some magazines and some radio programs report affirmative developments, where the action is, what is going on, what are new developments, what's working as well as what's wrong.

Indian tribal governments are very old as well as very new, especially new in being given any autonomy and respect. Sure, we make mistakes, but you must remember that sometimes we make no mistakes too. The problem is we do not know how to prove that we have made no mistakes. Often, you exaggerate, you portray the bad because it generates reader interest. You leave out the good and in doing so you inadvertently undermine the reputation, the integrity, and the stature of our leaders who are trying, trying very hard without training, without money, and without skills or experience.

Yet succeeding, not totally, but making progress, real progress, tangible progress, but progress that only becomes clear when one takes a longer time span of two, three, five, and ten years. The more you play up the moment, just this one moment, the less context you provide for any particular event, the more you will cripple our best efforts and undermine our strongest and most talented leaders.

Let me suggest also that you help us train our people in communications skills, media, radio, television, press, help train our school children, provide journalism training for our college students, help us learn so we can communicate internally with our reservation and externally with our state and local government, with the federal government, and with the American people. And also hire our native Americans, provide them with scholarships, or grants, or foundations, or fellowships so that they can learn. . . .

Second, there is local pressure, local prejudice and local self interest . . . and no one wants to hear about Indian rights, especially when these rights come into conflict with local emphasis and powerful interest. So it is very easy to set us up as the enemy of the people who pay electric bills in the Southwest, the enemy of the sport fisherman and tourism in the Northwest, the enemy of industrial development, hydroelectric power, and irrigation farmers, the enemy of the people of Maine and Rhode Island, the enemy of all of them. We are an available scapegoat for a nation that needs land, water, uranium, coal, oil, tourism, fishing, hunting, urban growth, industrial expansion.

In trying to cling to what little is ours, what little remains to us, we are set up as the enemy. We are likely to be viewed as evil and selfish people. That is unfair. For our entire world is grappling with limitations on growth, on pollution, on water. To make us the target is to pretend that if it were not for the Indians, America could still have unlimited growth, energy, land, and resources. If you took everything we have —native Americans have today—you would still face the same problems, the same limits, the same hard choices because at the bottom is a problem about the American way of life.

The dominant society, or the dominant culture, is essentially a culture that depends on material consumption. And here the native Americans have a special resource, for the native American culture is a nonmaterialistic culture with a very strong reverence for nature, a vital sense of community, an identity that does not rest on material wealth. We must ask you to find ways to help people understand that when Navajos and other native Americans reach for self-sufficiency— for political and economic self-sufficiency, governmental self-sufficiency—we are not declaring war.

Third, we need you to make a special effort on our behalf. We need your investigative reporting to be focused on two types of injustices that never see the light of day. (A) There are local injustices, consumer fraud, police brutality, refusal to extend credit, job discrimination, treatment of Indian children in schools, treatment of Indian peoples in hospitals. All of these need to be exposed. There is too little investigation of these patterns and practices. Sometimes we feel that we face a media blackout. (B) There is a broader and more fundamental breach of trust by the trustee of all native Americans, the federal government. You see, the federal government serves as trustee of our land, our resources. The federal government is our banker, our engineer, our forest ranger, and, yes, our doctor, our lawyer, and even our Indian chief. Because parallel to tribal government is a second government that exists on the reservation, and that second government is the BIA (Bureau of Indian Affairs). That trustee has certain basic responsibilities to preserve our assets, to invest them, to develop them for our benefit, to use reasonable judgment and prudence, to take reasonable precautions, to take reasonable risks. There have been and continue to be pervasive violations of minimal standards of trusteeship that are built into the system. It is built into the structure of the BIA.

We need your help in exposing these injustices, documenting them, bringing them to light if we are not to be the victim of our protector. This is your special strength. This is your special genius.

So there's a great deal of understanding that needs to occur between you and us. I feel that you, the people of the press, can do a great deal in this area. Ultimately, our fate rests upon the conscience of the American people, and the media, more than any other institution, will determine whether their conscience is asleep or awake when the fate of our people is decided.

Source: Panel discussion, "The American Indian," Associated Press Managing Editors convention, Portland, Ore., September 28, 1978.

And Peter MacDonald, Navajo tribal chairman, has the same message:

"In the Indian world we always say that before you judge a man you must walk several moons in his moccasins. Well, you need reporters who can understand the thinking about the concept of a dependent nation but also a sovereign nation. That's a very strange concept for America, but it does exist. And you need reporters who understand our attachment to our land base, our nonindustrial way of life, our values, and our needs."[9]

The separation of blacks and Hispanics from white society is not quite as total as reservation life, but it does exist as a function of residential patterns. And, as a result of the cultural backgrounds and residential socialization of blacks and Hispanics, they, too, have cultural perspectives which differ from that of the average white and which influence how they think within the overall context of American social structure. In some respects, Americans are not surprised at ethnic differences and, in fact, such differences often are encouraged. Much of the tourism business in this country is based on ethnic attractions.

Therefore, it should be no surprise that what is important to members of a group is predicated, at least in part, on their cultural perceptions of what they are and how that fits into the majority culture. Understanding of such influences can help a reporter avoid errors.

Frank del Olmo of the *Los Angeles Times* urges reporters to be sensitive to the backgrounds, history, and demographics of social groups. He notes one instance in which a common perception—that all Mexican-Americans are farm workers —is patently incorrect. Knowing that some 85 percent of the Spanish of this country, including Puerto Ricans and Mexican-Americans, are urban dwellers, he says, will make reporters a bit more sensitive and help them avoid incorrect preconceived notions about how a community will react to a given issue.

As another example, del Olmo points out that many Californians, including some political reporters, attribute the relatively low voter turnout among Mexican-Americans to lack of language skills or just apathy. There's some truth to that, he admits, but history teaches an additional lesson.

"Until as late as the 1950s, there were historic events that tended to force a Mexican-American community to be a little less than receptive toward dealing with the outside," he says. "When you see your neighbors being carted off by immigration agents, that's going to have an impact, and it doesn't surprise me that there still are a lot of the older generation who feel less than total commitment to being U.S. citizens. They were beaten into submission for about twenty years. So, twenty years from now, I think you'll see the younger generation—my generation—will probably be more typical in its voting patterns."

The women's movement in this country provides numerous similar examples. Even though women had battled since the nineteenth century against the idea that they should occupy a separate sphere, reporters who sought to cover the modern movement as it emerged in the 1960s found their biggest problem to be a general lack of understanding.[10] Some editors did not recognize the significance or the potential of the story. Many chose to ignore it, to treat it lightly, or to heap scorn upon it. Even today, with significant progress having been made, questions remain as to whether those in journalism understand what they are dealing with. Peggy A. Simpson of The Associated Press, for example, asks:

"Can the movement continue to make its case with the news media, let alone the general public? Can it educate reporters and via the newspapers tell the nation about the inequities that still remain and, in some cases, are worsening? Are the enormous changes throughout society affecting men as strongly as women, or seen as significant enough for editors to assign reporters to monitor them? Are new writers developing the expertise to go beyond personality conflicts between the White House and activists to report on conditions facing women in factories and typing pools, about the resentments of men facing serious challenges for jobs from women, about the anger of millions of women isolated in low-paid, dead-end work ghettos? Are reporters aware of the new frontier facing many women in professional jobs, or concerned about the conflicts between careers and personal relationships?"[11]

It's axiomatic in journalism that no reporter can effectively explain what he or she does not understand. It's also accepted that journalism exists to provide information about the community to the community. Yet, millions of persons are seeing neither understanding nor adequate information about their life styles, their problems, and their role as American citizens.

"If we accept a cliche that I think has a lot of validity, that newspapers are in a sense writing a first rough draft of history," says Dorothy Gilliam of the *Washington Post,* "then the importance of getting the black (Hispanic, Indian, female) perspective is of significance not only to blacks (or other groups), but to the wider audience. And it seems to me that one of the perceptions that is most difficult for whites to understand is what a great stake they have in racial harmony in this country. So it is not enough to simply say that we have done this, or we have done that in terms of pacifying blacks. The real issue has to be that both interests are served, when this job is done and done well."[12]

MAKING THE WHEEL SQUEAK

If you have a problem you want to discuss with someone, you first have to make sure that person is listening. It also helps if whatever you do to attract attention also makes the other person want to do something to help solve the problem. This is a lesson civil rights groups learned very early, and it's one being copied regularly these days.

"The handicapped have been really invisible except for the past couple of years," says Siggy Shapiro of WWDB-FM in Philadelphia. "We were kept in the closet, so to speak, and it hasn't been until recently that we ourselves banged down that door, burst out of the closet, had some really rambunctuous rallies in front of Secretary [of Health, Education and Welfare Joseph A.] Califano's home in Washington in 1977. People finally started to notice that we were around."

That's the point. Making people notice. This may be sought by being rambunctuous, it may be an effort to impress by congregating great numbers of people, or it may take the most extreme form—creating a disruption in the lives of citizens and government officials, perhaps even breaking the law. Social groups have, in fact, become very sophisticated in developing strategies that force others to pay attention. The specific actions take several forms:

Farmers from across the country disrupting traffic in Washington, D.C., by driving their tractors slowly down the city's main streets

Women traveling in large numbers to Washington to participate in an Equal Rights Amendment rally where prominent speakers from all walks of life urge support

Blacks staging sit-ins at restaurants, movies, and other public establishments in efforts to desegregate them

Hispanic homemakers, workers, and retirees packing San Antonio, Texas, city council meetings to demand that something be done to improve public services in their neighborhoods

LaDonna Harris, a Commanche and founder of Americans for Indian Opportunity, is one who has given considerable thought to the various strategies of attracting attention. She notes that when people see disruptive Indian actions at

Alcatraz, Wounded Knee (South Dakota), and Washington, D.C., they consider such actions irrational.

"We came to the conclusion that Indian people were acting rationally in an irrational situation," she says. "When there is no one paying any attention to you, you have to go crazy. Everybody says, 'How do you get things done in your organization?' And I say, well, I first try to seduce people into it. If they don't do that, then I do my crazy Indian woman act. And it works. It really works to go crazy on them, particularly government agencies.

"And so all that the Indian people were saying is 'We're here. We want you to pay attention to us. We're here. We have a right to exist, and we have a right to exist in the style that we believe in.' "[13]

The audience for such actions is fourfold. In the first place, groups may be seeking to persuade others to join the movement. Second, they have a message for those in power, be that the state or federal government, corporate executives, or local business operators. Third, they want the attention of citizens in the hopes of gaining sympathy or support for their cause.

USING THE MEDIA TO CHANGE SOCIETY

The media can be the best means of mass communication and con-sciousness-raising yet invented, especially when you have little money to spend bringing your ideas to the public. So take advantage of them if they invite you to an interview, a talk show, or other special-interest event. . . .

The second thing that we have learned about the media is that they can rip you off. The people of the media are always looking for ways to feed their programming. Do not let them take advantage of you. Too much publicity when you are not ready for it is as difficult to cope with as too little when you need it. You may never be able to control the rate and flow of media interest, but do not let them misrepresent your organization. Do not let them box you in and use you for something you are not. You are not merely a human interest story about "active senior citizens." You are a potentially powerful coalition of young and old. Your focus is not to arouse curiosity but to create human action and power to change society. . . .

The current fascination of the media with the "senior citizen" may pass. We must not confuse this enthusiasm, which may be temporary, with the very real, frightening, and continuous age-ism which we find everywhere in our society. We must point to the older citizen who is "in" with the media and to the younger individual who is not "in," for both are victims of this age-ism. The problems of youth may not be so apparent as those of the older adult, but they are just as real: minors are as dependent on the legal system and bureaucratic agencies as are older adults.

[From the organizing manual of the Gray Panthers.]

Source: As quoted in "Using the Media to Change Society," *The Center Maga-zine,* March-April 1975, p. 20.

The fourth audience is made up of news organizations which have the means of spreading the message. Often, the activities depend upon what the news media, particularly television, are most likely to cover. For example, in a study of a 2½-year strike of an Austin, Texas, furniture factory, Chicano union leaders admitted how they carefully orchestrated many of their plans with an eye toward the local media. And from that study came such comments as:

"We deliberately called the city council a bunch of rednecks. This got everybody interested, and they wanted to know what we were going to do. It was in the news all over." "We did not want a confrontation with the police. We were not equipped for one. But having the police there was an asset. It heightened tensions and gave the impression of a confrontation when in fact we were all working to avoid one. It sure brought out the media." "All of a sudden [after a letter was written to the Federal Communications Commission], they [the media] all wanted to talk with us about why we were striking. We started having press conferences about once a week, and the press would cover them."[14]

Journalists are aware of their role in such events. They have mixed emotions about them. On the one hand, they have the standard distaste for being manipulated, for being forced to cover the complaints of a group through stagings they cannot ignore. "Media events," the call them. Sponsors say such events would not be necessary if reporters did a better job of discussing their complaints and their frustrations. Sometimes there is truth to that statement, but reporters respond that too often the issues have been discussed thoroughly and the sponsors are being greedy in wanting constant attention and repetition.

The debate is unnecessary, however, because when an act—especially one which is illegal or disruptive—is committed in a public place, often in the presence of thousands of people, it must be covered. Of course, reporters have the option of deciding that the event was only theater and of little substance and thus giving it minimal play. But they must be on the scene.

Given the public nature and obvious newsworthiness of most of those events, reporters such as William Greider of the *Washington Post* don't worry much about manipulation. They point out that there's little distinction between such activities and a presidential press conference. So the major decisions concern how, not whether, to provide coverage and how to cope with some special journalistic problems they offer.

"I think probably the major frustration of speakers at a major rally—this used to be particularly true in the antiwar period—is that they cannot get the rhetoric into the newspaper because of the theater," Greider says. "You go to a monster rally, and the stories concentrate on 'God, look at this crowd' and 'There will always be some, maybe a lot of, violence.' Clashes between police and demonstrators, lots of colorful people smoking pot. The newspapers would be filled up with that. There may be very little of what speakers are saying. I'm sure the ERA people would say the same thing today. Or the anti-ERA people."

The activities, the disruption, the violence, the unusual nature of any rally or demonstration must be covered. And the task may require a team of reporters.

William Greider of the *Washington Post*

(*Washington Post* photo)

At the same time, however, "you have to give every group at least a clear shot at getting its rhetoric taken seriously," Greider says. Someone has to ignore the throngs and pay attention to the speakers, interview the sponsors, and attempt to get meaningful comments from the crowd.

In addition, every situation of this type has another side. Someone opposes. Someone disagrees. A government official may feel that the complaints are unfounded. What is being requested may be impossible in the eyes of those responsible for taking official action. Perhaps officials believe they have done as much as they can. Or they may agree with the complaints, promise action, or pass the buck. Perhaps reporters will be unable to do all of the follow-up concurrent with the rally or demonstration. It may be the next day or several days later. But the response is part of the story.

How circular the follow-up process gets depends upon the reporters' judgment. Sponsors of the rally may want to respond to the response. That may be valid. It may not. The decision is journalistic and is dependent upon individual circumstances.

However, in some instances there is a need for long-range follow-up. Issues, promises, plans of action all should be evaluated later. It's unfair and unwise to report the big splash and ignore how the water settles.

In San Antonio, for example, efforts to get city government to improve Hispanic neighborhoods produced a number of spinoff stories. For one thing, city leaders apparently responded, and the improvements are being made. For another, the success of the protest has contributed to a steady rise in Hispanic voter participation. And this increased activity later gave Hispanics a majority of the city council seats.[15]

MATTERS OF LANGUAGE AND STYLE

Language represents a three-pronged obligation for reporters. First, it is the means whereby they get the information to be presented on the printed page or over the air. Second, it is the tool used to present that information, and the success of communication efforts to a diversified audience depends upon its proper usage.

Third, how it is used can suggest meaning which goes beyond the precise message of the moment.

And those obligations become particularly crucial when the reporter is dealing with and about individuals who feel they have been objects of discrimination. They have sensitivity to language which goes beyond the dictionary. Sometimes it is language which provides part of the basis for social separation. Often the loudest complaints are about the specific words used. This means that news organizations must share that sensitivity. It's not that reporters must always accept the language suggestions made. They should, however, be willing to consider them and to make modifications when valid points have been made.

They Don't All Speak Standard English

Frank del Olmo of the *Los Angeles Times* is realistic about the reasons he has gotten, as a young reporter, some outstanding assignments. He was a member of that paper's Watergate team after only two years of professional experience. He has had foreign assignments and occasionally travels across the country in pursuit of specific stories.

"I've gotten many other kinds of fairly big assignments that normally might not have gone to a reporter of my youth and inexperience," he says. "But they needed somebody who spoke Spanish. I'm the guy who knows the language and can go there immediately and do the job. If anything, I would define my job as not so much a Chicano specialist as a Spanish-speaking specialist because, incredibly, the paper doesn't have that many reporters who speak Spanish."

Perhaps that's part of the reason journalism is criticized as not understanding significant portions of the population of this nation. Of course, not every newspaper or broadcast station could afford or even want a full complement of reporters who speak the many languages that contribute to the cultural diversity of this country. But when geography dictates that frequent contact will be made with Spanish- or German-speaking people, it makes sense that news organizations would have reporters on hand who can do it.

Speaking the source's language serves two purposes. Perhaps most important is the fact that it makes better communication. More information can be gathered and understood. But there is a broader implication—in development of empathy with sources and members of the audience. The natural assumption is that one who has taken the trouble to learn a language probably has greater interest in the group to whom that language is important. It's an instant means of overcoming what may be termed a "we-they" complex.

And then there's the matter of black English. Scholars don't agree about its origins, and there's debate over whether it should be accepted educationally. But the reporter who deals with blacks—especially ghetto blacks—has no choice but to accept it. It does exist for a large percentage of Americans of African ancestry. The ability to grapple with it may determine a reporter's understanding of black culture.

"If Black English were merely the concentration of a few quaint country usages from the rural areas of England, as the Establishment dialect geographers have made it out to be, the received opinion that the matter is trivial might be acceptable," says linguist J. L. Dillard. "But if, on the other hand, the disadvantaged Black has a historically different variety of English from that of the mainstream-culture white, the question remains open as to whether lack of communication is part of the racial trouble in this country."[16]

But reporters can't wait for scholars to reach agreement. Whatever their race, they must of course present the news in standard English and traditional grammatical form. At the information collection end of their job, however, in seeking to serve the society as a whole and this particular portion of it they must consider the advice given by two other black-language scholars:

"This is our rap. Will a rapid fading of our signals mean that it will not linger for reception at a reader's convenience? Well, that's where it's at baby, Black Language, and how you gonna get respect if you ain't learned it yet? Black Language documented from down on the ground Black People. The Black Man and Woman with a moving hip supermorphic body that goes along pimping with a creative and powerful mind, and sounds of Black Language blending in a beautiful crazy swinging way that says, 'That's our Language, Man, it's beautiful, logically grooving; I'm walking that walk and talking that talk and can you dig it.' "[17]

Sticks, Stones, and Words

That old bit about "sticks and stones and bones and words" is nonsense. Words do hurt. They can hurt deeply. They can demoralize. And this is especially true when they are used over and over again for long periods of time. That's why many of the complaints which social groups have about news media coverage find their most emotional expression in debates over specific word choice.

It matters only in degree whether the complaint concerns a truly derogatory word, represents oversensitivity, or is an expression of preference. Psychologically, if a group considers a word to be offensive, it is offensive. Being outside the dominant culture makes one more likely to grasp shades of meaning and intent and to want to break away from what is perceived as symbols of negative attitudes.

The problem is that certain terms, however legitimate their dictionary meaning, have become stereotypes and may be used to classify groups of individuals in a way which denies their individuality. The situation is worse when the stereotype is derogatory or has been given negative connotations. Thus, when the term "Negro," for example, came to be looked upon as a negative stereotype, a strong and unified move developed to replace it with "black."

There are those who criticize use of the term "illegal alien," saying it reinforces the image of what they call the "undocumented worker" as a law enforcement or public problem.[18] Likewise, some object to "senior citizen" because they feel it stereotypes older Americans as infirm, doddering, senile, and nonproductive.

Indians don't have discussions; they have "pow-wows." Indians do not take issue with authorities; they "go on the warpath." Shapiro provides yet another example:

" 'Cripple,' folks, is a no-no. By most standards among the handicapped community, 'cripple' is a totally negative term. It is ugly. It is nasty. And most handicapped people cannot abide by it. Also, 'wheelchair-bound' or 'confined to a wheelchair.' There are no chains around my chair. There are no ropes. I don't sleep in it. I don't make love in it, though some have tried. I don't spend my entire life in a wheelchair, and it is not a trap or a cage.[19]

How news organizations react to such attitudes depends, of course, upon their evaluation of the legitimacy of the complaint. It may depend upon how complex making the change would be. It may depend upon whether acceptable alternatives are available.

The fact that groups or individuals are honestly sensitive about a certain label should be given consideration. But that does not mean automatic acceptance. Reporters cannot please everyone. The language cannot be restructured every time someone gets a new idea. But neither is there a reason for stubbornness just because that's the way it's always been done.

Women: The Majority Minority

Census Bureau officials tell us that women outnumber men in this society. Demographic experts add that they control much of the nation's wealth. Yet their struggle has been essentially the same as that of minority groups who have sought equality of opportunity and fact. And, like minority groups, women have complaints about their treatment by the news media. That they have had some success with the news media is a fact of little dispute.

"Just a few years ago," says Sara Fritz of *U.S. News and World Report*, "any American newspaper might have carried a story saying: 'Margaret Thatcher doesn't look the part, but this glamorous mother of twins has shed her apron for a fling in British politics.' Stories belittling the ambitions of women have since disappeared from the pages of most newspapers—the result of a hard-fought feminist campaign begun in the early 1970s. . . . Yet some major issues involving the portrayal of women in newspapers remain unresolved."[20]

Part of that success came in 1977 when United Press International and The Associated Press issued new stylebooks in which they accepted some relatively new thinking about coverage of women. The importance of the major news agencies cannot be underestimated since most of the nation's newspapers and broadcast outlets tend to accept UPI or AP style as their own with only few modifications.

Perhaps the most significant contribution of the stylebooks was not in the recommendations about how to handle specific situations. Indeed, debates continue over some of the specific rules. But the news agencies did specify, "Women should receive the same treatment as men in all areas of coverage. Physical descriptions, sexist references, demeaning stereotypes, and condescending phrases should not be used."

Among specific examples, the stylebooks say that copy should not assume maleness when both sexes are involved (for example, use of the term "newsman" instead of "reporter"), that copy should not express surprise that an attractive woman can be professionally accomplished, that copy should not gratuitously mention family relationships when there is no relevance to the subject, that the same standards should be used for men and women in decisions of whether to include specific mention of personal appearance or marital and family situation.[21]

Whether news organizations are living up to these rules remains a subject of debate. One inconsistency often pointed to by feminists is the fact that many of the news media—including UPI and AP—continue to use courtesy titles for women and not for men. Such usage represents automatic reference to family relationships, they say, and is a waste of reporter time as well as an offense to some women. Few news organizations—with the *New York Times* representing a major exception—use courtesy titles for both men and women.

It appears inevitable that consistency of treatment will rule, and American journalism will eliminate use of "Miss" and 'Mrs." Some major news organizations already have, including both *Time* and *Newsweek,* the *Los Angeles Times* (with some exceptions), and three major news groups—Gannett, Knight-Ridder, and the Copley news services. AP and UPI, curiously, do not use courtesy titles on their sports wires.

Another source of contention lies in the structure of the English language, represented by male-oriented terminology: "chairman," "congressman," "mankind," "manmade," "fireman," and "man" as a collective ("the rights of man"). Here's where resistance has been greatest on the grounds that elimination of such references represents a major overhaul of the language. It may be relatively easy to use such substitute terms as "humanity" and "fire fighter" in some instances, and this is happening. But "chairperson" or "chair," as nonsexist equivalents of "chairman," are defined as awkward. The news agencies have adopted a middle-ground policy and use "chairman" or "chairwoman."

It may be that the importance of the debate over coverage of women and what is defined as sexist language is the debate itself. Whatever the specific conclusions, the news media are thinking about the implications of what they do. Whether this would have happened without pressure from women's groups makes little difference. It is an era of concern. A growing number of individual reporters and news executives have gained an awareness they did not have before.

Is Descriptive ID Needed?

Journalists, from day one, are trained to identify persons in the news. Name, age, address, title. But is it really necessary to describe a person in terms of race, sex, or physical status? Obviously, in many instances, this is an almost rhetorical question. Chances are good that Sarah Jones is a woman, the executive secretary of the National Association for the Advancement of Colored People is black, and the leader of Disabled in Action of Pennsylvania is handicapped.

But reporters often have options, and most say they would provide racial identification only when it is pertinent to the story. But when is it pertinent? Some say that, in the past, news organizations have been too quick to attach a racial label, for example, to crime stories, and that then becomes part of a broader complaint.

"Blacks and Hispanics commit crimes; their role as victims is slight. The victims are white. And the closer they are to the middle-class status of the paper's white editors, the bigger the story," says Clinton Cox of the *New York Daily News*. "With only the rarest exceptions, that is the picture of the New York City homicide world that emerges from the intellectual *Times*, the conservative *News* and the liberal *Post* week after week."[22]

While some research disputes this contention,[23] it does agree with the intuition of many. Without doubt, it is an accusation which has been made against most news organizations at one time or another. It is a problem which reporters must keep at the front of their minds.

UPI and AP try to be very specific in their instructions, listing four instances in which identification by race is acceptable: in biographical and announcement stories; when it provides the reader, viewer, or listener with a substantial insight into conflicting emotions known or likely to be involved in a demonstration or similar event; when describing a person sought in a search; when the event being reported involves conflict that cuts across racial lines.[24]

The broader goal, however, must be to avoid such identification. Calling specific attention should be the exception. Most news stories involve human beings caught in the act of being citizens. Sometimes those stories are negative, sometimes positive. But usually whichever category they fall in has little to do with anything more specific than human nature.

Again, advice from Siggy Shapiro:

"If I could urge you to do one thing, it would be to follow what I call the 'crip-in-a-crowd' approach. I would really like to see news coverage with background shots of a person in a wheelchair in a crowd. I'd like to see crips-in-a-crowd stories in the written and electronic media.

"One of my favorite photos was of a female psychiatrist in a recent five-part series in the *Philadelphia Inquirer* on how dismally mental patients are being treated in the communities since they've been released from hospitals. The woman was depicted in a picture counseling one of her clients. She was referred to in the story as a psychiatrist, Dr. So-and-so, with her credentials. She was in a wheelchair in the picture, and not one mention was made of that fact. She was just there as a human being doing her job. That's what I'd like to see more of."[25]

STREAMS FLOW INTO OCEANS

Journalists seldom work in abstractions. They seek the concrete, the specific. They prefer to demonstrate philosophy as it relates to life. They thrive on practi-

cal examples, realistic case studies, straightforward action, and logical applications. Thus it is with those whose responsibilities include coverage of
discrimination complaints and the drive for equality by some of this nation's
social groups.

By definition, "discrimination" must be either for or against someone or something. If a person or group is favored, there must be a person or group who is
not favored. Likewise, "equality" is a term which requires comparison. One
cannot be equal unless there is another party against which that equality is
measured. And both discrimination and equality have little meaning unless a
frame of reference is provided. Discriminated from doing, having, or being what?
Equality for what purpose?

And that's why it's a mistake to categorize coverage on the assumption that
blacks or women or elderly Americans represent exclusive categories. When one
analyzes specific problems of any of these groups, the finding often is that they
overlap, that the problems go beyond one group to the society as a whole. It's
a way of saying, "We're all in this together, and we'd better look at it from all
perspectives." Clarence Page of WBBM-TV in Chicago has learned this lesson.

Clarence Page of WBBM-TV, Chicago

"It's happened to me numerous times," he says. "I set out to write what I
thought was a black story or an ethnic story, and it turned out to be an education
or an economics story by the time I finished. It had little to do with race. This
kind of class consciousness is something that we've gotten to be aware of nowa-
days. But economics, inflation, energy are the news. That's where the action is
whether it's the black community or anywhere else. It's that poor people, once
again, get hit the hardest. They always do."

This message struck home with Page some years back when he was part of a
Chicago Tribune team which studied the history of blacks in that city. The team
found that three traditional issues had been dominant in the minds and lives of
blacks: jobs, housing, and schools. And it is Page's opinion that these are still the
issues.

"I think more and more people are realizing that race is declining in its
significance in America," Page says. "Civil rights leaders are shifting their thrust

from race to economics. The thing is, there is a widening gap between blacks who are making it economically and the blacks who are not making it. This is the modern tragedy now."

Examples abound of similar economic focus among other groups as, in effect, they seek their civil rights through efforts to gain economic self-sufficiency. Much of the Indian struggle, for example, concerns control of natural resources—water, coal, oil, and uranium, especially—found on the reservations. A major thrust of women and the handicapped is for employment and equality of pay.

But it's not all economic. The insistence on programs to help battered women and to counter growing problems of rape and/or sexual harassment—pushed predominantly by feminist groups on behalf of women—are law enforcement stories which cut across male-female lines. Two other so-called women's issues —the drives for modification of divorce and abortion laws and attitudes—are as much religion, family, and social as they are women's stories.

Thus, as streams gain greater prominence as they flow into larger bodies of water, specific problems do have a life of their own, but their meaning is greater when analyzed in a broader perspective. It is not likely that journalism, like schools, can function most effectively on a "separate but equal" philosophy.

How reporters deal with this depends upon the talents and wishes of the reporters. Consider, for example, the somewhat different approaches used by two reporters from the same newspaper, Warren Brown and William Greider of the *Washington Post.*

Warren Brown of the *Washington Post*

(*Washington Post* photo)

Says Brown:"I don't believe that because a person is 'one of the people,' he or she knows more about what is going on in the community. They don't know what is happening to them in the larger context. So I always research the community first. I go through clip files. I deal with research and development centers. Obviously, most chambers of commerce have a vested interest in telling you what is wonderful about that town, but in doing so and by the material they give you, they are telling you a lot more about that town. I deal with the Census Bureau, employment offices, and school boards.

"Then I go and talk to the person on the street. At least, I can sense how politically savvy they are, based on what I know. I can better fit in the quotes. I can tell when the quotes make sense in the story because of what I know about the community."

Greider's approach has only a slightly different twist. He seeks the larger perspective by using social statistics as the basis of evaluating comments or events. The most valuable source of such information, he says, is the U.S. Census Bureau, but he also uses statistics from accumulated public opinion polls and various other governmental agencies.

"I think it's a really useful technique in taking the numbers and putting one comparison next to another and seeing if they tell you something," he says. "That, at least, gives you a premise on what you're going out to look for. You've got to be able to go beyond that, obviously, because there are things happening which some groups are not ready to acknowledge. You take the numbers, and you talk to people and try to put some flesh on them."

This doesn't mean most stories he writes are statistical. It does mean a number of them have had three or four paragraphs which broaden the information or which say, "Look, what's happening in New Orleans is not unique."

Because of the need for such broader coverage, the attitude that news organizations can meet their needs by labeling a reporter as "minority writer" or some such title is placing too great a burden on that person. The ideal is that such coverage should be provided by the news organization's total staff as its members go about their business of covering issues of social concern.

Another part of that ideal would be elimination of the notion that one must be a member of a group to cover that group adequately. There may be certain short-term communication, attitudinal, and reporter interest advantages to have, say, a black reporter covering blacks. But, in the long run, special consideration must be given to the fact that this attitude runs counter to journalistic norms.

For a number of reasons, news organizations ordinarily do not want a member of any group covering that group. One reason is the potential for actual conflict of interest or the appearance of such conflict. Another is the added burden on that reporter, who must deal with the expectations of his or her colleagues.

The ideal must be functional integration of a news organization's staff, with reporters assigned to coverage areas in which they have expertise and interest. Sensitivity would be facilitated by that expertise as it is demonstrated in understanding and knowledge of specific social groups. And perspective would be broadened by greater individual representation in newsrooms of the social groups themselves.

NOTES

1. *Report of the National Advisory Commission on Civil Disorders,* New York Times Edition (New York: E. P. Dutton and Co., 1968), p. 10.

2. *National Advisory Commission on Civil Disorders,* p. 366.
3. *National Advisory Commission on Civil Disorders,* p. 21.
4. Comments made during a panel discussion, national convention of the Society of Professional Journalists, Sigma Delta Chi, Birmingham, Ala., November 16, 1978.
5. Robert C. Maynard, "This Far by Fear," in Marion Marzolf and Melba Tolliver, *Kerner plus 10* (Howard R. Marsh Center for the Study of Journalistic Performance, University of Michigan, 1977), p. 3.
6. Andrea L. Rich, *Interracial Communication* (New York: Harper and Row, 1974), p. 117.
7. *Interracial Communication,* p. 120.
8. *Kerner plus 10,* p. 12.
9. Panel discussion, "The American Indian," Associated Press Managing Editors convention, Portland, Ore., September 28, 1978.
10. For discussions of the role of women in journalism, see, for example: Marion Marzolf, *Up from the Footnote* (New York: Hastings House, 1977) and Maurine Beasley and Sheila Silver, *Women in Media: A Documentary Source Book* (Washington, D.C.: Women's Institute for Freedom of the Press, 1977).
11. Peggy A. Simpson, "Covering the Women's Movement," *Nieman Reports,* summer 1979, p. 22.
12. *Kerner plus 10,* p. 19.
13. "The American Indian" panel discussion.
14. As quoted in: Stephen E. Rada, "Manipulating the Media: A Case Study of a Chicano Strike in Texas," *Journalism Quarterly,* spring 1977, pp. 109–113.
15. Donald C. Bacon, "San Antonio's Battle to Blend Rival Cultures," *U.S. News and World Report,* November 24, 1980, pp. 58–59.
16. J. L. Dillard, *Black English* (New York: Random House, 1972), p. 25.
17. Malachi Andrews and Paul T. Owens, *Black Language* (Los Angeles: Seymour-Smith, 1973), pp. 26–27.
18. Felix Gutierrez, "Through Anglo Eyes: Chicanos as Portrayed in the News Media," paper presented to the History Division, Association for Education in Journalism convention, Seattle, Wash., August 1978, p. 15.
19. Society of Professional Journalists panel.
20. Sara Fritz, "A Change in Style," *Nieman Reports,* summer 1979, p. 24.
21. Howard Angione, Editor, *The Associated Press Stylebook and Libel Manual* (New York: Associated Press, 1977), p. 240.
22. Clinton Cox, "Meanwhile In Bedford-Stuyvesant . . . ," *Civil Rights Digest,* winter 1977, p. 39.
23. See, for example, Fred Fedler, "Newspapers, Blacks and Crime: Emphasis on People, Not Property, Affects Balance," paper presented to Mass Communication and Society Division, Association for Education in Journalism convention, August 1980.
24. *AP Stylebook,* p. 185.
25. Society of Professional Journalists panel.

Chapter 17

THE REVIVAL OF RELIGION AS NEWS

It's standard wisdom. If you want to avoid an argument, don't get involved in conversations about politics or religion. But reporters are independent souls, and they have proved it for years by ignoring the advice about politics. Now the door to the second subject is being opened, even if only slightly at this stage.

There's little question that one of the journalistic hallmarks of the second half of the twentieth century has been increasing attention to religion. Not just announcements of church and synagogue activities. Not just evangelical messages and summaries of sermons. Religion as news. Religion as a cultural force. Members of the clergy as individuals who handle large sums of money and who are influential leaders of social movements. Religious beliefs as factors which contribute to governmental and social decisions.

Admittedly, such a news emphasis is late in coming and slow to develop. But the signs are there. The arguments as a result of the coverage have started. Religious groups are complaining about the scrutiny, sometimes even threatening. They're organizing and learning how to deal with this new attention.

And within journalism, self-analysis is more frequent. Internal discussion and criticism are finding their way to the agendas of journalistic organizations. Professional reports often are more critical than even the public complaints. The Associated Press Managing Editors conducted its study and received these comments from Ronald I. Goble of the *Visalia* [California] *Times-Delta:*

God is not dead!

Editors, it is time we have a revival of our own.

Most of the church pages published across the nation are dead and in need of resurrection. And in this case we cannot count on the Lord to intervene.

While editors can always seek a little Divine direction, they must face the fact that the bulk of the task is up to them. There is no need for editors to wait for a booming voice from above, a flash of lightning or a vision before they get started.

We can start by fighting for more space for religion news. Editors should not count on advertising departments to fill two-thirds of the church page with church-related ads. We should want plenty of space for a good display.

Upgrade the position of church editor. Many newspapers rely on a Girl Friday or some part-timer to write the church news copy. That is a mistake. The coverage of religion should carry a much higher priority.

Editors need to focus on *people* in religion. Anytime we can involve readers with people and personalities, whether in the area of religion or other fields, we have a very readable story.

Few newspapers dig into the theological issues of the day. The controversies which are carried over the AP can easily be localized. Often all it takes is a couple of calls to clergymen in your area. Let's find out what our readers have to say about some of these issues. People and their opinions make the news.

There are a few fine examples of what can be done in the area of religion coverage. One of the most outstanding is *Crossroads,* published by the *St. Petersburg Times.* And the reason it is outstanding is because the editors and reporters are looking beyond the routine meeting notices we are all too familiar with.

That leads us back to more of our original statements that a revival is needed. And to make it more clear, Webster says that a revival is: renewed attention to or interest in something; a new presentation or publication; renewed religious interest.

Those of us in the newspaper business who have strayed from the flock need to be brought back into the fold. None has committed the unpardonable sin of rejecting the needs of readers, we would hope.

And while a word for most church pages is "sinful," those editors who see the light can find redemption. But their heart must really be in it.

The new word should be commitment. Without that, we are doomed to judgment by those we serve—our readers.

God help us![1]

This strong language would not be wasted on a coverage area considered unimportant. But it's representative of the intensity felt by many who note the disgrace of journalism for having virtually ignored for so many years a subject of pervasive and abiding public interest. Public interest in religion appears to wax and wane with time, but the concern is always there. Psychologists, anthropologists, and philosophers will attest that religion is a permanent and inevitable characteristic of being human.

"Every newspaper survey that has ever been taken in the last quarter century finds religion high on the list of reader interest, usually greater than politics or sports," says George Cornell of The Associated Press, perhaps the dean of the nation's religion reporters. "But newspapers continue to second-rate it as if it were a peripheral or secondary concern. That aversion stems, I think, not from attention to readership, but from habit—an old 'front page' notion that newspaper desks must be staffed by hard-bitten cynics, that religion is too controversial (which ordinarily is a measure of news interest), that religion is 'soft' and not 'hard' news. All of these are wrongheaded."

George Cornell of The Associated Press

Cornell and some of his colleagues are adamant that religion is news and must be covered as news, not as the view of any particular group. Religious organizations represent people speaking out of their deepest convictions, and what they say is an expression of social thought.

Religion news also is part of the mix that goes into determining national and international directions. For example, the World Council of Churches in 1957 called for a ban on above-ground testing of atomic weapons. The council's position was denounced as pro-Communist at the time, but four years later, the ban was signed into policy by the major powers.

Consider civil rights, a movement dominated by churches and church leaders. It's not surprising that the name most strongly associated with the movement, Martin Luther King Jr., is that of a minister. And in more contemporary times, perhaps the leading civil rights spokesman today, Jesse Jackson, is a member of the clergy.

But of equal significance to the local reporter is the fact that churches and synagogues often are at the front in tackling serious community problems. Recreation programs designed to give young people alternatives to roaming the streets often are supported, sponsored, or even operated by religious organizations. Efforts to clean up crime-ridden portions of town may be spearheaded by members of the clergy. Support for the poor, shelter for battered spouses, and even efforts to attract industry are seldom accomplished without involvement of religious leaders.

The best religion reporters know this. Perceptive religious leaders know it. And not only are more reporters being urged by people like Goble to do more about it, but similar advice is being given to churches and synagogues by people such as Charles M. Austin, who wrote a media handbook for churches:

"Religion is news. It's news because it deals with people, often at their deepest levels. Religion writers have learned that church news is not bazaars or bridge parties or bingo. For all its aberrations, the current spiritual revival touches many people and congregations. What you do in your churches is (or should be) just as important as what the local political party does or what the regional Women's Political Caucus gets into. It's your job to see that the newsy angles of your work get to the papers."[2]

RELIGION'S GHETTO: THE CHURCH PAGE

That kind of approach has not been typical. Standard coverage by American newspapers has been to devote a page or two or three to religion once a week, usually Saturday, and fill most of the space with advertisements from merchants who believe, as one newspaper announces, "the church represents the greatest force for good." Beyond that, one finds church notices, wire stories, perhaps a column by a local minister, and occasionally a feature story about some church activity.

Standard coverage by broadcasters, for the most part, has been to ignore the subject unless something controversial or exciting happens.

Historically, the typical church page was the natural result of the fact that news organizations placed little stock in the news value of religion and did not want to run the risk of offending church leaders and members. They simply did not have the guts to give religion the same scrutiny commonly devoted to politics or law enforcement. It's safe to stick to a bland diet of activities, pastoral changes, or comments under some minister's byline.

The church page often was produced (and still is, in many instances) by part-time personnel who devoted the end of the week to collecting miscellaneous trivia. Over time, these efforts were helped by increasing interest of advertisers, a growing flow of publicity handouts from religious organizations, and development of the syndicated inspirational column. And this resulted in a bland and highly standardized image of church life on the religion pages.[3]

There can be greater value to church or religion pages if a newspaper goes beyond the obvious announcements and tries to provide coverage of religious issues and personalities. That value depends on what reporters and editors decide to do.

Religion news must have the opportunity to compete with other news for locations in the paper, including page one. Given that circumstance, the church pages may be used for stories that are not of general interest but are important to the dedicated reader who turns to that section as sports fans turn to the sports pages or those interested in finance turn to the financial section. And the pages may be used informationally to provide facts on upcoming major community religious events, much as the political reporter would write that the governor is going to speak.

But too often that is not the case, principally because many editors do not view religion in the same light as other types of news, says Bruce Buursma, who has covered the subject for the Louisville *Courier-Journal* and *Chicago Tribune*.

Bruce Buursma of the *Chicago Tribune*

(*Chicago Tribune* photo)

"It's very easy for an editor, if you're going out on a Monday night to cover some local religious controversy, to say, 'Well, we're a little short on space for tomorrow's paper. Why don't you hold that thing until Saturday and put it on your church page?' And that destroys the immediacy of the thing, and it gives the impression to religion writers—and I think to the public too—that religion is an inferior subject to cover, and it doesn't carry as much interest as politics or crime or lust or whatever. Surveys show that's simply not true."

It's not true for two reasons. First, even in highly secular historic periods, religion remains a powerful, though subsurface, force in the lives of many people. Second, it tends to rise in its social importance to peaks of public concern and activity. Two such peaks helped transform religion reporting. One came immediately after World War II.

"The early postwar era saw a revival of religion," says William C. Simbro of the *Des Moines Register* and *Tribune.* "Church attendance became almost as much a part of the American Way of Life as the desire to own two cars and a boat and live in the suburbs. It was a time of interest in matters ecumenical. The World Council of Churches and the National Council of Churches emerged.

"In 1949, people covering religion in the secular press formed their own organization, the Religion Newswriters Association. Its formation was spurred by a fledgling journalistic interest in better religion coverage. Its influence has bolstered that interest. The RNA has approximately 100 members."[4]

This was the period in which religion began its move from the news ghetto. In some instances, church pages were abolished, and religion began to compete for space. Simbro credits magazines, particularly *Time,* for paving the way. The magazine put religion on the cover, and some larger newspapers began to follow suit.

Then came a time of seeming religious drought—the infamous 1960s—in which the mood, especially among younger people, was at least nonreligious if not antireligious. But even then, says Ken Briggs of the *New York Times,* forces were beginning to collect which would result once again in religious emphasis.

"There were quieter movements going on," he says. "The whole evangelical burgeoning was in a kind of germinating stage at that point. As secularism made its inroads and more people became detached from the basic teachings of religious faiths, the ignorance level rose to such a point that it was time for people to rediscover. There was a whole repository of wisdom, belief, ways of looking at the world that they had simply not been exposed to. And what we're dealing with in the late 1970s and 1980s, to a great extent, are young people whose emerging religious awareness became very apparent, very striking."

Briggs adds that the movement had to be personified in former President Jimmy Carter before the media could see it. And two other specific news stories emerged to heighten that interest. One was in the Catholic Church, with the 1978 papal deaths and elections and the growing debate over Catholic doctrine. The second was the controversial activities of the Moral Majority in and following the 1980 presidential election.

"I don't think there has been a single field of journalism that's undergone a more stunning transition than religion," Briggs says. "The emphasis has moved away from a kind of special treatment, deference, kid-gloves approach, and bulletin-board style to covering religion as a legitimate area of newsworthy activity which can subject the institutions and the movements to criticism as well as give an opportunity to really inform the people what they're about."

Journalism's response has been inconsistent. Some news organizations, as Goble's comments verify, stayed where they were. The bland church pages continued. Others have abolished the ghetto and put religion news on the same basis as other areas of coverage. And some—notably the *St. Petersburg Times* and the *Denver Post*—have maintained the special-section concept by establishing separate pullouts devoted extensively to religion. However, these publications are more than bulletin boards. They contain real news as well as announcements. And they are not restrictive. Reporters know that if they have a breaking story of importance, it may find its way to page one.

PATTERNS OF RELIGION COVERAGE

If it is a new wave of journalism to treat religion as bona fide news, it is logical to ask just what that means. It would be true, but overly simplistic, to say it means attempting to provide the full story. Equally true, but also simplistic, would be to say it means applying all the traditional textbook lists of qualities of newsworthiness. Perhaps the best question, really, is how the new religion coverage differs from treatment of the past.

For one thing, the best religion reporters are seeking to cover their subject much more broadly. This nation has been predominantly Christian with a rather substantial Jewish minority since its inception. News organizations have tended to reflect that. Attention has focused on the "big three"—Protestant, Catholic, and Jewish—and the result has been a widespread ignorance about other forms of organized religion, most of which are at least represented in this country. The smaller, often less organized, denominations were ignored, with the possible occasional exception of coverage in the locale in which they function. That's changing.

"We have a lot of space for religion," says Virginia Culver of the *Denver Post,* "and we run everything we know of that would make a good story. It makes no difference whether it's hard news or features or pictures. We don't make judgments that we will just cover Christianity or the big three or whatever. We cover anything. We cover all kinds of cults. If people think that's their religion, then that's their religion as far as we're concerned. We're not in the business of promoting religions or trying to stamp them out. All we do is report them."

Inexorably related to this breadth is an increasing effort to apply standard journalistic fairness to religion coverage. In spite of the dominance of the big three, this is a nation of religious pluralism, and that inevitably evokes emotional responses, even among reporters and editors. What is one person's true path to salvation is another person's bizarre cult. Sensitivity to a person's beliefs, even in the face of personal feelings, is important for the new breed of religion journalists.

"Faith transcends the rational, and that's their right," Buursma says. "A person who's going to be fair has to allow that kind of perplexing, emotional behavior. I try. And that's why I can feel comfortable writing about the Unification Church or the Church of Scientology or a church that worships somebody's left elbow. They have a right to do that, and I have to recognize that even though I don't subscribe to those particular methods of worship."

One of the reasons more journalists are finding themselves capable of reporting on beliefs and activities with which they personally disagree is that religion reporting is becoming more secular. At one time it was common, for example, for a newspaper or broadcast outlet on Easter or Christmas to place a Christian message on page one or the editorial page, perhaps an appropriate scripture passage. That's still done in instances, but it's a practice many news organizations have stopped. Such active promotion tends to undercut efforts to be fair and makes it difficult for reporters in the field to maintain credibility.

Another application can be found in efforts by some reporters to use more neutral language, rather than assuming general agreement on a denominational or biblical statement. To use statements like, "The Crucifixion was the most important event in history" or "When Jesus ascended into heaven . . ." is to take a side in matters not accepted by everyone, says John Dart of the *Los Angeles Times.*

John Dart of the *Los Angeles Times*

(*Los Angeles Times* photo)

"I try to provide specific attribution," he adds. "I would say, 'When, according to biblical accounts. . . .' A lot of religion writing in the past would not be this careful. But I think it's important. That kind of language doesn't violate the beliefs of anyone who accepts the statement as fact. It's just journalistic practice, and I believe it adds to the authenticity. I think that's the way we function best."

Application of such journalistic principles to religion reporting, of course, represents only part of the effort. Breadth must apply to more than increasing the number of religions covered. It also must involve development of personal or institutional philosophy about how the subject matter is to be approached. As reporters continue to experiment, focuses have evolved. They overlap, and no reporter can follow one or two exclusively. The best reporter will discover what combination best suits his or her personal style, news organization philosophy, and community needs.

Religion and Culture

No social institution, including organized religion, can function effectively for long in a way which is contrary to culture. It may hold to old patterns for a while, perhaps even years, but change is inevitable. And the reporter should be there to record that change and to relate it to the culture in which it occurred. And if analysis of culture provides a yardstick with which to measure the role of religion, the coin has another side. Religion provides a means through which reporters may analyze the culture.

"Religion always mirrors what's going on in the culture," Briggs says, "particularly religious institutions because they're conservative. They don't always react as quickly, and that's sometimes why they make news. Things work through the system more slowly, but then suddenly those cultural happenings begin to filter through and the church mixes them with its own peculiar and particular way of looking at the world. There is a transcendent element there that also brings something to the culture and makes the culture look at itself in ways it wouldn't otherwise."

That's why, he adds, he tries to take a thematic approach to his religion coverage. Balancing local coverage, event coverage, and national coverage is difficult, and the bigger picture is lost if the reporter fails to find and concentrate upon inherent cultural characteristics or actions.

Discovery of the bigger picture involves broad understanding. Religion impinges on just about every public concern and issue, from war to sex. Whether the issue is crime, foreign aid, the law, nuclear power, economics, labor disputes, consumer fraud, or the quality of television shows, religious presuppositions are involved. The basic question always is: What's the right, the just, the good solution? And that's a moral question bound up with religious premises about human obligations. The role which religious premise or organized religion plays in any public concern will both influence and be influenced by the culture.

And this point is well demonstrated in the following story by Briggs which represented an effort, after the mass suicides at Jonestown, Guyana, to understand the history and role of fringe groups in American culture:

Fringe Religions Find Fertile Soil in United States

BY KENNETH A. BRIGGS

Fringe religious groups, though always a feature of American life, have grown more eclectic and diversified in the last decade, increasing the possibility of explosive mixtures of belief and practice such as marked the People's Temple.

Nations and cultures have invariably experienced exotic and innovative religious outcroppings, but America, because of its tolerance for dissent, its idealism and its frontier individualism, particularly so.

"America, despite all its pressures to conform, officially [said] O.K. to the cults as long as they obeyed the law," said Dr. Langdon Gilkey, professor of theology at the University of Chicago.

The followers were there because, scholars say, young Americans, deprived of strong family ties, confused by rapid social change and untaught in religious tradition, were searching for meaning in their lives.

"The theology of the cult is always dependent on a message of salvation not believed to be available in ordinary experience," Dr.

Gilkey explained. "They are sometimes radically separated from the world, going into their 'embassy.' The world is a foreign continent and they, the ambassadors."

Many recently formed groups owe their origins to earlier movements. The People's Temple, founded in San Francisco by the Rev. Jim Jones after he took a small, unorthodox Indiana congregation west and away from what he perceived as intolerance, was spawned as an offbeat Christian church with official ties to the Disciples of Christ.

Ultimately it came to bear little resemblance to an established movement, and that, too, is not uncommon. Technological leaps have brought different religions into increasing contact, and the effect has been that the nation has become a kind of religious hothouse for incubating new varieties of spiritual life, often splicing parts of many faiths into startlingly different hybrids. . . .

Source: Kenneth A. Briggs, "Fringe Religions Find Fertile Soil in the United States," *New York Times,* November 28, 1978, p. A14. Copyright © 1978, The New York Times Co. Reprinted by permission.

Moral Influences on the Real World

Religion is not something individuals can separate from what they do. And this applies to public officials. Closely related to the cultural approach—but on a more intimate, personal level—is the matter of how individual beliefs influence, or even predict, the position of a public official on a specific issue. And this consideration, in the opinion of many, is an aspect of coverage which must rank among journalism's failures.

Wesley G. Pippert of United Press International, for one, says that "we in the press frequently have been uneasy, unable and perhaps even a little unwilling, in dealing competently with the moral dimension of public issues." Author of *The Spiritual Journey of Jimmy Carter,* Pippert notes that few reporters ever understood the impact of the former president's religious beliefs because they often ignored the evidence frequently placed before them. They seldom covered Carter's Sunday School teaching, for example.

"The thought of one of the most powerful persons in the world standing in front of a small group, speaking without benefit of researcher or speechwriter, reflecting on his values is astounding," Pippert says. "It is some of the purest Carter that we have, inasmuch as most other remarks are crafted by his stable of speechwriters."

Pippert says that, by analyzing Carter's religious background and beliefs, reporters could have discovered much more about the man, his approach to power, his views on the presidency, his insistence on human rights, his personal drive. Indeed, much was written about Carter being born again, but much of that coverage reflected a lack of knowledge and a lack of religious understanding.

"Every issue, of course, does not have a consuming moral nature," Pippert says. "It obviously would be just as wrong to make faith central in defining the religiously indifferent politician as it is to ignore a politician's religion if it is important to him or her. But I am saying that we miss a vital dimension to the news if we scoff at or skip over faith when it is an essential part of the story.

"Obviously, this is a big challenge. We need to be able to report and write about morality without being moralizing. When writing about morality, we need to understand what we're writing about. We must use words in a way that they mean the same thing to the reader or viewer as they mean to the person who spoke them. This ought to be on the agenda of academic journalists. It ought to be in the awareness of every editor and news director. It surely ought to be on the minds of every one of us who constitute the working press in our pursuit of the truth."[5]

Religion as Controversy

Get a group together, involve participants in something as personal and emotional as religion, and controversy is inevitable. The diverse beliefs of this nation's hundreds of religious groups and predictable variations within a given group make disagreement natural. Some news organizations in the past have ignored such controversy because they felt it was an internal matter or because they wanted to avoid alienating members of the community's churches or synagogues.

That is changing. Reporters know that a broad approach to coverage of such an important social institution must include the blemishes of that system as well as the successes. They know everyone is not going to like every story they write, but they can only hope their impartiality, completeness, and fairness will be respected.

Religious controversy comes in standard packages: philosophical disagreements over the purpose and appropriate activities of an organization; power struggles; corruption; and conflicts with outside groups or government or individuals. And a reporter's approach must be traditional journalism involving multiple points of view. Often there can be no solution; at times there may be compromise. In either event, it is the journalist's job to follow the story, satisfied with the pluralistic discussion being presented, until the issue is settled or fades away.

Taking a Solutions Approach

One of the best methods a reporter can use to gain satisfaction is to help define solutions as well as problems. American society in the 1960s and early 1970s went through an epoch of social criticism in which the approach usually was negative. Few dissidents at that time presented positive approaches to solving the problems which prompted their complaints. And, while it seemed more pervasive then, such criticism is not unusual at any time.

Perhaps reporters can help in the debate and at the same time strengthen their coverage by pushing for a solution to a controversial issue. Perhaps there will be no agreement, but coverage which provides readers, viewers, and listeners with alternative possible solutions has enhanced public understanding.

It needn't be controversial. Churches and synagogues in this country have problems, and their leaders would find stories about how others coped interesting and perhaps informative. This is a suggestion made to The Associated Press by Michael Yopp, managing editor of the Raleigh, North Carolina, *Times:*

"And I wish the AP would take a solutions approach to reporting religion," he said. "For instance, find a small church in—goodness help us—Middle America that is successfully keeping contributions in step with expenses and explain how it does it, or find an urban church that is keeping its younger members and explain how it accomplishes this."[6]

Religious Doctrine Is the Core

Explaining journalistically what people believe and why they believe it may be the biggest challenge of the religion reporter. The term is faith, and faith, by definition, is not explainable. For many, belief does not result from rational calculation. A particular doctrine is accepted. It's not a result of thought; it's the beginning of thought.

Add to this the fact that many believe church doctrine to be a personal or internal matter which should not be discussed publicly, especially by a person who is not within the fold. The mere mention of some subjects is a source of controversy heightened when the information does not agree specifically with an individual's personal interpretation. Many people are sensitive about their religious beliefs, and it's easier for them when those beliefs are not discussed.

The problem is compounded when religion reporters do not have backgrounds to tackle these sensitive and complex matters. One can argue forever as to whether they should be formally trained in theology—and more are these days—but the fact is that without formal training or very careful personal study, reporters are likely to heap scorn upon or shy away from stories which get into doctrinal matters.

This is unfortunate, and, says the AP's George Cornell, is a problem news organizations must continue to address.

"Newspapers and news services need specialists in religion coverage as much or more than they need specialists in sports, financial, scientific, or political coverage," he says. "It is true that religion is a universal subject, but it is far more complex than any of the others mentioned. It also is one in which there has been more misunderstanding and tribal—read denominational—misconceptions than in just about any other field.

"Those mutual misconceptions, fed by offhand scuttle-butt, backyard gossip, and ignorance, have been at the root of some of our sorriest social sores and prejudices. Religious illiteracy is rampant, particularly in our age, even in terms of many people's own religion."

Thus, if Cornell is right, and he is, the need for explanation of religious doctrine is as great for many of the traditional patterns of thought as it is for new ideas which work their way into public consideration. Some reporters do not want to tackle the old issues, the standard arguments, the historic debates. The normal excuse for this is that it's been done, all the arguments have been presented, no conclusion can be reached. That latter point may be true, but it's wrong to say all arguments have been presented. Genuine biblical scholars continue their study, and they tend to be ready sources for careful consideration of traditional doctrine.

Take, for example, the following *Newsweek* article, presented on Christmas Eve, 1979, as an analysis of one of the oldest questions.

Who Was Jesus?

BY KENNETH L. WOODWARD

As Christians around the world gather to celebrate the birth of Jesus, once again they recite the story of a child born to a virgin. The details are familiar yet fabulous: harkening angels, adoring shepherds, a mysterious star. But is the story true? To the literal-minded, the infancy narratives of Matthew and Luke are the opening chapters in the official biography of Jesus. To scholars of the New Testament, however, they are not history at all but something infinitely more important: symbol-laden stories created to dramatize a deeper mystery—that the Jesus who was born 2,000 years ago was truly Christ, the Lord.

Since the nineteenth century, scholars have sought to isolate "the historical Jesus" from "the Christ of faith" proclaimed in the Gospels. But today, most Biblical scholars no longer make such a facile distinction. For one thing, there are no firsthand written accounts of Jesus' life from which a verbal or visual portrait could be fashioned. For another, while there are eyewitnesses to his public ministry, it is highly unlikely that any of them can be identified with the authors of the four Gospels, which were written 40 to 60 years after his death. Thus scholars agree that the real Jesus can no more be separated from the theology of the Gospel writers than the real Socrates can be separated from the dialogues of Plato.

In their quest for the real Jesus, scholars today emphasize the creative role of the four evangelists. Each of the four Gospels, they say, presents a different portrait of Jesus fashioned to meet the needs of the community for which it was written and to rebut views of Jesus with which they disagreed. By using the modern tools of historical criticism, linguistics and literary analysis, Biblical scholars try to distinguish the layers of oral traditions embedded within each Gospel and to confront the essential mind-set—if not the actual words—of Jesus. "Primarily, the Gospels tell us how each evangelist conceived of and presented Jesus to a Christian community in the last third of the first century," says Father Raymond Brown, a leading expert on the Gospel of John and a professor at New York's Union Theological Seminary. "The Gospels offer only limited means for reconstructing the ministry and message of the historical Jesus."

Despite these limitations, New Testament scholars today know more about the Gospels themselves and the milieu in which they were formed than any previous generation of Biblical researchers. In the past decade alone, translations of several ancient texts from the period 200 B.C. to A.D. 200 have vastly enriched the Biblical trove. One is the Temple Scroll, longest of the Dead Sea Scrolls, which indicates that Jesus' strictures against divorce and other of his teachings were very similar to those held by the ascetic Essene sect at Qumran. Another is the recently translated Nag Hammadi codices, which contain gospels composed by second-century Gnostic rivals of orthodox Christians. And next year, Duke University professor James H. Charlesworth will publish the most complete edition of the Pseudepigrapha, a collection of some 53 texts by Jewish and early Christian scribes, many of which were regarded as sacred books by the Jews of Jesus' time.

Woodard's article continues for several pages with analyses of the pictures of Jesus presented by Matthew, Mark, Luke, and John, then concludes as follows.

Who was Jesus? Mark's Jesus dies alone, feeling forsaken but true to his Father's will. This Jesus will appeal to Christians who embrace life's tragedies with confidence. Matthew's Jesus dies only to return and promise his guidance to those who follow him. This Jesus will appeal to Christians who find assurance in the church. Luke's Jesus dies forgiving his enemies, knowing his Father awaits his spirit. This Jesus will attract Christians who have learned in life to trust God by imitating his mercy. John's Jesus dies in the confidence that he will return to the Father. This Jesus is for those Christians who have traveled the mystical way. All of these accounts express a truth; none of them is complete. All of these Jesuses are accessible only to those whose faith compels them on the search for "the way, the truth and the light."

Source: Kenneth L. Woodward, "Who Was Jesus?" *Newsweek,* December 24, 1979, pp. 48–55. Reproduced with permission from *Newsweek.* Copyright 1979, by Newsweek, Inc. All rights reserved.

Consideration of traditional doctrine in light of new knowledge and new theories represents a potentially exciting phase of a religion reporter's job. And one does not have to have the staff or the resources of a *Newsweek.* Biblical scholars are as close as the telephone or perhaps the nearest university campus; the results of their studies are published in journals and books; local members of the clergy have ideas to contribute. It does take time, it does take effort, and it does take conscious study. And it requires dedication, both by the individual reporter and by the news organization.

Seeking the Real Me

Although not unusual in history, one of the characteristics of the late twentieth century has been a turning inward, a concentration on self and rejection of organized religion. Such introspection represents efforts to "find myself" or "get my head on straight" in the hopes of gaining serenity and the ability to cope with the problems of life. This implies a time of spiritual hunger, says William C. Simbro of the *Des Moines Register* and *Tribune.*

That hunger has expressed itself in myriad forms: the movement of the "Jesus freaks" from drugs to religion, the charismatic movement in the Roman Catholic Church and "mainline Protestantism," the attendant growth of the Pentecostal churches, and fascination with Eastern religions, cults, mysticism, meditation, spiritualism, astrology, soul travel, revival of the "olde" religion of witches.

"These movements may not be congenial to the thinking of 'realistic,' hard-headed or cynical editors and reporters," Simbro says. "We may not be involved in them. But the movements are out there, they are vital to many of our present or potential readers, they have an impact on many facets of our nation and communities. For religion writers to trivialize them, ignore them or give them a light once-over is simply to fail to do their jobs."[7]

Covering the Institution

In the drive to broaden the scope of religion coverage, religion reporters—like their counterparts in other specialties—cannot forsake the obvious need for atten-tion to activities within local churches and synagogues and the church as an institution. Two-thirds of all Americans—132 million—are affiliated with estab-lished churches. On an average week, 42 percent of the country's people—90 million of them—gather to worship in these churches.[8]

To ignore what they do as part of the organization would be a serious error for any community-oriented news body. The raffles, bingo, groundbreakings, pastoral changes, programs, pageants, classes, meetings, and publications are what the churches are about. Call it trivia, call it mundane, call it less than exciting. But call it necessary to total coverage. And that's the key, if for no other reason than that any reporter must keep in touch with specific events and specific people to retain the broader perspective of religious trends and issues.

But institutional coverage is not necessarily just announcements. Every pro-gram has content, and that content represents a potential link to the broader picture. It is not necessary, of course, that every story become a thoughtful discussion of a serious religious issue. But the reporter who understands religion will find many opportunities to make a contribution to public understanding.

The solution lies in the perspective and understanding of the reporter. If he or she considers the assignment dull and incomprehensible, that will be the inevita-ble result. If he or she remains vigilant to the possibilities, more assignments will be less "hum" and more "drum."

THEY'RE LEARNING TO DEAL WITH REPORTERS

The complaint this time is from Simbro, but it's familiar among religion reporters, especially those who deal with small local churches and religious groups:

"Without question, the people you write about are more sensitive, defensive and nervous about what appears in the press than are any other sources. And, sad to say, they can be the nastiest. Which is why a religion writer on a Canadian paper some time back said that after receiving a series of death threats he wanted to switch to something safe, like the police beat."[9]

Simbro and his colleagues also report improvement in recent years, especially among representatives of the larger churches and religious organizations. The response has been best among Protestants and Jews, who some time ago learned how the system works and how to deal with it. Catholic leaders were slower, but they now can be just as open, direct, and communicative. As a generalization—perhaps unfair when applied to specific individuals in a community—representatives of smaller groups, more fundamental groups, and cults are least likely to be willing to talk candidly.

The fact that religion is the subject matter doesn't imply that reporters won't have to apply their normal skepticism to sources, especially ministers.

"One thing a reporter has to take into consideration," says Darrel Turner of the Religious News Service, an organization that supplies religious news to nearly 1,000 media clients, "is the fact that religious leaders who are involved in controversy are just as prone to cover up or misrepresent as government officials involved in controversy. I've had many examples of this in my own coverage. One should not assume that because somebody has a clerical collar that person is going to be more open and above board than someone who does not. But, on the whole, they tend to be cooperative."

In addition to individual religious leaders who have learned to deal with reporters, every major denomination—and, in fact, some of the nation's very large individual churches—have public relations arms. These are no different from their counterparts in other fields. They can be very helpful, both as suppliers of information and as initiators of story ideas. They can open doors. And they are subject to the same limitations of any PR outfit, so reporters are wise not to depend upon them exclusively.

Two Popes Comment on Reporters and the Media

The expanding relationship between journalism and religion is underscored by comments made early in their tenures by the two most recent popes. The popes stress that the times dictate working together, and they emphasize the need for responsibility and the importance of the task.

Pope John Paul I: "This pleasing meeting gives us a chance to thank you for the sacrifices and toil which you have faced during the month of August in serving world public opinion—yours, too, is a very important service—by offering to your readers, listeners and television viewers, with the rapid and immediate delivery required of your responsible and sensitive profession, the possibility of participating in these historical events, in their religious dimension, with their deep connection to human values and the expectations of today's society. . . .

"When major events happen and when the Holy See publishes important documents, you will often have to present the church, speak of the church, and sometimes comment on our humble ministry. We are sure that you will do it with love of truth and respect for human dignity because such is the goal of all social communications. We ask you to help safeguard in today's society a deep regard for the things of God and for the mysterious relationships between God and each of us, which constitutes the sacred dimension of human reality."[10]

Pope John Paul II: "My dear friends of the communications media: It would hardly be possible for me to depart from the United Nations without saying 'thank you' from my heart to those who have reported, not only the day's events, but all the activities of this worthy organization. In this international assembly, you can truly be instruments of peace by being messengers of the truth. You are indeed servants of truth; you are its tireless transmitters, diffusers, defenders. You are dedicated communicators, promoting unity among all nations by sharing truth among all peoples.

"If your reporting does not always command the attention you would desire, or if it does not always conclude with the success that you would wish, do not grow discouraged. Be faithful to the truth and to its transmission, for truth endures; truth will not go away. Truth will not pass or change.

"And I say to you—take it as my parting words to you—that the service of truth, the service of humanity through the medium of the truth is something worthy of your best years, your finest talents, your most dedicated efforts. As transmitters of truth, you are instruments of understanding among people and of peace among nations."[11]

RESOURCES FOR THE RELIGION REPORTER

Religion is not static. Reporters find themselves dealing with new ideas and new approaches. Keeping track of these ideas and approaches is possible. Even the local religion reporter has resources available and can read the major religious periodicals. Following are some that should be helpful.

Reference Material

Yearbook of American Churches, published annually by the National Council of Churches. Good for statistical information and for personnel lists of virtually every religious body in the country.

National Catholic Directory, published annually by P. J. Kenedy & Sons.

A *Bible,* of which several good translations are available. The most frequently used probably is the Revised Standard Version.

Concordance of the Bible, to provide ready answers to where a particular passage came from.

AP or *UPI Stylebook,* which contains relatively detailed background information on structure, officials, and beliefs of most major denominations.

Periodicals

Christian Century, published in Chicago, an ecumenical publication which does a good job of digesting current thought.

Christianity Today, published in Wheaton, Illinois, a leading conservative, evangelical publication.

National Catholic Reporter, Kansas City, Missouri, the best source of Catholic thought.

NOTES

1. Ronald I. Goble, "Church Pages and Religion: An Introduction," *Report of the APME Modern Living Committee,* 1979, pp. 2–3. Reprinted with permission from The Associated Press.

2. Charles M. Austin, *Let the People Know: A Media Handbook for Churches* (Minneapolis, Minn.: Augsburg Publishing House, 1975), p. 15.

3. Kenneth D. Nordin, "Non-Sectarian Religion: An Historical Interpretation of the Shape of Religious News in the American Daily Press," paper presented to the History Division, Association for Education in Journalism annual convention, Seattle, Wash., August 1978.

4. William C. Simbro, "Unheralded Religion News," *The Quill,* December 1979, p. 12. Reprinted courtesy of *The Quill,* published by the Society of Professional Journalists, Sigma Delta Chi.

5. Wesley G. Pippert, "Moral Considerations," *The Quill,* December 1979, pp. 19–21. Reprinted courtesy of *The Quill,* published by the Society of Professional Journalists, Sigma Delta Chi.

6. Michael Yopp, "Church Pages and Religion: The South," *Report of the APME Modern Living Committee,* 1979, p. 4.

7. "Unheralded Religion News," p. 13.

8. George Cornell, "Religion '77: From Flynt to Lefebvre," *ap log,* December 1977, p. 3.

9. "Unheralded Religion News," p. 23.

10. "The Journalists Meet the Pope," *Origins, NC Documentary Service,* September 14, 1978, pp. 199–200.

11. From remarks presented October 2, 1979, at the United Nations, quoted in "Something Worthy of Your Best Years," *The Quill,* December 1979, p. 12.

Appendix

HOW TO USE THE FEDERAL FOI ACT

The FOI Service Center

INTRODUCTION

The Federal FOI Act Is Simple, Quick, and Easy to Use

In America of the 1980s, all significant aspects of life are affected by the federal government. The press—including print and broadcast journalists, researchers, and scholars—has an obligation to inform the public about the policies and actions of government. Fortunately, the public's ability to receive information about government has been significantly aided in recent years by the federal Freedom of Information Act. This Act guarantees your right to inspect an enormous storehouse of government documents by making all records of government agencies presumptively available to you upon request.[1]

The FOI Service Center is a joint project of the Society of Professional Journalists, Sigma Delta Chi, and The Reporters Committee for Freedom of the Press.

The FOI Act was enacted in 1966. Since then, print and broadcast news reporters, authors, writers, and scholars have used the Act to help investigate a variety of news stories and historical matters. The FOI Act has been used to uncover important information on stories such as the Rosenberg spy trials, FBI harrassment of civil rights leaders, automobile design defects, consumer product testing, international smuggling operations, environmental impact studies, the salaries of public employees, school district compliance with anti-discrimination laws, sanitary conditions in food processing plants, and CIA spying on domestic political groups.

This pamphlet is designed as a general "Do-it-Yourself" Guide to help members of the press and the academic community understand how the federal FOI Act works. In its original form, the pamphlet was researched, written, and published by The Reporters Committee for Freedom of the Press in 1976. This new edition has been expanded and updated—taking into consideration new amendments to the Act and new court opinions, some of which have been helpful and others which have not.

This Second Edition of the pamphlet was researched and written by **The FOI Service Center,** a joint project of The Reporters Committee and the Society of Professional Journalists, Sigma Delta Chi. It will show you how to use the FOI Act as an effective investigative tool and comes complete with sample letters so that in most cases you should be able to deal with the government promptly and effectively by yourself. If you need assistance, however, please call **The FOI Service Center** and we will be pleased to help you.

THE FOI ACT

A Brief Overview of How the FOI Act Works

The Federal FOI Act gives "any person" access to *all* records of *all* federal agencies, unless these records fall within one of nine categories of exempt information which agencies are permitted (but not required) to withhold. Many times, an informal telephone request to the agency is all that is needed to achieve compliance with the law. If not, you have the right to make a formal, written request for documents. Once an FOI Act request is made, the burden is on the government to promptly release the documents or show that they are covered by one of the Act's exemptions.

At most agencies, a designated FOI Officer is responsible for responding to FOI Act requests. The agency must respond to a properly written FOI Act request within 10 working days. It may charge the Requestor the costs of locating and copying documents, and the fees charged must be "reasonable."

If the agency refuses to disclose all or part of the information, or does not reply within 10 working days to a written FOI Act request, the Requestor may appeal to the head of the agency. If the agency head denies the appeal or does not reply within 20 working days, the Requestor can file a lawsuit in the federal court most convenient to him, and the case must be heard promptly. If the Requestor wins in court, a judge will order the agency to release the records, award the Requestor attorneys fees and court costs, and may recommend employment sanctions against agency officials who improperly had withheld the information.

WHAT AGENCIES ARE COVERED BY THE FOI ACT?

The FOI Act applies to every "agency," "department," "regulatory commission," "government-controlled corporation," and "other establishment" in the Executive Branch of the federal government. This includes Cabinet offices, such as the departments of Defense, State, Treasury, Interior (including the Bureau of Indian Affairs), Justice (including the F.B.I., the Law Enforcement Assistance Administration and the Bureau of Prisons); independent regulatory agencies and commissions, such as the Federal Trade Commission, Federal Communications Commission and the Consumer Product Safety Commission; and, "government-controlled" corporations, such as the Postal Service and AMTRAK.

Some corporations that are wholly or partially funded by the federal government are covered by the FOI Act (such as Legal Services Corp.); others claim they are not (such as the Corporation for Public Broadcasting).[2] Presidential commissions are also covered by the Act. According to a recent decision of the U.S. Supreme Court, a private organization, established for the sole purpose of carrying out a government research contract and totally funded by the federal government, is not automatically an "agency" subject to the FOI Act.[3]

The FOI Act also applies to the Executive Office of the President (e.g. Office of Management and Budget), but not to the President or his immediate staff.

The Act does not apply to Congress, the federal courts, or private corporations. However, documents generated by these groups and filed with agencies of the federal government became subject to disclosure under the Act, the same as documents created by the agencies.

The FOI Act also does not apply to state or local governments. But most states have their own "open records" laws which permit access to state and local records. Information on how to use these state laws is available from **The FOI Service Center.**

However, if documents of a state or local government are submitted to a federal agency, they automatically become subject to the federal FOI Act. This would occur, for example, where a state or local agency that receives federal funds through the Law Enforcement Assistance Administration (LEAA) submits reports to LEAA accounting for how the funds were spent.

WHAT RECORDS ARE AVAILABLE?

The FOI Act is very broad. It covers all "records" in the possession or control of a federal agency. The term "records" is defined expansively to include all types of documentary information, such as papers, reports, letters, films, computer tapes, photographs, and sound recordings. But physical objects which cannot be reproduced, such as the rifle used to assassinate President John F. Kennedy, are generally not considered "records" under the Act. If in doubt as to whether the material you want is a "record," assume it is and request it.

When requesting records, you must "reasonably describe" the material you want. This does not mean you need to know a specific document or docket number. But your request should be specific enough so that a government employee familiar with the subject area of your request can locate the records with a reasonable amount of effort, either by physically inspecting files or by using computerized indices and retrieval systems.

WHO MAY USE THE FOI ACT?

An FOI Act request may be made by "any person." This means that all U.S. citizens, as well as foreign nationals, can use the Act. A request can also be made in the name of a corporation, partnership, or other entity, such as a public-interest group or press organization. Members of the press have no more and no fewer rights under the Act than other Requestors. To obtain information, you do not need to tell the agency why you are making a request, although advising the FOI officer that you are a journalist, author or researcher, and intend (if you do) to publish some or all of the requested information may encourage prompt consideration of your request.

FIRST: TRY AN INFORMAL REQUEST

The Agency May Give You the Files After a Phone Call

Anyone seeking information from government documents should first try to obtain the documents through informal means because the government may readily agree to supply all or part of them at your request. Assuming you know with reasonable specificity which records you want and which agency has them, call the Public Information or Press Officer at the agency involved, identify yourself as a newsreporter, researcher, or scholar, and ask for the information. It might be helpful to offer some explanation of why you want the documents. If you are turned down, then try the agency's FOI Officer, who may be persuaded to give you the documents you want without the necessity of filing a formal FOI Act request.

If necessary, use your right to make a formal FOI Act request as leverage in your efforts to persuade the agency to release the information you are seeking informally. Make a point of telling any officials with whom you speak that you intend (if you do) to make a formal request and, if denied, to take an appeal and file a lawsuit. However, only a written FOI Act request—not an informal, oral request—will place the agency under a legal duty to act on your request, establish your right to appeal if your request is denied and then, if necessary, to file a lawsuit.

HOW TO MAKE A FORMAL REQUEST

A Simple Letter Is All You Need

If the informal approach does not succeed, exercise your full rights under the FOI Act by making a formal request. To preserve all your rights under the Act, your formal request must be made in writing. It is very simple to make an FOI Act request; any reporter, author, or researcher should be able to write his or her own request letter. *See Sample FOI Act Request Letter, Appendix A*

Each federal agency subject to the FOI Act has a designated FOI Act Officer responsible for handling information requests. Large cabinet agencies, such as Defense and Agriculture, have separate FOI Officers for their various subdivisions and regional offices. If you are sure which subdivision of an agency has the records you want, send your request letter directly to that FOI Officer. Otherwise, send your request to the FOI Officer for the whole agency or department, who will then forward it to the appropriate divisions.

Sometimes, it is advisable to send the original of your request to agency headquarters with copies to divisions that you think might have the records you want. For example, a request to the National Labor Relations Board might be made to the NLRB's national office with copies to regional offices in areas of the country relevant to the subject of your research. If you are unsure which federal agency has the records you want, send requests to several agencies.

Address your request letter to the FOI Officer at the appropriate agency or subdivision. Mark the outside of the envelope "FOI Act Request," and send it registered mail, return receipt requested. Be sure to keep a photocopy of your letter and your receipt. Generally, a properly drafted request should contain the elements included in the Sample FOI Act Request Letter reproduced in Appendix A. In most cases, you should be able to prepare a simple request letter by yourself, but if you need assistance, call **The FOI Service Center.**

SEARCHING AND COPYING FEES?

Must Be "Reasonable"

Agencies may charge "reasonable" fees for the "direct" costs of searching for and copying the records you request. Search fees generally range from $4 to $6 an hour for clerical personnel and from $10 to $18 an hour for professional personnel, such as lawyers and accountants. Fees for computer time vary greatly among agencies, but charges of $60 to $70 an hour are common. Photocopying costs are normally $.10 per page. (The standard commercial copying fee is no more than $.10 per page and any government charge substantially in excess of that amount would appear to be unlawful.) Search fees may be charged even if few or no documents are located in response to your request. Agencies may not charge you for the time they spend examining files to determine what individual documents, if any, should be exempt from disclosure and deleting material in those documents.

Before making your FOI request, you may want to obtain an estimate of what the search and duplication fees might be. In some cases, the agency's FOI Officer can give you this information on the telephone. As an alternative, state in your request letter your willingness to pay fees up to a certain limit and ask to be contacted by telephone or letter if the fees are likely to exceed that amount. Then you can decide how much you want to pay. *See Sample FOI Act Request Letter, Appendix A*

The FOI Act requires agencies to publish in the Federal Register uniform schedules for search and reproduction fees. Fee schedules may be obtained by contacting the agency FOI Officer or from **The FOI Service Center.**

CAN FEES BE CUT OR WAIVED?

Yes, for the Press, Scholars and Authors

You may ask the agency to waive or reduce search and copy fees if you think the fees are too high or if the fee is fair but the volume makes it too expensive. The FOI Act provides that the agency "shall" waive or reduce fees when it decides that furnishing the information you request would "primarily benefit the general public," and therefore be in the public interest. Some agencies have adopted regulations specifically allowing fee waivers for requests made by indigents, non-profit groups, and, in a few cases, journalists.[4]

We believe journalists, scholars, and authors should be entitled to fee waivers in most cases because dissemination of public information through books and news media articles is generally in the public interest. If you are a journalist, author or scholar seeking a fee waiver, be sure to inform the agency of your intent to publish the information you have requested or otherwise use it as the basis for a planned article, broadcast, or book. Point out the "newsworthiness" or historical value of the work you are researching, particularly with regard to your news organization's circulation or broadcast area or the potential readership of your book. Also, try to show how publication of your work will be of "significant" benefit to a large number of people. This will help demonstrate that furnishing information to you will "primarily benefit the general public."

Also, experience shows that Requestors seeking relatively modest numbers of documents are more likely to be granted fee waivers than those whose requests encompass several thousand pages. In this regard, you may want to show that you have narrowed your request as much as possible and therefore have not sought to burden the agency with an overly-broad request.

A fee waiver request is included in the Sample FOI Act Request Letter, Appendix A.

INSPECTION VS. REPRODUCTION

A Personal Visit May Be Faster and Cheaper

You can visit the agency and inspect the documents in person if you think the time or expense involved in having documents copied by the agency would unduly delay your story or be too expensive. Most agencies will make a typewriter available to take notes on and, once you are there, may let you do a modest amount of copying without charge. The Public Information Office at the agency may be of assistance in this situation.

HOW TO MAKE A FORMAL APPEAL

It's Easy. But Here You Might Want to Argue Your Case

If your request is wholly or partially denied, you have the right to appeal to the head of the agency. An FOI Act appeal is a procedure anyone can take advantage of by means of a simple letter. *See Sample FOI Act Appeal Letter, Appendix B* Even if your request is only partially denied, we suggest you take what documents you are offered and appeal the rest.

You also have the right to appeal if your request was granted but you think the fees are too high, or if 10 business days have elapsed since the date of your request and you still have not received a reply from the agency (an additional 10 days may be available to the agency in "unusual circumstances"—such as a very large request or the need to search field office files—if the agency notifies you of this expected delay in advance.).

Some agencies regularly fail to meet these time requirements. For example, the FBI has a backlog of requests and normally takes six to twelve months to fully process a request. Due to the backlog, however, courts have been inclined to give the FBI an exemption from the response time rules. Other agencies where long delays may be anticipated include State, Justice, and the CIA.

Before making a formal appeal, it often is helpful to call the agency FOI Officer to try to negotiate for release of at least some of the documents that were denied. By agreeing to narrow the scope of your request or permitting deletion of some information the agency considers particularly sensitive, you may be able to persuade the FOI Officer to give you most of the documents you originally wanted.

If your negotiations are not successful, however, you should take the next step and make a formal appeal. Appeals are made to the head of the agency involved (for example, the Attorney General or the Secretary of Defense). Try to file your appeal within 30 days after the denial, although some agencies permit a longer time to appeal. In most cases, appeals are reviewed by agency personnel better trained in FOI Act matters than the lower-ranking employee who initially denied your request. In any case, only by making a written appeal can you place the agency under a legal duty to reevaluate your original request and only by a written appeal can you establish your right to bring an FOI Act lawsuit if your appeal is denied.

Your appeal can be a brief letter to the agency administrator reviewing your previous request and denial (attach copies of this correspondence) and stating your belief that the denial was improper. If the agency cited one or more exemptions as the cause for denying your request (for example, personal privacy or national security), consider arguing in your appeal that the requested documents do not fall within those exemption categories and, even if they did, the public would be greatly benefited by release of the information. You may also want to re-state your intent to take your case to court if the denial is upheld.

Again, keep a photocopy of your appeal letter, mark the outside of the envelope "FOI Appeal," and send the appeal letter by registered mail, return receipt requested.

You may also want to include some legal or practical arguments in your appeal letter. For this type of help, you can contact **The FOI Service Center** for cost-free assistance, or consult a private attorney. Generally, however, an appeal letter will be sufficient if it contains the elements included in *the Sample FOI Act Appeal Letter reproduced in Appendix B.*

HOW TO FILE YOUR FOI ACT LAWSUIT

The First Step Is Simple, Quick, and Relatively Inexpensive

If your appeal is denied, or if the agency fails to respond to your appeal within 20 working days, you may file an FOI Act lawsuit in the United States District Court most convenient to you. Though technically you have up to 6 years after the date on which your appeal was denied to file a lawsuit,[5] you should try to file the suit as soon as possible in order to demonstrate to the court your need for the information. The FOI Act provides that your lawsuit must be given "expedited" treatment in the courts, which means that your case, if properly filed, will be given precedence over other litigation.

Filing an FOI Act complaint should be relatively inexpensive and simple. Sometimes, as soon as a complaint is filed, the government will capitulate and release documents without further litigation. Federal courts do allow non-lawyers to file complaints they have against the government without the assistance of an attorney. If your case is a more or less routine denial of documents which you think are clearly covered by the FOI Act, you may wish to draft and file your own "short-form" complaint using *the Sample FOI Act Complaint reproduced in Appendix C.* In addition, consider also filing a "Motion for *Vaughn* Index" *using the Sample Vaughn Motion reproduced in Appendix D.* This is a routine motion under which the government will be required to give you an index describing the documents it is withholding and the justification it claims for withholding each piece of information.

If your case appears to be complex or involve special problems, however, you should probably obtain at the outset the services of a private attorney or contact **The FOI Service Center** for cost-free assistance. Legal briefs and court opinions from other cases are available upon request from **The FOI Service Center.**

After you file your complaint, the burden is on the government to come forward and justify the withholding of the information. Courts are becoming more demanding on the government for precise and detailed reasons as to why the government refuses to release the information. It is at this point—when the government replies—that you and your attorney, if you have one, will obtain a fairly accurate idea of how strong or weak the government's case is and how much it will cost to continue the lawsuit.

The Act provides for the payment of your attorney fees and court costs if a judge decides that you "substantially prevailed" in your lawsuit. This generally means that in court you won release of some significant portion of the information that had been improperly withheld by the government.

INFORMATIONAL NOTE: DISCIPLINARY ACTION

The FOI Act provides that an "arbitrary" or "capricious" withholding of information requested under the Act can subject the responsible agency employees to disciplinary action by the Office of Personnel Management. Punitive actions may include loss of salary. To date, however, only one case is known to have been referred for disciplinary action and in that case the government official was not punished. Nevertheless, it is a good idea to learn what particular officials are responsible for decisions to withhold records you request. Reference to the punitive provision in conversation with agency personnel may have the effect of encouraging compliance with your request. Use your discretion here.

INFORMATIONAL NOTE: DEPARTMENT REVIEW

As an alternative to immediately filing a lawsuit, you can request an informal review of your case by the Office of Information Law and Policy of the U.S. Department of Justice, the federal agency that currently has responsibility for overall administration of the FOI Act. If Justice Department officials conclude that another agency clearly acted unlawfully in denying your request, they will recommend that the other agency reverse its decision and release the records to you. However, the Information Law and Policy staff will perform this review only if you contact them before you file a lawsuit.

THE 9 FOI DISCLOSURE EXEMPTIONS

Reasons Why Government Can Keep Information Secret

The FOI Act includes nine exemptions or reasons allowing the government to refuse to disclose information. In brief, these exemptions cover documents relating to (in the order of their appearance in the Act):

1. national security,
2. internal agency personnel rules,
3. information specifically exempted by dozens of other federal laws already on the books—the "Catch-All" exemption,
4. trade secrets,
5. internal agency memoranda and policy discussions,
6. personal privacy,
7. law enforcement investigations,
8. federally regulated banks, and
9. oil and gas wells.

These exemptions (except for the "Catch-All" exemption) are not mandatory —which means that the government is permitted, but not required, to suppress the information. In other words, even if records fall within these categories they still can be released at the government's discretion. This is particularly true if you can show that disclosure would be "in the public interest."

Furthermore, even though a requested document contains some words, sentences, or paragraphs that may be covered by an exemption (or a file contains some documents that may be exempt), the FOI Act requires the government agency to release the remainder of the document or file after the exempt material has been edited out.

The type of information covered by each of the nine exemptions is discussed below:

EXEMPTION 1. NATIONAL SECURITY

Must Be "Identifiable Damage"

This exemption is basically designed to prevent disclosure of properly classified records whose release would cause at least some "identifiable damage" to the national security. The exemption covers records that are:

(A) specifically authorized under criteria established by an Executive Order to be kept secret in the interest of national defense or foreign policy (because unauthorized disclosure reasonably could be expected to cause at least identifiable damage to the national security),[6] *and*

(B) are in fact properly classified pursuant to such Executive Order;

Documents which generally fall under this section are those, like the Pentagon papers, that are officially stamped Top Secret, Secret, or Confidential, terms which are defined in a Presidential Executive Order.[7] The FOI Act, however, makes it clear that courts have a duty to determine whether the claim of national security classification is justified.

Under the current Presidential Executive Order information can be withheld only if its disclosure would cause some "identifiable damage" to the national security.[8] Furthermore, the Executive Order says the government "should" release the documents if "the need to protect [the information] is outweighed by the public interest in disclosure."[9]

Courts will not necessarily accept the government's determination that requested documents, if released, would damage national security. If you file a lawsuit, there is a good chance the judge will demand to examine the documents in secret. This opportunity for judicial review can be especially helpful in securing access to historical records, and documents which were obviously classified merely to prevent domestic political repercussions.

Remember that just because a few pages of a report are properly classified does not mean that the remaining non-sensitive portions can be cloaked in secrecy. In other words, the government must justify the withholding of each document and within each document must justify the withholding of every word, phrase, sentence, and paragraph. Also, merely because information is in the possession of the Departments of Defense or State does not necessarily mean it is classified.

EXEMPTION 2.   INTERNAL AGENCY RULES

For Housekeeping Details Only

This exemption generally covers agency management or "housekeeping" records which Congress decided would not be of interest to the general public. It applies to records that are:

related solely to the internal personnel rules and practices of an agency;

This provision is basically designed to relieve government agencies of the burden of maintaining for public inspection routine materials that are more or less trivial and in which the general public is assumed to have little or no interest. Examples include employee parking rules and agency cafeteria regulations. However, any documents which could be viewed as the subject of legitimate public concern—such as personnel management evaluation forms—may not be withheld under this exemption, according to a ruling of a federal appellate court.[10]

An unsettled issue is whether this exemption should cover agency staff manuals, such as instructions for prosecutors and guidelines for auditors. Courts have divided on this question. Generally, unless disclosure of such materials clearly would enable the public to circumvent agency regulations or laws, staff manuals will not be withheld under this exemption.

EXEMPTION 3.   "CATCH-ALL" EXEMPTION

A Major Secrecy Loophole

This exemption, the "Catch-All Exemption," is designed to exempt from disclosure information required or permitted to be kept secret by dozens of other federal laws. It covers records that are:

specifically exempted from disclosure by [another federal] statute . . . provided that such statute
(A) [clearly] requires that the matters be withheld from the public.
[This incorporates statutes such as the Census Act which prohibits use of information furnished under that Act "for any purpose other than the statistical purpose for which it was supplied."[11]], or
(B) establishes particular criteria for [discretionary] withholding [of the information sought] or [narrowly specifies] particular types of [informational] matters to be withheld;

(For example, this incorporates statutes such as the Consumer Product Safety Act, which requires the Consumer Product Safety Commission to withhold documents submitted by private companies if information contained in them is not "accurate,"[12] and the National Security Act, which exempts from disclosure "the names, titles, salaries, or number of persons employed by" the National Security Agency.[13])

Only statutes meeting either of the strict criteria of this provision can qualify as exempting statutes. In recent years, federal agencies have cited nearly 100 "Catch-All" statutes to justify withholding of documents.

Most of these laws have not been tested in court to determine whether they do, in fact, qualify as "Catch-All" exemptions. For example, courts have ruled that the "Catch-All" exemption could not be invoked under a provision of the Export Administration Act that permitted the government to withhold foreign trade information about private corporations unless it determined that doing so would be "contrary to the national interest."[14]

Similarly, the "Catch-All" exemption does not incorporate a provision of the Federal Aviation Administration Act of 1958 which allowed the Administrator of the FAA to withhold agency reports on airline operations when, in his opinion, disclosure would "adversely affect" the company that submitted the data and "is not required in the interest of the public."[15]

Fifteen "Catch-All" statutes most frequently cited by federal agencies are discussed below. The statutes described below that have been tested in court and found definitely to qualify as "Catch-All" exemptions are identified by an asterisk, following a citation to the United States Code:

1. Agricultural Adjustment Act (7 U.S.C. 1373)

This provision makes confidential the reports and records that farmers submit to the Agriculture Department concerning government loans, parity payments, consumer safeguards, and market quotas. It states that such data "reported to or acquired" by the Secretary of Agriculture "shall be kept confidential by all officers and employees" of the agency.

2. Census Bureau Records (13 U.S.C. 9)*

This statute is designed to protect the privacy of persons responding to U.S. Census Bureau questionnaires. It prohibits Commerce Department and Census Bureau employees from publicly disclosing the contents of completed individual Census forms, or from using Census information "for any purpose other than the statistical purposes for which it is supplied."

3. Federal Trade Commission (15 U.S.C. 57b-2(f))

This provision was designed to prevent government disclosure of a broad range of consumer information that business firms would prefer to keep secret. It permits the FTC to withhold "any material" it receives—voluntarily or by subpoena—in connection with any FTC "investigation" to determine whether federal laws administered by the agency may have been violated.

4. Consumer Product Safety Commission (15 U.S.C. 2055)*

This provision is designed to protect manufacturers from damage to their business reputations that could result from public disclosure of hazardous product reports received by the Commission. It requires that the Commission—prior to releasing information from which a particular manufacturer could be identified—take "reasonable steps to assure" the accuracy of the information.

5. Public Utility Information (16 U.S.C. 825(b))

This broad provision prohibits Department of Energy employees from disclosing information obtained by them "in the course of examination of books" or other financial records of public utilities or other agency licensees.

6. Central Intelligence Agency (18 U.S.C. 798)

This statute is generally designed to keep secret the procedures and methods by which the United States government intercepts foreign communications. It makes it a crime for anyone—including CIA employees—to disclose to unauthorized persons any classified information concerning "the communication intelligence activities of the United States or any foreign government."

7. Trade Secrets (18 U.S.C. 1905)

Under this criminal provision, government employees are subject to jail and/or a fine if they disclose "trade secrets" or other private business information which they obtain in the course of their government employment and which they are not specifically authorized by another law to disclose. Courts currently are in disagreement as to whether this statute qualifies for use under Exemption 3.

8. Bank Records (18 U.S.C. 1906)

This criminal provision is aimed at keeping secret the financial records of banks and bank users. It provides jail sentences and/or fines for bank examiners and employees of the General Accounting Office who have access to bank examination reports and who disclose without authorization "the names of borrowers or the collateral for loans" of federally regulated banks.

9. Tax Returns (26 U.S.C. 6103)*

This statute was designed to protect the privacy of individuals submitting tax returns to the Internal Revenue Service. It makes it a crime for any "officer or employee" of the United States to disclose any "return or return information" obtained by him in connection with this government employment, unless otherwise authorized to do so by federal law.

10. Patent Applications (35 U.S.C. 122)*

This statute protects the secrecy of scientific inventions prior to the time they are recorded by the Patent Office. It requires that "no information concerning" applications for patents may be disclosed by the Patent and Trademark Office without permission of the applicant or in such other "special circumstances" as the Commissioner of Patents may allow.

11. Veterans' Benefits (38 U.S.C. 3301)

This statute makes confidential most records in possession of the Veterans Administration regarding claims for benefits filed by veterans. In general, it prohibits disclosure of "all files, records, reports, and other papers" concerning "any claim under any of the laws administered by the Veterans Administration and the names and addresses of present or former personnel of the armed services, and their dependents . . ."

12. Postal Service (39 U.S.C. 410, 412)*

This statute is aimed at protecting the confidentiality of persons using the U.S. mails and of investigations conducted by the U.S. Postal Service. It prohibits Postal Service employees from disclosing the identities and addresses of "postal patrons," "mailing lists," and the agency's law enforcement investigation files.

13. Employment Discrimination (42 U.S.C. 2000c-5)

This statute is designed to keep confidential the employment discrimination charges filed with the Equal Employment Opportunity Commission. It provides that "any person" who publicly discloses information about discrimination charges or about the Commission's efforts to informally resolve them, shall be subject to a fine "not more than $1,000" or imprisonment up to one year, or both.

14. Central Intelligence Agency (50 U.S.C. 403(d)(3))*

This statute authorizes the director of the CIA to protect "intelligence sources and methods from unauthorized disclosure." A related provision, 50 U.S.C. 403g, exempts the CIA from any law requiring "disclosure of the organization, functions, names, official titles, salaries, or numbers of personnel employed" by the CIA.

15. **National Security Agency** (50 U.S.C. 402)*
This statute is designed to keep secret virtually all information about the National Security Agency, a division within the Department of Defense concerned primarily with communications security and foreign intelligence. It prohibits release of information concerning the "organization or any function" of the NSA, or "the names, title, salaries, or number of" persons employed by NSA.

EXEMPTION 4. TRADE SECRETS

Must Really Be a Secret

This exemption is basically designed to protect two different categories of information. One is "trade secrets," such as customer lists and secret formulae. The other is sensitive internal financial information about a company which, if disclosed, would cause the company competitive harm. The exemption covers:

trade secrets and commercial or financial information obtained from a person and privileged or confidential;

Under this exemption, a "trade secret" is generally considered to be information used in one's daily business that is commercially valuable, secretly maintained, and not generally known in the trade.

To withhold documents under the other part of the exemption covering "commercial or financial information," the government must be able to prove the information is "confidential." Courts have said such information is "confidential" only if its disclosure would be likely either (1) "to impair the government's ability to obtain necessary information in the future" or (2) "to cause substantial harm to the competitive position" of the person from whom the information was obtained.[16]

These are strict tests and require the government to show more than just a likelihood that some embarrassment or commercial loss might result to a business firm if its records are disclosed. This exemption applies only to information supplied to the government by individuals or private business firms. Government-prepared documents about a person or private firm based primarily on information the government generates itself or gathers from outside sources generally are not exempt.

EXEMPTION 5. EXECUTIVE PRIVILEGE

Agency Policy Drafts

This is the "executive privilege" exemption. It is mainly designed to protect working papers, studies, and reports prepared within an agency or circulated among government personnel as the basis of a final agency decision. The exemption covers:

> inter-agency or intra-agency memorandums or letters which would not be available by law to a party other than an agency in litigation with the agency;

This exemption is widely used by the government. Its purpose is to encourage open discussions on policy matters among agency personnel. Therefore, it covers documents such as preliminary policy drafts, letters between agency officials, and staff proposals. In most cases, these pre-decisional documents will remain exempt even after a final agency decision is announced, *unless* in the final decision the agency clearly adopts the position set forth in a particular pre-decisional document.

However, purely *factual* portions of pre-decisional documents are not exempt. For example, if a long policy memorandum containing advisory recommendations on a proposed federal building project also contains facts regarding the current price of construction materials, such facts must be segregated from the policy portion of the memorandum and released upon request. Also, final opinions and other "post-decisional" documents explaining an agency position are generally not exempt.

In addition, this exemption incorporates the attorney-client privilege, which protects most communications between an agency and its own attorney or another agency acting as its attorney, such as the U.S. Department of Justice. It also incorporates the attorney-work product privilege, which protects documents prepared by an attorney if their disclosure would reveal the attorney's theory of the case or planned trial strategy.

EXEMPTION 6.   PERSONAL PRIVACY

"Personnel" & "Medical" Files

The very nature of this exemption makes it difficult to lay down hard and fast rules about its scope. But it generally covers a person's intimate family-life details which in and of themselves are deemed not to be of significant public interest in view of the intrusion into the person's personal life that disclosure would cause. This exemption applies to:

> personnel and medical and similar files, the disclosure of which would constitute a clearly unwarranted invasion of privacy;

The kinds of intimate personal facts properly protected by this exemption include matters such as the legitimacy of children, medical condition, job evaluation, welfare payments, alcoholic consumption, and family relations. One way to avoid this exemption is to agree to have agency officials delete names or other identifying data from a document before it is released. Also, merely because a document is located in a government file labeled "personnel" or "medical," it is not automatically exempt. Each individual document must contain protected information in order to be withheld under this exemption.

Also, courts have ruled that persons who apply for or seek government contracts or other significant government benefits are deemed to have waived their rights to privacy as to personal information they submit to the government which might play an important role in the government's decision to grant them the contract or benefit.

For example, if a person applies for a government building contract and with this application encloses personal financial information to demonstrate his record of successful contract work, then he cannot argue that that information should be protected. This is in contrast, of course, to the person who goes for treatment to a public hospital and reveals personal medical information. No waiver of privacy rights is presumed in that case.

Furthermore, this exemption allows a balancing of privacy interests against the public need for disclosure. Therefore, this is one instance where your reasons for requesting information could be important. If your request involves this exemption, you should include a brief explanation of why you want the information and why the public interest in disclosure outweighs any possible privacy invasions. This will allow the agency to determine whether a potential invasion of privacy which could result from disclosure would be justified or "unwarranted."

EXEMPTION 7.   LAW ENFORCEMENT

Current & Pending Files Only

This exemption is primarily designed to protect the confidentiality of documents whose untimely disclosure would jeopardize ongoing criminal or civil investigations. The exemption covers:

> investigatory records compiled for law enforcement purposes, but only to the extent that the production of such records would:
> a. interfere with enforcement proceedings,
> b. deprive a person of a right to a fair trial or an impartial adjudication,
> c. constitute an unwarranted invasion of personal privacy,
> d. disclose the identity of a confidential source, . . . (or) confidential information furnished only by the confidential source (in a criminal or national security investigation),
> e. disclose investigative techniques and procedures, or
> f. endanger the life or physical safety of law enforcement personnel;

Congress amended this provision in 1974 in order to avoid broad agency claims of exemption for almost anything which could be called an "investigatory file." As amended, the Act requires the government to prove that documents were compiled for specific criminal, civil or other law enforcement purposes, and that disclosure actually would result in one of the six listed harms.

The exemption does cover most types of records related to the current investigation of a specific crime or administrative enforcement proceeding, such as interviews with witnesses, affidavits, and notes compiled by investigative officers. However, courts have stated that law enforcement compilations routinely made and kept, such as rap sheets, arrest and conviction records, and department manuals and rosters of law enforcement personnel, generally are not suppressable as "investigatory records."

The first of the six enumerated harms—covering interference with enforcement proceedings—is the one most often cited by the agencies. This exemption generally applies only when an enforcement proceeding has actually begun or when there is a "concrete prospect" that an ongoing investigation will lead to an enforcement proceeding. It does not apply after enforcement proceedings have ended, such as after a trial, conviction, and sentencing. Where an investigation drags on for many years due to lack of funds or exhaustion of leads, courts have said the exemption can be applied only as long as there remains a "concrete prospect" of enforcement proceedings.

As for subsection (c), which permits withholding on privacy grounds, a balancing of the protected privacy invasion against the public interest in disclosure is permitted, as under the main privacy exemption (Exemption 6). Subsection (d), which is designed to protect investigation techniques, generally applies only to secret techniques and procedures not generally known to the public. Routine scientific tests, like fingerprinting, are not covered.

EXEMPTION 8.   BANK REPORTS

This exemption applies mainly to reports prepared by federal agencies about the conditions of banks and other federally regulated financial institutions. It covers records that are:

> contained in or related to examination, operating, or condition reports prepared by, on behalf of, or for the use of an agency responsible for the regulation or supervision of financial institutions;

This little-used exemption applies to banks, trust companies, and investment banking firms and associations. Its purpose is to prevent disclosure of sensitive financial reports or audits that, if made public, might undermine public confidence in individual banks, or in the federal banking system. Agencies responsible for bank regulation that are most likely to invoke this exemption include the Federal Reserve System, the Comptroller of the Currency, and the Federal Home Loan Bank Board.

EXEMPTION 9.   OIL & GAS WELL DATA

This exemption is primarily designed to prohibit speculators from obtaining information about the location of oil and gas wells of private companies. It covers:

geological and geophysical information and data, including maps, concerning wells;

This provision is infrequently used. It covers geological information in files of federal agencies, such as the Bureau of Land Management in the Interior Department, the Federal Energy Regulatory Commission, and the Federal Power Commission.

THE PRIVACY ACT

How to Discover What the Government Knows About You

Due to revelations in the 1960s and 70s that agencies of the federal government had systematically monitored political activities of American citizens, many journalists, authors, and scholars would like to inspect their own dossiers in government files. The way to do this is to make a request under the federal Privacy Act, a law that gives you the right to see government records about yourself and to correct errors in them, if necessary.[17]

The Privacy Act, like the FOI Act, is relatively simple to use. Identify the agency that you think may have records about you—such as the FBI, CIA, or IRS. Send a letter, *using the Sample Privacy Act Request Letter reproduced in Appendix E.* In your request letter (which for broadest coverage should invoke both the Privacy and FOI Acts) you will need to give the agency enough information so it can be sure of your identity and know which files to search.

Among the types of information you may want to provide are: your full name, other names and nicknames you have used, your date and place of birth, history of foreign travel, home addresses, government employment, participation in political groups, demonstrations, etc. Decide for yourself how much of this type of information you want to disclose to the government.

You can request that the agency search its central files in Washington, D.C. as well as regional and local offices throughout the country. FBI headquarters in Washington, however, will not honor requests for searches of field office files. If you think one of the FBI's 49 field offices has records about you, you must make a separate Privacy Act request directly to that field office.

Unlike the FOI Act, the Privacy Act does not permit agencies to charge you for the time it takes to search for the records you have requested. Duplication fees are charged, however. These are normally at the rate of ten cents per page. Also, the Privacy Act does not require agencies to process your request within ten business days, as under the FOI Act.

However, under Guidelines issued by the Office of Management and Budget, agencies "should" acknowledge receipt of Privacy Act requests within 10 business days, advising whether the request will be granted, and provide access to the records within 30 business days.[18]

Federal agencies have different requirements for what type of proof of identification must be submitted by Privacy Act requestors. Generally, you can meet all agency requirements—including those of the FBI—by stating your full name, social security number, date and place of birth, and having your signature on the request letter notarized. It may also be helpful to enclose copies of a standard piece of identification, such as a birth certificate or driver's license.

One provision of the Privacy Act is of special interest to journalists, authors, and scholars. It prohibits federal agencies from maintaining any records "describing how any individual exercises rights guaranteed by the First Amendment" unless done under authorization of a statute or within the scope of an "authorized law enforcement activity."[19]

There have been few court cases to date interpreting this provision. It does appear, however, that this law prohibits the government from all necessary monitoring of the professional activities of members of the press, as well as authors, scholars, and researchers. If the government is found to maintain these types of records unlawfully, "in such a manner as to have an adverse effect on an individual," the Privacy Act permits that individual to file a civil suit against the agency and, in some cases, recover monetary damages and attorneys fees.

If you need help in using the Privacy Act, contact **The FOI Service Center** and we will be pleased to assist you.

NOTES

1. The FOI Act appears in the United States Code at 5 U.S.C. 552.
2. The Corporation for Public Broadcasting claims it is not covered by the FOI Act. However, Corporation spokesmen say FOI Act requests received by the Corporation are voluntarily processed in accordance with the FOI Act.
3. *Forsham* v. *Harris,* 445 U.S. 169 (1980).
4. Journalists making FOI Act requests to the following agencies are presumptively entitled to a waiver or reduction of fees, according to the agencies' own regulations: Department of Energy, 10 C.F.R. 1004.9(a)(1)(ii); Department of Interior, 43 C.F.R. 219(c)(3)(i); Small Business Administration, 13 C.F.R. 102.6(d)(2); Department of Defense, 32 C.F.R. 2861, et seq. *see* Enclosure 4—Fee Schedule B(3)(c); Federal Trade Commission, *see* FTC News Release "JO 73/FEES," 12/7/78.

   In addition, the following agencies reported in response to a Senate subcommittee questionnaire that they normally waive fees "for news media requests": Civil Service Commission, Postal Service, NASA, and Veterans Administration; *see* "Agency Implementation of the 1974 Amendments to the FOI Act," Report on Oversight Hearings by the Subcommittee on Administrative Practice and Procedure of the Senate Committee on the Judiciary, March 1980, at p. 87.

5. 28 U.S.C. 2401(a). The general statute of limitations for civil suits against the federal government is six years.

6. Executive Order No. 12065, 43 Fed. Reg. 28949 (July 3, 1978). at Sec. 1–3.

7. *Ibid.,* Sec. 1–1.

8. *Ibid.,* Sec. 1–301.

9. *Ibid.,* Sec. 3–303.

10. *Vaughn* v. *Rosen* (II), 523 F.2d 1136 (D.C.Cir. 1975).

11. 13 U.S.C. 9(a)(1); *see Seymour* v. *Barabba,* 559 F.2d 806 (D.C.Cir. 1977).

12. 15 U.S.C. 2055(b)(1); *see CPSC* v. *GTE Sylvania, Inc.,* 447 U.S.—(June 9, 1980).

13. 50 U.S.C. 402 note; *see Hayden* v. *National Security Agency,* 608 F.2d 1381 (D.C.Cir. 1979), *cert. denied,* 446 U.S.—(May 12, 1980); *Founding Church of Scientology of Washington, D.C., Inc.* v. *National Security Agency,* 610 F.2d 824 (D.C.Cir. 1979).

14. *American Jewish Congress* v. *Kreps,* 574 F.2d 624 (D.C.Cir. 1978).

15. 49 U.S.C. 1504; *see* Senate Report No. 94–1178 (1976), at p. 25.

16. *National Parks and Conservation Assoc.* v. *Morton,* 498 F.2d 765 (D.C.Cir. 1974).

17. The Privacy Act appears in the United States Code at 5 U.S.C. 552a.

18. OMB Regulations, 40 Fed. Reg. 28948, 28957-8 (July 9, 1975).

19. 5 U.S.C. 552a(e)(7).

APPENDIX A. SAMPLE FOI REQUEST LETTER

Tele. No. (business hours)
Return Address
Date

Name of Public Body
Address

To the FOI Officer:

This request is made under the federal Freedom of Information Act, 5 U.S.C. 552.

Please send me copies of (Here, clearly describe what you want. Include identifying material, such as names, places, and the period of time about which you are inquiring. If you wish, attach news clips, reports, and other documents describing the subject of your research.)

As you know, the FOI Act provides that if portions of a document are exempt from release, the remainder must be segregated and disclosed. Therefore, I will expect you to send me all nonexempt portions of the records which I have requested, and ask that you justify any deletions by reference to specific exemptions of the FOI Act. I reserve the right to appeal your decision to withhold any materials.

I promise to pay reasonable search and duplication fees in connection with this request. However, if you estimate that the total fees will exceed $____, please notify me so that I may authorize expenditure of a greater amount.

(Optional) I am prepared to pay reasonable search and duplication fees in connection with this request. However, the FOI Act provides for waiver or reduction of fees if disclosure could be considered as "primarily benefiting the general public." I am a journalist (researcher, or scholar) employed by (name of news organization, book publishers, etc.), and intend to use the information I am requesting as the basis for a planned article (broadcast, or book). (Add arguments here in support of fee waiver). Therefore, I ask that you waive all search and duplication fees. If you deny this request, however, and the fees will exceed $____, please notify me of the charges before you fill my request so that I may decide whether to pay the fees or appeal your denial of my request for a waiver.

As I am making this request in the capacity of a journalist (author, or scholar) and this information is of timely value, I will appreciate your communicating with me by telephone, rather than by mail, if you have any questions regarding this request. Thank you for your assistance, and I will look forward to receiving your reply within 10 business days, as required by law.

Very truly yours,

_____
(Signature)

APPENDIX B. SAMPLE FOI ACT APPEAL LETTER

Tele. No. (business hours)
Return Address
Date

Administrator
Name of Agency
Address

To the Administrator:

This is an appeal under the Freedom of Information Act, 5 U.S.C. 552.

On (date) I made an FOI Act request to your agency for (brief description of what you requested). On (date), your agency denied my request because (state the ground for denial cited by the agency, or that the agency failed to respond within lawful time limits). Copies of this correspondence are enclosed.

Please be informed that I consider the requested information clearly releasable under the FOI Act and consider your agency's denial to be arbitrary and capricious.

(Here, insert legal and "public policy" arguments in favor of disclosure, if you wish.)

I trust that upon re-consideration, you will reverse the decision denying me access to this material and grant my original request. However, if you deny this appeal, I intend to initiate a lawsuit to compel disclosure.

As I have made this request in the capacity of a journalist (author, or scholar) and this information is of timely value, I will appreciate your expediting the consideration of my appeal in every way possible. In any case, I will expect to receive your decision within 20 business days, as required by law. Thank you for your assistance.

Very truly yours,

_____
(Signature)

APPENDIX C. SAMPLE FOI ACT COMPLAINT
United States District Court
FOR_____

YOUR NAME,
your address

Plaintiff

v.

NAME OF AGENCY THAT HAS FILES   Civil Action No.—
agency address

NAME OF HEAD OF AGENCY   COMPLAINT FOR
agency address   INJUNCTIVE
                                             RELIEF
Defendants

   1.   This is an action brought under the Freedom of Information Act, 5 U.S.C. 552, to order defendants to produce certain documents for inspection and duplication.
   2.   This court has jurisdiction over this action pursuant to 5 U.S.C. 552(a) (4) (B).
   3.   Plaintiff is a newsreporter (researcher, author, historian) employed by (name of newspaper, station, university) who is investigating (brief description of subject matter of request) for the purpose of preparing an article (broadcast, book) for public dissemination.
   4.   Defendant (name of agency) is an agency of the Executive Branch of the U.S. Government and has possession of the documents that plaintiff seeks.
   5.   Defendant (name of head of agency) is Secretary (or other official title) of (name of agency) and made the final decision to deny plaintiff access to records of that agency.
   6.   By letter dated _____, addressed to _____, plaintiff requested access to (brief summary of request). A copy of this letter is attached as Exhibit 1.
   7.   By letter dated _____, plaintiff's request was denied by (name and title of agency official). A copy of this letter is attached as Exhibit 2.
   8.   By letter dated _____, addressed to _____, plaintiff filed an administrative appeal of the denial. A copy of this letter is attached as Exhibit 3.
   9.   By letter dated _____, plaintiff's appeal was finally denied by (name and title of agency official). A copy of this letter is attached as Exhibit 4.
   10.   Pursuant to the Freedom of Information Act, 5 U.S.C. 552, plaintiff has a right to inspect and copy the requested documents.

11.   Plaintiff has exhausted his administrative remedies.

WHEREFORE, plaintiff requests (1) that this Court take jurisdiction of this cause, (2) that this Court order defendants to provide him with the requested documents for the purpose of inspection and copying, (3) that this Court award him his costs and disbursements in this action as provided in 5 U.S.C. 522 (a) (4) (E), (4) that this Court expedite this proceeding as provided in 5 U.S.C. 522 (a) (4) (D), and (5) that this Court grant such other and further relief as it may deem just and proper.

Dated: City and State
      Date   _____

                            (Name of Plaintiff or Plaintiff's Attorney)
                                      address

APPENDIX D. SAMPLE VAUGHN MOTION
United States District Court
FOR _____

YOUR NAME,
  your address

  Plaintiff

  v.   Civil Action No.——

NAME OF AGENCY THAT HAS FILES
  agency address

NAME OF HEAD OF AGENCY
  agency address

  Defendants

MOTION UNDER *VAUGHN* V. *ROSEN* TO REQUIRE
DETAILED JUSTIFICATION, ITEMIZATION AND INDEXING

Plaintiff (your name) moves this Court for an order requiring Defendants (name of agency and agency head) to provide within 30 days of the filing of the Complaint in this action, a detailed justification for allegations contained in Defendants' answer and previous administrative denial that the requested documents are exempt from disclosure under the Freedom of Information Act, 5 U.S.C. 552, including an itemization and index of the documents claimed to be exempt, correlating specific statements in such justification with actual portions of the requested documents, see *Vaughn* v. *Rosen,* 484 F.2d 820 (D.C.Cir. 1973), *cert. denied,* 415 U.S. 977 (1974).

Respectfully submitted,

_____
(Name of Plaintiff or Plaintiff's Attorney)
address

Dated: City and State
       (date)

APPENDIX E. SAMPLE PRIVACY ACT REQUEST LETTER

Tele. No. (business hours)
Return Address
Date

Name of Agency
Agency Address

To the FOI/Privacy Act Officer:

This request is made under the Freedom of Information Act, 5 U.S.C. 552, and the Privacy Act, 5 U.S.C. 552a.

Please provide me copies of all records about me in your files. To assist your search, I am providing the following additional information about myself (Here, list whatever additional personal data you don't mind revealing to the agency, such as other names used, social security number, date and place of birth, places of residence, foreign travel, government and other employment, political activities, etc.)

If you determine that any portions of these documents are exempt, I will expect you to delete those portions and release the remainder of each document to me.

I promise to pay lawful fees in connection with this request up to a limit of $____. If the estimated fees will be greater than that amount, please contact me by telephone so that I may authorize a larger expenditure.

If you have any questions regarding this request, please contact me by telephone. Thank you for your assistance. I will look forward to receiving your prompt reply.

Very truly yours,

_____
Signature
Your Full Name
Social Security Number
Date and Place of Birth

Your Signature Should Be Notarized

Index